The Holiday in His Eye

THE SUNY SERIES

HORIZONS OF CINEMA

MURRAY POMERANCE | EDITOR

The Holiday in His Eye

Stanley Cavell's Vision of Film and Philosophy

William Rothman

Cover: Stanley Cavell, photo courtesy of Harvard University

Published by State University of New York Press, Albany

© 2021 State University of New York

All rights reserved

Printed in the United States of America

No part of this book may be used or reproduced in any manner whatsoever without written permission. No part of this book may be stored in a retrieval system or transmitted in any form or by any means including electronic, electrostatic, magnetic tape, mechanical, photocopying, recording, or otherwise without the prior permission in writing of the publisher.

For information, contact State University of New York Press, Albany, NY
www.sunypress.edu

Library of Congress Cataloging-in-Publication Data

Names: Rothman, William, author.
Title: The holiday in his eye : Stanley Cavell's vision of film and philosophy / William Rothman.
Description: Albany : State University of New York Press, [2021] | Series: SUNY series, horizons of cinema | Includes bibliographical references and index.
Identifiers: LCCN 2021024192 | ISBN 9781438486055 (hardcover : alk. paper) | ISBN 9781438486062 (pbk. : alk. paper) | 9781438486079 (ebook)
Subjects: LCSH: Cavell, Stanley, 1926–2018. | Philosophy, American—20th century. | Motion pictures—Philosophy. | Motion pictures—Aesthetics.
Classification: LCC B945.C274 R68 2021 | DDC 191—dc23
LC record available at https://lccn.loc.gov/2021024192

10 9 8 7 6 5 4 3 2 1

A man is but a little thing in the midst of the objects of nature, yet, by the moral quality radiating from his countenance, he may abolish all considerations of magnitude, and in his manners equal the majesty of the world. I have seen an individual, whose manners, though wholly within the conventions of elegant society, were never learned there, but were original and commanding, and held out protection and prosperity; one who did not need the aid of a court-suit, but carried the holiday in his eye; who exhilarated the fancy by flinging wide the doors of new modes of existence; who shook off the captivity of etiquette, with happy, spirited bearing, good-natured and free as Robin Hood; yet with the port of an emperor,—if need be, calm, serious, and fit to stand the gaze of millions.

—Ralph Waldo Emerson, "Manners"

in memory of Stanley Cavell

Contents

Preface		xi
1	Cavell Reading Cavell	1
2	Introduction to *Reading Cavell's "The World Viewed"* (*with* Marian Keane)	9
3	Sights and Sounds (*with* Marian Keane)	23
4	The Acknowledgment of Silence (*with* Marian Keane)	37
5	Cavell's Philosophy and What Film Studies Calls "Theory"	59
6	Response to Vivian Sobchack's *The Address of the Eye*	67
7	*Pursuits of Happiness*: Cavell in Transition	71
8	In Defense of *Pursuits of Happiness*	81
9	Viewing the World in Black and White	89
10	Cavell's Creation	103
11	Nostalgia Ain't What It Used to Be	119
12	Cavell on Film, Television, and Opera (excerpts)	135
13	*Cavell on Film*: Introduction	153
14	The Same Again, Only a Little Different: Cavell's Two Takes on *The Philadelphia Story*	167

15	Cavell, Emerson, Hitchcock: Reflections Inspired by Stanley Cavell's *Cities of Words*	175
16	On Richard Allen's "Hitchcock and Cavell"	187
17	Introduction to *Must We Kill the Thing We Love? Emersonian Perfectionism and the Films of Alfred Hitchcock*	203
18	On Stanley Cavell's *Band Wagon*	217
19	"Excerpts from Memory": Autobiography, Film, and the Double Existence of Cavell's Philosophical Prose	241
20	Stanley Cavell, Victor Perkins, and the Personal	251
Afterword		257
Works Cited		261
Index		265

Preface

When Stanley Cavell came to Harvard in 1963, the charismatic young professor allowed me, a skinny undergraduate philosophy major with a penchant for mathematical logic, a love of movies, and a full head of hair, to enroll in a graduate aesthetics seminar devoted to film. In *The World Viewed*, Cavell calls that seminar a failure. As I never tire of saying, it didn't fail me.

For Cavell, the seminar was of value insofar as he took its failure as a challenge to think more deeply about what a serious study of film might require, how it might fruitfully proceed. And this led to his second course on film at Harvard, one he cotaught with Robert Gardner, the anthropological filmmaker and film artist. In "Anecdote of a Season," a tribute to Gardner published in 2007 in *The Cinema of Robert Gardner*, Cavell wrote that "super-8 cameras were made available to students, a reading list was provided, and discussions were held to relate the experience of filming, and its results, to philosophical reflection on film" (Barbash and Taylor 1997, 19–21). In his essay on the Cavell–Gardner relationship for our 2016 book *Looking with Robert Gardner*, Charles Warren writes, "Cavell says about the co-taught course that its ambition was to found a study of film where art and the way of thinking of artists and, on the other hand, intellectual reflection more familiar to universities, actually speak to each other and listen to each other, as they did at music conservatories like Juilliard, where Cavell had studied before that Road to Damascus moment when he came to the realization that philosophy, not music, was his calling" (Meyers, Rothman, and Warren 2016, 65).

In the fall of 1971, Alfred Guzzetti, who was teaching filmmaking at Carpenter Center, persuaded several Harvard departments to pitch in to purchase a print of Jean-Luc Godard's *Two or Three Things I Know About Her*. Guzzetti writes, "Interest spread to a number of faculty members concerned either centrally or peripherally with film; in a short time, a study group had formed" (Guzzetti 1981, 8). It included Cavell and his close friend Michael Fried, and met every week for the academic year 1971–1972.

In 1972, Cavell played a crucial role in securing a Luce Foundation grant for a visiting professorship in film history. The position was awarded to Vlada Petric, who was the first recipient of a doctorate from the New York University Cinema Studies Department.

The following year, Cavell helped arrange for Harvard's participation, along with New York University and the State University of New York at Buffalo, in a three-year series of seminars on the problems of film scholarship and reaching. The first two years, I was an assistant professor in cinema studies and participated as a member of the NYU contingent, but these meetings made me homesick for Harvard—especially when Cavell described to me the course on film comedy he was planning to give. In teaching the course, which he offered in 1974, as he put it in the introduction to *Pursuits of Happiness*, "thoughts of remarriage as generating a genre of film began presenting themselves" to him (Cavell 1981b, 275). The third year, I was a member of the Harvard contingent, where I felt I belonged.

In the early 1970s, Cavell also worked diligently to help establish the Harvard Film Archive, with Petric its first curator, and to persuade the powers that be at Harvard to elevate Guzzetti's position to a tenured professorship. And he applied for, and received, an ambitious National Endowment for the Humanities grant, "Toward the Humanistic Study of Film," that made it possible for Harvard, in the words of his grant proposal, "to add a set of eight courses to the present curriculum in film and to develop new teaching and research tools" to "help secure the humanistic incorporation of film into universities."

With interludes as a visiting lecturer in philosophy at Berkeley and—enjoying the last gasp of the countercultural 1960s—a year of traveling in Europe and Africa, I lived in Cambridge, Massachusetts, between 1961, when I entered Harvard College, and 1973, when I completed my doctoral dissertation in philosophy—Cavell was my committee chair; Hilary Putnam and Robert Nozick the other members—and accepted a position as Assistant Professor in Cinema Studies at New York University.

In 1976 my sentence at NYU was commuted when, under the terms of the NEH grant, Cavell invited me to return to Harvard to help develop the kind of film curriculum he envisioned, one with no walls separating filmmaking from film studies, or film studies from philosophy or other branches of the humanities.

Cavell also persuaded Harvard University Press to establish the Harvard Film Studies series, with myself as the initial series editor. Among the first books in the series were Guzzetti's shot-by-shot reading of Godard's *Two or Three Things I Know About Her*, based on his contributions to that 1971–1972 seminar; Cavell's *Pursuits of Happiness*; and my own *Hitchcock—The Murderous Gaze* (1982, 2012)—all exemplary, in their different ways, of the "humanistic study of film" Cavell's NEH proposal envisioned.

For almost a decade, Harvard's Carpenter Center for the Visual Arts was to be home to myself; to Marian Keane; to Nick Browne; to Vlada Petric and the Harvard Film Archive; to Robert Gardner and the Film Study Center he founded; to Gilberto Perez, for the time he was a Mellon Fellow at Harvard; to Alfred Guzzetti, whose 1975 film *Family Portrait Sittings* was the subject of one of my first published essays; to visiting filmmakers such as the great Dušan Makavejev; and to brilliant students, Richard Pena and Mira Nair among them, who all took Cavell's vision to heart.

Carpenter Center was also a home away from home to Charles Warren, Norton Batkin, Alan Cholodenko, and Pepe Karmel, among others, all based in different departments. And Cavell was across the street in Emerson Hall.

Those were the days!

In that inspiring and nurturing environment, where thought-provoking conversations were an everyday occurrence, I wrote *The Murderous Gaze* and published numerous essays that were later to find their way into *The "I" of the Camera: Essays in Film Criticism, History and Aesthetics* (1988, 2004), my second book. In writing about film, my commitment, like Cavell's, was—and is—to open myself to film's own ways of expressing thoughts; to let each film reveal itself—and myself—to me; to allow the film to help teach me how to view it, how to think about it, how to find what I had at heart to say about it.

In the mid-1980s, when grant support had run its course, Cavell was unable to persuade Harvard, which was gearing up for a major fundraising drive and had imposed a moratorium on new tenure lines, to fund the additional permanent positions our visionary film program needed to be self-sustaining. And so, some of us went our separate ways. We kept faith with the program's vision, even as we never stopped regretting that our collective voice had been silenced—a voice that could have made a crucial difference within film studies as it was forging its identity as an academic field.

Petric, Gardner, and Guzzetti remained; Giuliana Bruno joined the faculty and taught her specialized courses; filmmakers as gifted as Ross McElwee and Robb Moss were hired to teach production; filmmakers of the stature of Raul Ruiz and Chantal Akerman were brought in as visiting artists; and the Harvard Film Archive continued its exemplary programs of screenings, lectures, and special events. But film at Harvard had become too fragmented, too lacking in a unifying vision, to fulfill the curricular role Cavell had envisioned for it. He continued to respect the serious and talented individuals who continued the teaching of film at Harvard, but he no longer had faith that a film program at Carpenter Center would be exemplary of "the humanistic incorporation of film into universities." Nor did he believe that some other Harvard department would, or could, foster such a curriculum.

With our collective voice silenced, there was little effective opposition, within the fledgling field of film studies, to the seductive but pernicious idea that, as I put it in "Excerpts from Memory," the legitimacy of film studies "could only be established by the 'higher authority' the field called 'theory'"—as if by adopting for the study of film systems of thought that claim to provide an unchallengeable place to stand outside our own experience, a field lacking an intellectual tradition of its own could acquire the authority of a science, an authority unattainable by acts of criticism accountable to experience (59).[1]

In choosing this path, the field divorced itself, to quote from the introduction to *Reading Cavell's "The World Viewed,"* from "the philosophical perspective of self-reflection apart from which we cannot know what movies mean, or what they really

---

1. Page references are to this volume.

are" (15). In Cavell's view, as he put it in a remark at a 1999 symposium I invoke more than once in the essays that follow, the study of film cannot be a "worthwhile human enterprise" if it "isolates itself" from the kind of criticism Walter Benjamin had in mind when he argued that "what establishes a work as art is its ability to inspire and sustain criticism of a certain sort, criticism that seeks to articulate the work's idea; what cannot be so criticized is not art" (4, 164). By privileging "theory" over criticism, academic film studies actively reinforced the philistine attitude of superiority to movies that Cavell saw as a mission of the serious study of film to transcend or overcome.

Years later, Harvard did make a serious commitment to the study of film by hiring David Rodowick—an ideal choice—to anchor a degree-granting graduate program. But by then, sadly, the identity of film studies as an academic field had become all but unalterable. Harvard had squandered its opportunity to play a leading role in shaping the field of film studies. And to this day, the "humanistic incorporation of film into universities," as Cavell envisioned it, has not fully been secured. In later years, Cavell would speak of this as the greatest disappointment of his professional life. That this never stopped feeling like an open wound to him accounts, I suspect, for the total absence of references in *Little Did I Know: Excerpts from Memory* (Cavell 2010), his philosophical memoir, to his years of tireless efforts to secure a place for film at Harvard worthy of his vision.

Two years after Harvard had made its fateful decision, Cavell persuaded the organizers of its ambitious new core curriculum program to include a course on moral reasoning. We might say that Cavell designed this course to stand alone, in the company only of other "core" courses but in the absence of the kind of curriculum in film he had long envisioned. Perhaps it is more accurate to say that Cavell packed so much substance into this extraordinarily demanding and challenging course that it constituted a curriculum in itself.

Cavell was to teach his moral reasoning course at Harvard every year until he retired from full-time teaching in 1997. After he retired from Harvard, he reprised it at the University of Chicago. And two decades after he initially taught the course, he used his lectures as the basis of his magisterial *Cities of Words: Pedagogical Letters on a Register of the Moral Life* (2005). As I put it in "Cavell, Emerson, Hitchcock," this book "pairs chapters on thinkers of the magnitude of Aristotle, Plato, Locke, Hume, Kant, Nietzsche, Freud, and Cavell's Harvard colleague John Rawls—as well as Shakespeare, Ibsen, Henry James, and George Bernard Shaw, who are treated, in this context, as the significant thinkers these artists also were—with chapters on individual films. . . . And Emerson is the linchpin that clinches Cavell's case" (177).

In 1985, when I left Harvard, my wife Kitty and I, turned screenwriters, almost succeeded in coproducing (with a New Zealand production company and Conacine, the Mexican government's boutique film studio) a Hitchcock-inspired romantic comedy thriller revolving around an ancient Mayan artifact. Gabriel Figueroa was slated to shoot the film, and Eli Wallach was on board (it was a rare chance for him to play a Mexican who shaved). But then, in a double whammy, the New Zealand tax law changed, causing feature film production to fall from thirty to zero a year, and the Mexican peso collapsed.

For the next three years, Kitty and I continued to try to get film projects off the ground even as we traveled the world leading the International Honors Program on Film, Television, and Social Change in Europe and Asia. In 1989, we wrote and produced (with the National Film Development Corporation of India) the 35-mm feature film *Unn*, directed in the state of Kerala by the visionary Indian director G. Aravindan. And we signed a contract to coproduce a film with the Shanghai Film Studio. When the Tiananmen Square massacre aborted that project, the time had come for me to be a film studies professor again—only a little differently this time. After concurrent stints as a visiting professor at both UCLA and USC, I happily accepted my present position at the University of Miami in the only city in the continental United States that looks a bit like the South India with which Kitty and I had fallen in love.

We have no regrets.

During our vagabond years, filled with mind-expanding experiences, I didn't expect that I would ever again be—or wish to be—a film studies professor. And yet, I never stopped thinking philosophically about film. I continued as a series editor of the Cambridge University Press Studies in Film series, and in 1988 published *The "I" of the Camera*, for which I wrote new essays on D. W. Griffith's *Birth of a Nation* and *True Heart Susie*, on the ending of Chaplin's *City Lights*, and on Jean Renoir's *The River*.

In reclaiming my identity as a film studies professor, I made two resolutions I have kept faith with ever since. One resolution, which has proved hugely consequential to my life as a writer, was to continue to publish the kind of philosophical film criticism I believed in, loved, and had made my own. In this spirit, I wrote my third book, *Documentary Film Classics* (1997), in which I "read" five landmark documentaries in the manner of the readings of five Hitchcock films in *The Murderous Gaze*. I subsequently edited and contributed introductions and essays to two additional books on documentaries, *Jean Rouch: A Celebration of Life and Film* (2007) and *Three Documentary Filmmakers* (2009), and later coedited (with Charles Warren and Rebecca Myers) *Looking with Robert Gardner* (2016). In 2004, I put together a new edition of *The "I" of the Camera*, doubled in size by the addition of essays written subsequent to 1988. In 2012, I published, for SUNY's Horizons in Cinema series, an expanded edition of *The Murderous Gaze*, augmented by a chapter on *Marnie* that is now the longest in the book. Two years later, I published *Must We Kill the Thing We Love? Emersonian Perfectionism and the Films of Alfred Hitchcock* (2014). And in 2019, I published *Tuitions and Intuitions*, a new book of essays.

My second resolution, which has proved equally consequential, was to do everything in my power to provoke the field of film studies to acknowledge the profound implications, for the serious study of film, of Cavell's vision of a marriage of film studies and philosophy. For in 1990, academic film studies in the English-speaking world was more than ever straitjacketed by "theory." The field as a whole accepted as unquestionable doctrines a number of claims or assumptions—I think of them as dogmas—that were anathema to Cavell and to me. Within film studies, for example, it was dogma that, as Marian Keane and I would put it in our introduction to *Reading Cavell's "The World Viewed,"* classical Hollywood movies "systematically subordinate women by aligning the camera with the male gaze, among other means, and, more generally, that movies are pernicious ideological representations to be decoded and resisted, not treated as works of art capable of instructing us as to how to view them" (18).

It was also dogma that "the stars projected on the movie screen in classical movies are 'personas,' discursive ideological constructs, not real people; that the world projected on the screen is itself an ideological construct, not real"; and—this view is emblematic of philosophical skepticism—that "reality itself"—the one existing world—"is such a construct, too."

In 1990, to celebrate my return to film studies, I wrote, as a labor of love and in a white heat of inspiration, "Cavell's Creation," the earliest of the essays in *The Holiday in His Eye*. (It was published three years later in *Pursuits of Reason: Essays in Honor of Stanley Cavell* (Cohen, Guyer, and Putnam 1993). "Cavell's Creation" is in some ways quite unlike the other essays in *The Holiday in His Eye*, but it's one for which I have a special fondness, despite its excesses and eccentricities. I must admit that I am perhaps a bit inordinately proud of the way the essay anticipated, or prophesied, Cavell's late turning to autobiography in *A Pitch of Philosophy: Autobiographical Exercises* (1994) and ultimately *Little Did I Know* (2010). I think of his turning to autobiography as one of the most consequential events in his life as a writer.

Although Cavell's work had long been profoundly enabling for me, I had never before made his writings an explicit subject of study in writings of my own. I credit the joyful and liberating experience of writing "Cavell's Creation" for bringing home to me how rewarding it is to read Cavell's writing with the kind and degree of attention I had learned to devote to films I cared about—the kind and degree of attention required to know one's own mind, as Cavell liked to put it.

As I said, I wrote "Cavell's Creation" to celebrate my return to film studies. But in 1990, "theory" had for almost two decades lulled the field into ever deepening dogmatic slumbers. 1990 was the year, for example, that *Critical Inquiry* published a letter by Tania Modleski, who was considered within film studies to be a leading feminist theorist, that (absurdly) impugned Cavell's integrity as a scholar, along with his pained but devastating response (which he included in *Contesting Tears* as a postscript to his reading of *Now, Voyager*).

The following year, the Society for Cinema Studies (it hadn't yet added "Media" to its name) rejected the panel on Cavell that I had proposed for its annual conference. My suspicion that this panel proposal had been rejected because the name "Cavell" had raised a red flag, that Cavell was blackballed or blacklisted, in effect, was confirmed by a member of the conference committee, who made me swear not to divulge his name. I complained so vehemently that SCS compromised, still rejecting the Cavell panel but accepting my paper ("Cavell's Philosophy and What

Film Studies Calls 'Theory,'" which it added to a panel with the inoffensive title "Film Theory II." I've included it in *The Holiday in His Eye*, although in retrospect I regret that the paper failed to make clear that the real target of my critique was not the work of such serious thinkers as Roland Barthes, Jacques Derrida, Michel Foucault, Julia Kristeva, and Jacques Lacan, who were ascendant in the intellectual life of post–May '68 France, where they were in conversation—and debates—with each other. What my paper derisively calls "theory" is what *became* of their systems of thought when the field of film study in America, in search of a way to prove its legitimacy, reduced their serious ideas to slogans that students could readily be trained to parrot.

I was also added to a panel of speakers asked to make brief remarks (which I've included in this book) at a plenary session devoted to "multiculturalism," the official conference theme. From that podium, I undertook to show how the language of the call for submissions of conference papers and panel proposals was symptomatic of the field's unhealthy regime of conformity. My remarks concluded by rebuking SCS, the field's primary professional organization, for dictating that its members were "to affirm that human beings speak in many voices" but, in so affirming, "were all to speak in one voice."

Unlike Woody Allen and Groucho Marx before him, who didn't want to belong to any club that would have him as a member, I resented having to renew my membership in a field that didn't value my kind of work. Hence the angrily polemical tone of my SCS paper and my remarks at the plenary session. This anger spilled over to other early pieces I've included in *The Holiday in His Eye* (the two unpublished reviews I've put together as "In Defense of *Pursuits of Happiness*" and my response to Vivian Sobchack's *The Address of the Eye*). In these pieces, my anger was directed at the reader, whom I addressed as a representative of a field I wanted to shame into waking up to the value of Cavell's work—and my own. Hardly an approach likely to succeed.

Among the later essays in the book, the only one in which anger repeatedly flares up is "On Richard Allen's 'Hitchcock and Cavell.'" In that piece, though, the anger in my words isn't directed at a reader I take to be hostile. My anger isn't even directed at Richard Allen personally, whom I think of as a friend and toward whom I harbor no hostility. And please rest assured, dear reader, that I'm not angry at you. Why should I be? If you were hostile to what I have to say about Cavell's writing, if you didn't want to be a friend, why would you be reading these words? If I didn't want you to be a friend, why would I be writing them?

By the end of the 1990s, my friend and comrade-in-arms Marian Keane and I both recognized, the tyrannical reign of theoretical systematizing had loosened its grip on film studies. Few still had the stomach for doing "theory." But few were willing, or able, to do the work of contesting its doctrines, clearing away the debris and ideological landmines that so cluttered the field's intellectual landscape that they were formidable obstacles to moving forward. The field may have stopped privileging "theory" over criticism, but it no more favored criticism—much less criticism that is also philosophy—than it had in the heyday of "theory." Only now criticism was being subordinated to what the field called "historiography" (the word "history" being insufficiently scientific-sounding). Because research into the history of film was being conducted within an academic field still wearing the ideological blinders bequeathed by "theory," it was still "theory" that was setting the agenda.

At least, that was how Marian and I saw it. We were convinced that academic film studies had reached an impasse at which the field couldn't move forward without *undoing* "theory." And that it couldn't fully awaken from its dogmatic slumbers without looking back, with an open mind, and achieving a new perspective on its own history. And it was clear to us that at every juncture within the history of film studies, Cavell had blazed a path that the field had chosen not to follow—roads not taken to regions that still remained to be explored. And so, Marian and I wrote *Reading Cavell's "The World Viewed": A Philosophical Perspective on Film*.

Reading Cavell's "The World Viewed" is not angry or polemical. In it, we simply read Cavell's brilliant and beautiful little book, from beginning to end, with the kind and degree of attention its writing calls for—the kind and degree of attention it takes to discover that, and how, it reads itself. What better corrective could there be to the notion that prevailed within the field—it is still all too widely believed—that Cavell's prose is imprecise, opaque, and self-indulgent, and his arguments, if there are any, impossible to follow?

The book's introduction described our method:

> In the pages that follow, whenever a passage thwarts our comprehension, we keep thinking the passage through until we arrive at an interpretation that sustains our conviction—until an intuition dawns in us, prompted by Cavell's words, as to what those words are saying in this context, what prompted the author of *The World Viewed* to use precisely these words on precisely this occasion, and what prompted us until now to resist this understanding. In striving to arrive at words of our own we can trust to express our understanding of the words Cavell had arrived at ("to follow out in each case the complete tuition for a given intuition"), we read *The World Viewed* in a way that quite literally follows Cavell's thinking with the attention necessary to decipher our own. And, at each point, our writing invites readers to check Cavell's words, and ours, against their own experience, their own understanding. (20)

I've included in *The Holiday in His Eye* the introduction and two key chapters of *Reading Cavell's "The World Viewed"* (all parts predominantly written by me). They earnestly reflect our hopefulness, at the time, that reintroducing *The World Viewed* to the field of film studies, demonstrating that the book *can* be read and how it calls for being read, would move the field to take seriously the philosophical alternative that Cavell's way of thinking offered. "Theory," with its dogmas and faux-scientific pretensions, had caused film studies and philosophy, happily married in Cavell's writings, to divorce. Wasn't it time for their remarriage?

In 1971, when *The World Viewed* originally appeared, Cavell was disappointed by its reception, or its lack of reception, as he would be by the reception, or lack of reception, of the expanded edition (augmented by "More of *The World Viewed*") he published in 1979—the year he completed his philosophical masterwork *The Claim of Reason*. When Cavell read our book, he told me that he was deeply moved by it; we had given *The World Viewed* back to him, was the way he put it. But he also gently warned that Marian and I shouldn't expect our book to spark a revolution within film studies, as we were hoping. In his words: "The field has already had its revolution." I only gradually came to understand, and accept, what he was telling us.

In writing his early essays, and in putting them together to make *Must We Mean What We Say?*, his first book, Cavell understood himself to be embracing, and in a sense *completing*, a revolution in philosophy exemplified by the appeals to ordinary language in Ludwig Wittgenstein's *Philosophical Investigations* and the essays of J. L. Austin. The postscript to *Reading Cavell's "The World Viewed"* characterizes the aspiration of *Must We Mean What We Say?* as "raising the procedures of ordinary language philosophy to an explicit self-consciousness" (Rothman and Keane 2000, 234). And the postscript summarizes Cavell's reasons for believing his own practice of philosophy to be revolutionary.

Did *We Mean What We Say?* actually spark a revolution within philosophy? Not if we take that to mean that it provoked a radical change within the field as a whole, a paradigm shift in its agenda and its sense of its own identity as an intellectual discipline. When *Must We Mean What We Say?* was published, even most philosophers who were impressed by it doubted that it was really philosophy. Cavell persevered, though, and eventually gained sufficient acceptance among academic philosophers to be elected president of the Eastern Division of the American Philosophical Association. But philosophy *as Cavell understood and practiced it* was never during his lifetime—and is not now—ascendant within the field of philosophy as a whole. For most philosophy professors and their students then and now, Cavell's revolutionary understanding and practice of philosophy had little if any impact on their own philosophical procedure. On the other hand, I would wager that virtually every major American philosophy department has at least one faculty member whose work Cavell's writings have influenced and inspired—in many cases, radically transformed. And the same can be said for major universities all over the world.

In literary studies and other fields on which Cavell's writings have a bearing, such as literary studies, American studies, and religious studies, Cavell's ideas are widely, if hardly universally, acknowledged as significant contributions. Few serious Shakespeare scholars, or Emerson scholars, simply dismiss his work. But the Society for Cinema and Media Studies (né Society for Cinema Studies) repeatedly rebuffed requests to formally acknowledge his lifetime of achievement. The field of film studies is unique in harboring a long-standing animus against Cavell. How is this to be explained?

The study of literature, of course, has a tradition as old as literature itself. When the theoretical frameworks ascendant in post–May '68 France took literary studies in America by storm, this reflected a widespread perception, especially among young professors in the field, that the traditional modes and methods of literary criticism were exhausted. But when film studies, following literary studies, embraced what it called "theory," the field was just beginning to develop its own critical terms and methods. Lacking a tradition of its own, film studies embraced "theory" in the hope of gaining recognition as a legitimate academic field in its own right. For film studies, the reign of "theory" was singularly tyrannical because it could lay claim to being "the only game in town"—as if questioning its anointed doctrines was tantamount to denying the field's legitimacy, calling into question its very existence. For film studies professors of my generation, Cavell's writings were all but universally condemned—without being seriously read—as *heresies* that posed an existential threat to the field. For better or worse, film studies professors of my generation have mostly faded from the scene. And the animus against Cavell has mostly faded with them. At least in principle, the field is now open to taking Cavell seriously in a way it hadn't been ever since its earliest years, when by turning to "theory" it turned away from philosophy.

In recent years, of course, there has emerged a flourishing academic field, or subfield, which boasts its own professional organization with its own annual conference and online journal, that answers to the name "Film Philosophy" (sometimes with, sometimes without, a hyphen between the words). Surely, this was a welcome development. But it doesn't signify that Cavell's vision of a marriage of film studies and philosophy has triumphed, that film's "humanistic incorporation into universities," as he envisioned it, has been secured. After all, "Film Philosophy" is predicated on a marriage of two academic fields but, as I've said, in neither of these fields, as it stands, is Cavell's way of thinking ascendant. From my point of view, the good news is that the organizers of the 2019 Film Philosophy Conference welcomed the panel on the continued relevance of Cavell's work to film studies, which I proposed with Catherine Wheatley (whose important book *Stanley Cavell and Film: Scepticism and Self-Reliance at the Cinema* was about to be released). And Andrew Klevan—there's no keener reader of Cavell—was chosen to be one of the keynote speakers. The bad news is that Cavell's revolutionary understanding and practice of philosophy had no discernible influence on the vast majority of papers presented at the conference.

Within the field of film studies as a whole, taking Cavell seriously is still a lonely enterprise. Cavell died in 2018, yet in the titles of the roughly 1,800 papers at the Society for Cinema and Media Studies Conference the following year, the name "Cavell" appears exactly two times—in the title of a paper for a panel on Hannah Arendt, and the title of a paper pairing Cavell with Gilles Deleuze—the only time the name "Deleuze" appears at all, by the way.

Within American universities, being French is still a formidable selling point for a film theorist. But despite the considerable attention within the field to his *Cinema* books, Deleuze doesn't occupy, any more than Cavell does, anything like the exalted position once bestowed upon the likes of Jacques Lacan. As I observed in the introduction to *Tuitions and Intuitions*, when I was on the 1992 Society for Cinema Studies Dissertation Committee, of the fifteen dissertations I was given to read, "fourteen described their goal as developing a Lacanian approach to film studies (the one holdout being a dissertation about films made from x-rays, a topic not amenable to a Lacanian approach, since only baby Superman could see his own mirror image with x-ray vision)" (Rothman 2019, 8).

To indulge in understatement, neither Deleuze's ideas nor Cavell's hold much sway within film studies, a field in which only a tiny minority have seriously *read* their writings. Even in the heyday of "theory," to be sure, virtually no one in the field actually read Lacan, either. But Lacan, unread, can readily be reduced to parrotable slogans. Deleuze, unread, cannot be. Neither can Cavell. And yet, when I recently did a cursory search for "film + Cavell" on the University of Miami libraries website, I was surprised to discover that the search returned literally hundreds of journal articles and dozens of books. Some are by writers whose work on Cavell I know and admire. But the majority are by writers, mostly young (by my standard, which is quite a low bar these days), whose names weren't familiar to me. This bodes well for the future.

In the heyday of "theory," it was common for writers within film studies to buy into and propagate the myth that "everyone"—including their readers—knew that Cavell's thoughts about film had already, *somewhere*, been discredited. That practice seems largely to have died out. But the practice of buying into and propagating the myth that Cavell was simply a bad writer, and that "everyone"—including the reader—already knew this, has very much not died out. Rhetorically, the effect is to authorize the reader, for whom feeling superior to Cavell may or may not be a preexisting condition, to feel entitled to look down on his writing.

In her 1991 book *The Address of the Eye*, for example, Vivian Sobchack, championing Merleau-Ponty's brand of phenomenology as an alternative to "theory," asserted, as I put it in the unpublished review of her book I've included in *The Holiday in His Eye*, that Cavell "can legitimately be dismissed"—her wording implies that within film studies Cavell *is* dismissed, and rightly so—for lacking "systematic rigor," for being "enthusiastic but methodless," and for thus appearing "at best metaphysically arcane, at worst metaphorically vague and mystically poetic."

Richard Allen's 2006 essay "Hitchcock and Cavell" wouldn't have sparked my anger so much if I hadn't been so acutely aware how common it still was, even at that late date, for writers within film studies to encourage their readers to assume—or to assume that their readers already assumed—an attitude of superiority to Cavell. That attitude was not only utterly unearned—Cavell was a major American philosopher, after all—but precluded reading his writings with the kind and degree of attention it takes to follow his thinking.

Sadly, even some writers in the field of film studies who do take Cavell's work seriously seem to feel the need, at times, to play to, rather than confront and contest, the notion that "everyone" knows that Cavell is a bad writer. I'm thinking, for example, of Jennifer Fay and Daniel Morgan, who observe, in their introduction to "Cinema, Modernism, and the Perplexing Methods of Stanley Cavell," the valuable special issue of *Discourse* they coedited, that Cavell "takes stock on occasion, and sometimes maddeningly, of erroneous recollections of plot and character that he refused to correct in subsequent editions of *The World Viewed*" (Fay and Morgan 2021, 4). They don't point out that Cavell devoted the early pages of the preface to the 1979 expanded edition to reflections on the handful of erroneous descriptions in *The World Viewed* that he had become cognizant of. (As far as I am aware, there are no such glaring misdescriptions in Cavell's later writings, when he had access to video copies of the films he was discussing.) So why should any reader, having been forewarned of such a misdescription, find it "maddening"—especially a reader like Morgan, the author of *Late Godard and the Possibilities of Cinema* (2013), a masterful study of works that, on first encounter, anyone who is not already mad would find maddening? If Ray and Morgan testify that they find some Cavell passages maddening, who am I to doubt them? My gripe is with their failure to be specific, thus making it impossible for readers to check the authors' testimony against their own experience. And in saying that in later editions Cavell "refused to correct" erroneous recollections, the word "refused" is no less gratuitous than their use of "maddeningly." It serves no purpose other than to intimate, without literally saying it, that Cavell's "refusal" was wrongheaded. Perverse.

Rhetorically, "maddeningly" and "refused" function as winks and nods to indicate that Ray and Morgan are not dissociating themselves, or at least not completely, from readers who look down on Cavell's writing, and that they are keeping enough distance from Cavell to read him objectively. Then, too, Ray and Morgan named their special issue "Cinema, Modernism, and the Perplexing Methods of Stanley Cavell" even though they are astute readers who are *not* perplexed by Cavell's methods. Whatever perplexity they may have experienced when they first read *The World Viewed*—and it could not have been greater than the perplexity Morgan must have felt when he began thinking through Godard's late works—they rose to the challenge of thinking their way through Cavell's book to arrive at an interpretation they find convincing. The word "perplexing" functions only as another signifier of the authors' "objectivity," another wink and nod to readers who believe in a myth about Cavell's writing that Ray and Morgan don't actually believe in—as if avoiding alienating readers who believe in that myth took precedence over opening their eyes—and, perhaps, took precedence over unguardedly declaring their conviction in *The World Viewed*. It's probably more accurate to say, though, that it reflects a less than full commitment to Cavell's way of thinking. After all, from where I stand, from the perspective articulated in *Reading Cavell's "The World Viewed,"* Ray's and Morgan's interpretation of *The World Viewed* is partial and skewed, fixated as it is on the concept of modernism—a term that drops out of Cavell's lexicon at a later stage of his thinking.

Catherine Wheatley is another astute reader who takes Cavell's work seriously but felt the need, in the first chapter of her otherwise admirable study *Stanley Cavell and Film*, to play to, rather than confront, the notion that "everyone" knows that Cavell is a bad writer. There, she devotes page after page to quoting, without contesting, harsh rebukes by authors so smug in their sense of superiority to Cavell's writing, so oblivious of their own failures to follow his thinking, that they don't even deign to cite specific passages. If Wheatley believed that these rebukes had merit, she would not—could not—have written the insightful and appreciative chapters that follow. But in the opening chapter, sadly, she doesn't attempt to defend Cavell against these baseless attacks. By refraining—in this case, "refusing" may be an apter word—from declaring where she stands, she allows, and inadvertently encourages, her readers to assume that she is letting these authors speak for her. Thankfully, however, as *Stanley Cavell and Film* unfolds, Wheatley's conviction in Cavell's ideas about film indeed, her love for his writing—movingly reveals itself. And her own book overcomes or transcends its needlessly guarded opening and becomes a powerful lesson in the value of self-reliance, a lesson Wheatley is grateful to Cavell's writing for helping her to learn—and to teach. I can't help but muse that if academic presses could still afford to keep true copy editors on staff, an editor who was passionate about her craft would have undertaken to open Wheatley's eyes to the need to jettison these rebukes or else to rebuke them herself. (Here, I'm thinking fondly of Joyce Backman at Harvard University Press who, fifty years ago, was the copy editor for *The Murderous Gaze*. Her countless queries and comments were meant not only to push me to improve the manuscript in ways small and large, but to teach me how to edit my own writing.)

In a different category is Noel Carroll, a highly regarded philosopher whose work I generally respect and whose character, as a human being, I admire. In "Revisiting *The World Viewed*," his contribution to *The Thought of Stanley Cavell and Cinema* (LaRocca 2020), the invaluable anthology edited by David LaRocca, Carroll, to his credit, never resorts to language that is condescending or patronizing toward *The World Viewed*. He writes, "The book, I think, it is fair to say is not an easy read," but doesn't try to account for its difficulty by suggesting that Cavell was a bad writer (Carroll 2020, 41). When he adds that *The World Viewed* has "a reputation, in some quarters, for obscurity," he is dissociating himself from the denizens of those unsavory "quarters," not from Cavell. He remarks, sensibly, that a reason for the book's difficulty is that Cavell is involved in doing a number of things at the same time. However, Carroll's list of those "things"—proposing a philosophy of film; distilling philosophical insights from individual films; doing film criticism; doing traditional philosophy, including political philosophy—is revealing for what it leaves out. It leaves out, for example, the interlocking concerns that led Cavell to characterize his book as a "metaphysical memoir": the writing's self-referential aspect, its prompting as a response to what he describes as the breaking of his "natural relation" to movies—a response whose philosophical dimension can't be separated from its personal or autobiographical dimension, or from its historical dimension (the book's reflections on the moment in history, and in the history of film, at which its own writing was prompted).

Carroll observes that Cavell's diverse concerns "interweave in ways that can seem digressive." But he defends *The World Viewed* by saying, "I think it possesses a reasonably continuous, through-argument, despite the apparent digressions" (Carroll 2020, 41–42). And so, Carroll sets out how he will be proceeding in his essay.

First, he will trace what he takes that argument to be "by way of an extended commentary," then "review the argument critically," highlighting what he sees "as potential problems" (Carroll 2020, 42).

If I were writing an article for an academic philosophy journal about Carroll's essay, I would do well to follow such a procedure. But to proceed that way with *The World Viewed* is to fail to acknowledge what is revolutionary about Cavell's way of doing philosophy. Carroll's claim, in effect, is that Cavell's apparent digressions aren't really digressions because they support the book's "through-argument"—as if in Cavell's book there were a hierarchy of ideas, a pyramid with the conclusion of the "through argument" at the apex.

Cavell was well trained in the methods of analytical philosophy and, when he had a motivation to do so, was capable of constructing arguments with ironclad logic. But for Cavell, philosophy is not all about arguments, not about proving claims to be true or false. For Cavell, as for Emerson, philosophical ideas are born from intuitions. And what might seem digressions are like riffs in jazz; they aren't really digressions because for Cavell every intuition, potentially, is of value in its own right, not merely as a step in a single "through argument." But to redeem its potential value, to transform an intuition into an idea, a thought, much less a thought with a bearing on philosophy, what Emerson calls "tuition" must be paid; the intuition has to be given expression, expressed in a way that is *meant*, not proven to be true.

For all his respect for *The World Viewed*, Carroll has a long-standing gripe against Cavell's view of film—one that goes back almost fifty years to Carroll's days as a protégé of Annette Michelson in the NYU Cinema Studies doctoral program—a time in the history of the field of film studies on the eve of its surrender to "theory." Michelson, who had admired *Must We Mean What We Say?*, was hostile to *The World Viewed* because of what she perceived as Cavell's hostility to the tradition of "anti-illusionistic" cinema, from *Man with a Movie Camera* to contemporary films by the likes of Stan Brakhage and Michael Snow, that she championed.

Carroll writes, "Cavell charges that films in this tradition that declare that cinema is a matter of light and movement do not strike him as having the force of art. But that is something to be proven, not merely asserted." Note, however, that Cavell is not saying that such films *lack* the force of art. That might well be a claim requiring something akin to a proof (although it's unclear how one might go about proving such a claim). What Cavell is saying is that such films *do not strike him* as having the force of art. And that is not a claim that requires, or even allows for, proof. Thus, it is *not* "incumbent on Cavell," as Carroll insists, "to show why films such as Stan Brakhage's *The Text of Light* (1974) lack the so-called force of art" (Carroll 2020, 59). To be sure, Carroll could, by means of an act of criticism that marshaled evidence drawn from his own experience—not from some theory or other—make a case for *The Text of Light* as a work of art. But if Cavell still didn't experience Brakhage's film as having the force of art, no act of criticism can prove him wrong. Criticism isn't all about proofs. Neither is philosophy, as Cavell understood and practiced it.

What I say in "On Richard Allen's 'Hitchcock and Cavell'" applies equally to Carroll. Carroll proceeds in identifying and characterizing Cavell's "through argument" the way Allen proceeds in identifying and characterizing what he calls "Cavell's philosophy": by summarizing or paraphrasing, only occasionally quoting—and then, out of context—Cavell's actual words. You can't do that with Cavell. Like Allen, Carroll "often gets Cavell almost right, but with Cavell's writing, or Emerson's before him, getting him almost right means getting him completely wrong" (188).

In *Reading Cavell's "The World Viewed,"* as you will see, Marian Keane and I were able quite straightforwardly to refute, simply by citing the actual words of *The World Viewed*, Carroll's claim, in his book *Philosophical Problems of Classical Film Theory* (1988), to have exposed a problem with Cavell's argument and thereby disproved his view of film's relation to reality. In "Revisiting *The World Viewed*," written twenty years after the publication of *Reading Cavell's "The World Viewed,"* Carroll still counts this as one of the "potential problems" he finds in *The World Viewed*. I can't demonstrate this in detail here, although it is a claim whose truth or falsity is amenable to proof, but it is clear to me that all of the "potential problems" he cites in "Revisiting *The World Viewed*" only seem like problems to him because of his misreadings of Cavell's text. I can't help but believe that if he had read *Reading Cavell's "The World Viewed,"* or read it with the kind and degree of attention Marian and I devoted to Cavell's book, Carroll would have written a very different essay—or not written an essay about *The World Viewed* at all.

In truth, Carroll's essay is rife with instances in which he gets Cavell completely wrong—and not always by getting him almost right. To pick an example at random, Carroll writes, "Film fulfills the wish for invisibility. We can view the world unseen. This satisfies a desire for anonymity of modern privacy" (Carroll 2020, 53). But Cavell's idea is not that film satisfies our desire for anonymity; modern human beings like us are all too familiar with feeling anonymous. What film does is to relieve us of responsibility for this unnatural condition, making our sense of being invisible to the world seem like our natural condition.

Here's another example. Carroll writes, "Cavell intends his ruminations on the ontology of film to be taken symbolically, as 'mythological descriptions of the state of someone in the grip of a movie'" (Carroll 2020, 54). Ending the sentence by quoting Cavell's own words may seem to assure that Carroll is getting him right. But here is Cavell's whole sentence:

> When at the end of my book I say, "The actors are there . . . in your world, but . . . you cannot go there now. . . . In a movie house, the barrier to the stars is time," I was counting on having earned the right to expect my reader to take these expressions symbolically, as mythological descriptions of the state of someone in the grip of a movie. (Cavell 1979b, 211)

What Cavell is saying, perfectly clearly, is that these *particular* "expressions," not "his ruminations on the ontology of film" in general, are to be taken symbolically. This is a misreading with major consequences.

Here's an even more consequential example. It's crucial to Carroll's interpretation of *The World Viewed* that although Cavell sometimes waffles—I don't believe he really does—on the question of film's relation to modernism, his book's "through argument" hinges on the claim that film's ontology makes it *impossible* for it to be a modernist art. But *The World Viewed* never makes such a claim. Indeed, Cavell makes clear that he accepts certain "art films" of the 1960s as modernist. And *The World Viewed* characterizes the present moment of film's history—the book was published in 1971—as one in which, even as traditional movies continued to be made, film was, however belatedly, entering what he calls a "modernist environment."

In any case, Cavell's thinking about film's relation to modernism deepens over the years. In his 1981 essay "*North by Northwest*," for example, he writes, in a passage you will encounter again in the pages that follow, "What I found in turning to think about film was a medium which seemed simultaneously to be free of the imperative to philosophy and at the same time inevitably to reflect upon itself—as though the condition of philosophy were its natural condition" (Cavell and Rothman 2005, xxii). In Cavell's view, as I point out in "Stanley Cavell, Victor Perkins, and the Personal," painting only brought itself under its own question, in the way Cavell takes to be defining for philosophy, "when painters like Manet could no longer make paintings they believed in without breaking with the tradition they wished to keep alive. But being 'under its own question' *is* film's tradition, *The World Viewed* argues" (254).

In *Must We Mean What We Say?*, Cavell suggests that the essential fact about the modern in art or philosophy "lies in the relation between the present practice of an enterprise and the history of that enterprise, in the fact that this relation has become problematic" (Cavell 2002, 6). But if "being under its own question," which is philosophy's tradition, is film's tradition, too, what could modernism in film—or in philosophy, for that matter—possibly be? And so, in later stages of Cavell's thinking, he stops using the word "modernism," which played such a key role in *The World Viewed*. And, as I suggest in "Cavell Reading Cavell," it's no coincidence that this occurred simultaneously with his discovery of Emerson.

In this context, I can't resist adding a little anecdote. When I submitted my proposal for *The Holiday in His Eye* to SUNY Press, one of the two external reviewers who were sent the proposal, although generally positive, complained that it contained some claims that were obviously false. That may be; who am I to say? But the sole instance cited was my assertion, in "Cavell on Film, Television, and Opera" and in earlier draft of this preface, that Cavell was the only major philosopher in the English-speaking world who had made writing about film an essential part of his work. Why did this reviewer think that this claim was obviously false? Because I had left out Noel Carroll. Judged by the standards that prevail within Anglo-American philosophy departments, it may seem obvious that Carroll is a major philosopher. I hope my preceding remarks make clear why, judged by my standards—judged from the perspective of the way of thinking that underwrites, and is underwritten by, the essays in *The Holiday in His Eye*—it is obvious that he is not. This is an issue open to debate, of course. But to assert that my claim is obviously false is to dismiss it out of hand—the way all of Cavell's ideas about film were for so long dismissed out of hand within film studies.

In 2019, Sandra Laugier and Elise Domenach organized an international conference ("La pensée du cinéma: En hommage à Stanley Cavell") at the Sorbonne. At all the conferences on Cavell's work that followed his death in 2018, there were thoughtful papers addressing his film books. But the Sorbonne conference was the only one focused exclusively on Cavell's thoughts about film. There were dozens of papers, most of a very high standard, presented by speakers from England, Italy, Belgium, Switzerland, Germany, the United States, Canada, Peru, Japan, and all regions of France.

Gratifyingly, there were many young speakers whose work I hadn't been familiar with. There were also many distinguished scholars I'd already had the pleasure of getting to know at earlier conferences. To name a few (in alphabetical order): Hugo Clémot, Alice Crary, Elise Domenach, Piergiorgio Donatelli, Russell Goodman, Andrew Klevan, Victor Krebs, David LaRocca, Sandra Laugier, Daniele Lorenzini, Richard Moran, Paola Marrati, Stephen Mulhall, Jean-Philippe Narboux, Naoko Saito, Paul Standish, Kate Rennebohm, and David Rodowick. And there are so many more I could add from other conferences—again to name only a few: Steven Affeldt, Norton Batkin, Avner Baz, Charles Bernstein, Rex Butler, Jay Cantor, Bill Day, Robert Egelman, Juliet Floyd, Paul Franks, Eli Friedlander, Tim Gould, Toril Moi, Naomi Scheman, Robert Sinnebrink, and Andreas Teuber.

Just running through these lists of names sparks memories of the wonderful experiences I've had, over the years, at conferences where conviction in the value of Cavell's work wasn't alienating but, rather, a common bond, the source of a sense of belonging to a true community of scholars—an international community, spanning diverse intellectual disciplines, that no doubt has far more members than the Society for Cinema and Media Studies.

A corollary to the widespread notion that Cavell was a bad writer is the equally pernicious myth that those for whom his work is singularly important are nothing but members of a cult who mindlessly follow the cult leader, rather than readers who have learned the value of attending to his writings with the attention required to follow his thinking and their own. Thus, as I note with annoyance in "On Richard Allen's 'Hitchcock and Cavell,'" Allen feels free to call me, in a footnote, "Cavell's disciple"—as if my books and essays were devoted to proselytizing the Gospel of Cavell *as opposed to* thinking for myself, "paying the tuition" for intuitions of my own. As Cavell put it in *Must We Mean What We Say?*, if philosophy, as he understood and practiced it, "is esoteric, that is not because a few guard its knowledge, but because most guard themselves against it" (Cavell 2002, xxvii).

What Marian Keane and I say about *The World Viewed* in our book about Cavell's book can equally be said about all his writings:

> That the writing of *The World Viewed* possesses accuracy and consequentiality means that its thinking *is* worth following with the attention we devote to it. It also means that attending to the words of *The World Viewed* can be singularly difficult. Yet apart from facing this difficulty, it is not

possible to know what makes the book worth attending to in this way. Apart from reading *The World Viewed* in a way that is worthy of it, it is not possible to know the book's true worth. (21)

Emphasizing the difficulty of Cavell's writing, however, risks lending credence to the pernicious notion that he was such a bad writer that reading his prose cannot but be a frustrating, unpleasant experience. As you will discover from the essays that follow—unless you find my prose frustrating and unpleasant—I find Cavell to be a *great* writer, one whose prose I find inspiring, liberating, empowering—and *pleasurable*. You will discover, in short, that I *love* reading Cavell. And if you aren't a reader who already knows this, I hope you will discover why his writings are worthy of love.

As I read them, Cavell's writings are rigorous philosophy, but they are also well-wrought aesthetic objects. Cavell studied composition at Juilliard before the intuition dawned in him that philosophy, not music, was his calling. But it's not that he abandoned his dream of becoming a serious composer. His compositions are his writings. For me—and for so many others—the experience of reading a Cavell book or essay, like listening to great music, is meaningful, and of value, in and of itself—a source of unending pleasure not in spite of but thanks to its difficulty or, more precisely, its particular way of being difficult, its way of continually challenging the reader to follow the thinking it expresses, savoring the ways Cavell pays the tuition for his intuitions.

"On Stanley Cavell's *Band Wagon*," my reading of two essays on Fred Astaire in Cavell's collection *Philosophy the Day After Tomorrow* (2005b), concludes by claiming that these essays at once exemplify and articulate an idea of criticism "as a form of gratitude, or of gratitude as a form of criticism that aesthetic objects can move us passionately to express. That idea, and the kindred idea that there is room for praise within philosophy, are among Cavell's most praiseworthy contributions, worthy of gratitude, to philosophy today, tomorrow, and the day after tomorrow" (240).

And, as I might well have added, they are also among Cavell's most praiseworthy contributions, worthy of gratitude, to film studies. His writings—and, I'd like to think, mine—are specific antibodies to the virus, which for so long infected the field and whose toxic effects still linger, that to think seriously about film, the first and most crucial thing we must do is break our attachment to movies that are meaningful to us, movies we love. As I put it in "Cavell, Emerson, Hitchcock," if we stop letting films move us, "we cannot think seriously about their value to us, why we seek our attachments to them, how they attract us, what rightful call they make upon us. That is, we cannot think seriously about films at all" (182).

In part, all the essays in *The Holiday in His Eye* were written in praise of Cavell's writings, which have moved me to express my gratitude. My essays are, unabashedly, expressions of love. Like certain of his own writings, they are akin to what in Cavell's important late essay "Performative and Passionate Utterances" (Cavell and Rothman 2005, 155–91) he calls "passionate utterances" or "expressive utterances." If I stop letting myself be moved by Cavell's writings, I couldn't think seriously about their value to me, why I seek my attachment to them, how they attract me, what rightful call they make upon me. Then I couldn't think seriously about them at all. And I couldn't rightfully call upon you, dear reader, to be moved by his writings, too.

∽

Reading Cavell's "The World Viewed" promised a companion volume: a retrospective of the numerous and diverse writings on film, apart from *Pursuits of Happiness* and *Contesting Tears*, that Cavell wrote in the years between the publication of *The World Viewed* and our book about his book. *Cavell on Film*, which I edited and for which I wrote the introduction, was that volume. And it was much more, for it also contained many pieces, on such a wide range of topics and films that it should have laid forever to rest the idea that he was fixated on the past—written between 2000 and 2005, when *Cavell on Film* was published—a period of great productivity for Cavell.

Some of the writings in *Cavell on Film* may strike the reader as relatively slight occasional pieces. But my introduction makes the case that these pieces bring home with special vividness that Cavell, like Emerson, was committed, on philosophical principle, to finding something out of the ordinary in the most ordinary of occasions. As Cavell himself came increasingly to appreciate, it was a crucial feature of his aspiration and achievement as a writer that, as I put it in my introduction to *Cavell on Film*, "every one of Cavell's writings is an occasional piece. Every one of his writings acknowledges, responds to, its particular occasion" (162). For Cavell, philosophy "is not a realm of abstract thought. It is an activity performed by human beings *in* the world, an activity best performed in a spirit of adventure. Philosophy is a way of rising to its occasion" (162).

I've also included in *The Holiday in His Eye* excerpts from the essay "Cavell on Film, Television, and Opera" that I wrote for Richard Eldridge's invaluable volume *Stanley Cavell* (2003). It explores the relationship of Cavell's writings on film to his thoughts on television and opera. Like *Cavell on Film*, this essay is a corrective to other erroneous but widely held views about Cavell, that he was fixated on the small set of Hollywood comedies and melodramas of the 1930s and 1940s that he wrote books about, hence that he was living in the past, as if the field of film studies, not to mention the world, had simply passed him by.

Like a number of the essays in *The "I" of the Camera* and *Tuitions and Intuitions*, "Seeing the World in Black and White" and "Nostalgia Ain't What It Used to Be," among those in *The Holiday in His Eye* that take Cavell's writing less as a subject of study in its own right than as a starting point for reflections, of a kind Cavell himself mostly refrained from engaging in, on the vicissitudes within the history of cinema of the philosophical and moral outlook—in his later writings, he named it "Emersonian perfectionism"—that was ascendant in Hollywood, as it was in America, in the New Deal years, subsequently suffered repression, but has continually resurfaced in American culture—for example, in Cavell's writings (and my own). The particular picture of the trajectory of film history that emerges in *The Holiday in His Eye* is mine, not his. But my essays pay the tuition for intuitions that would not—could not—have dawned in me were it not for Cavell's writings.

Along with the chapters from *Reading Cavell's "The World Viewed"* and the introduction to *Cavell on Film*, the majority of the essays in *The Holiday in His Eye* treat Cavell's writings both as objects of reading and as a means or touchstone of reading, to invoke the characterization in *Cities of Words* of the privileged role Emerson's writings play in that book. "Cavell, Emerson, Hitchcock," "On Stanley Cavell's *Band Wagon*," the introduction to *Must We Kill the Thing We Love?*, "Excerpts from Memory," and "Stanley Cavell, Victor Perkins, and the Personal" all take the form of philosophical investigations of aspects of his writings. So, too, do the recent papers I presented at several of the international conferences on Cavell's work that took place in the wake of his death in 2018: "Cavell Reading Cavell," "*Pursuits of Happiness*: Cavell in Transition," and "The Same Again, Only a Little Different: Cavell's Two Takes on *The Philadelphia Story*."

Collectively, the studies of Cavell's writing in *The Holiday in His Eye* advance a particular interpretation of the trajectory of his authorship as a whole. This interpretation takes Cavell's embrace of Emerson in the late 1970s to have been, as I put it in "Cavell Reading Cavell," a "seismic event—as consequential as the publication of *Must We Mean What We Say?*, which began his philosophical life; *The Claim of Reason*, which declared his existence as the only kind of philosopher who could have written such a book or could have wanted to; and *Little Did I Know*, which closed the book on his life in philosophy" (6).

In these explicit studies of Cavell's writing, too, I pay the tuition for intuitions that would not—could not—have been mine if it weren't for intuitions Cavell articulated in his writings—in particular, his intuitions about his own authorship. Nonetheless, the interpretation of the trajectory of Cavell's authorship that emerges in these essays, like that of the trajectory of film history, is mine, not his. But I would not—could not—have arrived at this interpretation apart from achieving a new perspective on my own writing. My awakening to the fact that, like Cavell, I was, or had become, an Emersonian perfectionist was a seismic event in my own life as a writer—as consequential as the aesthetics seminar so long ago that Cavell deemed a failure; the publication of *The Murderous Gaze* and *The "I" of the Camera*, in which I found my voice writing about films I loved; and the resolutions I made to myself upon reclaiming my identity as a film studies professor.

∾

Two challenges I faced in putting together the present collection were deciding what to include—more poignantly, what to leave out—and the order in which to present the essays. Earlier, I called *Tuitions and Intuitions* a "companion volume" to *The Holiday in His Eye*. In part, I mean by this that so many of the essays in the former—among them, "Film and Modernity," "André Bazin as Cavellian Realist," "Hats Off for George Cukor!," "Space and Speech in the Films of Yasujiro Ozu,"

"Precious Memories in Philosophy and Film," "Seeing the Light in *The Tree of Life*," and "A Film That Is Also a Handshake: Philosophy in the Films of the Dardenne Brothers"—are as focused on Cavell's writings as any of the essays in *The Holiday in His Eye*. Concerns about length made me resist, reluctantly, the temptation to double dip, so I have refrained from including any of those pieces.

Because in *The Holiday in His Eye* my primary concern is with Cavell's authorship, not mine, I've also resisted the temptation to present the essays in the order in which I wrote them (whether putting the oldest or the newest essays first). I've chosen, rather, to let the position of each essay be determined by the place of the Cavell work that essay primarily addresses within the trajectory of his authorship—from *Must We Mean What We Say?*, to *The World Viewed*, to *Pursuits of Happiness*, to *A Pitch of Philosophy*, to *Contesting Tears*, to *Philosophy the Day After Tomorrow*, to *Cities of Words*, and to *Little Did I Know*. It is the central claim of "Cavell Reading Cavell" that the practice of returning to his earlier writings, continuing their thinking from a transformed perspective that those writings enabled him to achieve, was essential to Cavell's philosophical enterprise, as it was to Emerson's. That is why I've decided not only to include "Cavell Reading Cavell" in *The Holiday in His Eye*, but to place it first, despite the fact that its primary focus is *Must We Mean What We Say?*, which is not at all a book about film.

It is my hope that presenting my essays in this order helps make it perspicuous how each of Cavell's writings, while written to stand on its own, also returns to, and continues, the thinking in writings that came before it and anticipates, and invites, being returned to. To invoke an Emerson metaphor: each of Cavell's writings draws a circle around the circles drawn by his earlier writings. That this is a feature that Cavell's writing has in common with Emerson's is a recurring theme in *The Holiday in His Eye*. Cavell shares with Emerson the knowledge that, as he put it in the preface he wrote for the 2002 edition of *Must We Mean What We Say?*, "philosophical ideas reveal their good only in stages" (Cavell 2002, iii). Each of my essays, too, was meant to stand on its own, but *The Holiday in His Eye* as a whole has a trajectory, or so I'd like to think, that resonates with, and illuminates, the trajectory of Cavell's authorship.

My goal in publishing *The Holiday in His Eye* at this propitious moment—a moment when academic film studies is, in principle, open to taking Cavell's writings seriously—is to do my part in helping to assure that his glorious vision of a marriage of film studies and philosophy as humanistic enterprises, as *moral* enterprises, will inform and inspire both fields as they go forward into the uncharted future.

∽

My debt of gratitude to Murray Pomerance, the editor of SUNY's Horizons of Cinema series, for his enthusiastic support of this volume, for our many years of friendship, and for his own work, which resonates deeply with my own, keeps accruing interest at such a high rate that I don't see how I can ever repay it.

The essays in this book span so many years of my life that there is no way I can acknowledge individually here all the colleagues, students, and friends to whom this book is indebted. Marian Keane, George Toles, and Andrew Klevan—along with Gilberto Perez, Victor Perkins, and Charles Warren, three friends whose loss deeply saddens me—will have to stand in for the rest. Among all the organizers of the conferences and colloquia devoted to Cavell's work to whom I am grateful, Sandra Laugier has earned special recognition for the indispensable role she has played over the years in helping to keep alive, and to spread worldwide, understanding of the importance of his work.

Everyone Stanley Cavell's work has pleased, instructed, moved, and inspired has reason to be thankful to Cathleen Cavell, whose understanding, support, friendship, and love Stanley cherished and relied on as much as I cherish and rely on my wife Kitty, the love of my life.

1

Cavell Reading Cavell

Must We Mean What We Say? has been important in my life since I was Stanley Cavell's student half a century ago. But once I threw my lot with the fledgling field of film studies and found my voice writing philosophically about movies I loved, I rarely felt the need to open that book; I'd already learned from it what I required for my own work. When Marian Keane and I wrote *Reading Cavell's "The World Viewed,"* I did reread *Must We Mean What We Say?* to detail ways Cavell's little book about film continued its thinking. But that was twenty years ago. Since then, my writing has focused almost as much on Cavell as on film, but I primarily immersed myself in his late writings. When I returned to Cavell's first book to prepare for a paper I presented in 2019 at a conference at Boston University called "Continuing Cavell: *Must We Mean What We Say?* at Fifty," I was overwhelmed by the sense that Cavell's later thought is all there in his early essays, but no less by the magnitude of what separates them. What separates them is also what joins them: a body of work that movingly stands in for an exemplary human life.

In sorting through the emotions rereading *Must We Mean What We Say?* stirred up in me, it helped to have had a most reliable guide: Stanley Cavell. There's no better reader of Cavell, no better guide to reading Cavell, than Cavell. For his own writing—the way he wrote, why he wrote that way, and how, given what his writing *is*, it calls for being read—was one of his abiding subjects. The new preface he wrote for the 2002 edition of *Must We Mean What We Say?*, for example, is his profound response to returning, more than three decades after its publication, to his first book.

Revised from a paper presented at the "Continuing Cavell: *Must We Mean What We Say?* at Fifty" conference, Boston University, 2019. Many thanks to the organizing committee: Rob Chodat and Juliet Floyd (Boston University), Sandra Laugier (University of Paris I Panthéon-Sorbonne), Naoko Saito (Graduate School of Education, Kyoto University), and Paul Standish (University College London, London Institute of Education).

This practice of returning to his earlier writings, continuing their thinking but from a transformed perspective, was essential to Cavell's philosophical enterprise. I am thinking, for example, of his new preface, written in 1998, to the paperback edition of *The Claim of Reason*; the innumerable passages in his books and essays in which he "goes back" to earlier writings, such as "More of *The World Viewed*," included in the 1979 expanded edition of *The World Viewed*, or his recounting, in "What Is the Scandal of Skepticism," of his use in *The Claim of Reason* of Descartes's Third Meditation. Then there is *The Claim of Reason* itself, in which part 4 responds to, departs from, and in that way continues the thinking in the first three parts, which he adapted from his earlier dissertation. And *Cities of Words*, doubly a return in that he adapted it from lectures for a course called Moral Reasoning he first offered at Harvard almost twenty years earlier, and because in it he returned to movies he'd written about in *Pursuits of Happiness* and *Contesting Tears*. But the definitive instance of Cavell reading Cavell is *Little Did I Know*, which tells the story of his life up to the completion of *The Claim of Reason*, a story in which the philosophical and the personal are inseparable. Then again, his late turn to autobiography was itself anticipated in his early writing. It was already a theme in *Must We Mean What We Say?* that philosophical appeals to ordinary language have a personal or autobiographical dimension.

Must We Mean What We Say? begins with a foreword, "An Audience of Philosophy," that exemplifies another of Cavell's ways of returning to his earlier writing. The last-written essay, it addresses the book as a whole and articulates a perspective only completing the rest of the essays enabled him to achieve. It is a foreword that doubles as an afterword and asks to be read twice—as if the reader's logical next step, after reaching the book's end, is to begin it again but from an altered perspective. "An Audience for Philosophy" does not, as Cavell's later forewords-that-are-also-afterwords will do, also chronicle the occasions of the writing of the individual essays in terms that, anticipating *Little Did I Know*, reveal the mutual implication of the philosophical and the personal. But, like them, it brings its book full circle and, to invoke Ralph Waldo Emerson, draws a circle around the circles drawn by the other essays, enabling *Must We Mean What We Say?* to take a step beyond the steps its individual essays take—as if, like Emerson's essay "Experience" as Cavell was to read it, the book gives birth to itself. That Cavell embraced this practice so early can be seen, from the perspective of his late writings, as a manifestation of the profound affinity with Emerson that he would come to recognize only in stages, to borrow a term from his preface to the 2002 edition of *Must We Mean What We Say?*, where he writes:

> I understand the presence of notable, surprising anticipations to suggest something specific about the way, or space within which, I work, which I can put negatively as occurring within the knowledge that I never get things right, or let's rather say, see them through, the first time, causing my efforts perpetually to leave things so that they can be, and ask to be,

returned to. Put positively, it is the knowledge that philosophical ideas reveal their good only in stages. (Cavell 2002, iii)

When Cavell adds that it isn't clear "whether a later stage will seem to be going forward or turning around or stopping, learning to find oneself at a loss," he is not registering a concern that a new stage might be a step back. He is distinguishing three ways a philosophical idea might "reveal its good" (an odd locution that I take to be forging a link, which asks to be returned to, with his essay, then hot off the press, "The Good of Film" [Cavell and Rothman 2005, 133–48]). The three ways are going forward; changing direction—that is, undergoing a conversion; and—here his wording resonates equally with Ludwig Wittgenstein and with Emerson—"learning to find oneself at a loss" (Cavell 2002, iii). Cavell is saying that the philosophical ideas in *Must We Mean What We Say?*, as there expressed, were at an early stage of "revealing their good." They "left things" so that they might be, and *asked* to be, returned to, each such "return" being a new departure whose own "good" reveals itself only in stages.

In the new preface to *Must We Mean What We Say?*, Cavell observes that he was struck, in returning to the book's earliest essay, by "a double anticipation" in a formulation in which he speaks of Socrates "coaxing the mind down from self-assertion—subjective assertion and private definition—and leading it back, through the community, home. The sense of the philosopher as responding to one lost will become thematic for me as my understanding of Wittgenstein's *Investigations* becomes less primitive than it was"—and, I would add, this happened when he discovered Emerson. "The literary or allegorical mode of the formulation," Cavell adds, "is something I recognized early as a way of mine of keeping an assertion tentative, that is, as marking it as a thought to be returned to" (Cavell 2002, v).

In the new preface, he cites the wonderfully aphoristic line in "An Audience for Philosophy," "If philosophy is esoteric, that is not because a few men guard its knowledge but because most men guard themselves against it," both as a response to the call of students at the time for relevance in their studies—count me among them—and as an instance of his practice of invoking an arresting concept, like "esoteric," that "halted" him, made him learn to "find himself at a loss." The pertinence of this practice, he goes on, "I felt strongly in connection with ordinary language practice (how could we become alienated from the words closest to us?—but then again, from what others?), but which I would not be able to speak about with much consequence until years later" (Cavell 2002, xi)—until part 4 of *The Claim of Reason*, for a start.

In "The Avoidance of Love," Cavell remarks, "If philosophy can be thought of as the world of a particular culture brought to consciousness of itself, then one mode of criticism (call it philosophical criticism) can be thought of as the world of a particular work brought to consciousness of itself" (Cavell 2002, 313). The term "philosophical criticism" acknowledges a distinction between his readings of *King Lear* and Beckett's *Endgame*, which one might want to call literary criticism, and the other essays, which are evidently philosophy, while affirming that the kind of criticism his readings exemplify *is* philosophy. But it was in a 1989 interview, when his philosophical ideas about these matters were at a later stage of "revealing their good," that Cavell entered his memorable claim that "any place"—Cavell's readings show that *Endgame* and *King Lear* are such places—"in which the human spirit allows itself to be under its own question *is* philosophy" (Fleming and Payne 1989, 59).

When criticism is of a work of philosophy, when it questions a work that is itself under its own question, it "allows itself to be under its own question," too. Philosophical criticism *is* philosophy. And philosophy, as Cavell understood and practiced it, *cannot but be* criticism. In a work of *philosophical* criticism it is the work itself that is "at every moment answerable to itself, that is allowed to do the questioning, that allows the questioning to happen, that is compelled to answer candidly every question it asks itself—being so compelled is what "being answerable" means. Such a work renders moot the distinction between criticism and philosophy by bringing to consciousness of itself the world of a particular work *and* the world of its culture—the language, the form of human life to which the work gives expression.

In a 1999 Sorbonne colloquium organized by the indispensable Sandra Laugier, Cavell remarked that the study of film cannot be a "worthwhile human enterprise" if it "isolates itself" from the kind of criticism Walter Benjamin had in mind when he argued that "what establishes a work as art is its ability to inspire and sustain criticism of a certain sort, criticism that seeks to articulate the work's idea; what cannot be so criticized is not art" (Cavell and Rothman 2005, xxvi). Nor, I would add, is it *philosophy*. A philosophical work seeks to articulate its *own* idea. But a philosophical idea, as Cavell would in stages come to recognize, "reveals its good" only in stages. I suppose it is the idea of this book, which I hope has some "good" to reveal, that every one of Cavell's writings is a work of philosophical criticism. And that this cannot be separated from the feature of his writing this essay has so far dwelled on, that Cavell wrote so that his words could be returned to, *ask* to be returned to, enabling his philosophical ideas to "reveal their good" in stages. The "good" of his writing, for Cavell, was its efficacy in bringing the world of each work, the world of the entire body of his work, the world of philosophy, the world of his culture, our culture, *his* world, *our* world, to consciousness of itself.

Must We Mean What We Say?, Cavell observes in his 2002 preface, "freed me for I suppose the most productive nine months of my life, in which I recast the salvageable and necessary material of my Ph.D. dissertation as the opening three parts of what would become *The Claim of Reason* and completed small books on film and Thoreau. I consider those small books to form a trio with *Must We Mean What We Say?*, different paths leading from the same desire for philosophy." Finding paths from the trio's *achievement* of philosophy, however, proved problematic. In his preface to the 1999 edition of *The Claim of Reason*, Cavell noted that he felt confident enough with his work in *Must We Mean What We Say?* to announce there the imminent publication of his dissertation. The rashness of this announcement showed itself to him when he completed drafts of *The World Viewed* and *The Senses of Walden* and, as he puts it, "the conclusions so far achieved in the dissertation revision seemed to me outstripped by those pieces." Soon enough, he would discern "the direction" the revision was "hauling itself toward" Cavell 1999, xxii). It "had to do with the connection of the two concluding essays of *Must We Mean What We Say?*, the reciprocation between the ideas of acknowledgment and of avoidance, for example as the thought that skepticism concerning other minds is tragedy" (Cavell 2002, xxxii). But how he might *arrive* at such a conclusion was "distinctly less clear."

In his preface to the 1999 edition of *The Claim of Reason*, Cavell tells us that to work his way through this blockage he began what he calls a "limited philosophical journal"—it was like a journal because, in his words, "the autonomy of each span of writing was a more important goal than smooth, or any, transitions between spans," and because "there would be no point, or no hope, in showing the work to others until the life, or place, of which it was the journal, was successfully, if temporarily, left behind, used up" (Cavell 1999, xxiii). Returning to this passage after so many years, I was stunned by its uncanny similarity to Cavell's description in *Little Did I Know* of the procedure he adopted to work his way through a comparable blockage when he was seeking to get his "philosophical memoir" on track. And what *Little Did I Know* tells us about the consequence of completing *The Claim of Reason* is that after his success in blazing philosophical paths between acknowledgment and avoidance, between skepticism concerning other minds and tragedy, between his "trio" and *The Claim of Reason*—his success in putting his dissertation behind him—he was never again to doubt his ability to go on within philosophy.

"Philosophy's all but unappeasable yearning for itself is bound to seem comic to those who have not felt it," Cavell's 1981 essay "*North by Northwest*" begins. "To those who have felt it, it may next seem frightening, and they may well hate and fear it, for the step after that is to yield to the yearning, and then you are lost" (Cavell and Rothman 2005, 41). To put his dissertation behind him, Cavell had to find himself lost. *The Claim of Reason* declared his existence as a philosopher. That's why *Little Did I Know* ends with that book's publication. In turn, *Little Did I Know* brought to an end the period of Cavell's life that began where the story it tells ends—the period in which he fully yielded to his yearning for philosophy. Writing the book that tells this story is inseparable from the story it tells. Telling the story brought its meaning home. *Little Did I Know* is not only "under its own question"; it finds the answer it seeks. With the writing completed, the life of philosophy of which it was the journal was successfully left behind—for good. For Cavell, philosophy had achieved its end. In writing *Little Did I Know*, Cavell's way of "walking in the direction of the unattained but attainable self," to again invoke Emerson, was by looking back. Then again, "looking back" was also a return—to a place he had never been.

In *The Claim of Reason*, Emerson's name appears once, in passing, as it does in *Must We Mean What We Say?* In *The World Viewed* and, remarkably, *The Senses of Walden*, Emerson's name rarely appears. The year he completed *The Claim of Reason*, 1978, was also the year he wrote "Thinking of Emerson," following it two years later with "An Emerson Mood." Cavell's discovery of Emerson was a seismic event—as consequential as *Must We Mean What We Say?*, which began his philosophical life; *The Claim of Reason*, which declared his existence as the only kind of philosopher who could have written such a book or could have wanted to; and *Little Did I Know*, which closed the book on his life in philosophy. *Pursuits of Happiness* invoked Emerson more than a few times, but had he written "Thinking of Emerson" and "An Emerson Moment" *before* beginning his book on the Hollywood comedy of remarriage, Emerson would surely have played as privileged a role as in *Cities of Words*, where Cavell returns to those films to continue thinking about them—the same again, only a little different. It wasn't until the Moral Reasoning course he began teaching in the late 1980s, and the publication of *In Quest of the Ordinary* and *This New Yet Unapproachable America*, in *Conditions Handsome and Unhandsome* and the essays later collected in *Emerson's Transcendental Etudes*, that he acknowledged the full magnitude of Emerson's importance for his own work and declared himself to *be* an Emersonian perfectionist, the way in *Must We Mean What We Say?* he had declared himself to be a modernist. Or had he?

In "A Matter of Meaning It," Cavell embraced a distinction between the modern and the traditional, in philosophy and out. "The essential fact of (what I refer to as) the modern lies in the relation between the present practice of an enterprise and the history of that enterprise, in the fact that this relation has become problematic." The passage goes on, "The various discussions about the modern I am led to in the course of these essays are the best I can offer in explanation"—thanks to Emerson, his late writings will have a better explanation to offer—"of the way I have written, or the way I would wish to write" (Cavell 2002, xxiii). But nowhere does Cavell call himself a modernist.

I find a clue to this in his essay "*North by Northwest*," which follows the line I quoted, which invokes philosophy's "yearning for itself," with "From such a view of philosophy I have written about something called modernism in the arts as the condition of their each yearning for themselves, naming a time at which to survive, they took themselves, their own possibilities, as their aspiration—they assumed the condition of philosophy" (Cavell and Rothman 2005, 41). *Must We Mean What We Say?* was, its essays assert, written from within a "modernist situation," but that doesn't make it modernist. If "yearning for itself" is philosophy's *tradition*, what could *count* as modernism within philosophy?

When Cavell observes, in the preface to *The Claim of Reason*, that Wittgenstein's *Philosophical Investigations*, "like the major modernist works of the past century at least, is logically speaking, esoteric," he doesn't say that it *is* a modernist work, only that, like such works, it seeks "to split its audience into insiders and outsiders (and split each member of it)" (Cavell 1999, xxiii). "A Matter of Meaning It," in characterizing *Must We Mean What We Say?* as *modern* philosophy, suggests that its writing, like Wittgenstein's, "seeks to split its audience." But in *The Claim of Reason* Cavell leaves it an open question—an instance of "leaving things so that they can be, and ask to be, returned to"—whether his writing *is* esoteric in this sense. And when he does return to this question in *Cities of Words*, his answer is "No."

In "A Matter of Meaning It," Cavell writes, "Innovation in philosophy has characteristically gone together with a repudiation—a specifically cast repudiation—of most of the history of the subject. But in the later Wittgenstein, the repudiation of the past has a transformed significance, as though containing the consciousness that history will not go away, except through our perfect acknowledgment of it (in particular, our acknowledgment that it is not past." Cavell adds, "'The past' does not in this context refer simply to the historical past, it refers to one's own past, to what is past, or what has passed, within oneself. One could say that in a modernist situation 'past' loses its temporal accent and means anything not present" (Cavell 2002, xxiii). Wittgenstein describes his later philosophy "as an effort to 'bring words *back*' to their everyday use," as though "the words we use in philosophy, in any reflection about our concerns, are *away*" (Cavell 2002, xxiii). Unacknowledged, history, too, is "away." To acknowledge that history is not past is to bring it back, to acknowledge its presentness, which is—paradoxically, it might seem—to acknowledge its pastness, enabling it to "go away" in the sense that we can leave it behind; we are free to move on.

When Cavell adds that later Wittgenstein seems to contain the consciousness that "one's own practice and ambition can be identified"—he says "identified," not "pursued," but for the modernist artist, as for the modern philosopher, *pursuing* and *identifying* one's practice and ambition can't be separated—"only against the continuous experience of the past" (Cavell 2002, xxiii). Using the word "one's" rather than "his" acknowledges that this is a *general* feature of the modernist situation in which Cavell, too, finds himself. The word "against," connoting opposition, seems to reinforce the word "repudiation," as if to underscore that in a modernist situation a work can declare what it is, what it was intended to be, solely through its repudiation of the history it rejects. That's how I used to understand "A Matter of Meaning It." But that can't be right. One of the leading philosophical ideas in *Must We Mean What We Say?*, an idea Cavell never stopped returning to, most consequentially in his discovery of his affinity with Emerson, is that history has to be *acknowledged*, not repudiated.

Fortunately, there's another way of interpreting the word "against" in the formulation "one's own practice and ambition can be identified only against the continuous experience of the past." In the last chapter of *The World Viewed*, Cavell uses "against" in a way devoid of any association with repudiation. He invokes the concept of "the ground of consciousness," the "further reality film pursues," what he calls "the reality of the unsayable"—an "arresting concept," if there ever was one (Cavell 1979b, 148). In characterizing the unsayable as the ground of consciousness, Cavell means "ground" as distinguished from "figure." His point is that only against the unsayable as a background can the figures of consciousness stand out, be apparent to us, *identifiable*. Similarly, in the modernist situation the "continuous experience of the past" is the ground, the background, one's practice and ambition require if they are to stand out, to be experienced, in the present, as figure. But then the past, too, must be experienced in the present, experienced—experienced *continuously*—as present. For in modernism, as Cavell understood it, an art cannot but assume the condition of philosophy and, as he will at a later stage put it, philosophy is answerable to itself *at every moment.*

In *Little Did I Know*, Cavell tells us that after completing *The Claim of Reason* "going on" in philosophy was no longer problematic for him. If the "essential fact" about the modern is that "the relation between the present practice of an enterprise and the history of that enterprise has become problematic," how could he go on thinking of his work as modern, as opposed to traditional, philosophy? That distinction had become moot for him. And so, the words "modern" and "modernism" dropped out of his lexicon. And it's no coincidence that this occurred simultaneously with his discovery of Emerson.

When writing *Must We Mean What We Say?*, Cavell, like Wittgenstein, found himself in a modernist situation in relation to the tradition of analytical philosophy in which he had been trained. Reading Emerson opened Cavell's eyes to the fact that he had also inherited, without realizing it, an alternative philosophical tradition, founded in America by Emerson, embraced by Emerson's great reader Thoreau and, in Europe, Emerson's devoted readers Nietzsche (and, through Nietzsche, Heidegger) and Bergson (and, through Bergson, Deleuze) and kept alive in American culture and in *himself* by the films he watched in the years going to the movies was a normal part of his week. Cavell didn't find himself in a modernist situation in relation to *that* tradition. By the late 1980s he was ready to give a name—"Emersonian perfectionism"—to the way of thinking he had come to recognize as his own, no less than Emerson's. In finding Emerson, Cavell found himself.

Then, thankfully, he was *really* lost.

2

Introduction to *Reading Cavell's "The World Viewed"*

with Marian Keane

Although it has been three decades since film studies declared its independence as an academic field, and despite its at times explosive growth, the field has not yet fully secured its existence, intellectually. It has engendered few if any great works of criticism, few if any impressive intellectual achievements, few if any major contributions to American letters, to the intellectual life of the university, or to our culture at large.

Academic film studies now finds itself at a crucial juncture. There is a pervasive sense within the field that the poststructuralist interpretive frameworks that have dominated it for a quarter of a century no longer compel conviction. Ably championed by David Bordwell and Noel Carroll, among others, a cognitivist alternative, eschewing interpretation altogether, is poised to enter the breech. But neither poststructuralism nor cognitivism can provide a sense of liberation to the many students and teachers of film who feel moved to give voice to their own experience of movies.

Our most urgent purpose in writing this book is to introduce, or reintroduce, Stanley Cavell's *The World Viewed: Reflections on the Ontology of Film* to the field of

---

From William Rothman and Marian Keane, *Reading Cavell's "The World Viewed": A Philosophical Perspective on Film* (Detroit: Wayne State University Press, 2000). Reprinted with permission. Unless otherwise indicated, page numbers refer to the 1979 expanded edition of *The World Viewed*. The first five paragraphs of this chapter are taken from a presentation given at New York University, shortly before the book was published.

film studies. We believe that Cavell's brilliant and beautiful little book, when read in a way that acknowledges its philosophical achievement, is capable of providing inspiration and encouragement to a field that has forsaken, or forgotten, its passion for the art of film. *The World Viewed* can help the field to move forward by reclaiming, and reaffirming, its original calling.

We are also writing for Cavell's many readers, cutting across disciplinary lines, who appreciate the importance of his explicitly philosophical works but have not yet fully grasped why he has given film the attention he has given it, nor fully grasped the place of *The World Viewed* within the totality of his writings about film. *The World Viewed* opens with the words, "Memories of movies are strand over strand with memories of my life." And writing about movies has been strand over strand with Cavell's philosophical life from this, his second book, published between *Must We Mean What We Say?* and *The Senses of Walden*; to *Pursuits of Happiness: The Hollywood Comedy of Remarriage*, companion piece to *The Claim of Reason*; to *Contesting Tears: Hollywood Melodramas of the Unknown Woman*, his latest book about film.

That *The World Viewed* derives philosophically from the essays that comprise *Must We Mean What We Say?*, Cavell's first book, is a recurring theme in what follows. So is the magnitude of the difference between the two works. For one thing, *Must We Mean What We Say?* does not pose to the reader the same degree or kind of difficulty as *The World Viewed*. Indeed, none of Cavell's other writings is difficult in the same way as his first book about film. No other book by Cavell seems to require a companion volume to guide readers in following its thinking. Nor, we suspect, would composing a companion to any of Cavell's other works be as challenging, or as gratifying, as the writing of the present book has proved to be. *The World Viewed* is one of its author's greatest achievements, yet it remains perhaps his most unknown work. The reading of *The World Viewed* that we present in these pages represents a journey of discovery for us, and we take pleasure in the prospect of sharing our discoveries with others.

∽

Between World War II and the Cold War, there was an all-too-brief period when thoughtful people everywhere were joined in recognizing humanity's awesome responsibility for creating a new world order. American films like *The Best Years of Our Lives* and *It's a Wonderful Life* reflected this moment's humanistic spirit. In Japan, it was reflected in the great postwar films of directors like Yasujiro Ozu, Kenji Mizoguchi, and Akira Kurosawa. Perhaps most notably, the guarded optimism of this moment was expressed by the remarkable Italian films that comprised the so-called Neorealist movement (Vittorio De Sica's *Bicycle Thieves*, Roberto Rossellini's *Rome: Open City*, and Luchino Visconti's *La Terra Trema*, for example), which so profoundly moved viewers—and inspired filmmakers—throughout the world.

Liberated France, like Italy, was flooded in the late 1940s with American movies that had not been available during the war. André Bazin, in his thoughtful and eloquent reviews and essays, articulated a realist alternative to the privileging of montage by Sergei Eisenstein and other Soviet filmmaker/theoreticians in the 1920s. Bazin's guiding conviction was that by virtue of the privileged role reality plays in the film medium, cinema had a unique role to play in helping to create a more humane world order. He championed films he saw as committed to such a goal. Although there was an anthropological aspect to his writing, and despite his fondness for mathematical metaphors, Bazin's aspiration was not to posit a rational, scientific basis for film's power, but to acknowledge the medium's mysteries, which were rooted in mysteries intrinsic to reality itself.

In the 1950s, the ambitious screening programs at the Cinémathèque Française presided over by the charismatic Henri Langlois enabled Parisians to immerse themselves, in a way never before possible, in the entire range of cinematic history. In the Paris of the 1950s, many of the best young minds were steeped in the past and present achievements of the art of film. They felt, as Bazin did, that film had a political or moral mission. But they were also in love with movies, convinced that at their best they were of transcendent value in and of themselves. A new understanding and appreciation of film, a new film culture, was emerging.

The famous journal *Cahiers du Cinéma* was a yardstick of the growth of this new film culture. The regular contributors to *Cahiers* were nurtured by Bazin, but their views differed in a number of respects from those of their mentor. For the likes of François Truffaut, Jean-Luc Godard, Eric Rohmer, Claude Chabrol, and Jacques Rivette, what was of greatest value about film was less the medium's unique relationship to reality than its possibilities for self-expression. Bazin never grasped what his younger protégés saw in the work of some of the "auteurs" they most admired (Hitchcock, for example). Nor did he share their burning desire to make films. In the pages of *Cahiers*, they were expressing exciting new ideas about film's aesthetic possibilities, ideas rooted in their understanding and appreciation of the history of the art of film. And, by the end of the 1950s, the French film industry, struggling to stay afloat, was ready to provide these young critics/theorists with opportunities to make films of their own in which they could put their ideas into practice.

If the 1950s represented a privileged moment in the emergence of film as a subject for serious criticism, this was in part because it represented a privileged period in the history of the art of film. Directors whose careers had begun in the 1940s who openly declared themselves to be film artists—Ingmar Bergman, Federico Fellini, Michelangelo Antonioni, and Robert Bresson among them—were gaining international recognition. Hollywood auteurs of a new generation, such as Nicholas Ray and Vincente Minnelli, were striking out in new directions, exploiting the new technological possibilities such as widescreen. And the "old masters" like Jean Renoir, Carl Dreyer, Alfred Hitchcock, John Ford, and Howard Hawks (and Orson Welles, who straddled both generations) were still at the peak of their form.

A striking feature of *Cahiers*' critical perspective was the conviction that the art of cinema was as much to be located inside as outside the commercial mainstream. There were popular films and genres that had never been taken seriously by intellectuals, yet were among the greatest achievements of the art of cinema, and great directors, authentic auteurs like Alfred Hitchcock, Howard Hawks, and John Ford, who had presided over their creation.

In the 1950s and early 1960s, the *Cahiers* critics were demonstrating that numerous popular movies—so familiar, so much a part of our lives as to be taken for granted—were profoundly meaningful works of artistic self-expression. And in order to back up their claims, the *Cahiers* critics strove to develop new critical terms—"mise en scène," for example—and new critical practices, such as shot-by-shot analysis, that might prove adequate to address the artistic significance of films that had always been regarded as escapist "entertainments."

The other side of the fact (first pondered by art historian Erwin Panofsky) that film had remained popular rather than esoteric, avoiding the obscurity that was the fate of other arts in the modern period, is that the achievements of so many of film's greatest directors, who were able at will to tap into the powers of the medium, remained critically unacknowledged for so long. Unlike great jazz musicians, who were unrecognized by the culture at large but fully appreciated within their community of aficionados, many of the greatest filmmakers remained unknown even among their peers. The emergence of the new film culture exemplified by *Cahiers* meant that the absence of recognition, the unknownness that was the other side of the popularity of film, seemed to be coming to an end. Not coincidentally, this was happening at precisely the historical moment when filmmakers could no longer take for granted their ability to tap into the powers of the medium, the moment when the traditional genres were losing their hold over popular audiences.

That is, a new understanding and appreciation of the value of popular film emerged at the precise moment its traditions seemed to be breaking down. It was the moment film, its audience fragmenting, was ceding to television its position of dominance, the moment what could be called modernism was emerging in film— the "New Wave" films the *Cahiers* critics went on to make were catalysts in the emergence of a modernist cinema—as it had emerged so much earlier in arts such as painting, music, and poetry. The 1950s represented at once a high-water mark of the art of cinema and the moment it was for the first time possible to imagine that film as a *traditional* art was coming to an end. (After all, the great art of silent cinema became extinct at the very moment of its greatest flowering.)

A new film culture was emerging in America, too, especially in New York, which had succeeded Paris as the scene of the most important developments in modernist painting. Like Paris in the 1920s, New York in the 1950s was a center for an avant-garde cinema (the so-called New American Cinema) that identified itself with the avant-garde art world, not with popular movies. Jonas Mekas, who felt that film as an art owed nothing to Hollywood, was a leading critical voice of this movement. But Mekas shared the pages of *Film Culture* and the *Village Voice* with Andrew Sarris, who concurred with the *Cahiers* critics in regarding the best Hollywood films as at least the equal in artistic achievement to the most esteemed works of self-declared film artists.

In France, the new film culture was an intellectual and cultural movement, but not one driven to establish itself as an academic field. As late as the mid-1970s, film had not gained a foothold in American colleges and universities, either. But it was in America, not France, that film studies first demanded recognition as a legitimate academic subject.

The immediate impetus for film's large-scale entrance into American colleges and universities was the political upheaval of the 1960s. Pressures for including film in the curriculum came primarily from students. This reflected the fact that a new appreciation of film and its history had already come to exist among students. And it reflected the fact that young Americans felt that film, like rock music, was integral to their so-called counterculture.

Film's entrance into the American academy was opposed by faculty members and administrators who argued that a mass medium like film lacked the artistic stature to make it a subject of study comparable to established arts such as music, painting, or literature. The advocates of film studies, in turn, attacked the assumption that popular art was inferior to "high art." A half-century earlier, similar battle lines had been drawn over the worthiness of modern literature as a subject of study. The goal of those championing film's admission into the academy was to assure that films would not only be studied, but studied in a way that took seriously their artistic achievements, their own ways of thinking about society, about human relationships, and about their condition as films.

The legitimacy of studying film sociologically (as an alleged cause of "juvenile delinquency," for example), or within a context of experimental psychology, was not at issue. Those were not the kinds of study film's advocates were struggling to establish. What we were championing, rather, was a study of film that undertook to acknowledge the value of film as a medium of artistic expression. In America in the late 1960s and early 1970s, the fledgling field of film studies was struggling, against powerful forces inside and outside the university, to win recognition for film as a worthy subject of serious criticism, and at the same time to win recognition for the study of film as a legitimate intellectual discipline.

As the preceding account implies, when the case for the academic study of film was originally made to American university administrations and faculties, film studies predominantly envisioned itself as a new field of criticism. The works to be studied were to encompass, but not be limited to, ordinary movies, in particular American movies of what the field has since come to call the classical period (the 1930s and 1940s, especially). And the new field predicated its claim for legitimacy on the conviction that the artistic achievements of cinema, importantly but not exclusively the achievements of American classical cinema, called for serious critical acknowledgment, and on the corollary conviction that no existing academic field has established methodologies capable of engendering the kind of criticism film called for. The medium of film was different from every other medium. Film studies could not validly begin by adopting preexisting theories, taking for granted their applicability to film, but only by reflecting philosophically on the testimony of movies themselves, the testimony of our experience of movies. Films called for the creation of new terms of criticism, new modes of critical thought capable of taking instruction from films' own ways of thinking.

From the beginning of film history, it has remained a mystery what it is that actually takes place within and among silent viewers sitting in those darkened theaters. In the 1930s and 1940s, film could be said to have been our culture's dominant medium of expression. And yet public discourse about film (no doubt this was true of private conversation as well) has virtually never probed in a serious way our experience of movies, never attempted to articulate what movies really mean to us, our understanding of what they have to say to us. Movies address matters of intimacy and do so in a language of indirectness and silence. If we are to understand film's historical importance, or its present impact upon society and upon our lives, we must bring this experience, this knowledge, to consciousness.

Movies exercise a hold on us, a hold that, drawing on our innermost desires and fears, we participate in creating. To know films objectively, we have to know the hold they have upon us. To know the hold that films have on us, we have to know ourselves objectively. And to know ourselves objectively, we have to know the impact of films on our lives. No study of film can claim intellectual authority if it is not rooted in self-knowledge, our knowledge of our own subjectivity. In the serious study of film, in other words, criticism must work hand in hand with the perspective of self-reflection that only philosophy is capable of providing. To back up its declaration of independence as an intellectual discipline, the field of film studies needed to found itself, intellectually, upon a philosophical investigation of the ontology of the medium, and the art, of film. Such was the challenge *The World Viewed* took upon itself.

The World Viewed embraces Ludwig Wittgenstein's methodological principle that we can find out what kind of object a thing is by investigating expressions that show the kinds of things that can be said about it. In all of his writings, Cavell proceeds (like Wittgenstein, and like Cavell's own professor of philosophy, J. L. Austin) by appealing philosophically to what we ordinarily say and mean. As we will explain in the book's appendix, Cavell's appeals to ordinary language (like Freud's procedures of free association, dream analysis, investigation of verbal and behavior slips, noting and analyzing "transferred" feeling, and so on) are procedures for acquiring self-knowledge. They are appeals to facts—about language, the world, ourselves—so obvious we cannot simply fail to know them. When what we fail to know is so obvious we cannot simply fail to know it, our ignorance cannot be cured by additional information, or by defining words or introducing new ones; it is a refusal to know. In investigating the kind of knowledge of which self-knowledge is a paradigm, Cavell employs philosophical procedures that enable one to acquire self-knowledge. Without knowing oneself, one cannot know what self-knowledge is.

To be sure, in *The World Viewed* there is an almost complete absence of the kinds of remarks about philosophy in general, and about his own philosophical procedures in particular, that are everywhere to be found in *Must We Mean What We Say?*, Cavell's first book. This does not mean that in *The World Viewed* philosophy plays a less central role, however. In *Must We Mean What We Say?*, Cavell undertook philosophical investigations of many subjects, including his own philosophical procedures. In *The World Viewed*, philosophy is not part of the subject, not one subject among many, not a subject addressed by some remarks but not by others; philosophy *is* the subject, is *the* subject, of the book. This is not to deny that the book's subject is film. The point is that in *The World Viewed* philosophy and film are joined in a conversation so intimate as to constitute a kind of marriage (the kind of happy marriage envisioned by the "remarriage comedies" Cavell will go on to study in *Pursuits of Happiness*). *The World Viewed* enables us to know that a marriage of film studies and philosophy is possible. As will emerge in the course of our reading, *The World Viewed* also enables us to know that such a marriage is not only possible; it is necessary. Philosophy cannot deny or avoid the subject of film. And it is not possible to think seriously about film apart from the perspective of self-reflection only philosophy is capable of providing.

To think seriously about film, *The World Viewed* is capable of teaching us, we must forsake the wish—without denying the depth of its motivation—for a scientific methodology that would provide an unchallengeable place, a place outside our own experience, to stand. To embrace theory as a higher authority than our experience of movies, as the field of film studies has done, is to divorce the study of film from the philosophical perspective of self-reflection apart from which we cannot know what movies mean, or what they really are. It is to compound, rather than undo, their unknownness, to reinforce the philistine attitude of superiority to movies, and to their audiences, that it was the field's original mission to transcend or overcome.

When *The World Viewed* was published, however, the emerging field, for understandable historical reasons, altogether missed, or failed to take to heart, the true significance of the book's philosophical perspective. From its first large-scale entrance into American universities, film studies had cast its lot with criticism, and academic criticism in America was in the throes of a theoretical revolution, as a succession of powerful new theoretical frameworks and methodologies arrived from France.

One decisive early moment in this development was the publication in the late 1970s of Peter Wollen's *Signs and Meaning in the Cinema*, an attempt to apply the structuralism of the French anthropologist Lévi-Strauss to the study of the work of cinematic "auteurs" such as John Ford or Howard Hawks, and to genres of popular film such as the western. Another is the work of the French film theorist Christian Metz, who championed a semiology of cinema, a scientific study of cinema's systems of signs or "codes."

In the aftermath of the political events of May '68 in Paris, there was a major shift in the new French thought. This shift was made available to English-speaking film students through a series of translations published in the British journal *Screen*. The most influential of these essays was the first to be translated: a reading of John Ford's *Young Mr. Lincoln* written collectively by the editorial staff of *Cahiers du Cinéma*. The *Young Mr. Lincoln* essay was significant less for the details of its reading—often misreading—of this particular film than for its attempt, the first of many, to incorporate the poststructuralist theories—mutually incompatible, one might well have thought—of the psychoanalyst Jacques Lacan, the Marxist philosopher Louis Althusser, and the literary critic / semiologist Roland Barthes.

With this essay, *Cahiers du Cinéma* found itself recanting its earlier affirmation of popular cinema as an art. *Cahiers* was now condemning films like *Young Mr. Lincoln*, as it was condemning popular cinema as a whole, as a repressive ideological apparatus.

The proper task in studying a film like *Young Mr. Lincoln*, the *Cahiers* piece argued, is not to acknowledge the film's thinking, but to expose its ways of not thinking, its systematic ways of repressing thought. The field's new goal was not to grasp the astonishing capacities for meaningfulness that movies have discovered within the singular conditions of their medium, but to expose the ways they are determined by the "codes" of the "dominant ideology." And the *Cahiers* editors assumed, on theoretical grounds, that those codes, and that ideology, were already fully known by them.

This shift from valuing films as meaningful works of art whose own ways of thinking are capable of teaching us how to think about them to repudiating films as pernicious ideological constructs whose solicitations are to be resisted was not motivated by the *results* of criticism. The *Cahiers* editors simply took for granted that their newly adopted Althusserian and Lacanian theoretical framework authorized them to detach themselves from their own experience and provided them with scientific knowledge of the film they were studying. The essay's "conclusions" were dictated from above, as it were, by the higher authority of the theoretical systems they were applying to the film. And their privileging of theory over criticism, their denial of critical acts rooted in empirical experience, their forgoing of the philosophical perspective of self-reflection that *The World Viewed* had shown to be necessary for securing the independence of the study of film as an intellectual discipline, increasingly set the agenda, and the tone, for the field of film studies in the 1970s and 1980s—as if by bowing down to a higher authority a field lacking an intellectual foundation of its own could vicariously acquire the authority, the intellectual stature, of a science.

And yet, when film studies in America—following and leading parallel developments in the study of literature—turned to the new French thought, it was attempting to *receive* philosophy, unaware that it was also forgoing philosophy. In response to America's traumatic experience of the late 1960s and early 1970s, when America was torn, every American was torn—agonizingly, ecstatically—between thinking and avoiding thought, American intellectuals were turning to Europe in quest of ways of thinking that were freer, truer to their experience, than the traditional ways of thinking that were tearing America apart. But Americans were also turning to Europe to find relief from thinking about their own troubling experience.

In a 1989 interview with the philosopher James Conant, Cavell observes that the ascension of French theory was to be welcomed, because academic criticism in America "had been terribly undertheorized, much too dismissive and afraid of philosophy" (Conant and Cavell 1989, 64). Nonetheless, the fact that America "had to receive philosophy into the study of literature . . . at the hands of the French," Cavell goes on, "strikes me as an irony and a pity, however understandable the historical forces at play." That is because "the price of this reception, in the context in which literary studies have shunned philosophy as practiced in America, is that what is called philosophy by departments of literature is not by American criteria simply to be called philosophy."

When Cavell says that literary studies "have shunned philosophy as practiced in America," he is straightforwardly stating a fact, as he is when he says that "what is called philosophy by departments of literature is not by American criteria simply to be called philosophy." Behind these facts stands a further fact: Between philosophy as practiced professionally in America and England (where so-called analytical philosophy prevails) and philosophy as practiced in Europe (where philosophy edges closer to literature than to science or mathematics) there is a history of mutual ignorance, incomprehension, and distrust.

At one level, all of Cavell's work is engaged in extending Wittgenstein's and Austin's efforts to transform analytical philosophy radically from within. As this suggests, Cavell's own professional training locates him on the English-speaking side of this continental divide. Recognizing that both traditions have equal claim to the mantle of philosophy, however, his writings aspire to overcome or transcend this rift within philosophy by making it a subject for philosophy. His aim is to bring the two traditions into closer alignment, or, rather, to achieve a perspective from which it becomes perspicuous how intimately they are aligned, as if they represent two halves of the same mind, not opposed positions to be reconciled. In this spirit, he repeatedly returns to the surprising affinities he finds between Wittgenstein and Heidegger (the latter being, for Cavell, the modern philosopher who effects a critique and transformation of the Continental tradition comparable to Wittgenstein's critique and transformation of the Anglo-American tradition).

When *The World Viewed* was published in 1971, some film journals dismissed it on the erroneous ground that it advocated a realist theory derived from the writings of Bazin. Others, equally erroneously, took it to advocate a Clement Greenberg–derived formalism. However, the book's continuing reception by the field of film studies, or, rather, its continuing nonreception, cannot be attributed to simple mistakes about its theoretical claims. If that were the only problem, correcting those mistakes would be all it would take for film studies to accommodate the book's way of thinking. Nor can the field's neglect of the book be attributed to a deliberate effort to repress its thinking. It takes no effort to deny or avoid *The World Viewed*'s thinking. What takes effort is to follow the book's thinking, to read it in a way that acknowledges its philosophical aspiration and achievement.

It is commonly supposed within the field of film studies that the writing of *The World Viewed* is vague and impressionistic. This only confirms that the field has simply not known how to read the book. For one thing, to read *The World Viewed* in a way that acknowledges its philosophical aspirations and achievement, it is necessary to free oneself from prejudicial theories as to how philosophy has to *look*—the theory that it must proceed systematically by formal arguments, for example, or must employ rhetorical strategies of poetic persuasion. In the Conant interview, Cavell observes that if you give up those traditional routes to conviction in philosophy (as both Wittgenstein and Heidegger felt it necessary to do), "then the question of what achieves philosophical conviction must at all times be on your mind." Cavell's answer is that conviction must be achieved by the writing itself, by "nothing other than this prose just here, as it's passing before our eyes" (Conant and Cavell 1989, 59).

The sense that the words on the page must achieve conviction on their own is one key to Cavell's writing. This sense is conjoined with another, which he wishes, as he puts it, to "radicalize": the sense "that philosophy is at all moments answerable to itself, that if there is any place at which the human spirit allows itself to be under its own question, it is in philosophy; that anything, indeed, that allows that questioning to happen *is* philosophy" (Conant and Cavell 1989, 36).

It is because it is under its own question, answerable to itself, that philosophy is capable of providing a perspective that cannot be provided by any other discipline, "a perspective of self-reflection that the human being cannot avoid, or cannot escape without avoiding" (Fleming and Payne, 313),

A further key to Cavell's writing can be found in *Disowning Knowledge*, a volume of his readings of Shakespeare's plays. Cavell observes that those readings work out his intuition that "Shakespeare's plays interpret and reinterpret the skeptical problematic—the question whether I know with certainty of the existence of the external world and of myself and others in it," hence that "the advent of skepticism as manifested in Descartes's *Meditations* is already in full existence in Shakespeare, from the time of the great tragedies in the first years of the seventeenth century" (Cavell 1987, 3).

In calling his guiding idea an intuition, Cavell distinguishes it from a hypothesis. "Both intuitions and hypotheses require what may be called confirmation, but differently." A hypothesis requires evidence, and "must say what constitutes its evidence. (I know what it means to say that lighter objects fall to earth at the same rate as heavier objects . . .) An intuition, say that God is expressed in the world, does not require, or tolerate, evidence but rather, let us say, understanding of a particular sort" (Cavell 1987, 3).

The World Viewed incorporates insightful remarks about a diversity of matters pertaining to film's origins; its historical development; its characteristic forms and genres; the myths and the human types around which those genres revolve; the medium's ability, until recently, to stave off modernism, to continue to employ without self-consciousness traditional techniques that tap naturally into the medium's powers; and so on. In addressing such matters, *The World Viewed* incorporates equally insightful remarks about particular films, genres, stars, and cinematic techniques. Almost invariably, Cavell's intuitions run counter to views generally accepted without question within the field of film studies. Within film studies, for example, it remains an unquestioned doctrine that "classical" movies systematically subordinate women by aligning the camera with the male gaze, among other means, and, more generally, that movies are pernicious ideological representations to be decoded and resisted, not treated as if they were works of art capable of instructing us as to how to view them. And it remains another unquestioned doctrine that the stars projected on the movie screen in classical movies are "personas," discursive ideological constructs, not real people; that the world projected on the screen is itself an ideological construct, not real; and, indeed, that reality itself—the so-called real world—is such a construct, too. In providing convincing alternatives to views the field has tended to treat as gospel, *The World Viewed* is capable of freeing film studies to explore regions that have remained closed to it, and to recognize that what has closed off those regions is the field's own refusals to question the unquestionable, its willingness to embrace theoretical frameworks as gospels it has already received.

"Primary wisdom [is] intuition," Ralph Waldo Emerson writes, "whilst all later teachings are tuitions." Thus, Emerson is called a philosopher of intuition, Cavell observes, adding that it is not typically noticed that Emerson is at the same time a teacher of what he calls "tuition." "I read him as teaching that the occurrence to us of intuition places a demand upon us, namely for tuition; call this wording, the willingness to subject oneself to words, to make oneself intelligible (Tuition so conceived is what I understand criticism to be.)" (Cavell 1987, 4–5). It would not be incorrect to call Cavell, too, a philosopher of intuition, as long as we keep in mind that he is at the same time a teacher of tuition. If the potential value of *The World Viewed* to the serious study of film is a function of the fruitfulness of its intuitions, it is no less a function of the exemplary discipline by which its writing—word by word, sentence by sentence, paragraph by paragraph, chapter by chapter—"follows out in each case the complete tuition for a given intuition."

Once an intuition occurs to Cavell—that Shakespeare's plays interpret what Cavell calls the "skeptical problematic," for example, or that there is a genre of Hollywood comedies in which the thrust of the plot is not to get a man and woman together but to get them together again—he takes it upon himself to find words he can trust to make his intuition, to make himself, intelligible. Cavell's writing always aims both to exemplify the importance of intuition and to teach tuition, the rigorous discipline of finding words to achieve a critical perspective that enables a certain kind of understanding to take place. From his earliest essays to his most recent work on autobiography, opera, and Hollywood melodrama, Cavell's writing aims, as he says, "to follow out in each case the complete tuition for a given intuition" (with an echo of Wittgenstein, he adds, "Tuition comes to an end somewhere") (Cavell 1987, 5).

In *Conditions Handsome and Unhandsome: The Constitution of Emersonian Perfectionism*, Cavell remarks that despite the attention recently accorded Emerson, there remains resistance among philosophers to recognizing his *philosophical* achievement. And yet Emerson is a thinker, Cavell writes, with the accuracy and consequentiality one expects of a mind "worth following with that attention necessary to decipher one's own" (Cavell 1990, 1). Our point of departure in the present volume is that *The World Viewed*, too, is an expression of a mind "worth following with that attention necessary to decipher one's own."

Crucially, Cavell's wording implies that if we follow our own thinking with the attention necessary to follow Emerson's, we will know that our minds, too, are worth following this way. We will find ourselves thinking with the accuracy and consequentiality necessary to achieve the perspective of self-reflection only philosophy is capable of providing. Cavell's words intimate something else as well. Without following our own thinking, we cannot know the minds of others. And without following the thinking of others, we cannot know our own minds, cannot have conviction in our thoughts, cannot claim them as our own. That the achievement of selfhood requires the simultaneous acknowledgment of otherness is a guiding philosophical principle for Cavell. This principle is inextricably bound up with the fact that, as his writing continually brings home to us, deciphering our own minds can be singularly difficult, difficult in a singular way.

In "The Avoidance of Love: A Reading of *King Lear*," written on the eve of the theoretical revolution that was to transform academic criticism in America, Cavell observes that the success of the so-called New Criticism was "a function of the way it is *teachable*. You can train someone to read complex poems with sufficient complexity, there is always something to say about them" (Cavell 2002, 269). In the Conant interview, Cavell remarks that the theoretical systems that have held sway over academic criticism in the intervening decades likewise possess the feature he calls "extreme teachability" (Conant and Cavell 1989, 66).

Philosophy, as Cavell practices it, is difficult in a way that precludes its being "extremely teachable." There is no *system* for training students to achieve the perspective of self-reflection *The World Viewed* exemplifies. Yet there are practical methods for teaching, and learning, this demanding discipline. The pages that follow demonstrate such a method, which begins and ends by attending to Cavell's utterly specific words ("to this prose just here, as it's passing before our eyes"). To achieve conviction in *The World Viewed*, one must follow its thinking. To do so, one must follow one's own thoughts as they are prompted by the words on the page (as those words follow Cavell's thoughts as they are prompted by the films in his experience). Without achieving a perspective of self-reflection, it is not possible to acknowledge *The World Viewed*'s achievement of such a perspective. (The achievement of selfhood requires the simultaneous acknowledgment of otherness, and vice versa.)

In characterizing Emerson's thinking as "consequential," Cavell means both that it has consequences (its radicalness resides in its power to change our way of thinking, hence our world) and that it is consecutive, ordered (each thought has consequences for those that follow). To demonstrate that *The World Viewed*, too, possesses "consequentiality," we proceed by reading the book from beginning to end. For the sake of convenience, we divide our reading into seven sections. Within each section, we address each chapter, at times each page, each line, in consecutive order.

In the pages that follow, whenever a passage thwarts our comprehension we keep thinking the passage through until we arrive at an interpretation that sustains our conviction—until an intuition dawns in us, prompted by Cavell's words, as to what those words are saying in this context, what prompted the author of *The World Viewed* to use precisely these words on precisely this occasion, and what prompted us until now to resist this understanding. In striving to arrive at words of our own we can trust to express our understanding of the words Cavell had arrived at ("to follow out in each case the complete tuition for a given intuition"), we read *The World Viewed* in a way that quite literally follows Cavell's thinking with the attention necessary to decipher our own. And, at each point, our writing invites readers to check Cavell's words, and ours, against their own experience, their own understanding.

That the writing of *The World Viewed* possesses accuracy and consequentiality means that its thinking *is* worth following with the attention we devote to it. It also means that attending to the words of *The World Viewed* can be singularly difficult. Yet apart from facing this difficulty, it is not possible to know what makes the book worth attending to in this way. Apart from reading *The World Viewed* in a way that is worthy of it, it is not possible to know the book's true worth. That is the intuition for which the present volume undertakes to follow out the complete tuition. The potential value of *The World Viewed* for the serious study of film is a function both of the fruitfulness of its guiding intuitions and the exemplary scrupulousness by which the book's prose—chapter by chapter, paragraph by paragraph, sentence by sentence, word by word—"follows out in each case the complete tuition for a given intuition."

To be sure, there are a number of intuitions crucial to his later work that had not yet occurred to Cavell during the period he was writing *The World Viewed*. It had not yet fully dawned on him, for example, the extent to which his own way of thinking inherited Emerson's understanding and practice of philosophy. Thus, nowhere in *The World Viewed*, or in *Must We Mean What We Say?* before it, does Cavell invoke Emerson's concepts of intuition and tuition in characterizing his own philosophical method, as he does in the 1989 Conant interview. Not coincidentally, during the period he was writing *The World Viewed*, it had not yet fully dawned on Cavell the extent to which the unique combination of popularity and artistic seriousness of American movies, especially of the 1930s and 1940s, was a function of their inheritance of "focal concerns of American transcendentalism . . . , concerns for society, for human relationship generally," as Cavell puts it in his conversation with Conant (Conant and Cavell 1989, 38).

In *Pursuits of Happiness* and *Contesting Tears*, Cavell's intuition that Hollywood movies inherited Emerson's philosophical concerns, conjoined with his intuition that he has inherited these concerns, too, led to the astonishing further intuition that his own philosophical procedures are underwritten by the ways American movies think about society, human relationships, and their own condition as films. It is in the very movies that were for so many years an ordinary part of Cavell's week that Emerson's ways of thinking remained alive within American culture, available as an inheritance. Apart from the role Hollywood movies played in Cavell's education, it would not have been possible for a philosopher who received his professional training within an analytical tradition that has never acknowledged Emerson as a philosopher to have "inherited" Emerson's ways of thinking at all.

But that intuition awaited the significant heightening, and deepening, of Cavell's work that coincided with the publication, all in 1978, of his first essay on Emerson ("Thinking of Emerson"); his reading of *The Lady Eve*, which was to become a cornerstone of *Pursuits of Happiness*; and completion of his monumental *The Claim of Reason*.

3

Sights and Sounds

with Marian Keane

The starting point of chapter 2 is that movies have to do with the projection of reality, of "live persons and real things in actual spaces," as Cavell puts it in "More of *The World Viewed*" (165–66). In arguing that the unprecedented role reality plays in film must be his starting point in reflecting on what film is, Cavell is aware he is bucking a "pervasive intellectual fashion, apparently sanctioned by the history of epistemology and the rise of modern science, according to which we never really, and never really can, see reality as it is" (165). Cavell resists this fashionable skepticism because of his conviction that "a general dismissal of reality depends upon theories (of knowledge, of science, of art, of reality, of realism) whose power to convince is hardly greater than reality's own" (165). (The Lacanian/Althusserian theoretical framework that for so long dominated academic film studies in America, as well as semiology, deconstruction, and cultural theory—at least as film studies embraced them—are instances of theories that dismiss reality in general as a mere ideological construct.)

The question of the role reality plays in film was in any case forced on him, Cavell testifies, by reading Erwin Panofsky and André Bazin. Nonetheless, it is incorrect to think of Cavell as a Bazinian realist, as American film studies has in the main labeled him. (It may well be incorrect to think of Bazin himself as the kind of realist he is often claimed to be, but that is another question.) In 1971, when *The*

Chapter 2 of William Rothman and Marian Keane, *Reading Cavell's "The World Viewed": A Philosophical Perspective on Film* (Detroit: Wayne State University Press, 2000). Reprinted with permission. Unless otherwise indicated, page numbers refer to the 1979 expanded edition of *The World Viewed*.

World Viewed was published, *Cahiers du Cinéma*, once a bastion of Bazin-inspired film criticism, was advancing a systematic critique of the ideological underpinnings of realism. *The World Viewed*, too, articulates a powerful critique of realist theories of film.

While agreeing that movies are, as Bazin puts it, "committed to communicate only by way of what is real," Cavell rejects the "unabashed appeals" to nature and reality inherent in Panofsky's view that "the medium of the movies is physical reality as such" or Bazin's view that "the cinema (is) of its essence a dramaturgy of Nature" (16). "What Panofsky and Bazin have in mind," he suggests, is that "the basis of the medium of movies is photographic, and that a photograph is *of* reality." But Panofsky and Bazin do not ask the question that guides the thinking of *The World Viewed*, or do not ask it in the same way: What *becomes* of reality when it is projected and screened? What *becomes* of objects and persons in the world when film displaces them from their "natural sequences and locales"? (This issue is the explicit subject of Cavell's important essay "What Becomes of Things on Film?" [Cavell and Rothman 2005, 1–10]).

"On film reality is not merely described or merely represented," Cavell writes (166). Movies project and screen reality rather than describing it, as (some) novels do, or representing it as (some) paintings do. Insofar as movies represent reality, they do so *by way of* projections, not representations, of reality. The difference between projections and representations is one of the central themes of *The World Viewed*. Equally central is the difference between reality and projections of reality—what film's mode of displacing reality comes to, what film's transformations of reality make possible (and what they make necessary). These themes are linked, in turn, to yet another: the difference between film and painting—what their difference comes to, what it makes possible, and necessary, for each. In attempting to understand what film is, Cavell employs the procedures of ordinary language philosophy to work through ways film differs from other kinds of things, ways what we say about film differs from what we say about other kinds of things.

One way *The World Viewed* develops these themes is by reflecting on the historical fact that modernist painting came to forgo the representation of reality. Embracing Michael Fried's interpretation of the origins and history of modernist painting, Cavell argues that painting contemporary with the advent of motion pictures (in common with other representational arts, such as the novel) had been "withdrawing from the representation of reality as from a hopeless, but always unnecessary, task" (Fried 1968, 16).[1] According to *The World Viewed*, when painting

---

1. Among Michael Fried's early writings, Cavell cites "Art and Objecthood," Artforum (June 1967), reprinted in Minimal Art, ed. Gregory Battock, 16–47 (New York: E. P. Dutton, 1968); "Manet's Sources," Artforum (March 1969): 28–79; "Shape as Form," Artforum (November 1966), reprinted in Henry Geldzahler's catalogue, New York Painting and Sculpture: 1940–1970 (New York: E. P. Dutton, 1969); and Three American Painters (Cambridge: Fogg Art Museum, Harvard University, 1965). Paul J. Gudel's Michael Fried and Philosophy: Modernism, Intention and Skepticism (New York: Routledge, 2017), a lucid account of the complex relationships among these three quite different writers, provides an extremely useful overview of Fried's work. Gudel's account makes clear that despite the fact that they are generally, and for good reason, lumped together, there are

withdrew from representing reality, photographic media like movies did not take up that task. Reality plays a central role in film, but its role is not that of being represented. Then again, reality continued to play a central role in painting, too, even when painting was forced to forgo representation and likeness.

One of *The World Viewed*'s guiding intuitions is that the role reality plays in movies cannot be accounted for without addressing the ontological differences between photography and painting. Another is that the differences between photography and painting cannot be accounted for without addressing the mysterious relationship between a photograph and the things (and/or persons) in that photograph. Cavell takes an initial stab at characterizing this relationship: "A photograph does not present us with 'likenesses' of things; it presents us, we want to say, with the things themselves" (17). His Wittgensteinian or Austinian "we want to say" alerts us to his awareness that it sounds paradoxical, or even obviously false, to say that photographs present us not with likenesses of things but with the things themselves. But "photographs do not present us with things themselves" sounds equally paradoxical or false. As always, Cavell's aim in appealing to what we ordinarily say and mean is not to convince readers without proof, but to call upon us to prove something to ourselves, to test something against ourselves.

In accordance with the principle that we can find out what kind of object anything is by investigating expressions that show the kind of thing said about it, the lesson Cavell draws from the fact that we do not know how to characterize the relationship between a photograph and the things and persons in that photograph is that we do not know how to place photographs ontologically. We are perplexed as to what they are.

Cavell specifies a source of our perplexity. "We might say that we don't know how to think of the *connection* of a photograph and what it is a photograph of. The image is not a likeness; it is not exactly a replica, or a shadow, or an apparition either, though all these . . . share a striking feature with photographs—an aura or history of magic surrounding them" (18).

An audio recording is not ontologically unplaceable the way a photograph is. A recording (of a French horn, say) is a copy (in principle, an all but perfect copy) of something (the sound made by that horn). There is no comparable "something"—no thing separable in principle from the object in the photograph, the way the sound of a horn is separable from the horn itself—that a photograph is a copy of.

> We said that the record reproduces its sound, but we cannot say that a photograph reproduces a sight (or a look or an appearance). . . . What

---

important differences between Fried and Cavell, on the one hand, and Greenberg, on the other. For example, Greenberg is reluctant to acknowledge openly that the function of paintings is to be looked at, which is a fact about painting that both Fried and Cavell face directly. (In Gudel's view, these matters are complicated by the fact that there often seem to be two Greenbergs, one concerned to acknowledge what the other is concerned to repress. We might add that in this way there never seem to be two Frieds. And two Cavells.)

you see, when you sight something, is an object—anyway not the sight of an object. Nor will the epistemologist's "sense-data" or "surfaces" provide correct descriptions here. . . . If the sense-data of photographs were the same as the sense-data of the objects they contain, we couldn't tell a photograph of an object from the object itself. To say that a photograph is of the surfaces of objects suggests that it emphasizes texture. . . . I feel like saying: Objects are too *close* to their sights to give them up for reproducing; in order to reproduce the sights they (as it were) make, you have to reproduce *them*—make a mold, or take an impression. (19–20)

The implication of this painstaking passage is not that photographs reproduce the objects in them, but that photographs are not recordings. To speak of a photograph as if it were a recording, as Bazin does, is to forget how different these things are, to fail to acknowledge what each, in its difference, is, what makes each singular and special.

Cavell also finds himself unable to accept Bazin's suggestion that photographs are visual molds or impressions. To speak of photographs as molds is to forget how different photographs and molds are from each other. In particular it is to forget that "molds and impressions and imprints have clear procedures for getting *rid* of their originals, whereas in a photograph, the original is still as present as it ever was. Not present as it once was to the camera; but that is only a mold-machine, not the mold itself" (20). By speaking of them as molds, Bazin forgets what it is about photographs that we find so perplexing. When we forget this, we not only forget something about photographs; we also forget something about ourselves, something about our own experience that it is perplexing for us to think about, to try to place.

"A child," Cavell observes, "might be very puzzled by the remark, said of a photograph, 'That's your grandmother'" (18). The puzzled child does not yet know (as we might put it) what a photograph is, has not yet learned to say and mean the kinds of things we ordinarily say and mean about photographs. This object she is beholding is not her grandmother in the flesh. Then how can she point to it and say, "That's my grandmother"? How can it be her grandmother—who is not now present—she is seeing? The child's puzzlement also reveals that if she does not (yet) know what kind of thing a photograph is, simply pointing to a photograph of her grandmother and saying "that's your grandmother" is unlikely to teach this to her.

Characteristically, Cavell's example, however casual it may appear, is a resonant one. To know that an object is a photograph is to know something about its origins. To know that it is a photograph of one's grandmother is to know something as well about one's own origins—about how one entered the picture, about how one enters into *this* picture. The scene of instruction Cavell invokes intimates a connection, explored within *The World Viewed* as a whole, between the way it is mysterious to us what photographs are, how they have entered the world, and the way it is mysterious to us what we are, how we have entered the world.

As Cavell notes, "Children are very early *no longer* puzzled by such remarks, luckily" (18). Children quickly learn to say and mean the kinds of things we ordinarily say and mean about photographs. And, Cavell's "luckily" implies, they are fortunate to

Sarah Shagan Rothman (Bill Rothman's grandmother)

Catherine O'Brien Keane (Marian Keane's grandmother)

learn these ways of speaking. The fact that very soon children are no longer puzzled by remarks like "that's your grandmother" said in the presence of a photograph does not mean they have arrived at a solution to the mystery the existence of photographs once posed to them. When we stop to think about it, the fact that when we look at photographs we see things that are not present remains as mysterious to us as it ever was. The fact that ordinarily we do not stop to think about photographs, that we forget our original puzzlement, is itself a puzzling fact (about photographs and about ourselves) that we do not ordinarily stop to think about.

"It may be felt that I make too great a mystery of these objects," Cavell writes. "My feeling is rather that we have forgotten how mysterious these things are, and in general how *different* things are from one another, as though we had forgotten how to value them" (19). When we forget how mysterious photographs are, how different they are from all other kinds of things, we forget something of value about photographs. When we forget this, we forget how mysterious we are (how different human beings are from other kinds of beings, how different we are from each other). We forget how to value our own lives, our own experience. We forget something of value about being human.

∽

To this point in chapter 2, Cavell has not provided a definition of "photograph." Nor does the remainder of the chapter provide such a definition. Neither does the chapter go on to advance a *theory* to explain the ontology of the photographic image. Cavell does not attempt to counter Bazin's theory that photographs are recordings or molds, for example, with a comparable theory of his own. The claim made by chapter 2 as a whole is that to advance such a theory—to theorize that photographs are, say, indexical signs, or ideological constructs, or media texts—is to attempt to explain away the mystery that when we look at a photograph we see things that are not present. In Cavell's view, theory is not to be used, as it so often is, to deny the puzzlement internal to our experience of photographs, the puzzlement internal to what, in our experience, we know photographs, and know ourselves, to be. To use theory that way is to escape only by avoiding the perspective of self-reflection that only philosophy is capable of providing.

Because Cavell's claim is that it is mysterious to us what photographs are, it is no evidence against his position that it may be difficult or impossible to spell out a coherent realist theory of photography. Hence the objections Noel Carroll raises against Bazin in *Philosophical Problems of Classical Film Theory*, whether or not they fairly address Bazin's position, do not apply to Cavell's. Nonetheless, Carroll takes them to apply to *The World Viewed* as well. "Bazin believes," he writes, that

> a photographic image is always an image of . . . the objects, places, events, and persons that gave rise to it. A photographic image re-presents its model. . . . Bazin himself does not really supply an argument for this point. The leading contemporary Bazinian, Stanley Cavell, however, does.

Cavell initiates his argument by asking what it is that films reproduce. (Carroll 1988, 98)

As we have seen, however, Cavell does not initiate his argument in chapter 2 by asking what films "reproduce" or "re-present." Acknowledging our impulse to say that a photograph presents us not with reproductions, likenesses of things, but with the things themselves, Cavell's question is what it is that a photograph of an object *presents*. Perhaps it is inattentiveness to Cavell's words (to "this prose just here"), or perhaps it is a reluctance to tackle head-on the opinion common within film studies that Cavell is a Bazin acolyte, that leads Carroll to assert that Cavell argues that "'sights' are rather queer metaphysical entities that might better be banished from one's ontology in the name of parsimony. . . . But if it is not the sight or the appearance of the object that a photographic image represents, then it must be the object itself that is represented" (Carroll 1988, 100).

But Cavell's argument is not, as Carroll supposes, that objects do not have sights the way French horns have sounds, that for this reason a photograph of an object cannot represent the sight of that object, and that therefore it must be the object itself that the photograph represents. Cavell argues, rather, that a photograph does not bear the relationship to *anything* that a recording bears to the sound it reproduces. A photograph does not reproduce the sight or appearance of an object that is in it, but neither does it reproduce the object itself. Cavell's point is that there is no thing that a photograph reproduces. And he concludes from this that photographs are not copies or recordings at all. Nor do photographs represent ("*re*-present") the objects that appear in them, for the reason that in a photograph the original is still as present as it ever was.

When Cavell asserts that what makes photographs different from all other kinds of things in the world, what makes their singularity so singularly difficult to place, is the mysterious fact that when we look at a photograph we "see things that are not present," he anticipates an objection: "Someone will object: 'That is playing with words. We're not seeing something not present; we are looking at something perfectly present, namely, a *photograph*'" (19). As if on cue, Carroll voices precisely the objection Cavell anticipates: "But why must we believe that something or anything is in fact re-presented via photographic representation? . . . . What photography does is to *produce* a stand-in for its model" (Carroll 1988, 102). Cavell's reply to his own imagined interlocutor is equally telling as a rejoinder to Carroll: "That is affirming something I have not denied. On the contrary, I am precisely describing, or wishing to describe, what it means to say that there is this photograph here" (19).

Cavell's point is that the relationship between an object or person in a photograph and the photograph itself is different from that object or person's relationship with any other kind of thing in the world. Merely saying that a photograph "produces a stand-in for its model" does not illuminate the way photography's kind of stand-in is different from other kinds of stand-ins—from counterfeits, fakes, or straw men, for example, which are intended to be passed off for the real thing, or from proxies or agents, which are not.

Ordinarily, a stand-in stands in for a different person or thing. There are criteria for distinguishing between the two, although in some cases it may require special expertise to apply those criteria. However, the person(s) and/or thing(s) the photograph is *of* and the person(s) and/or thing(s) *in* that photograph are not separate individuals. There can be no criteria for distinguishing them for the simple reason that they are one and the same. To speak of photographs as stand-ins, then, is not in itself to account for the singular relationship between a photograph and the person(s) and/or thing(s) in that photograph. It is to forget, once more, how different photographs are from other kinds of things.

Again, chapter 2 in no way claims to explain away what we find perplexing in the relationship between photographs and the person(s) and/or thing(s) in them. The chapter only calls upon us to stop forgetting how mysterious it is to us that when we look at photographs we see persons and things that are not present.

Although *The World Viewed* does not accept Bazin's suggestion that cameras are mold-machines, it does endorse his view that, as Cavell puts it, "photographs are not *hand*-made; they are manufactured," that there is an "inescapable fact of mechanism or automatism in the making of these images" (20). The mystery of photographs is their capacity to allow persons and things in the world to present, to reveal, *themselves*.

In our experience of teaching *The World Viewed*, students frequently take umbrage at the idea that in photography the world itself plays such an active role. They take Cavell to be asserting that there is no art to photography. However, nothing could be further from his intention than to deny that photography can be an art. He is not denying that photographs can be composed like paintings, for example, or otherwise shaped or manipulated. His claim is that there is an inescapable *element* of mechanism or automatism in the making of photographs, not that there is *nothing but* mechanism or automatism in their making.

Although Cavell agrees that it is a significant fact about photographs that they are not handmade, he rejects what he takes to be Bazin's claim that the element of mechanism or automatism in the making of photographs enables them to satisfy "once and for all and in its very essence, our obsession with realism" (20). This claim is misleading because it denies photography the status of a medium. The fact that photography enables the things and persons in the world to present or reveal themselves does not mean that there is no difference between a photograph and the things or persons in that photograph.

Then what does the fact of automatism in the making of photographs mean, what does it come to? "Getting to the right depth of this fact of automatism," this fact that film enables the world to present or reveal *itself*, is a task the remainder of chapter 2 undertakes. Rather, these extraordinarily dense two and a half pages *begin* to undertake this task. "Getting to the right depth of this fact of automatism" is a project that occupies the entirety of chapters 2 through 5 and, indeed, the whole of *The World Viewed*. This must be so, given that the relationship of film and painting is a central concern of the book, and given Cavell's conviction that the concept of automatism is a key to thinking through that relationship.

As a first step in "getting to the right depth of this fact of automatism," Cavell argues that it is misleading to say, as Bazin does, that "photography has freed the plastic arts from their obsession with likeness,' for this makes it seem (and it does often look) as if photography and painting were in competition, or that painting had wanted something that photography broke in and satisfied (21). Bazin's formulation implies, in effect, that painting wished to be photography. But painting's aspiration was always to create *paintings*, and its obsession was not with likeness but with *reality*. The obsession with reality that led painting to create ever more perfect likenesses ultimately forced painting, in Manet, to forgo likeness "because the illusions it had learned to create did not provide the conviction in reality, the connection with reality, it craved" (21).

Photography did not free painting from likeness, nor from the idea that a painting had to be a picture (that is, *of* or *about* something else)," until long after the establishment of photography; and then not because it finally dawned on painters that paintings were not pictures, but because that was the way to maintain connection with (the history of) the art of painting, to maintain conviction in its powers to create paintings, meaningful objects in paint (21). Furthermore, painting's final denial of objective reference was not a complete yielding of connection with reality. On the contrary, it was precisely the craving for connection with reality that likenesses were no longer able to satisfy that motivated this denial. Objective reference no longer enabled painting to satisfy this craving, Cavell argues, because it no longer enabled painting to provide a convincing sense of *presentness*—our presentness to the world, the world's presentness to us.

The concept of presentness, crucial to *The World Viewed* as a whole, is taken up at length in the pivotal chapter 15 ("Excursus: Some Modernist Painting"). Suffice it to say here that Cavell does not give the word some special meaning, does not use it as a technical term. "Presentness," as it occurs in *The World Viewed*, is an ordinary noun like "whiteness" or "blackness," a noun formed from the word "present" in accordance with the familiar grammatical rules of the English language. What the word "presentness" means, what presentness is, hinges on what "present" means, on what the present, or being present, is, on what we mean when we speak of the present, or speak of someone or something *as* present. ("Presentness" is *not* synonymous with "presence," as in Jacques Derrida's critique of "the metaphysics of presence.")[2]

---

2. Cavell's relation to Derrida is a large subject, as large a subject as the historical split between the Anglo-American and Continental branches of the Western philosophical tradition. Several extended discussions of Derrida's writing appear in "Nothing Goes Without Saying: Reading the Marx Brothers" (Cavell and Rothman 2005, 183–92), *A Pitch of Philosophy: Autobiographical Exercises* (Cavell 1994), *Philosophical Passages: Wittgenstein, Emerson, Austin, Derrida* (Cavell 1995), and "Naughty Orators," Cavell's reading of *Gaslight* in *Contesting Tears* (Cavell 1996). In these discussions, Cavell challenges Derrida's use, or misuse, of Austin's concept of "performative utterances" and reflects more broadly on the affinities and differences between Derrida's work and his own, with a focus on the procedures and anxieties of learning, of teaching and being taught, hence of inheriting, and refusing or otherwise failing to inherit, a tradition, a language, a culture, a form of human life.

That objective reference no longer enables painting to provide a sense of presentness reflects a fundamental change in the human form of life, in Cavell's view. At some point, "the unhinging of our consciousness from the world interposed our subjectivity between us and our presentness to the world." For modern human beings, "our subjectivity became what is present to us; individuality became isolation" (22). *The World Viewed* returns again and again to this idea of the unhinging of our consciousness from the world. At one level, Cavell locates it at a particular historical moment (the Protestant Reformation, the theater of Shakespeare, the birth of modern philosophy in Descartes's experience of skeptical doubt). He also suggests that it can be located (as it were psychoanalytically) at a particular moment in the life of every modern human being; once having taken place, it is also repeated again and again in that individual's life. That is, *The World Viewed* understands the "unhinging of our consciousness from the world" to be a historical event and also a mythical event, like the Biblical fall from grace. Picture it as a spiritual and psychological and political cataclysm that presents us with a new fact (or is it a new consciousness of an old fact?) about ourselves, about our condition as human beings. We now feel isolated by our subjectivity. It is our subjectivity, not a world we objectively apprehend, that appears present to us. Nor do we objectively apprehend our own subjectivity; our subjectivity, too, appears present to us only subjectively, as if our consciousness has become unhinged from our subjectivity no less than from the world. "So far as photography satisfied a wish," Cavell goes on, it satisfied "the human wish, intensifying in the West since the Reformation, to escape subjectivity and metaphysical isolation—a wish for the power to reach this world, having for so long tried, at last hopelessly, to manifest fidelity to another" (21).

It is crucial not to misconstrue this point, as Douglas Lackey does in his review of *The World Viewed* in the *Journal of Aesthetics and Art Criticism*. Misquoting Cavell as claiming that "photography satisfied . . . the human wish to escape subjectivity and metaphysical isolation," Lackey understands Cavell to mean that photography *succeeded* in satisfying this human wish that painting had failed to satisfy (Lackey 1973, 271).

This ignores Cavell's insistence that painting and photography were never in competition. It also fails to recognize that Cavell would find it as appropriate to say of modernist painting as of photography that "so far as it satisfied a wish" the wish it satisfied is the human wish to escape subjectivity and metaphysical isolation. Cavell's underlying point is that insofar as photography and modernist painting succeeded—and insofar as they failed—in satisfying this wish, they satisfied it—and failed to satisfy it—in fundamentally different ways.

Cavell's crucial "so far as" pointedly leaves open the possibility that photography's satisfaction of this wish was less than complete. The thrust of *The World Viewed* as a whole is that although film appeared to have solved the problem of reality by "magically" neutralizing the need to represent reality in order to connect with it, movies actually "brought the problem of reality to some ultimate head," as "More of *The World Viewed*" puts it (195). In Cavell's understanding, our wish to escape subjectivity cannot be separated from our wish to achieve selfhood. Selfhood cannot be achieved apart from reaching this world, apart from escaping the metaphysical isolation that has become our condition. Cavell's idea is that selfhood cannot be achieved apart from the acknowledgment of otherness (the acknowledgment of us by others, and our acknowledgment of others). Hence, he writes, "Apart from the wish for selfhood (hence the always simultaneous granting of otherness as well), I do not understand the value of art. Apart from this wish and its achievement, art is exhibition" (22)—"exhibition" being a concept *The World Viewed* will go on to investigate.

Merely to represent (as expressionism does) our terror of ourselves in isolation, which is our *response* to this new fact of our condition, is to *exhibit* our isolation, to theatricalize our isolation and thereby seal our fate. Cavell argues that for modern human beings, for creatures like us who find our subjectivity interposed between our selves and the world, photography and modernist painting exemplify different routes to overcoming theatricality, to reaching this world and achieving selfhood. Modernist painting accepts the recession of the world so as to maintain painting's conviction in its own power to establish connection with reality. It acknowledges "that endless presence of self" in order to permit us "presentness to ourselves, apart from which there is no hope for a world" (23). "To speak of our subjectivity as the route back to our conviction in reality is to speak of romanticism," Cavell writes.

> Hence Kant, and Hegel; hence Blake secreting the world he believes in; hence Wordsworth competing with the history of poetry by writing out himself, writing himself back into the world. A century later Heidegger is investigating Being by investigating *Dasein* . . . and Wittgenstein investigates the world . . . by investigating what we say, what we are inclined to say, what our pictures of phenomena are, in order to wrest the world from our possessions so that we may possess it again. (22)

In passages like this, *The World Viewed* acknowledges its own roots within romanticism. Cavell, too, is a philosopher who investigates reality by investigating what we say, our pictures of phenomena. He is a philosopher who seeks by writing to restore himself to the world, who calls upon us to wrest the world from our possessions so we may possess it again. *The World Viewed* begins with its author's acknowledgment that what he calls his "natural relation" to movies has been broken. His book calls upon us to acknowledge that we, too, are no longer possessed by the world of movies the way we once were, that we no longer possess the world of movies the way we once did. In giving thought to our new sense that the world of movies has become lost to us, Cavell proceeds by investigating, philosophically, what we say, what we are inclined to say, about the phenomena of movies.

By investigating "what our pictures are of movies," by investigating an experience of movies he calls upon us to acknowledge as ours as well, *The World Viewed* calls upon us to make our experience present to us. The goal is to wrest the world of movies "from our possessions so that we may possess it again"—not to enable us to restore the relation to movies that once came naturally to us, but to enable us to achieve a new relation to movies, to the world, to ourselves.

> Movies are photographic. Photography's route to "reaching this world," as opposed to modernist painting's route, is by overcoming the endless presence of subjectivity. Photography maintains the presentness of the world by accepting our absence from it. The reality in a photograph is present to me while I am not present to it . . . through no fault of my subjectivity. . . Photography overcomes subjectivity in a way undreamed of by painting, a way that could not satisfy painting, one which does not so much defeat the act of painting as escape it altogether: by *automatism*, by removing the human agent from the task of reproduction. (23)

With this idea that photography produces images of reality automatically, without subjectivity intervening, Cavell feels he is getting "to the right depth of this fact of automatism." And we are now prepared to say why Cavell believes it is misleading to claim that the inescapable element of automatism in the making of these images enables photography to overcome, once and for all, and in its very essence, our obsession with realism. First, because our obsession was never with realism but with *reality* (with reaching this world, attaining selfhood). Second, because photographs are not more realistic than paintings. That photographic media communicate by way of what is real does not make them inherently realistic. Indeed, it makes no more sense to speak of photographs as realistic than to speak of reality as realistic. Realistic as opposed to what? Fantastic? What could be more fantastic than reality? Reality is real, not realistic.

After all, as Cavell will go on to remind us, reality is precisely what it is that fantasy can be confused with. When objects and persons in the world are projected and screened, they are displaced from their natural sequences and locales. This displacement, which enables movies to depict the fantastic as readily as the natural—a point crucial to *The World Viewed* as a whole—itself acknowledges their material reality. Only what exists in the world can be photographed, subjected to photography's way of displacing things and people. And what exists in the world already bears the stamp of our fantasies.

As we have seen, *The World Viewed* resists what Cavell calls the "pervasive intellectual fashion" that holds that we do not, cannot, really know reality. Cavell resists this skepticism on the ground that reality's powers of compelling conviction are at least as strong as that of any theory. If appeals to theory cannot ultimately defeat our conviction in reality, unabashed appeals to reality like Bazin's or Panofsky's cannot ultimately free us from skeptical doubt. If reality is precisely what fantasy can be mistaken for (and what can be mistaken for fantasy), reality is also precisely what it is whose existence human beings are capable of doubting (as Cavell puts it, the possibility of skepticism is internal to the conditions of human knowledge). There is no particular feature or set of features by which the world on film can be distinguished from reality. The objects and persons projected on the screen appear real for the simple reason that they are real. And yet, these objects and persons do not really exist (now), and we are not (now) really in their presence.

The role reality plays in movies enables them to depict the fantastic as readily as the natural and makes the world on film what in "More of *The World Viewed*" Cavell will call "a moving image of skepticism." But for Cavell it is a fundamental principle that the possibility of skepticism is internal to the conditions of human knowledge. That we cannot know reality with absolute certainty is a fact about human knowledge, a fact about what knowledge, for human beings, *is*. It does not follow from this fact that we cannot really know the world, or ourselves in it.

4

The Acknowledgment of Silence

with Marian Keane

Naturalness has been withdrawing—nature itself has been withdrawing—from film. But "nature's absence," as Cavell puts it in chapter 15, "is only the history of our turnings from it." If nature has been turning away from film, film has been turning away from nature, indeed, from its own nature. Increasingly, chapter 16 argues, film itself, denying its own nature, has come to take over the task of exhibition; "film's growing doubt of its ability to allow the world to exhibit itself" has led it to a "new theatricalizing of its images." We now have a new sense of film, chapter 17 in turn suggests, a sense that the camera must now, in candor, acknowledge not its being present in the world but its being outside its world. Chapter 18 argues that the "new rush of technical assertions . . . are, insofar as they are serious, responses to [this] sense of withdrawing candor." It lists some uses of these devices to determine the limits, the conditions of film's existence, they discover.

Recapitulating this survey in chapter 19, *The World Viewed*'s final chapter, Cavell finds that he has emphasized silence, isolation in fantasy, and the mysteries of human motion and separateness. "This new emergence of the ideas of silence and fantasy and motion and separateness takes us back, or forward, to beginnings"—to film's origins, to *The World Viewed*'s own "obscure promptings."

For it isn't as if, long after our acceptance of the talkie, we know why the loss of silence was traumatic for so many who cared about film. What

---

Chapter 19 of William Rothman and Marian Keane, *Reading Cavell's "The World Viewed": A Philosophical Perspective on Film* (Detroit: Wayne State University Press, 2000). Reprinted with permission. Unless otherwise indicated, page numbers refer to the 1979 expanded edition of *The World Viewed*.

was given up in giving up the silence of the voice? Why suppose there will be some simple answer to that question, that there was some single spell broken by the sound of the human voice? For the voice has spells of its own. I think this issue now underlies all the explorations in film to which I have alluded. (147)

In *Must We Mean What We Say?*, Cavell made clear his understanding that ordinary language philosophy is about whatever ordinary language is about—"the necessities common to us all, those necessities we cannot, being human, fail to know. Except that nothing is more human than to deny them" (Cavell 2002, 96). In exploring the "silence of the voice," movies are exploring the limits of ordinary language, which is what modern philosophy, as Cavell understands and practices it in *The World Viewed*, is exploring as well. No one appreciates more fully than Cavell, who was committed to raising the procedures of ordinary language philosophy to an explicit self-consciousness, the diversity of roles speaking plays in our human form of life. Why should silence be expected to play fewer roles than speaking? If talkies gave up the silence of the voice, that silence, in the so-called silent cinema, was an endless source of aesthetic possibilities.

The title of the final chapter of *The World Viewed*, "The Acknowledgment of Silence," is yet another formulation with almost punning double meaning: Silence is to be acknowledged, but silence is also the form the acknowledgment is to take. And, we might note, Cavell understands the silence of the voice not only to be a feature of movies, a feature that movies seemed to lose when they became talkies, but a feature of moviegoing, too. The conversation of companions was internal to the "natural relation" to movies whose loss prompts the writing of *The World Viewed*. There is a silence internal to that relation, too—a silence Cavell is breaking by undertaking this writing. (There is also a silence that the writing of *The World Viewed* aspires to achieve by trusting its words to lead to its necessary conclusion.)

> The technology of sound recording soon overcame the actor's stiff bondage to the microphone, and the camera was free to stray again. But the technology did not free it from a deeper source of bondage in the idea of synchronization itself. On the contrary, the possibility of following an actor anywhere with both eye and ear seemed to make their bonding necessary. No doubt that source has to do with the absolute satisfaction of a craving for realism, for the absolute reproduction of the world—as if we might yet be present at its beginning. But there is a further reality that film pursues, the further, continuous reality in which the words we need are *not* synchronized with the occasions of their need or in which their occasions flee them. (147–48)

Cavell is not referring here to "the various ways dialogue can stand at an angle to the life that produces it," nor to occasions in which words that could have been said for some reason remained unsaid ("times in which the occasion is past when you can say what you did not think to say," or "when the occasion for speech is blocked by inappropriateness or fear, or the vessels of speech are pitched by grief or joy"). What he has in mind are such examples as

> the pulsing air of incommunicability which may nudge the edge of any experience and placement: the curve of fingers that day, a mouth, the sudden rise of the body's frame as it is caught by the color and scent of flowers, laughing all afternoon mostly about nothing, the friend gone but somewhere now which starts from here—spools of history that have unwound only to me now, occasions which will not reach words for me now, and if not now, never. (148)

These examples seem obscure, to say the least. Isn't that Cavell's point? These words are being used to invoke private moments one cannot know without having experienced them. For these are occasions—like the memorable movie occasions Cavell cites in chapter 1—whose passing is marked by an absence of words.

It is not that we lack the words needed to convey our experience of such moments. When we lack words, we can invent them. In the kinds of occasions Cavell has in mind, when words are not reached now and if not now never, words are not lacking but "out of reach"—not the ineffable but the unsayable, "time's answer to the ineffable," as he provocatively puts it, registering the idea that the barrier separating words from the unsayable, like the barrier separating the one existing world from the world on film, is not space but time (148). "I am not asking for more stream-of-consciousness," Cavell insists. "Stream-of-consciousness does not show the absence of words as the time of action unwinds; it floats the time of action in order to give space for the words." What he is asking for is "the ground of consciousness" upon which he "cannot but move." This is the "further reality that film pursues"—what Cavell calls the "reality of the unsayable" (148).

In characterizing the reality of the unsayable as the "ground of consciousness," Cavell means "ground" as opposed to "figure." It is only against the unsayable as a background that the figures of consciousness are able to stand out, to be apparent to us. He also means "ground" in the sense of "grounding," as opposed to "floating," for example—if stream of consciousness floats the time of action, the unsayable is the solid ground we must have beneath our feet if our need for horizons, for uprightness and frontedness, is to be satisfied, if we are to walk in the gait that is natural for human beings on earth. Thus, this passage echoes chapter 15's characterization of the modernist paintings Michael Fried calls "objects of presentness," which exist

> as abstracts of intimacy, declaring our common capacity and need for presentness, for clear separateness and singleness and connection, for horizons and uprightness and frontedness, for the simultaneity of a world, for openness and resolution. They represent existence without assertion;

authority without authorization; truth without claim, which you can walk in. It is out of such a vision that Thoreau in *Walden* . . . speaks of nature as silent. (118)

Chapter 15's invocation of *Walden* here adumbrates the deep connection that emerges in chapter 19 between the unsayable and the mysteries of human movement and separateness that, chapter 18 argues, motivate recent serious uses of devices like slow motion, freeze frames, and flash insets. It also helps us to recognize that, when in *The World Viewed*'s final chapter Cavell characterizes the unsayable as the ground of consciousness, part of what he means is that it is the unmoving ground we human beings need beneath us if we are to find our feet, to walk, to move from place to place, from thought to thought, to express ourselves in any medium.

By calling the unsayable "the ground of consciousness upon which I cannot but move," Cavell may seem simply to be asserting that he would be unable to move were he not standing upon terra firma such as this. But what his words literally say is that standing upon this unmoving ground he cannot *but* move, that is, he cannot stand still. This is a characterization of human consciousness in general: It is not possible for human beings to stop thinking. For human beings who find ourselves standing upon the unmoving ground of consciousness that is the unsayable—Cavell speaks of the unsayable as a "continuous reality," keeping in play the distinction between montage and continuity that runs through the chapter—movement, change, thought, expression, is not only possible but necessary. Always to be moving, always to be moved, always to be subject to montage, we might say, like Buster Keaton in *Sherlock Jr.*, is the fate of human consciousness, a condition of our existence as human. And, as Cavell's use of "I" here suggests, this formulation also refers specifically to his own consciousness, the thinking exemplified by the writing of *The World Viewed*. The continuous reality of the unsayable is the ground upon which *this* thinking, *this* writing, moves from "place" to "place."

The reality of the unsayable is what Cavell now finds in "film's new release from the synchronization of speech with the speaker, or rather in its presenting of the speaker in forms in which there can be no speech," as in the serious uses of cinematic devices enumerated in chapter 18. "The possibilities of moving pictures speak of a comprehensibility of the body under conditions which destroy the comprehensibility of speech," Cavell asserts. "It is the talkie itself that is now exploring the silence of movies" (149).

Cavell does not have in mind things movies have begun to say that traditionally had remained unsaid by them, or topics they have begun to address for the first time. He has in mind, rather, ways movies have begun exploring the possibilities and limits of the movie itself—of film's way of enabling the world to express itself, its way of "speaking the being of the world" directly (as every art, in Cavell's view, wishes in its own way to do). He has in mind attempts movies are making to determine wherein, for film, the unsayable is to be located; to survey the boundary between the unsayable and the merely unsaid; to discover what, for film, silence *is*.

"A silent movie has never been made," Cavell reminds us in one of the chapter's most eloquent passages.

> We called some silent after others acquired speech; but that was to register the satisfaction of the world's reproduction, as if the movie had until then been thwarted from that satisfaction, as if the actors and their world had been inaudible. But they were no more inaudible than the characters in radio were invisible. . . . No person or object we could be shown could be the ones called into existence by those sounds. . . . No word we could hear could be the word spoken by that figure of silence. (149)

Before they became talkies, movies were not silent; they projected "a world of silence." So-called silent movies had their own ways of "speaking the being of the world" directly. A world exhibited to sight expresses itself without what Cavell calls the "clumsiness of speech, the dumbness and duplicities and concealments of assertion, the bafflement of soul and body by their inarticulateness and their terror of articulateness." Hence it is a world of "immediate intelligibility" (as radio's world of sound is a world of "immediate conviction").

> We are told that most silent-film stars had to be replaced because his or her voice disappointed our expectations, but that a few satisfied us and crossed the boundary intact. No; no one did; all were replaced, some by themselves. We were universally disappointed. The new creations of synchronized sight and sound were merely powerful enough to distract us from the disappointment, and they deserved to. Now the disappointment is waking again. With talkies we got back the clumsiness of speech, the dumbness and duplicities and concealments of assertion, the bafflement of soul and body by their inarticulateness and by their terror of articulateness. Technical improvements will not overcome these ontological facts; they only magnify them. These ontological facts are tasks of art, as of existence. The advent of sound broke the spell of immediate intelligibility—a realistic renunciation, given the growing obscurity of the world. Then the task is to discover the poetry in speech. It will not be the poetry of poetry. It seemed at first as if it ought to have been, as if when the filmed world expressed itself in speech it would have the same absolute intelligibility as its exhibition to sight. But every art wants the expression of the world, to speak the being of it directly, and none can simply hand its own powers to the others. . . . The best film dialogue has so far been the witty and the hard-nosed. . . . They work . . . because they provide natural occasions on which silence is broken, and in which words do not go beyond their moment of saying; hence occasions in which silence naturally asserts itself. For the world is silent to us; the silence is merely forever broken. (149–50)

The arts of poetry and music incorporate the world's silence and "speak the world's being" directly in ways that the world itself, unmediated by art, cannot. In talkies, the filmed world expresses itself in speech. But film speech, like ordinary speech, does not have the immediate intelligibility, the lucidity, of the world of silence exhibited in so-called silent films. Then how can talkies be capable of conveying the reality of the unsayable? How can they be capable of "speaking the being of the world" directly? How can sound film be a medium of art at all?

Talkies are capable of conveying the reality of the unsayable, Cavell suggests, by showing experience that is beyond the reach of words. In order to find new ways of showing this, he argues, movies have begun exploring the possibilities of presenting speakers in forms in which there can be no speech. However, he adds, "there is another half to the idea of conveying the unsayable by showing experience beyond the reach of words."

> It is by freeing the motion of the body for its own lucidity. The body's lucidity is not dependent upon slowing and flashing and freezing it and juxtaposing it to itself over cuts and superimpositions. It was always part of the grain of film that, however studied the lines and set the business, the movement of the actors was essentially improvised—as in those everyday actions in which we walk through a new room or lift a cup in an unfamiliar locale or cross a street or greet a friend or look in a store window or accept an offered cigarette or add a thought to a conversation. . . . Our resources are given, but their application to each new crossroads is an improvisation of meaning, out of the present. (152–53)

Film speech cannot incorporate the world's silence the way poems can. In and out of the movie house, the poetry of speech—the capacity of ordinary language to convey the reality of the unsayable—emerges, rather, from "the fact that just that creature, in just those surroundings, is saying just that, just now" (153). In chapter 17, in the course of staking out the analogy summed up by his formula "The camera is outside its subject as I am outside my language," Cavell remarks, "When my limitation to myself feels like a limitation of myself, it seems that I am always leaving something unsaid; as it were, the saying." But the "saying itself"—one's saying of these particular words now, for one's own private reasons—is not something one is leaving unsaid; it is something unsayable—unreachable by words.

In movies, the synchronization of speech and speaker assures that the "saying itself" is not left out of the picture. In movies, the unsayable is always real; experience is always beyond the reach of words. It is part of the "natural vision of film," as Cavell puts it, that actions move "within a dark and shifting circle of intention and consequence, that their limits are our own, that the individual significance of an act (like that of a word) arises in its being this one rather than every other that might have been said or done here and now, that their fate (like the fate of our words) is to be taken out of our control (153).

It is part of the "natural vision" of film that movies appear automatically to satisfy "the explicit wish of human action since Kierkegaard and Nietzsche summed up Protestantism and Stanislavsky brought theater into line" to "act without performing, to allow action all and only the significance of its specific traces, the wound embracing the arrow and no self-consciousness to blunt or disperse that knowledge" (153). Thus, Cavell observes, movies automatically give Berthold Brecht "an unanticipated version of his wish for the epic in theater and the alienated in acting"—not the dissociation of actor and character, but "their total coalescence, allowing a dissociation or freeing of action from speech." Movies automatically satisfy Brecht's wish for "the turning of the spectator into somebody who just looks on (i.e., the absence of the 'involvement' of the spectator in the events on a stage, but without 'forcing him to make decisions'" (153–54).

As this last point suggests, however, movies do not automatically satisfy Brecht's wish for detached lucidity that directly issues in effective action for change. After all, movies have not effected the radical changes in the consciousness of individuals and society that Brecht espoused. And yet, of course, Brecht's art, too, failed to effect radical change. In Cavell's understanding, it is a fact that "art alone is not going to achieve the change of consciousness which its own reception also requires." Acknowledging this fact, Cavell points out, devastatingly, that it ought to be part of epic theater

> to contain the confrontation of its own continuous failing—every night our knowing the truth of our condition and every day dawning just the same—in order to make this failing neither palatable nor bitter, but to make it something we can live with faithfully, in consciousness, and with readiness for the significant detail when it really is ours to act upon. (154)

When Cavell adds that movies also automatically give Brecht "the vision that everything in the world other than nature is a human construction, humanly open to change," his point is that Brechtian theater, too, can change, can come to acknowledge, rather than deny, the moral the conclusion of chapter 18 sums up with the formulation "You do not know in advance what may arise as a significant detail."

There is no telling in advance the impact a movie is going to have, the place it will come to occupy in our lives. "The impact of movies is too massive, too out of proportion with the individual worth of ordinary movies, to speak politely of involvement. We involve the movies in us," Cavell writes. "They become further fragments of what happens to me, further cards in the shuffle of my memory," he goes on, reprising a theme that figures prominently in the preface (154). (In this formulation, the word "montage" could be substituted for "shuffle." We might note, however, that the opening line of the preface, "Memories of movies are strand over strand with memories of my life," uses a contrasting metaphor, one that shifts the emphasis from montage to continuity. When one picks a card from a shuffled deck, the card one chances to pick determines one's fortune. Viewed from the perspective of the preface, however, the fabric of Cavell's life appears as whole cloth to him, no matter the particular strands from which it happens to be woven.)

The movies we involve in our lives, Cavell is saying, are among the cards that at any moment we might draw, determining our fortunes. They are also "like childhood memories whose treasure no one else appreciates, whose content is nothing compared with their unspeakable importance for me." And they are like memories of traumatic childhood experiences we wish, rather, to forget.

> St. Augustine stole a pear; lots of children have. Rousseau got a spanking with his pants down; lots of little boys have. Why seems it so particular with them? Everybody has his stolen pear, and his casual, permanent seductions; if they are to know their lives, those are to be known. Parents are forever being surprised at their children's memories. Some find it amusing or quirky of them to remember such details; some boast, on that evidence, of their child's intelligence. The parents do not know what is important to the child, and their amusement and boasting mean that they are not going to try to learn. (154)

When Cavell poses the question "Why seems it so particular with them?" his wording echoes the question Hamlet's mother asks when she cannot fathom the way her son is grieving over his dead father. (The final paragraph of the chapter explicitly invokes *Hamlet*.) Enraged by his mother's blindness and lack of feeling, Hamlet replies that his grief does not merely *seem* "so particular to him," it *is* so—it is his and no one else's. Lots of children have stolen pears. Lots of little boys have gotten spankings. But these events, as St. Augustine and Rousseau wrote about them, not only *seem* but *are* "so particular to them." Had they not "spoken" about these events, we could not have known their importance.

"Everybody has his stolen pear, and his casual, permanent seductions," as Cavell puts it. If we are to know our lives, if we are to know ourselves, we must know the events that are so particular with us that they are of "unspeakable importance" to us. If we do not speak of these things, others cannot know their importance. Even when we do speak of them, their importance remains "unspeakable," unsayable, beyond the reach of words. To know ourselves, we must acknowledge the reality of the unsayable in our own experience, the ground of consciousness upon which we cannot but move. "The movie's power to reach this level"—film's capacity to become unspeakably important to us, like childhood memories we wish to treasure, or to forget—"must have to do with the gigantism of its figures, making me small again," Cavell remarks, adding, "it must also have to do with the world it screens being literally of my world" (154).

During the performance of a play, Cavell observes in "The Avoidance of Love," the audience occupies the same time but not the same space as the figures on stage. "I have been told," he writes in *The World Viewed*, "that [this] is obviously false: In a theater we obviously are in the same room as the actors, whereas at a movie we obviously are not" (155). But this objection wrongly assumes, first, that by crossing the footlights we would enter the space of the characters as well as the actors, when all we would accomplish would be to interrupt the performance. "The sacredness of the stage still holds," Cavell writes. "Not any longer because certain figures are authorized to be there," but because characters in a play have a past and future we cannot have been part of; like gods, they exist in a space that differs metaphysically from ours (155). Second, the objection wrongly assumes that we cannot enter the world of a movie because breaking through the screen, say, would not accomplish this. Cavell reminds us, however, that in a movie house, as in Plato's Cave, reality is *behind* us. ("[Reality] will become visible," he adds, "when you have made yourself visible to it, presented yourself" [155].)

When we view a movie, the stars are *there*, in our world. To get to them, though, we would have to go where they are. As things stand, we cannot go there *now*, but their space is not metaphysically different from the space we occupy; it is the same human space that ours is. During the performance of a play, we are forbidden to "cross the line between actor and incarnation, between action and passion, between profane and sacred realms." In a movie house, there is no line we are forbidden to cross. As Cavell provocatively puts it, "the barrier to the stars is time" (155). (In Cavell's understanding, time is also the barrier that separates our experience from words when words are out of reach.)

The world on film is all profane, all "outside"; there is no realm from which the stars, or we, are barred. "They and we could have been anywhere, may be anywhere next," Cavell writes. "The discontinuities in the environment of a film are discontinuities not of space but of places" (155–56). Remaining fixed in space, we somehow get from place to place but do not discontinuously go from one place to the other. For us, the discontinuities are those of attention: One after another, bits of the world are presented to our attention, and we must somehow put them together into *those* lives, as we put together our own lives. That at any given moment we find ourselves in a given place on earth, or on earth at all, is contingent. But it is necessary, not contingent, that at any given moment we find ourselves in *some* place. Placement is a necessity of our human form of life. And the absolute reality and placement of people in movies is a necessity of their appearing on film at all.

> I think everyone knows odd moments in which it seems uncanny that one should find oneself just here now, that one's life should have come to this verge of time and place, that one's history should have unwound to this room, this road, this promontory. The uncanny is normal experience of film. Escape, rescue, the metamorphosis of a life by a chance encounter or juxtaposition—these conditions of contingency and placement underpin all the genres of film, from the Keaton and Chaplin figures who know nothing of the abyss they skirt, to the men who know too much. (156)

In movies, the absolute reality and placement of people are conditions of their appearance. Thus, film escapes Aristotelian limits according to which the possible has to be made plausible.

It was a great achievement of realistic theater when Ibsen created an event, a suicide, in itself so improbable and in the character so right that he could rely on his play to rebuke the curtain line—"But people just don't do things like that!"—with the force of fact. That is the ordinary condition of the audience of film. Things like that don't happen in the world we go our rounds in—your father does not turn out to be a foreign spy, one's life does not depend upon finding a lady with a strange hat whom no investigation or headline can unearth, one man does not hold another by his sleeve from the top ledge of the Statue of Liberty, people do not . . . turn into werewolves and vampires. . . . But there they are. (156–57)

Summing up the implications of the fact that the absolute reality and placement of people in movies are conditions of their appearance, Cavell writes, "There is nothing people do not do, no place they may not find themselves in." People in movies escape the Aristotelian limits that constrain characters in plays. People in movies are *free*. It is noteworthy, moreover, that the formulation "There is nothing people do not do, no place they may not find themselves" does not distinguish the condition of people in movies from the condition of people outside movies—from our own condition, for example. The formulation applies to us, to the reality of our freedom, as surely as to the "human somethings" in movies.

When Cavell next asserts, "That is the knowledge which makes acceptable film's absolute control of our attention," his formulation serves to remind us that movies do, in fact, exert absolute control of our attention—at any given moment, the movie singles out the bit of the world we are to attend to (157). Deploring film's control of our attention and attributing it specifically to montage, Bazin championed techniques (long takes, deep focus) that he believed would minimize film's constraints on our freedom. Cavell accepts it as a fact about film that its control of our attention is absolute. In a note, he contrasts film with painting, which allows attention absolute freedom ("nothing will happen that is not before your eyes"), and with music, which asserts absolute control of our attention, as film does, but justifies this control by continuously rewarding our attention (157 n). By contrast, Cavell argues, what makes acceptable film's absolute control of our attention is *knowledge*—precisely the knowledge that "there is nothing people do not do, no place they may not find themselves."

When Cavell asserts that this knowledge "makes acceptable film's absolute control of our attention," he means that it is because we know we are free that we find film's control of our attention acceptable. He also means that when we accept film's absolute control of our attention, when we allow our freedom to be constrained in this way, we are rewarded with this knowledge of our freedom. Movies bring home the knowledge, or self-knowledge, that "we exist in the condition of myth," as Cavell puts it, that "we do not require the gods to show that our lives illustrate a story which escapes us; and it requires no major recognition or reversal to bring its meaning home" (157).

∽

At this point in the final chapter of *The World Viewed*, there is a blank space on the printed page, a typographical silence, as it were, that separates the body of "The Acknowledgment of Silence"—and the body of the book of which it is the final chapter—from the haunting four-paragraph coda that is the book's conclusion. It may well seem uncanny that we should find ourselves just now at this point, that the writing of *The World Viewed* should have unwound to this silence.

"Let me recall how we got to this point."—These were the words with which the final chapter of *The World Viewed* opened. There, "this point" meant the "point" that the conclusion of chapter 18 asserted, or reasserted, that "a 'possibility' of a medium can be made known only by successful works that define its media," that in modernism "a medium is explored by discovering possibilities that declare its necessary conditions, its limits." "This point" also meant the "place," unlocatable in advance of writing *The World Viewed*, to which this writing had arrived as chapter 19 opened, a point from which the writing could see its way to complete its exploration of the possibilities of the new medium of philosophy it has discovered, to go on to the ending it finds necessary, to declare its own limits, to achieve, and acknowledge, its own silence.

As the title "The Acknowledgment of Silence" suggests, the final chapter of *The World Viewed* is about film's capacity to acknowledge the world's silence. And it is about the capacity of film's silence to acknowledge reality beyond the reach of words. It is also about the capacity of *this* writing to acknowledge silence, and about the capacity of silence—what the writing of *The World Viewed* consigns to silence—to acknowledge the reality of the unsayable, to "speak the being of the world" directly.

The coda begins with the line "The knowledge of the unsayable is the study of what Wittgenstein means by physiognomy" (157). Wittgenstein's extended sketches of the kind of study he envisions, which begin with an investigation of the concept of "seeing as," occur in part 2 of *Philosophical Investigations*, where he "gives various examples in which some drawn figures (like some words, in some places) can be taken variously." One of his examples is our old friend the duck-rabbit. Another is a triangle that can be seen as fallen over. Others are drawings of faces and descriptions of postures "in which, as Wittgenstein puts it, different aspects of them can dawn, and in dawning strike us" (158).

For a philosopher thinking about the subject of film, Wittgenstein's discussion of "seeing as" has "what looks like a ready-made application," Cavell observes (158). The application he has in mind is the so-called Kuleshov experiment in which an actor's face was shown to alter its aspect when intercut with a bowl of borscht, a dead woman, and a little girl with a teddy bear. "Bazin," Cavell writes, "in a series of fine passages on the topic, turns this fact against what its admirers have taken it to show, *viz.*, the omnipotence of montage in film's narrative." Rather, "Bazin takes the demonstrated power of montage to show its weakness, because the inherent ambiguity or mystery of the human face is denied in presenting a context which forces one definite interpretation upon us" (158).

48 | The Holiday in His Eye

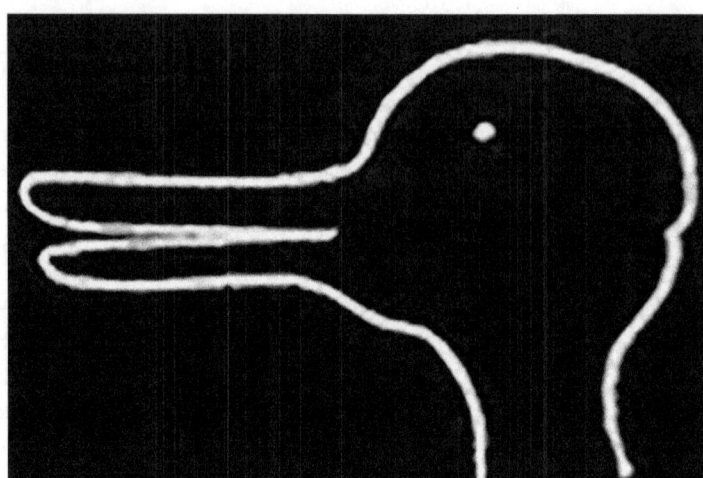

But in a sketch of a Wittgensteinian study, Cavell probes the issue more deeply. Linking up with chapter 2's investigation of what makes photographs different from other kinds of things, this passage brings home again the singularity, and the mysteriousness, of photographs.

> Shown (a photograph of) a human face, I might, as in the case of the duck-rabbit, be struck right off with one of its possible aspects. This is unlike the case of the triangle, in which to read it as "fallen over" I have to imagine something in connection with it, surround it with a fiction. But like the triangle and unlike the duck-rabbit, I *can* surround the face with a fiction in order to alter its aspects. And unlike the triangle and the duck-rabbit . . . , I must surround the face with a reality—as though the seeing of a reality is the imagining of it; and [the face] may itself either dictate or absorb the reality with which I must surround it, or fascinate me exactly because it calls incompatible realities to itself which vie for my imagination. (158)

If we are shown a photograph of a person's face, we are seeing the face of a real human being, someone who was in some particular place, surrounded by some particular reality, when the photograph was taken. What that place happened to be, what we imagine it to be, is utterly contingent; we can always imagine that person in some other place, surrounded by a different reality. But we cannot imagine the person in no place, surrounded by no reality at all ("We must surround the face with a reality, as though the seeing of a reality is the imagining of it"). Absolute reality and placement, which are conditions of the existence of people and things in the world, are conditions of their appearance in photographs as well. Because "the endless contingency of the individual human being's placement in the world," as Cavell puts it in "More of *The World Viewed*," cannot be separated from what is mysterious about human existence, the inherent ambiguity, or mystery, of the human face is not denied when, through montage, a shot of a face is presented in a context that surrounds it with a *particular* reality (181).

Nor is the inherent ambiguity, or mystery, of the human face on view in a given shot denied by the fact of recurrence of an actor in his type. The visible incarnation of character into star, and of star into successive characters, limits a performer's "range of expression, the physiognomical aspects which may dawn (one film working in montage to another), but it also threatens the limit" (158–59). Again, what a human being is capable of becoming on film is not determinable a priori; film does not fix in advance the range of the human.

Having seen Humphrey Bogart in several films, his physiognomy and gestures may seem so familiar that we feel we know the limit of what a man of his type is capable of expressing on screen. But it is possible for a new film—*The Treasure of the Sierra Madre* or *The African Queen*, for example—to place him in an unanticipated environment in which his familiar mannerisms take on an unanticipated significance or power, or in which he finds himself moved to perform unanticipated gestures to express ideas or feelings true to his type, but never before revealed by him on screen.

Indeed, it can be internal to a type that it threatens its own limit, Cavell writes. "This does not require the explicitness of *Dr. Jekyll and Mr. Hyde*. The threat is present when Harpo inevitably finds his harp. Then the usual frenzy of his information and gluttony and satyromania are becalmed in the angelic sounds with which this man of whistles and honks and noiseless roars and sobs can also express himself, the camera doting on the innerness of that face" (159).

This surfacing of the idea that within our knowledge of a face there is a region of unknownness, that "innerness" is something human faces on film, no matter how familiar, are capable of expressing, along with the idea that the camera tends to "dote" on familiar faces expressing innerness, leads Cavell to contemplate what he calls the "special use of unknown faces for their sheer impression upon us (as familiarly in Dreyer and Fellini)" (159).

What Cavell has in mind, in particular, are situations in which directors require faces with the capacity "both to invite and to refuse the imposition of imagination" (159), faces "which do not merely happen to be unknown but whose point, whose essence, is that they are unknown," as he puts it in "More of *The World Viewed*." Not just any unfamiliar face will have this quality. "It must be one which, on the screen, conveys unknownness; and this first of all means that it conveys privacy—an individual soul's aliveness or deadness to itself," hence its aliveness or deadness to others (182).

In Carl Dreyer's *The Passion of Joan of Arc*, for example, Maria Falconetti's face conveys unknownness by conveying a "sheer impression" that she is a woman who is alive to herself, as she is alive to others. (As so often in *The World Viewed* and in all of Cavell's writings about film, it is a woman, not a man, who serves as an exemplary representative of humanity.) By contrast, the faces of the bishops who interrogate and condemn Joan (with the memorable exception of the young bishop played by Antonin Artaud) convey the "sheer impression" that these are men who have no inner life, or none they are willing to express. Like the men in the film melodramas and operas Cavell studies in *Contesting Tears* and *A Pitch of Philosophy*, men who claim the authority to judge a woman, a claim the woman rightfully rejects, these bishops "want and want not to hear the woman's voice; to know and not to know what and that she desires" (Cavell 1994, 132). On screen, the denial of human potentiality expressed in the deadness of these men's faces is no less mysterious than the embrace of freedom that the woman's face, in its aliveness, expresses.

"The inflection of meaning available to a type is the background against which the inflexibility of a face commands its power of mystery," Cavell observes (159). The limit of the expressiveness of a performer's face on film, when viewed against the background of the range of expression available to the performer's type, enables the inherent ambiguity, or mystery, of the face to stand out, enables its unknownness to command its power of mystery. And Cavell follows this formulation with another whose wording parallels it, the parallel sentence structure underscoring the mysterious analogy upon which the transition hinges. "Film's promise of the world's exhibition is the background against which it registers absolute isolation" (159).

On film, there is no place a person cannot be. What it means for a person to be in a given place at a given moment of a given film is a function of what Wittgenstein calls "physiognomy"—a function of the range of expression available to a person of this type, the aspects this face is capable of registering, the aspects that can possibly "dawn" in such a face. Whatever the character this person happens to be incarnating in a particular film, whatever the place in which that character happens to find himself or herself, whatever the character's response to being in this place, there is something in his or her physiognomy—his or her type—that remains inflexible, fixed. The inflexibility of a particular human face—the limit of the expressiveness available to its type—is the "unmoving ground" that makes this face capable of being expressive, incapable of not being expressive.

Film's "rooms and cells and pinions hold out the world itself," Cavell's next sentence asserts (159). There is no "place" that cannot be exhibited on film. And yet, whatever bit of the world is exhibited at any given moment, something remains inflexible, fixed, in the physiognomy of the world on film. What is this "unmoving ground" that makes film capable of exhibiting the world, makes film incapable of not exhibiting the world? It is the very fact that film's "rooms and cells and pinions hold out the world itself." Whatever bit of the world is being exhibited at any given moment, it is the world itself, the world as a whole, that film "holds out." Holding the world out to us, holding the world out from us, holding us out of the world, film registers our isolation from the world projected on the movie screen.

Film's "fullest image of absolute isolation is in Dreyer's *Joan of Arc*," Cavell goes on, "when Falconetti at the stake looks up to see a flight of birds wheel over her with the sun in their wings. They, there, are free. They are waiting, in their freedom, to accompany her soul. She knows it. But first there is this body to be gone through utterly" (159). In this passage, Dreyer uses montage to surround Falconetti's face with a *particular* reality. Yet this does not deny this woman's face its inherent ambiguity, or mystery. Indeed, if no film sequence more fully registers absolute isolation, as Cavell asserts, it is equally true that no sequence more fully registers the power of mystery that the human face on film, when it reveals an individual soul's aliveness to itself, is capable of commanding.

Even as flames consume her body, the image of these wheeling birds, the sun in their wings, "waiting, in their freedom, to accompany her soul," asserts absolute control over Joan's attention, seals the denial of her freedom, and seals her isolation, as well. No one in Joan's world sees these birds. All others are riveted—in horror or in fascination or in righteous vengeance—to the spectacle of this woman's body engulfed in flames. And yet, this image also holds out the promise of freedom, and of the end of her isolation. Once this body is utterly consumed, she will be free, and no longer alone: That is Joan's faith.

This invocation of Joan burning at the stake is the culminating instance of the fire imagery that runs through *The World Viewed*. When Cavell characterizes the birds Joan sees as flames are consuming her body as *wheeling* over her, we might also note, this surprising—but quite accurate—word links the book's recurring fire imagery with the trope of the wheel or circle that plays such a crucial role in *King Lear*, as "The Avoidance of Love" interprets it (Cavell 2002, 340). In "The Avoidance of Love," Cavell takes Lear's climactic line "I am bound upon a wheel of fire" as an expression of the character's recognition that "his life is whole, like a wheel which turns," that our actions move "within a dark and shifting circle of intention and consequence" (as Cavell puts it earlier in chapter 19 of *The World Viewed*), that "their limits are our own, that the individual significance of an act (like that of a word) arises in its being this one rather than every other that might have been said or done here and now, that their fate (like the fate of our words) is to be taken out of our control" (153).

"To satisfy the wish for the world's exhibition, we must be willing to let the world as such appear," the penultimate paragraph of *The World Viewed* begins. "According to Heidegger, this means that we must be willing for anxiety, to which alone the world as world, into which we are thrown, can manifest itself; and it is through that willingness that the possibility of one's own existence begins or ends" (159). Without this willingness, we cannot really exist, we can only haunt the world. For this wish to be satisfied, however, we must "be willing to allow the self to exhibit itself without the self's intervention" (159). We must be willing to allow ourselves to exhibit ourselves *completely*, to open ourselves *completely* to being known (by others, by ourselves), to make ourselves *completely* intelligible. "The wish for total intelligibility is a terrible one," Cavell writes with grave eloquence.

> It means that we are willing to reveal ourselves through the self's betrayal of itself. The woman in *Hiroshima* is almost there: "I betrayed you tonight," she says in a monologue to her dead lover, looking at herself in the mirror, confessing her new lover. [Indeed, confessing that she has confessed her old love to her new lover.] It does not mitigate the need for acknowledgment that her old lover is dead, because what

she has betrayed is her love for him, which is not dead. As things stand, love is always the betrayal of love, if it is honest. It is why the path of self-knowledge is so ugly, hence so rarely taken, whatever its reputed beauties. The knowledge of the self as it is always takes place in the betrayal of the self as it was. That is the form of self-revelation until the self is wholly won. Until then, until there is a world in which each can be won, our loyalty to ourselves is in doubt, and our loyalty to others is in partialness. (159–60)

Early in our reading of the preface, we suggested that what prompts its opening paragraph is the entirety of the book whose completion it announces, but that this would not become apparent until we reached the book's ending. Now that we have arrived at that place, we can recognize that the preface not only announces that the writing of the body of the book has been concluded; it adumbrates the book's conclusion. It sustains the serenely elegiac mood, in the face of all but unendurable loss, that characterizes the writing of *The World Viewed* as it nears its conclusion. And it manifests the philosophical perspective whose achievement *is* the book's conclusion, its conclusive achievement.

In the haunting opening sentence of the preface ("Memories of movies are strand over strand with memories of my life"), we can now recognize, Cavell is speaking to us from the spiritual "place" to which the writing of *The World Viewed* transports him, the position he chooses to occupy, and to honor. This position grants him a philosophical perspective on his experience of movies, on the "natural relation" to movies he had enjoyed for a quarter of a century, on the loss of that relation, and on the writing that transported him to this "place," writing that is also an act of self-betrayal. (In the fabric of *The World Viewed*, made from the words he has found he could trust to render his experience intelligible, as in the fabric of his experience itself, memories of movies are strand over strand with memories of his life.)

In the preface, Cavell suggests that it is the business of *The World Viewed* as a whole to find a sufficient answer to the questions "What broke my natural relation to movies?" and "What was that relation, that its loss seemed to demand repairing, or commemorating, by taking thought?" To the reader beginning the book, what prompted this suggestion cannot but be obscure, as we suggested. Now that we have followed the book's thinking to the verge of its conclusion, we can recognize that *The World Viewed* is the answer Cavell takes to be sufficient to these questions. What breaks Cavell's natural relation to movies cannot be separated from the writing of *The World Viewed*, which concludes with this self-revelation, this declaration of self-knowledge.

In composing his metaphysical memoir of the period in which he enjoyed a "natural relation" to movies, in achieving this philosophical perspective on his life of regular moviegoing and the companionship it incorporated, Cavell commemorates the passing of that life, the death of the moviegoer who lived it. *The World Viewed* commemorates a world of movies and moviegoing that has passed into Cavell's memory. It commemorates, as well, the moviegoer its author no longer is, the companions with whom he no longer shares his experiences. In this writing, Cavell mourns the loss of that world, the death of that self. In the final paragraph of *The World Viewed*, he at once closes the book on his "natural relation" to movies and raises its writing to its highest plane. *The World Viewed* concludes with its fullest acknowledgment that the beauty and significance of its writing, its promise of "the pain and balm in the truth of the only world: that it exists, and I in it," is born of loss.

"A world complete without me which is present to me is the world of my immortality," the paragraph begins (160). During the period he enjoyed a "natural relation" to movies, the world on film, to Cavell, was a "world complete without me which is present to me." Hence to him the world on film was "the world of my immortality." In the world on film, he could not die, because it was a world into which he had never been born. And in viewing the world on film, he was not alone; he was with companions who were as free from mortal cares, in the world on film, as he was. Both the freedom and the companionship the image of the wheeling birds promises to Joan, even as flames consume her body, were given to Cavell, as if his body had already been utterly gone through.

That the world which is complete without one and yet is present to one is the world of one's immortality "is an importance of film—and a danger," the paragraph goes on. When Cavell specifies the danger ("It takes my life as my haunting of the world, either because I left it unloved (the Flying Dutchman) or because I left unfinished business (Hamlet), one might suppose he is thinking simply of the fact that one is not thrown into the world on film, as Joan is, or as we are thrown into the one existing world in which our lives begin and end (160).

Viewing the world on film from the outside, we haunt that world, rather than staking our own existence within it. But what would be the danger in that? No harm could come from our haunting the world on film if it were not for the massive way we involve movies in our lives. The danger in his taking the world on film to be the world of his immortality, Cavell's words literally say, is that it takes *his own life* to be a haunting of the world.

If we accept the world on film as complete without us, and if we accept the world on film *as* the world as a whole, it follows that we also accept that there *is* no world apart from the world on film. This means we accept that the world that is complete without us, the world we merely haunt, is *the* world, the world in which we live, the world in which movies are strand over strand with our lives. It means we accept that our lives *are* our haunting of the world. This means that, like the Flying Dutchman or the Ghost in *Hamlet*, we must forgo all hope of marrying our fantasies to the world, all hope of reaching this world and achieving selfhood. "So there is reason," Cavell concludes, "for me to want the camera to deny the coherence of the world, its coherence as past: to deny that the world is complete without me" (160). In acknowledging his wish for film to deny its own nature, he is yet again calling upon us to acknowledge that what is true for him, in this case, is true for us, too.

If *The World Viewed* is a work of mourning, it is also a work of self-revelation. Its path, rarely taken, is the path of self-knowledge. This means that it is a work of philosophy. It means that it is a confession, as well. When Cavell sums up the painful moral of *Hiroshima, mon Amour* with the beautiful but chilling words "As things stand, love is always the betrayal of love, if it is honest," he is confessing something about the writing which accords these words their privileged place. *The World Viewed* is an expression of Cavell's love for film, a love that is as alive to him as it ever was. But in confessing his love, he is betraying his love. For until our world becomes a place in which each human being can win his or her self, "the knowledge of the self as it is always takes place in the betrayal of the self as it was."

Cavell has reason to want the camera to deny that the world is complete without him, to deny that the world on film is the world as a whole, "to deny the coherence of the world on film, its coherence as past." He has reason to want nature to turn away from film, for film to turn away from its own nature, for his "natural relation" to movies to end. On the verge of ending, the writing of *The World Viewed* confesses its motive for wishing the world of movies and moviegoing, the world whose passing it commemorates, to be past. And Cavell confesses his own motive for wanting his moviegoer self, whose passing he mourns, to die.

There remains one last piece of testimony that the author of *The World Viewed* must, in candor, offer. Without taking back what has just been confessed, the book's final words enable a new physiognomical aspect to dawn. "But there is equal reason to want it affirmed that the world is coherent without me," Cavell writes. "That is essential to what I want of immortality: nature's survival of me. It will mean that the present judgment upon me is not yet the last" (160).

During the period of his life in which going to the movies was a normal part of his week, Cavell enjoyed a "natural relation" to movies. This relation is now lost. Gone. What broke this "natural relation," *The World Viewed* confesses, cannot be separated from the fact that its author wanted—wants—this world of movies and moviegoing to be past. This does not mean he wants movies, or his experience of movies, simply to be over and done with. It is the central thrust of *The World Viewed* that what movies have from the beginning promised, their way of "speaking the being of the world" directly, is as much as ever to be wanted. And that it is still possible for film's promise—letting the world and its children achieve their candidness—to be kept.

If the fact that our "natural relation" to movies is gone cannot be separated from our wishing it to be gone, the fact that film is still capable of keeping faith with its nature cannot be separated from our still wishing for film to keep its promise, to affirm that the world is capable of being coherent without us. That is essential, Cavell says, "to what I want of immortality: nature's survival of me."

We want nature to survive *us*, to survive our turnings away from nature, our turnings away from our own nature (from what is inflexible, fixed, in human physiognomy, the unmoving ground upon which we cannot but move). If nature has survived all our violence and betrayals, this means that human nature, too, has survived. It means it is not yet too late for us to keep faith with our nature, to declare ourselves, to reach this world and achieve selfhood. For Cavell this means, as he puts it in the hopeful final line of *The World Viewed*, that "the present judgment upon me is not yet the last" (160).

Knowing Cavell's disappointment at the response to *Must We Mean What We Say?*, it is tempting to suppose that, when he wrote this strangely apocalyptic line, Cavell was anticipating the world's all but total rejection of *The World Viewed*, as if he were fantasizing that because nature will survive him, because the world will go on after he is gone, there will be future judgments upon him, and future judgments, as well, upon those who have passed the present judgment upon him, and that in the end, at that point past imagination at which happiness and truth coalesce, justice will be done (and be seen to be done).

Surely, however, when Cavell invokes what he calls the "present judgment upon me," he is (also?) referring specifically to the judgment he has just brought upon himself by confessing that he wanted his moviegoer self to die, that he wanted his "natural relation" to movies to be broken, that he is in that way implicated in, responsible for, film's turning away from nature, from its own nature. How is Cavell to be judged for that? Who is to judge him? For he calls upon us to acknowledge that we, too, want the world of our "natural relation" to movies to be broken, that we, too, are responsible. If justice is to be done (and seen to be done), the judgment passed upon Cavell must be passed upon us, and upon the world. If film is still capable of holding a coherent world, if nature has survived our turning away from it, it means that the present judgment—the judgment Cavell has brought upon himself, the judgment he has brought upon the world, the judgment the world has brought upon itself—is not yet the last judgment. The Last Judgment, the end of the world, is not yet at hand.

When Joan looks up and sees the birds wheeling above her, the sun in their wings, she knows that, in Cavell's words, "They, there, are free. They are waiting, in their freedom, to accompany her soul." If these birds were not free, if they were waiting not because they wish to be her companions but because they are her servants, their presence would confirm the present judgment upon Joan, the judgment she brought upon herself—that she is a witch—when she recanted her false confession. But these birds are not the unnatural familiars of a witch; in their freedom, they are part of nature, as she is. What Joan knows, in knowing that these birds are free and that they will survive her, is that nature will survive her. Terrible flames are utterly consuming her body, but in her image of these wheeling birds, the sun in their wings, is the knowledge that she, too, is free.

Joan knows that these birds are free, Cavell asserts; she knows that they are waiting, in their freedom, to accompany her soul; she knows it is her nature to be free. But how can he know these things? How can Cavell know what Joan knows, the reality, particular to her, with which she surrounds what she sees at this moment in which words are out of reach? In claiming to know what this woman knows at this moment, Cavell is not "identifying" with her in the sense of imagining that she and he are one, not appropriating her experience, claiming the right to speak for her in his own voice. After all, he would hardly call this film's "fullest image of absolute isolation" if he believed that it denied this woman's innerness, her privacy, her separateness from him. This woman's experience is hers, not his; she is who she is, as he is who he is. Her silence, as it expresses itself on film, speaks the being of the world directly.

We might say that Cavell claims to know what Joan knows on the basis of knowing the particular reality he would surround this image with if he were in her situation. And yet, how Cavell can know what he would know if he were in Joan's situation is no less a mystery than how he can know what she knows. How can he know such a thing about himself unless he knows that he *is* in her situation, that her life illustrates his own? But how can the author of *The World Viewed*, as he is composing the final words of his book, so much as imagine this?

Dreyer's idea, Cavell observes in "More of *The World Viewed*" about the filmmaker's late masterpiece *Gertrud*, is that "the condition of privacy, of unknownness, of being viewed—the human condition—is itself the condition of martyrdom, the openness to interrogation and rejection" (205–06). If we exist in the condition of myth, if our lives illustrate a story whose meaning escapes us, if any life may illustrate any story, if any change may bring its meaning home, why should it not be possible for Cavell to find that Joan's life illustrates his own?

St. Augustine stole a pear; lots of children have. Rousseau, like lots of little boys, got a spanking with his pants down. For years, going to the movies was a normal part of Cavell's week, as it was for millions of Americans. And for Cavell, as for most regular moviegoers, the natural relation to movies has been broken. Why seems this so particular to him?

The breaking of the natural relation to movies is so particular to Cavell, *The World Viewed* makes clear, because among all of us who have involved movies massively in our lives, among all of us who have lost our "natural relation" to movies, he is the one prompted by that loss to think philosophically about what movies are and what makes them important. Cavell is the one prompted to step forward to write this book, to take upon himself the burden of its writing, to accept the necessity of the loss it mourns, to confess his own implication, to make himself intelligible, to open himself, like Joan, to interrogation and rejection. He is the one capable of enabling the writing of *The World Viewed* to achieve the silence that is its necessary conclusion. Now that the body of the book has been utterly gone through, he is the one who must set this writing free, must now fall silent to acknowledge that he is outside these words as he is outside the world on film.

As we have said, for Cavell to acknowledge his outsideness to the world on film is for him to acknowledge his commonality with us, because that is a condition we share. For him to acknowledge his outsideness to the words of *The World Viewed* is for him to declare his separateness from us, because only he is capable of performing that acknowledgment, as only we are capable of acknowledging it. That he is outside the words of *The World Viewed* means that these words are autonomous, complete without him, free to acknowledge the reality of the unsayable, free to speak the being of the world directly. That is Cavell's faith.

In its obscurity and in its fervor, *The World Viewed* registers an isolation in Cavell's temperament, an isolation the writing itself brings to a head, the way the writing of *Walden* brings Thoreau's isolation to a head. The author of *Walden* builds his house in the woods so that he may abandon it in the hope of finding his way, changed, to a changed world. But *Walden* does not end by placing its author in the world again, does not chart his way forward, or his way back. When he abandons his house, he departs from all settled habitation, all conformity of meaning, in order to walk a path of philosophy, a path of self-knowledge, which is an uncharted path. And he hopes that we, too, will find such a path for ourselves.

In the writing of *The World Viewed*, Cavell walks a path of philosophy, too, hoping that philosophy might enable him to be free, and in good company, in a world that is fit for human beings to inhabit. In this writing, the self is not yet wholly won. But in it he finds a way to speak truthfully and in his own voice—to speak within philosophy, which means to speak as an ordinary human being, to speak in a way others can comprehend—of what he loved and loves, of who he was and is. Therein lies the sense of liberation *The World Viewed* is capable of providing. For this writing is capable of bringing home to us—capable of reminding us that film is capable of bringing home to us—the wonder of our lives. The wonder is that our aliveness to ourselves has survived, hence our capacity for hope, and that we still wish for our own further chances.

We have added an appendix to the present volume in which we collect, and ponder, some of the remarks about Cavell's understanding and practice of philosophy that are to be found in *Must We Mean What We Say?*

In a forthcoming volume, we will trace the trajectory of Cavell's writings about film subsequent to *The World Viewed*. In placing those writings in the context of the development of Cavell's philosophical project as a whole, that volume will also place his understanding and practice of philosophy in the context of the history of the field of film studies, and place that field's development in the context of philosophy as Cavell understands and practices it. Viewed from the philosophical perspective Cavell's writing exemplifies, it becomes evident that every major crossroads in its brief history there are paths of discovery never taken by film study, paths that are as worth exploring as ever, paths not even marked on the field's road maps.

The theories that have dominated film study both embrace skepticism and claim to defeat it. They assure us that we have nothing to lose by accepting the view that knowledge is impossible, even as they assure us that they provide systems of thought capable of according film study the authority of a science, a certainty unattainable by acts of criticism accountable to our experience. *The World Viewed* denies us both assurances. It denies us the assurance that in our postmodern age there is no truth, that no interpretation is worth more than any other; and it denies us the opposite assurance that by conforming to its system of thought we can acquire truths that have been scientifically validated. It denies us the assurance that there are no longer villains; and it denies us the assurance that we are heroes capable of vanquishing evil capitalism, or patriarchy, or bourgeois ideology, or a hegemonic American culture that imposes lies on unthinking masses.

Continually turning in on itself, *The World Viewed* continually turns us to ourselves, calls upon us to go forward, to reach this world and achieve selfhood. We are forever being told that we live in an age that has moved beyond modernism.

But on what authority are we to accept it as given that we have been released from our condition as modern human beings, that we no longer believe in art's saving importance, that we no longer wish to master the self's fate, or no longer believe such mastery to be possible? Assuming that the language of the self has been discredited as a basis for serious thought, some will condemn Cavell's aspiration as romantic, not recognizing that their despair of selfhood is no less romantic. Others will condemn Cavell's thinking as irrational, not recognizing the irrational aspect of their own positivist faith. They, too, will assume that the language of the self has been discredited.

Yet apart from the language of the self we have no language with which to converse with others. The language in which we voice our thoughts and feelings is not a private language, it is our common language. The language of the self *is* the language of others, Cavell's writing teaches us. In reminding us of the importance of turning to our own experience, *The World Viewed* reminds us of the importance of turning to others. It reminds us of the importance of conversation, the importance of expressing ourselves with conviction and enthusiasm and the equal importance of acknowledging others. Therein lies the book's greatest potential usefulness to the serious study of film. Film studies is a field that has forgone conversation for so long that it has forgotten something about what conversation is, forgotten the value of community.

5

Cavell's Philosophy and What Film Studies Calls "Theory"

At the time of its first large-scale entrance into American universities in the late1960s, the fledgling field of film studies cast its lot with criticism. Criticism was about to undergo radical transformation, in academic departments of literature above all. One does not have to be a weatherman to know that, in the past two decades, the academic study of literature has been swept by a succession of winds from the east—structuralism, semiology, Althusserian Marxism, Lacanian psychoanalysis, Derridean deconstruction, and the rest of the now familiar litany of theoretical imports, which, despite their mutual incompatibilities, have become more or less collapsed into a single entity typically known in America simply as "theory."

Historically, film studies constituted its present identity as an academic field, or its present idea of its own identity, by embracing "theory," which meant, in part, by embracing a particular picture, or theory, of what a theory is. In taking its own enterprise to be authorized by the higher authority of "theory," a field groping for assurance that it had a legitimate identity of its own envisioned itself as acquiring, in a single bold stroke, the authority of a science—an authority unattainable by acts of criticism accountable to a critic's experience of individual works. In film studies, as in the study of literature, "theory" superseded such acts of criticism and dictates

---

Paper presented—under circumstances described in the preface—at the 1991 annual meeting of the Society for Cinema Studies ("Media" had not yet been added to the organization's title). As I note in the preface, when I read this paper from my present perspective, I regret that I had failed to make clear that what my paper derisively calls "theory" is what *became* of the ideas articulated by serious thinkers like Louis Althusser, Roland Barthes, Jacques Derrida, Michel Foucault, Julia Kristeva, and Jacques Lacan when the fledging field of film study in America, in search of a way to secure its legitimacy, reduced their thoughts to a set of slogans that students could readily be trained to parrot.

the agenda for a field that has come increasingly to speak in one voice, excluding or silencing all others.

This is not the place to trace in detail the specific sequence of events that led the field of film studies up the garden path to its present state. In such an account, the publication of a number of particularly influential essays and books, and especially their reception, would represent decisive moments (Peter Wollen's *Signs and Meaning in the Cinema*, for example; the series of translations in the British periodical *Screen* of articles from the radicalized post–May 1968 *Cahiers du Cinéma*, most influential among them the famous, or infamous, piece on *The Young Mr. Lincoln*; and Laura Mulvey's equally famous, or infamous, "Visual Pleasure and Narrative Cinema"). But an equally decisive moment was the publication, in 1971, of Stanley Cavell's *The World Viewed*. What made the publication of Cavell's brilliant little book of philosophy such a formative moment for film studies was not its reception by the field, but its all but complete nonreception. To this day, academic film studies, albeit with exceptions, has still failed to acknowledge the book's philosophical way of thinking. What I am implying is that, historically, the field constituted its present self-image at once by turning to "theory" and by turning away from philosophy.

Within film studies, no serious objections have ever been raised to the leading claims of *The World Viewed* or, for that matter, those of *Pursuits of Happiness*, Cavell's study of the Hollywood genre he calls the "comedy of remarriage," or those of his other writings about film (most recently the series of essays, the major part of a forthcoming book, on the films he calls "melodramas of the unknown woman"). Nonetheless, there seems to be a pervasive impression within the field that "theory" has long ago decisively discredited Cavell's way of thinking and that, in any case, contemporary film studies has advanced so far in its thinking that it would be beneath its dignity, as well as unproductive, for it to undertake to offer arguments at this late date against a figure who is obviously too naïve, and/or too reactionary, to take seriously.

Of course, to those of us who appreciate the seriousness of Cavell's philosophical aspirations, not to mention the magnitude of his achievement as a philosopher, the field's attitude of superiority is itself a clear indication that academic film studies, not Cavell, is naïve. Or perhaps it is an indication of the field's disingenuousness. For having staked its self-image, its belief in its own intellectual legitimacy, on the higher authority of "theory," the field has a clear motivation for wanting to deny Cavell's philosophical claims, to deny the claims of philosophy itself—to deny philosophy's claims without taking the risk of confronting them.

The World Viewed, subtitled "Reflections on the Ontology of Film," addresses the question of what film is, what makes a film a film and not another kind of thing. Cavell understands this question about film's ontology also to be a question about what Ludwig Wittgenstein would call the "grammar" of our concept of "film." Cavell understands this Wittgensteinian question, in turn, also to be a question about the roles films play in our lives in the world. Characteristically, Cavell addresses this question by reflecting on the roles films have played in his own life. On philosophical principle, he holds his claims about the ontology of film accountable to his experience. And his writing continually calls upon us to test these claims against our own experience.

In his opening pages, Cavell tells us that when he was writing *The World Viewed* he felt he was writing a "metaphysical memoir" of a period of his life, the period in which the experience of going to the movies was a normal part of his week. *The World Viewed*, he writes,

> is not the story of a period of my life but an account of the conditions it has satisfied. A book thus philosophically motivated ought to account philosophically for the motive in writing it. What broke my natural relation to movies? What was that relation, that its loss seemed to demand repairing, or commemorating, by taking thought? (Cavell 1979b, xix)

From within what Cavell calls the "natural relation to movies," film appears magically to satisfy a wish, a wish we may not even have recognized as our own: the wish for the world re-created in its own image, which is also the wish to be able to view the world unseen, free from responsibility for events within it. And by appearing to satisfy this wish, Cavell suggests, film seems to us to confirm something already true of our existence:

> In viewing films, the sense of invisibility is an expression of modern privacy or anonymity. It is as though the world's projection explains our forms of unknownness and our inability to know. The explanation is not so much that the world is passing us by, as that we are displaced from our natural habitation within it, placed at a distance from it. The screen . . . makes displacement appear as our natural condition. (Cavell 1979b, 39)

It is the fact that its material basis is photographic that enables film to have the power to make our displacement appear natural, Cavell proposes. A consequence of the fact that film is photographic is that film images are not representations, not signs, as "theory" insists they must be. Their relation to the world is not that of signification or reference: People and things in a photograph are not objects the photograph signifies or to which it refers, they are the photograph's *subjects*. The subjects of a photograph are not created by the photograph; they are, or at least were, real, really in the world. Nor is their relation to the photograph arbitrary or conventional. They are active participants in the photograph's creation.

For Cavell, the fact that photographs are "of" the world does not mean that they assure our presence or presentness to the people and things they present to us. The reality that is present to us in a photograph is also absent, is present as absent, or absent as present; in any case, we cannot possess it fully. But for us, reality itself cannot be fully possessed. Reality is present as absent, or absent as present—reality already participates in the condition of photography, in effect. To speak in this way is not to deny that reality is real; it is to characterize what reality is—what reality is ontologically, what "reality" is *grammatically*. Reality itself, what is really in our presence, is what we are already absent from, what we have already absented ourselves from.

> Film's displacement of the world confirms, even explains, our prior estrangement from it. The "sense of reality" provided on film is a sense of that reality, one from which we already sense a distance. Otherwise the thing it provides a sense of would not, for us, count as reality. (Cavell 1979b, 226)

Obviously, in speaking this way, Cavell is a far cry from the figure philosophers call the "naïve realist," who has never even imagined that what we call "reality" may not actually be real. Yet as far as "theory" is concerned, anyone who believes, as Cavell does, that real people and things are "in" a photograph can only be naïve—as naïve, and for the same reasons, as anyone who believes that reality itself is real.

The truth is that "theory" does not acknowledge even the possibility that a philosopher could speak seriously in the way Cavell does about such matters. When it denies that reality is real, "theory" takes itself to be making a sophisticated new claim, a claim that goes beyond, and radically undermines, anything that could be dreamed of by philosophy, not recognizing that, within philosophy, this denial is old, as old as philosophy itself. The name philosophy has given it is "skepticism."

Indeed, in arguing that what we call "reality" is not real but only that which we represent to ourselves as real and hence is only a reflection of our own representations, "theory" employs one of skepticism's oldest formulations. And it revises this classical formulation only minimally when it specifies that our representations are constructed in accordance with "semiological codes" or when it adds that these "codes" are "ideological" (metaphysical, logocentric, bourgeois, capitalist, patriarchal, and/or phallocentric, depending on the vintage of "theory").

Ironically, the new terms employed in these revisions are so far from being perspicuous, philosophically speaking, that their effect is to weaken the classical formulation of philosophical skepticism—to make it less interesting, philosophically, and less of a threat to philosophy. When has skepticism ever been so naïve as to assert, hilariously but with a straight face, that it has proved its claim with scientific certainty, proved it beyond the possibility of doubt, that is, beyond the possibility of skepticism?

Cavell's work has shown us that the entire modern history of philosophy can be viewed as dominated by a fixation on what he calls the "skeptical problematic," the idea that philosophy is locked in a kill-or-be-killed conflict with the skeptic who denies that the world can be known with certainty. Cavell's philosophical practice is everywhere guided by the intuition that philosophy cannot "cure" its fixation by silencing the skeptic but only by transcending the primitive notion that skepticism is a mortal threat to philosophy. The war of words between philosophy and skepticism has been going on for centuries, but the "mother of all battles" has yet to be fought between them because—and this is one of Cavell's leading intuitions—each depends on the other for its existence and its very identity: Skepticism is "other" to philosophy, yet its voice is also internal to philosophy. Philosophy's true interest is not in silencing skepticism but in acknowledging its voice, acknowledging the ways this voice motivates, and is motivated by, philosophy. Acknowledging "the truth of skepticism," as he sometimes calls it, does not make Cavell a skeptic.

In aligning his own philosophical aspiration with the attainment of such an acknowledgment, Cavell claims continuity with Emerson, Thoreau, Nietzsche, Heidegger, Wittgenstein, and Austin, among others—philosophers who have been dispossessed by the academic field of philosophy as it has been constituted, or constituted itself, in America. Cavell's aspiration is to claim the inheritance of this philosophical tradition, to claim it for philosophy, to enable philosophy to claim it as its own.

To claim this inheritance, philosophy has to attain a new perspective—it is also an old perspective—on itself. As Cavell envisions it, what is called for from philosophy is not a new piece of knowledge, but an acknowledgment. In calling upon the field of philosophy to acknowledge his philosophical voice, to acknowledge this voice as a voice of philosophy, Cavell is calling upon philosophy, philosophy is calling upon itself, to take a stand on its own identity. (It is part of the grammar of the concept of "self," part of what a self is ontologically, if you will, that, as Cavell puts it, "having a self requires taking a stand upon the self.")

In the reflections that comprise *The World Viewed*, then, as in his subsequent writing about film, Cavell is not naïvely oblivious of the claims of "theory," he is rejecting those claims. But in rejecting them, he is taking their motivations seriously. And he is not taking the opposing side, philosophy's traditional side in its age-old quarrel with skepticism (although he is taking that side's motivations seriously as well). Speaking in his own voice, Cavell is demonstrating, exemplifying, a philosophical alternative—a way of thinking philosophically, a philosophical perspective, whose possibility is not acknowledged either by "theory," as we have seen, nor by any practice of philosophy that remains fixated on silencing the skeptic.

When film studies dismisses philosophy as naïve, illegitimate, and in any case irrelevant to the aspirations of the field, and does so solely by appeal to "theory," which it recognizes as a higher authority, philosophy has a right to protest. We recognize no authority higher than philosophy. On the other hand, we also would not wish for film studies to anoint philosophy, rather than "theory," as the higher authority to which it defers. Philosophy does not aspire to be a higher authority to any other field—or to itself.

I am not alone in having struggled over the years to persuade or provoke the field of film studies to stop excluding philosophy, to stop denying philosophy's claims out of hand, even as Cavell has struggled to persuade or provoke the field of philosophy to acknowledge film as a philosophical subject. I do derive perverse pleasure, now and then, from mocking academic film studies for believing so naïvely that philosophy can be denied simply by appeal to a higher authority. But it provides no enduring satisfaction simply to dismiss film studies as naïve. By denying the aspirations of philosophy, film studies is also denying its own philosophical aspirations, its own aspirations to philosophy. It is denying my aspirations for studying film. And I don't really find this funny.

As I have said, Cavell believes that the academic field of philosophy, too, including the branch we call "aesthetics," has a history of denying the aspirations of philosophy as he understands them—a history of denying the perspective on its own identity that it is philosophy's identity to seek, in Cavell's view, a history of repressing the tradition within philosophy with which Cavell's writing claims continuity. Cavell's aspiration as a philosopher is to enable philosophy to free itself, to awaken, from its history of repression—its repression of an aspect of its own identity, its repression of his philosophical perspective, his way of thinking philosophically. ("In order to have a self, it is necessary for the self to take a stand on the self.")

When film studies turned away from philosophy to embrace "theory," the field understood itself to be attaining freedom from the bondage of ideology, from a tyranny that Derrida takes to have its source in what he calls the "metaphysics of presence." For Derrida, what is most repressive in the tradition of philosophy is a function of its supposed promotion of voice over writing. For Cavell, who sees matters very differently, "it is evident that the reign of repressive philosophical systematizing . . . has depended upon the suppression of the human voice" (Cavell 1984, 48).

Cavell's implication is not that all human beings, or individual human beings, speak or ought to speak in one voice. There can never be only one human voice: voices are always in conversation. But conversation can always be refused. When a voice is lost to itself or to other voices, or silenced, it can only be "recovered" by conversation, not by the silencing of other voices. Conversation requires points of convergence or agreement between speakers and a common language, but conversation also requires that voices be separate, different from each other. "To imagine a language is to imagine a form of life," what we might call a culture. But what is a culture, a language, a form of life, a voice, a human being? And what has the study of film, and what has philosophy, to teach us about such matters?

In Cavell's view, film studies has been fixated, not freed, by what the field calls "theory." Like the field of philosophy, film studies must awaken from its "trance of thinking" if it is to fully acknowledge its own subject, if it is to recover its own voice.

Statement Read at Plenary Session of the 1991 Society for Cinema Studies Annual Meeting

Most of my friends in the Society for Cinema Studies had so little expectation of finding real conversation at this conference that they stayed away. Many are too disillusioned even to suggest changes that might enable future conferences to shake things up a little. But in a hopeful spirit, I strongly urge one reform: Until we really exist as an intellectual community secure in its own identity, let us declare a moratorium on conference "themes."

This year's call for submissions is symptomatic of the field's unhealthy conformity. "In the past several years," it begins, "the Society for Cinema Studies has encouraged attention to issues of race, ethnicity, class, gender, sexual orientation and national origin." Yet the statement studiously avoids specifying what these "issues" are. The implication is that we do not need to be told because we already know. There is a consensus.

The statement continues, "Thus it seems appropriate to ask in a more intense way critical, philosophical and historical questions about the notion of multi-culturalism in relation to the traditional areas of research in film and/or television studies." Despite the "thus," this sentence in no way logically follows. First, because it slips in the term "multi-culturalism" as if no SCS member could possibly believe there might be anything problematic in lumping together under one rubric such diverse concepts as race, ethnicity, class, gender, sexual orientation, and national origin. Second, because whether it is now "appropriate" to ask a question depends, among other things, on what that question is. The statement does not specify the questions it has in mind but rather maintains that studied vagueness whose implication is that we all agree on what questions count as "appropriate."

The statement then announces that SCS is "encouraging" papers that consider "these issues" from "any vantage point that seems valuable." "Seems valuable" to whom, and from what vantage point? Proposals that do not see eye to eye with the assumption that we all see eye to eye on these matters are implicitly discouraged. Not surprisingly, no nonconforming proposals are included in the list of "possible ideas." Equally unsurprisingly, when I nonetheless submitted a nonconforming proposal for a panel on the implications of Stanley Cavell's writing, it was rejected.

Cavell's writing urges us to speak about film in our own human voices, in words accountable to our own experience but unsanctioned by any "higher authority." His writing thereby threatens the comforting illusion that the legitimacy of the field of film studies has been definitively established by the "higher authority" our field calls "theory." From a Cavellian perspective, the reign of theoretical systematizing over film studies, like its reign over philosophy, bears a repressive aspect. Of course, no serious intellectual grounds were made known to me for excluding my proposed panel from the conference agenda. There are no such grounds. But none were needed.

Every gathering of scholars should be a celebration of the diversity of human voices. No one in this room embraces human diversity more wholeheartedly than I. But such an affirmation must not be reduced to the status of an agenda. This year, it has been dictated to us that we are to affirm that human beings speak in many voices. But, in so affirming, we are all to speak in one voice.

6

Response to Vivian Sobchack's *The Address of the Eye*

In the preface of her challenging new book, Vivian Sobchack remarks that in a field dominated by Lacanian psychoanalysis and Marxism, "writing a book on the 'phenomenology' of the film 'experience' was both a lonely and suspect enterprise." First, because "'experience' seems"—to her, not to me (nor to any serious reader of the great essay of that name by Ralph Waldo Emerson)—"a mushy, soft, term," a "remainder (and reminder) of the sloppy liberal humanism"—I'm doing my best to avoid gagging on this sentence—"that retrospectively characterized cinema studies before it was informed by the scientific methods and technically precise vocabularies of structuralism and semiotics" (Sobchack 1991, xiv).

Second, because phenomenology was "regarded as idealist, essentialist, and ahistorical. It was also seen as extremely naive" (Sobchack 1991, xiv). But what motivated Sobchack to turn to phenomenology—in particular, the existential phenomenology of Maurice Merleau-Ponty—was her admirable desire to speak of "more possibilities than either psychoanalytic or Marxist theory currently allows." Sobchack writes, "Lacanian psychoanalysis may be fine"—or may not be fine, I would add—"for disclosing the 'unconscious' of patriarchal texts and the power and constitutive nature of an experienced 'lack,'" but not for "describing the pleasure and plenitude of an experience that includes—but is also in *excess* of—'sexual difference.'" Marxist theory, too, however accurately it has "teased out the ideological objectives of the cinematic 'apparatus' and its representations," fails to account for her experience

---

This review of Vivian Sobchack's *The Address of the Eye: A Phenomenology of Film Experience* (Princeton: Princeton University Press, 1991) was commissioned by *Film Quarterly*, which decided against publishing it. (I wonder why.) I like to think of it as one of five (uneasy) polemical pieces I've included in the present volume.

in and out of the movie theater. Refusing "to be completely contained" by the terms of contemporary film theory, her writing "cries out," as she puts it, "the particularity of her lived experience" (xv). An admirable ambition, in my book. And yet . . .

Sobchack characterizes her specific task as describing "the origin and locus of cinematic signification and significance in the experience of vision as an embodied and meaningful existential activity." By "literally 'fleshing out' contemporary film theory," she wishes to restore to film studies "the existential experience of the medium's openness and the spectator's freedom" (Sobchack 1991, xvii). This is a wish borne by my own writing, too. However great my sympathy for her goals, though, and however much I admire her considerable achievement, I find myself skeptical when, in her closing pages, Sobchack claims to have *succeeded* in realizing her wish—claims success in sharing with the field the insight that "there is originality and existential freedom as well as cultural constraint in the film experience, and that both the film and spectator are subjects of vision (as well as objects for vision)" (xvii).

This insight, Sobchack asserts, "is no less meritorious for being intuitive—or, for that matter, simple." Right on! Unfortunately, though, she feels the need to add, "Given the dominant context and turn of contemporary reflection on questions of cinema, for others to share this insight" with her required "rigorous elaboration" (Sobchack 1991, xviii). Ay, there's the rub. Freedom is the intuition she wishes to share with the field of film studies. But freedom is incompatible with the field's limited and limiting conception of what *counts* as "rigorous elaboration." Yet Sobchack accepts as a "requirement" that her writing conform to this conception. Alas, conform it does. Merleau-Ponty's prose, lucid and elegant, contrasts all too strikingly with Sobchack's sentences, laden with so many technical terms, and so many clauses, that their cumulative effect, over more than three hundred pages, is less rigor than rigor mortis.

To be shared, an intuition has to be acknowledged. No kind or amount of "rigorous elaboration" necessarily compels conviction; nor is any kind or amount necessarily required. The field of film studies cannot acknowledge Sobchack's "simple insight"—her own writing cannot render her intuition intelligible—cannot pay the tuition for the intuition, as Emerson would put it—without freeing itself from a conception of "rigorous elaboration" that denies this intuition, that denies, indeed, the efficacy of intuition itself. But even as she "cries out" her wish to "begin again," her writing resists the necessary change, takes conformity to the field's conception of "rigorous elaboration" to be a "requirement" for communicating with the field at all.

Merleau-Ponty died in the early 1960s. By reinscribing his eloquent philosophical voice into the conversation from which, historically, contemporary film theory emerged, *The Address of the Eye* gives film studies a new perspective on its own history. That is one of the book's important contributions to the serious study of film. But it fails to take the further step of acknowledging *philosophy's* perspective(s) on that conversation—fails, for example, to place phenomenology meaningfully within the history of Western philosophy. In particular, Sobchack reduces Edmund Husserl, a seminal figure in the emergence of phenomenology as a movement within philosophy, as a mere foil for Merleau-Ponty. And she allows Martin Heidegger, a major philosophical source for Merleau-Ponty—only a bit part in *The Address of the Eye*, and Heidegger's own philosophical sources—most crucially, Friedrich Nietzsche and, standing behind Nietzsche, Emerson—no part at all. Nor does *The Address of the Eye* even broach as a topic Merleau-Ponty's relationship to Anglo-American analytical philosophy in general, or to Ludwig Wittgenstein and J. L. Austin in particular.

Seemingly unaware that modern philosophy has long since accepted that it may itself be ungrounded, Sobchack turns to existential phenomenology in search of a "ground" for film studies. Lacking an internal perspective on philosophy, she believes, for example, that Stanley Cavell's *The World Viewed*, the work of a major American philosopher she thinks of as merely a phenomenologist manqué, can legitimately be dismissed for lacking "systematic rigor," for being "enthusiastic but methodless," and for thus appearing "at best metaphysically arcane, at worst metaphorically vague and mystically poetic" (Sobchack 1991, 29).

Within film studies—that is, within its world of pervasive avoidance of philosophy—dismissing Cavell is no "lonely and suspect enterprise," of course. But from a philosophical point of view, it is naïve to assume, as Sobchack does, that we can know a priori what kind of "elaboration" is needed in order to share a simple insight. And it is doubly naïve for her to claim that she has succeeded in "recovering the cinema from objectification and alienation, recovering for the spectator her lived body, her subjectivity, her intentionality, and some measure of existential freedom and responsibility" (Sobchack 1991, 303). Such an immodest claim fails to recognize, first, that an insight cannot be shared without being acknowledged. Second, that I alone can "recover" my lived body, my subjectivity, my intentionality; I cannot do it for others, and others cannot do it for me.

In a climactic passage, Sobchack argues that, while contemporary film theory is satisfied merely to "deconstruct" the Cartesian *cogito* ("I think, therefore I am"), existential phenomenology goes further by reconstructing the proposition "in a way that admits presence, subjectivity, and integrity as they are always qualified by a particular (and always social) lived-body 'being-in-the-world': I see, therefore I am embodied" (Sobchack 1991, 304). But in *The Claim of Reason*, Cavell goes further still. Being embodied, while necessary, is not *sufficient* to assure my existence as a human being in the world. I *am* free, as Sobchack puts it, perhaps unaware she is channeling Emerson, "to realize and make visible in action the possibility of becoming other" than I am. But to *realize* the possibility of my existence in the world, Cavell would add, I must *claim* my freedom (always simultaneously acknowledging the freedom of others). That is, the *cogito* is an act I must perform—must *risk* performing—for myself. *The Address of the Eye* cannot perform it for me, nor provide a "system" or "method" that mitigates the risk.

In a blurb on the book jacket, Dudley Andrew celebrates *The Address of the Eye* for wishing "to erase the alienated discourse of academic film theory." But this misses the book's own pattern of equivocation. Sobchack does wish to "begin again"—but without questioning the supposed "scientific rigor" or the "power and utility of both psychoanalytic and Marxist film theory as they are presently applied to cinema." This is wishing to have one's cake and eat it too.

Phenomenology emphasizes "systematic rigor," Sobchack insists. Yet she says, "Phenomenological inquiry is less a set of steps to be applied programmatically to phenomena than it is a series of *critical commitments* made by the researcher to respond openly to the phenomena of consciousness and to her own consciousness of phenomena." Phenomenology's claim to rigor ultimately resides in its openness to experience, not in adherence to any "system." But Sobchack pulls back from the full implications of this principle. She pulls back, for example, from unequivocally acknowledging that insofar as it lacks openness to experience, contemporary film theory, which is nothing if not systematic, is anything but rigorous. It is fruitless for academic film studies to turn to philosophy in search of a "ground." What academic film studies above all stands to learn from philosophy, a discipline that brooks no equivocation, is that to claim its freedom, to justify its existence, the field must be willing to call a spade a spade.

7

Pursuits of Happiness

Cavell in Transition

A year after the publication in 1969 of *Must We Mean What We Say?*, Stanley Cavell observes in the elegant preface he wrote for the 2002 edition, the effect on him, as he put it,

> of putting the book behind me, or perhaps I should say, of having it to stand behind, freed me for I suppose the most productive, or palpably so, nine months of my life, in which I recast the salvageable and necessary material of my Ph.D. dissertation as the opening three parts of what would become *The Claim of Reason* and completed small books on film (*The World Viewed*) and Thoreau (*The Senses of Walden*). I consider those small books to form a trio with *Must We Mean What We Say?*, different paths leading from the same desire for philosophy. (Cavell 2002, xxix)

The first three parts of *The Claim of Reason* might well be included to form a quartet, but not if that would relegate them to playing second fiddle. In any case, I take the fourth part of *The Claim of Reason*, completed in 1978, and *Pursuits of Happiness*, which in 1978 he was already writing, to form a duo—but not, I would say, different paths leading not from the same *desire* for philosophy, but from the trio's *achievement* of philosophy.

This essay was adapted from a paper presented at the "Democratic Affections: Film, Philosophy, and Religion in the Thought of Stanley Cavell" conference, the University of California at Santa Barbara, 2019, organized by Thomas Carlson, Dominique Jullien, and Andrew Norris (Political Science).

The year 1978 was also when Cavell wrote "Thinking of Emerson," in which he experienced a newfound sense of Emerson's philosophical seriousness. He followed that essay two years later by "An Emerson Mood," which goes further in acknowledging, and exploring, the profound affinities with Emerson he had come to intuit. It was not until the late 1980s, however, in *In Quest of the Ordinary*, *This New Yet Unapproachable America*, *Conditions Handsome and Unhandsome*, and the essays later collected in *Emerson's Transcendental Etudes*, and in the Harvard core course he called Moral Perfectionism, that the full magnitude of Emerson's impact on Cavell's understanding of his own aspiration and achievement as a philosopher became clear. And with the publication in 2005 of *Cities of Words*, based on his lectures for the Moral Reasoning course, Cavell acknowledged that Emerson had assumed a privileged place in his thinking.

In the acknowledgment section at the end of *Pursuits of Happiness*, Cavell tells us, "Thoughts of remarriage as generating a genre of film began presenting themselves to me during a course of mine on film comedy I gave in 1974 at Harvard's Carpenter Center for Visual Studies" (Cavell 1981b, 275). It was in 1975 that Cavell first presented his reading of *Bringing Up Baby*. In 1976, he gave a version of the film comedy course designed to "test out those ideas as rigorously as I knew how." Thus, Cavell conceived of the book that became *Pursuits of Happiness* on the eve of his discovery of Emerson. Surely, his immersion in thinking about the distinctly American movie genre he named "the comedy of remarriage" was instrumental in motivating him to return to Emerson, only differently this time, and in enabling him to read Emerson's essays in a way he had never before been able, or willing, to do.

In *Pursuits of Happiness*, Emerson is invoked more than a few times. And yet, if Cavell had written "Thinking of Emerson" and "An Emerson Moment" *before* he had he started writing *Pursuits of Happiness*, I don't doubt that Emerson would have played a far more prominent role, as he does in *Cities of Words*. Already in the 1983 essays "The Thought of Movies" and "A Capra Moment," published two years after *Pursuits of Happiness*, Emerson does take center stage. In *Pursuits of Happiness*, one key invocation of Emerson is the quote Cavell chose to caption the wonderful frame enlargement, in the chapter on *The Awful Truth*, of Cary Grant, who manifestly *does*, in Emerson's words, "carry the holiday in his eye" and *is* "fit to stand the gaze of millions."

When Cavell writes, near the end of the *Philadelphia Story* chapter, "Dexter's demand to determine for himself what is truly important and what is not is a claim to the status of a philosopher," Emerson, the champion of "self-reliance," is surely the kind of philosopher Cavell takes Dexter to be. And although he's not yet prepared to claim this in so many words, Cavell is Emerson's kind of philosopher as well. The passage goes on, "But is what Dexter claims to be enormously important, a matter of one's most personal existence, to be understood as of national importance? How is the acceptance of individual desire, his form of self-knowledge, of importance to the nation?" (Cavell 1981b, 150) And these questions motivate the chapter's closing pages, which go on to answer them. Or do they?

Cavell writes, "I take Dexter at the conclusion of *The Philadelphia Story*, when he says to Tracy 'I'll risk it, will you?' to be saying that he'll both risk their failing again to find their happiness together, and also finally risk his concept of that happiness" (Cavell 1981b, 157). Is such happiness *possible*? Is it even *conceivable*? In this context, Cavell invokes Matthew Arnold's concept of the "best self." "Arnold wishes to work out," Cavell writes, "the rule of the best to mean the rule of the best self, something he understands as existing in each of us. It is of course common not to know of this possibility, but more natures are curious about their best self than one might imagine, and this curiosity Arnold calls the pursuit of perfection. 'Natures with this bent,' Arnold says, 'emerge in all classes, and this bent tends to take them out of their class and make their distinguishing characteristic not their Barbarianism or their Philistinism, but their humanity'" (157).

Here, Cavell does something he rarely does in *Pursuits of Happiness* by drawing explicitly on ideas about the ontology of film he had worked out in *The World Viewed*: "the photogenetic power of the camera as giving a natural ascendency to the flesh and blood actor over the character he or she plays in a film"; "the camera's tendency to create types from individuals, which I go on to characterize as individualities" (Cavell 1981b, 157). In this way, Cavell sets up his point that

> there is a visual equivalent or analogue of what Arnold means by distinguishing the best self from the ordinary self and by saying that in the best self, class yields to humanity. He is witnessing a possibility or potential in the human self not normally open to view, or not open to the normal view. Call this one's invisible self; it is what the movie camera would make visible. The originality inspired by the love of the best self that Arnold calls "genius." So much he might have been confirmed in by Emerson, whom he admired, and by Thoreau, if he read him. But when he goes on to call the best self "right reason" he parts company with American transcendentalism. The rule of the best self is the source of the new authority for which Arnold is seeking, the authority of what he calls culture, of what another might call religion, the answer to our narcissism and anarchy. It was his perception of society's loss of authority over itself . . . that prompted Arnold to write *Culture and Anarchy*. In it he distinguishes two forms of culture or authority, the two historical forces still impelling us on the quest for perfection or salvation; he names them Hebraism and Hellenism. (Cavell 1981b, 158)

The governing idea of Hellenism, Cavell goes on, "is spontaneity of consciousness; that of Hebraism, strictness of conscience." The world "ought to be, though it never is, evenly and happily balanced between them." Arnold finds that his moment of history requires a righting of the balance in the direction of spontaneity of consciousness more than it needs further strictness of conscience. "The more one ponders what Arnold is driving at," Cavell continues, "the more one will be willing to say, I claim, that Dexter Hellenizes (as, in their various ways, do Shakespeare and Tocqueville and Mill) while Tracy Hebraizes (as Arnold says all America does)" (Cavell 1981b, 159)—although, I would add, Arnold never heard American jazz or saw a Hollywood movie.

Emmanuel Lévinas had a different take on the distinction between "Hellenizing" and "Hebraizing." His brief against Western philosophy, which was born in Greece, was that, by "Hellenizing," it has always excluded, or repressed, the ethical standpoint, particular to the Hebrew language and the worldview specific to Judaism. As Hilary Putnam observes in an eloquent and appreciative essay, Lévinas, an Orthodox Jew, was addressing a predominantly Gentile audience in his philosophical writings, but his goal wasn't to convert Gentile philosophers to Judaism—to persuade them, for example, to observe the traditional dietary laws and the entire panoply of *mitzvot* that collectively transform every act we might perform in our daily lives—this is the domain Cavell calls "the ordinary"—into a sacrament, an act God *commands* us to perform, or to perform in a certain way, or to refrain from performing.

The aspiration of Lévinas's philosophical writings, as Putnam reads them, was to convert philosophy into an ethical practice—a practice that accepts its absolute responsibility to the ethical standpoint, particular to the Jewish tradition, that philosophy had always repressed. For Lévinas, ethics, philosophy's Other, is *higher* (Putnam 2008, 68–80 passim). By contrast, Cavell's aspiration, like that of Emerson before him, was to bring the "Hellenic" and "Hebraic" ways of thinking together, or back together, as if philosophy and ethics were not in opposition to each other, but were two halves of the Western mind. Cavell's wish, like Emerson's, was to achieve, in philosophy and in life, a marriage or balance between Hellenizing and Hebraizing, between philosophy *and* life, between saying what one means and meaning what one says, between being rational and being moral and, when he was tickling the ivories—or, for that matter, when he was composing his philosophical writings—between improvisation and structure.

In his late essay "What Is the Scandal of Philosophy?," Cavell reflects on the striking resemblance—yet the strikingly different conclusions or morals the two philosophers draw—between Lévinas's pivotal use of the passage in Descartes's *Third Meditation* designed to prove the existence of God from the otherwise inexplicable presence within him of the idea of an infinite being, and Cavell's own use of the same Descartes passage in *The Claim of Reason* in connection with the role of God in establishing for myself the existence, or relation to the existence, of the finite Other.

Lévinas's idea is that my discovery of the other, my openness to the other, requires "a violence associated with the infinite having been put into me"—"put into me" being Lévinas's transcription of Descartes's insistence that "the idea of God I find in myself I know cannot have been put there by a finite being, for example, by myself." In Cavell's words, "This event creates as it were an outside to my existence, hence an isolated, singular inside" (Cavell 2006, 145). At the same time, "it establishes the asymmetry of my relation to (the finite) other in which I recognize my infinite responsibility for the other." But, Cavell asks, when the idea of the infinite is "put into me," why should it be *infinite* responsibility for this other that is revealed, rather than, as Cavell maintains, "infinite responsibility for myself," together with "finite responsibility for the claims of the existence of the other upon me, claims perhaps of gratitude or sympathy or protection or duty or debt or love? In an extreme situation. I may put the other's life (not just her or his wishes or needs) ahead of mine, answerable to or for them without limit" (144). Although my responsibility to the finite other is finite, I have an infinite responsibility to myself, in Cavell's view—an absolute obligation to express myself, to make myself intelligible to myself as well as to others.

Cavell writes, "What the marriage in *The Philadelphia Story* comes to, I mean what it fantasizes"—or what his essay is fantasizing that the film is fantasizing—is "a proposed marriage or balance between Western culture's two forces of authority, so that American mankind can refind its object, its dedication to a more perfect union, toward the perfected human community, its right to the pursuit of happiness." And Cavell adds,

> It would not surprise me if someone found me, or rather found my daydream, Utopian. But I have not yet said what my waking relation to this daydream is, nor what my implication is in the events of the film. Our relation to the events of the film can only be determined in working through the details of the events of significant films themselves. And specifically, as I never tire of saying, each of the films in the genre of remarriage essentially contains considerations of what it is to view them, to know them. (Cavell 1981b, 159)

These last words help set up the chapter's splendid conclusion, which calls attention to "the events of the ending of the film," events that have, as Cavell puts it, "a peculiar bearing on the issue of viewing" (Cavell 1981b, 159). Reluctantly, I'll resist the temptation to spend all the time I have left reading Cavell's reading of the ending of *The Philadelphia Story* and cut directly to the chapter's last sentences:

> The ambiguous status of these figures and hence of our perceptual state will have the effect of compromising or undermining our efforts to arrive at a conclusion about the narrative. For example, shall we say that the film ends with an embrace, betokening happiness? I would rather say that it ends with a picture of an embrace, something at a remove from what has gone before, hence betokening uncertainty. Will someone still find that my daydream is not sufficiently undermined by this uncertainty, and still accuse me of Utopianism? Then I might invoke Dexter's reply to George's objection to his, and all of his kind's, sophisticated ideas: "Ain't it awful!" (Cavell 1981b, 159)

Cavell's shot-by-shot reading of this passage, another rarity not only in *Pursuits of Happiness* but in his writings about film in general, identifies the aspiration of *The Philadelphia Story*—or its fantasy of its aspiration—to be a marriage of Hellenism and Hebraism that might "bring American mankind a step closer to reclaiming its right to pursue happiness" (Cavell 1981b, 159). And isn't Cavell declaring this also to be his own aspiration in writing this chapter, or his own fantasy of his aspiration?

Cavell is claiming here that *The Philadelphia Story* is meant to leave us in a state of uncertainty as to whether it is *merely* a daydream, as opposed to a daydream we *can* bring closer to reality. Shouldn't that uncertainty be enough to keep the film, or Cavell's account of the film, from being dismissed as a Utopian fantasy? And yet, by giving Dexter the last word, by indeed letting Dexter speak *for* him, isn't Cavell overcoming or transcending that uncertainty by taking Dexter's side? Isn't Cavell in effect saying—saying to us—"I'll risk it, will you?" Or is this little scene Cavell is sketching, in which he responds to an interlocutor accusing him of spinning a Utopian daydream, part of the daydream he is spinning?

What I'm suggesting is that the uncertainty Cavell locates within *The Philadelphia Story* is mirrored by an uncertainty I am locating within his reading of the film. Then what is *my* "waking relation" to *Cavell's* daydream? If his reading of *The Philadelphia Story* convinces me of the film's "national importance," if I don't take it to be *merely* a daydream, couldn't someone accuse *me* of Utopianism? Then I would have to determine for myself how to respond. And I, too, might well find myself saying: "I'll risk it. Will you?"

In saying that Matthew Arnold diverges from American Transcendentalism by identifying the best self with "right reason," Cavell doesn't *explicitly* take sides. But surely, he's on the side of Thoreau and Emerson. At least, his best self is. And although it seems accurate enough to say that Tracy Hebraizes, is it really true that Dexter Hellenizes? This would suggest that Tracy and Dexter are equal in moral authority. They once were, but at some time between the brief prologue and the body of the film, Dexter undergoes a transformation, a conversion to humanity— although this happens off camera, as a comparable conversion does in Hitchcock's *Notorious*. (It's not until *North by Northwest*—and, I might add, Leo McCarey's *An Affair to Remember*, also made in 1959—that a Cary Grant character undergoes such a transformation on camera, in front of our eyes.) By the time Dexter walks into Sidney Kidd's office and sets the events of the narrative in motion, he has already become a philosopher of Emerson's—and Cavell's—stripe.

If Dexter has truly become an *Emersonian* philosopher, he does not need his "spontaneity of consciousness" to be balanced with Tracy's "strictness of conscience." He has already found in *himself* that "saving balance" between "Hellenizing" and "Hebraizing." That's what gives him both the desire and the authority to help empower Tracy to balance her Hebraism with Hellenism and recognize her own "best self"—and Dexter's. "He not busy being born is busy dying," Bob Dylan sang, channeling Emerson, who knew that what he called the "wonderful way of *life*" must be *strictly* followed if one's "best self" is to rule. Surely, in writing this chapter, Cavell sought, and found, a "saving balance," a true marriage, between "Hellenizing" and "Hebraizing." Hadn't he always? His equal commitment to saying what he means and meaning what he says *was* his aspiration to marry "Hellenizing" and "Hebraizing."

Arnold called himself a perfectionist. But he wasn't *Cavell's* kind of perfectionist. Emerson was. At the time he wrote *Pursuits of Happiness*, Cavell had walked far on the path that would lead him to give the name "Emersonian perfectionism" to the kind of perfectionism that he, like Emerson, believed in and aspired to practice. He wasn't quite there yet when he wrote *Pursuits of Happiness*. But he was a lot farther along that path than I was. In *Pursuits of Happiness* Cavell observes that in 1978 "William Rothman and I offered a course jointly that took off from the material I had developed about remarriage and related it to other genres in (primarily) the Hollywood constellation of genres and to other films in which the actors and directors worked who were mainly responsible for the comedy of remarriage" (Cavell 1981b, 275).

The course we cotaught seemed to me at the time, through no fault of Cavell's, a failure. By 1978, his understanding of the remarriage comedy genre was already largely set. This meant, for example, that what most piqued his interest in Yasujiro Ozu's *Late Spring* was its focus on a father for whom his daughter's happiness is the most important thing in the world—not a traditional Japanese father, but a kindred spirit to the woman's father in an American remarriage comedy, as is the father in Hitchcock's *Stage Fright*. I understood why, given Cavell's concerns, he would gravitate to the father–daughter relationship in these films. But I didn't yet understand why, given *my* concerns, I, too, should find it thought-provoking.

Cavell was born in 1926, a year before *The Jazz Singer*, so the films Cavell watched during the quarter of a century in which going to the movies was an ordinary part of his week were, with few if any exceptions, "talkies." And while "talkies" are *films* and thus subject to the ontological conditions *The World Viewed* investigates philosophically, it was also a medium unto itself, a medium that, to borrow that book's terminology, film's material basis is capable of supporting. And, for Cavell, the comedy of remarriage is itself a medium, one that the medium of the "talkie" is capable of supporting.

That each comedy of remarriage is a personal expression of its director is what is "Hellenizing" about the genre; what is "Hebraizing" about the genre is that it has "laws" that each of its members must strictly follow. Hence *Pursuits of Happiness*'s claim that it is a "law" of the genre that each film must at some point acknowledge the woman in the film *as* the flesh and blood actress who incarnates her, thereby acknowledging that it is a film, not unmediated reality. But what *Pursuits of Happiness* primarily focuses on, what remarriage comedies themselves primarily focus on, as Cavell reads them, are the ways they find, different for each film, to obey the "law" of the genre requiring each film to earn its membership by entering into conversation with the other members. Obeying this "law" requires each film to achieve its own perspective on the genre as a whole, to enter the ongoing conversation among the genre's other members. It is no wonder, then, that Cavell, for whom ordinary language is both a medium of philosophy and an inescapable subject for philosophy, should find the comedy of remarriage, which revolves around conversation, takes the form of a conversation, and is *about* conversation, to be not only a subject of interest *to* philosophy, but to be itself a medium *of* philosophy

But I am saying all this after the fact. In the course Cavell and I taught together, my lectures were at cross-purposes to his. I had already begun writing *Hitchcock—The Murderous Gaze*, and my way of thinking about authorship was as firmly set as his way of thinking about genre, which was in any case so different from any of the theories of genre that then prevailed—and largely still do—within academic film studies, and so different from the way I was thinking about film, that I didn't know how to make my lectures responsive to his, even though I was talking about films I loved and had a lot to say about, such as Griffith's *True Heart Susie*, Chaplin's *City Lights*, Murnau's *Sunrise*, Sternberg's *Morocco*, Lubitsch's *Trouble in Paradise*, Hawks's *Twentieth Century* and *Only Angels Have Wings*, as well as *Late Spring* and *Stage Fright*. The task I faced was all the more challenging for me because Cavell's own thinking had become so unsettled by his new encounters with Emerson that he was at a pivotal moment of his own philosophical life. He was blazing a path through unexplored territory—a path I wasn't yet ready to take.

In *Must We Mean What We Say?* and *The World Viewed*, Cavell declared his affinity with J. L. Austin, his own professor of philosophy, and with the Wittgenstein of *Philosophical Investigations*. By characterizing his own writings as *modern* philosophy, Cavell, who was then in regular conversation with Michael Fried, also declared his affinity with modernist artists, declaring himself to be writing from within what he called the "modernist situation." In *Pursuits of Happiness*, though, references to modernism are altogether absent. Nor would the concept of modernism ever again figure significantly in Cavell's writings.

Then, too, in *The World Viewed*, Baudelaire played a central role in the book's reflections on film's emergence at the moment in the history of the traditional arts in which realism was the burning issue and modernism was emerging. And yet, as Cavell would suggest in "An Emerson Mood," Emerson came closer than Baudelaire to prophesying the advent of film's mode of viewing the world. How different would *The World Viewed* have been if Cavell had written it *after* the encounter with Emerson that led him to write "Thinking of Emerson" and "An Emerson Mood"? And how different would *Pursuits of Happiness* have been had Cavell begun writing it after completing those two essays? But perhaps this last question is moot, given that he had been thinking about the genre he was to call "the comedy of remarriage" as early as 1974, and that, as I've suggested, his thinking about this quintessentially American genre must have played a role in sparking a desire to—and a sense that he *had* to—return to Emerson, and in empowering him to read Emerson in a way that enabled him to recognize that Emerson's writing is at every moment "answerable to itself," "under its own question."

By the end of the 1980s, Cavell had paid in full, in his writing and teaching, the tuition for his intuition, first expressed a decade earlier in "Thinking of Emerson" and "An Emerson Mood," that his own writing had profound affinities with Emerson's. All of this thinking, and writing, about Emerson led Cavell to a further intuition. When he was writing the trio of *Must We Mean What We Say?*, *The World Viewed*, and *The Senses of Walden*, and preparing for publication the first three parts of *The Claim of Reason*, Cavell, like Wittgenstein and Austin, found himself in a "modernist situation" in relation to the tradition of analytical philosophy in which he had been trained. He felt he had no choice but to write philosophy in a way that was radically different from the mode of philosophical analysis that was, and largely still is, dominant within English-speaking philosophy departments. But Cavell had also inherited, at first unknowingly, concerns and procedures of an alternative philosophical tradition, founded in America by Emerson, embraced by his great reader Thoreau and, in Europe, by his devoted readers Nietzsche (and, through Nietzsche, Heidegger), and Bergson (and, through Bergson, Deleuze), and kept alive within American culture, and in *himself*, by the films Cavell watched during the quarter of a century in which going to the movies was a normal part of his week. Cavell didn't find himself in a "modernist situation" in relation to *this* tradition. And by the end of the 1980s, he was finally ready to give a name—"Emersonian perfectionism"—to the way of thinking philosophically that he had come to recognize as his own, no less than Emerson's. Looking back from this transformed perspective, *Pursuits of Happiness* can be seen as a new departure, but also as a transitional work, a way station on the path that would lead to *A Pitch of Philosophy*, *Philosophy the Day After Tomorrow*, *Cities of Words*, and, finally, his philosophical memoir *Little Did I Know*.

8

In Defense of *Pursuits of Happiness*

Response to David Shumway's "Screwball Comedies: Constructing Romance, Mystifying Marriage," *Cinema Journal* 30, no. 4 (Summer 1991): 7–23.

Although there seems to be a pervasive impression within film studies that Cavell's writings have long ago been discredited on theoretical grounds, no serious objections have ever been raised within the field to the leading claims of *The World Viewed* or, for that matter, those of *Pursuits of Happiness* or Cavell's other writings about film. David Shumway's "Screwball Comedies: Constructing Romance, Mystifying Marriage" might seem an exception. It certainly is meant to give the impression that it is raising serious objections to the leading claims of *Pursuits of Happiness*. In truth, this impression is illusory, for Shumway's essay not only does not pose a serious challenge to *Pursuits of Happiness*; it conveys no sense whatever of the nature and value of Cavell's philosophical project. It does not acknowledge or address Cavell's way of thinking at all. For example, Shumway writes:

> Despite the fact that the focus of Cavell's argument is marriage, he neglects the feminist perspective almost entirely and the significant body of feminist film studies almost completely. This is certainly a major reason for his failure to understand the cultural work of the genre. (Shumway 1991, 7)

These are two of the five (uneasy) polemical pieces I've included in *The Holiday in His Eye*. They were written as reviews to be published in film studies journals, but I never submitted either for publication. Instead, I used passages from my response to David Shumway in my essay "Screwball Comedy" for Roy Grundmann, ed., *The Wiley-Blackwell History of American Film* (Oxford: Wiley-Blackwell, 2012). And Nicole Richter's judicious review of the Glitre book (in *Modern Language Notes* 122 [2007]: 1197–1200), duly appreciative but critical of the book's treatment of Cavell, relieved my sense of urgency about going on record to defend *Pursuits of Happiness*.

To claim that *Pursuits of Happiness* neglects the feminist perspective is to fail to acknowledge one of the book's leading claims, which is that the Hollywood genre of the remarriage comedy represents, among other things, a stage within the development of feminism. And how can *Pursuits of Happiness* be charged with neglecting "the significant body of feminist film studies" when Cavell's book was published in 1981, incorporates essays written in the mid-1970s, and exemplifies ways of thinking about film and films that go back to *The World Viewed* and, indeed, to essays Cavell published as early as the 1950s? If there is a question of scholarly propriety, that question isn't why *Pursuits of Happiness* doesn't systematically refer to "the significant body of feminist film studies," but why so-called "feminist film studies" has almost completely failed to acknowledge *Pursuits of Happiness*. Not only have feminist film theorists not offered detailed responses to *Pursuits of Happiness*; few have even acknowledged its existence, nor acknowledged that it is *possible* to think about these films, about film, the way Cavell does, a way that is no less feminist than their way.

From within Cavell's way of thinking, it is *because* feminist film criticism has not acknowledged the possibility of thinking the way his writings exemplify that, like academic film studies as a whole, it has largely been fixated, despite *Pursuits of Happiness*'s evidence to the contrary, on the assumption that classical American movies must be ideologically pernicious agents of patriarchal ideology and cannot possibly be capable of thinking seriously about the subjectivity of women. And, from within Cavell's way of thinking, what the field calls "feminist film criticism," like film studies as a whole, has been fixated on doctrines that cannot be reconciled with the ontological conditions of film as he had worked them out philosophically in *The World Viewed* (for example, the doctrine that in classical cinema the viewer's relationship to the film image can be adequately characterized by the psychoanalytic concept of the fetish).

In other words, when Shumway attributes what he calls Cavell's "failure to understand the cultural work of the genre" to a failure to recognize the perspective of feminist film studies, he is failing to recognize the failure of feminist film theorists to acknowledge Cavell's philosophical perspective. That is, Shumway is failing altogether to acknowledge Cavell's way of thinking, failing to acknowledge it *as* a serious way of thinking.

And when Shumway presumes to specify—on no discernible intellectual grounds—the "cultural work" of the genre, what it *is* about the genre that he takes Cavell to have failed to grasp, it is again obvious to any serious reader of Cavell that Shumway has utterly failed to grasp his way of thinking.

Shumway writes:

> The major cultural work of these films is not the stimulation of thought about marriage, but the affirmation of marriage in the face of the threat of a growing divorce rate and liberalized divorce laws. What an analysis of screwball comedies will show is that romance functions as a specific ideology that is used by these films to mystify marriage. (Shumway 1991, 7)

By not just *claiming* but on every page *demonstrating* that remarriage comedies are thinking seriously about such matters as the nature of marriage, society, and change, *Pursuits of Happiness* is not "failing to consider" that these films "mystify marriage," as Shumway charges, or that they are in the grips of a pernicious ideology of romance. Cavell's writing *shows*, on every page, why claims like Shumway's are wrong. These films *do* affirm the marriage, the remarriage, of their leading couples, as Cavell claims. But the films also acknowledge the present failure of marriage as a social institution. They do not mystify the institution of marriage as it stands. They entertain a utopian vision of marriage as it could become—if only we, and society, change.

And by demonstrating how remarriage comedies incorporate acknowledgments of film's unique ontological conditions, Cavell demolishes another of Shumway's claims, that the remarriage comedy is simply a subgenre of romance and thus applies the same set of assumptions and "performs the same cultural work that many of the most important forms of cultural production (novels, operas, poems, etc.) had been performing throughout the period of bourgeois hegemony" (Shumway 1991, 7). What is singular about the remarriage genre, what makes this singularity important, is what *Pursuits of Happiness* is about. Here, too, Shumway does not raise a serious objection to Cavell's way of thinking. He simply fails to acknowledge it.

But enough is enough. It is not my business here to presume to say what Cavell's way of thinking *is*. *Pursuits of Happiness* is fully capable of speaking for itself, as is all of Cavell's writing. But who in the field of film studies is willing, and able, to listen?

∼

Response to Kathrina Glitre's *Hollywood Romantic Comedy: States of the Union, 1934–1965* (Manchester: Manchester University Press, 2006).

The position that Kathrina Glitre stakes out in the chapter on the 1930s in *Hollywood Romantic Comedy: States of Union, 1934–1965* is very close to that of *Pursuits of Happiness*. She, too, sees what she calls "screwball comedy" as having a privileged place, ideologically, among classical genres. Virtually point by point, her claims recycle Stanley Cavell's, but—and this is all too typical of one way that Cavell's writing is often treated within the field of film studies—instead of fully acknowledging the magnitude of her indebtedness to the American philosopher's seminal work, she restricts herself to taking nitpicking issue with him on a few points she thinks he gets wrong. This evidently helps her to feel justified in avoiding acknowledging the "big picture" in Cavell, the seriousness of his philosophical project.

Cavell does not address "material history," Glitre claims, without seriously asking herself what she means by that term—whether, for example, "material history" includes or excludes intellectual history, hence the history of philosophy. In any case, she doesn't seriously ask herself what, if not "material history," *Pursuits of Happiness* does address. What is Cavell's project? What is the relevance, if any, to the concerns of film studies?

I will not try to address these questions here, but simply single out a number of points on which Glitre—mistakenly, I believe—takes issue with Cavell.

—Glitre says that Cavell mystifies marriage by using the same word to refer to the legal state and to the ideal heterosexual relationship. (By the way, Glitre's use of the word "heterosexual" here is gratuitous. Cavell harbored no inclination to deny the possibility that two men, or two women, could achieve such a relationship.) To avoid confusion, as she puts it, Glitre opts for using the word "marriage" to refer only to the legal state. But where, exactly, does she think Cavell's use of the word causes confusion? Rather than sowing confusion, Cavell, on philosophical principle, uses the word "marriage" as we ordinarily use it, refusing to mask its ambiguity. In the same spirit, in *The World Viewed* Cavell uses the words "medium" and "automatism," which likewise have two senses—senses whose relationship we do not, in fact, already know how to think about, just as we do not already know how to think about the relationship between our concept of a "true" marriage and marriage as a legally defined civil state. What validates a marriage, what makes a relationship a true marriage, is a question that, if we stop to think about it, perplexes us. And it is a burning political issue today, one that splits America down the middle. In Cavell's view, comedies of remarriage, at one level, are concerned with thinking through this question. They are *philosophical*.

Glitre recognizes that the relationship the couples in remarriage comedies achieve changes the "constitution" of marriage. But this means, in part, that they change the concept of marriage, our understanding of what marriage is, what constitutes it—its "grammar," as Cavell understands it. Of course, there is what Emerson would call a "discrepance" between marriage as it exists as a civil institution in today's imperfect America and the examples of what a marriage can be that remarriage comedies envision. What these films are saying is that our society stands in need of change. Radical change? Not in the Marxist sense. It's not a change that would be guaranteed by a Marxist revolution. It's a change that cannot happen unless we change. The hopefulness of these films, and especially the earliest of them, *It Happened One Night*, is in their faith that Hollywood movies have the power to provoke their viewers—in effect, all of America—to think differently. (I think of Capra's *Meet John Doe* as marking the end of this "innocent" period.) America has to change, not by assuming a new identity, but by being more perfectly what it is, what it understands itself to be.

—Glitre says that comedies of remarriage are "anti-romance." This misses Cavell's point. What they mock is not romance, but conventional representations of romance. One has to be a sucker to believe in the romantic powers of moonlight, as *The Lady Eve* hilariously shows. But part of the film's point is that we *are* suckers; that is inseparable from what it is to be human. In *The Awful Truth*, when Lucy says that she can't help still being in love with that crazy lunatic, or in *It Happened One Night* when Peter confesses that he's crazy enough to love Ellie, the genre is asserting at once the power and the irrationality, the incomprehensibility—call it the *mystery*—of love. Love is real, but reality in these films is mysterious. Magical. And in the world on film, whose origins, mythically, are in magic, as *The World Viewed* suggests, there is no barrier separating what is natural from what is magical. Thus, Glitre is wrong to say that, unlike Shakespeare's "green worlds," in the "green world" of these films there is no magic. In these films, romance—its constitution—changes, becomes the same but different. And the goal is to bring romance home. Glitre says that these films are on the side of the extraordinary, not the everyday, but Cavell's chapter on *The Awful Truth* explicitly denies this. The goal is to live both every day and every night, in a spirit of adventure, breaking down the walls that separate holidays from the everyday. Or, we might also say, to break down the wall, the barrier-that-is-no-real-barrier, that separates the world on film from our ordinary lives.

—Glitre jumps all over Cavell—she is not alone in this—for what she thinks is his uncritical, unexamined, embrace of the patriarchal fantasy that it is the business of men to create women—as if he believed that, for men, achieving autonomy, self-reliance, is no problem, hence that, in and out of these films, women are the problem. In light of Cavell's work as a whole—*Contesting Tears*, for a start—this charge is manifestly unfounded. One Cavellian response would be that it is *in these films*—in the myth these films underwrite and are underwritten by—not in the one existing world, that the creation of women *is* the business of men. In the myth, of course, not every man is up to this task or challenge. Thorvald in *A Doll's House*, for example, is not; nor is King Westley, George Kittredge, or any character played by Ralph Bellamy. To be worthy, a man has to dream of finding a woman who will, as Peter puts it in *It Happened One Night*, jump into the surf with him and enjoy it as much as he does. Call this a "real man," as Peter thinks of his dream woman as a "real woman." Peter finally acknowledges that he is such a man, no matter how he tried to deny it to others and to himself, and that Ellie is such a woman. Dexter in *The Philadelphia Story* is definitively such a man, or becomes one in the gap between the film's comical prologue and the moment he walks into Sidney Kidd's office and sets the narrative in motion. At the heart of the genre's myth is less a "patriarchal fantasy," then, than a fantasy of the overcoming or transcending of patriarchal fantasies, in particular the fantasy that there is a natural hierarchy in which women are inferior to men, or at least want different things. (Compare the film *Female* [Michael Curtiz, 1933], in which the George Brent character describes his dream of finding a woman who will stand beside him and thereby help *him* to achieve.)

Glitre says that Cavell envisions the man in a comedy of remarriage as "bestowing" an education upon the woman by, for example, lecturing her—as if in these films the measure of education or creation were the attainment of *knowledge*. Rather, it is the recognition of the *limits* of knowledge, the acknowledgment of the unknowable—what in *The World Viewed* and in his late book *Philosophy the Day After Tomorrow* Cavell calls the *unsayable*. In a comedy of remarriage, the man plays an essential role in this process, whether consciously (Dexter) or unwittingly (Hopsy in *The Lady Eve*). But this doesn't mean that the man "bestows" an education on the woman. The key condition is that the man, whether he is consciously aware of this or not, *wishes* for his "dream woman" to be *real*, to be separate from him, self-reliant—an autonomous human being, a "self" in her own right.

Pursuits of Happiness isn't saying that it is the way things really are, or should be, that a woman, if she is to fully exist in the world, needs a man to preside over her education. But in this movie genre, that *is* the way things are. But it is not by lecturing the woman that the man performs his role, helps the woman to open her own eyes, to think for herself. When men lecture women in comedies of remarriage, they never speak with unquestionable authority. Glitre is caricaturing Cavell when she says that it is "ironic" that he is able to provide a persuasive diagnosis of Peter's problem. Of course, Cavell recognizes full well that the men in the films have their own problems, their own limitations. The man's felt need to lecture the woman, to *assert* his authority, *is* a problem he will have to overcome or transcend if he is to be worthy of the woman.

Observing that Dexter claims for himself the status of a philosopher, Cavell characterizes him as an "Emersonian sage"—as a philosopher of Cavell's own stripe, in other words. Dexter's creation *as* a philosopher is a matter that *The Philadelphia Story* doesn't explicitly address. Nor is Cavell's own creation as a philosopher a matter that *Pursuits of Happiness* explicitly addresses. And yet, as I argue in "Cavell's Creation," the origination of philosophy—historically and phenomenologically, as it were—is a fundamental concern within Cavell's philosophical project as a whole, as his late autobiographical writings make explicit.

To say, as Cavell does in *Pursuits of Happiness*, that in *The Awful Truth* Lucy plays an essential role in helping Jerry to open his eyes is not to deny that Jerry plays an essential role in Lucy's own education. What completes Lucy's education is her recognition that, whether or not she trusts Jerry, she is in love with him. (Or is it her recognition that she *does* trust Jerry, that she has faith in his love for her? Or that her love for him is not conditional on his loving her?) She wants him to declare his love—in effect, to propose marriage—all over again. So, she accepts the challenge of winning him again.

Glitre says that Cavell dismisses the women's own intentions. But these women will go on to see themselves, as well as the men, "the same but differently." They will come to recognize that their real intentions were not what they had thought they were.

—Glitre is almost correct when she observes, taking this to be a problem with Cavell's account of the remarriage comedy genre, that in only two of the six films does the woman's father play the kind of role he plays in *It Happened One Night* and *The Lady Eve*. Actually, the father in *The Philadelphia Story* plays such a role as well, so we're talking about half the films Cavell considers definitive of the remarriage comedy genre. The presence of such a Shakespearean father, as we might call it, so perfectly exemplified by the fathers in Hitchcock's *Stage Fright* and Ozu's *Late Spring*, and whose absence is so painfully felt by the woman in Ophuls's *Letter from an Unknown Woman* and Capra's *Meet John Doe*, might seem to invalidate Cavell's claim that the presence of such a father is a defining feature of the remarriage comedy genre. A possible response to this would be to say that if the woman's father appears in a remarriage comedy, this is the kind of father he has to be, the kind of role he has to play.

Another possible response would be to say that in a comedy of remarriage the man has to be, in effect, both husband *and* father to the woman; he has to be on the side of her happiness, her creation (just as the woman has to be all things to the man). The most telling response, though, would be to appeal to Cavell's conception of genre, as he begins to think it through in *Pursuits of Happiness*, which holds that the members of a genre can be understood to have every feature in common; they can find a way to compensate for the lack—or apparent lack—of a particular feature, the way in *It Happened One Night* the fact that the couple is on the road compensates for its (apparent) lack of a "green world." In *The Awful Truth*, say, Lucy has no Shakespearean father who is a presence in the film. How does the film compensate for the (apparent) lack of this feature, what keeps this from being a deal-breaker that excludes the film from the genre? That is a question to be addressed by criticism, in Cavell's view.

—There is an element of Cavell's account one might have expected Glitre to critique on feminist grounds, but which she refrains from criticizing. I'm thinking of the feature that it is a "law of the genre," as Cavell puts it, that the man must at some point *claim* the woman, must assert his exclusive right to marry her—not to *possess* her, as if she were an object, but what is the difference, since marriage, unlike friendship, is an *exclusive* relationship? No doubt, the idea that it is a "law of the genre" that the man must claim the woman is linked to Cavell's intuition that in comedies of remarriage the man has a "taint of villainy" (a feature that plays a central role in the genre he calls the "melodrama of the unknown woman," which he claims is derived from the comedy of remarriage by a process he calls "negation").

But it is complicated. In *The Philadelphia Story*, Cavell suggests, Dexter claims Tracy when he punches Connor in the jaw before Tracy's fiancé George has a chance to do so. And yet, later, when Connor proposes to Tracy, Dexter waits—and must wait—silently, allowing—and compelling—Tracy to think for herself. Similarly, in *It Happened One Night*, Peter "claims" Ellie by declaring, not to her but to her father, that he loves her. But Ellie, who has already told her father that she loves Peter, is nonetheless free, during the wedding ceremony, to make up her own mind as to whether she will go through with her marriage to King Westley.

Here, as elsewhere, Glitre makes the serious mistake—and she is far from alone in this—of assuming, taking it as a given, that *Pursuits of Happiness*, and the films it addresses, are to be repudiated on feminist grounds. This is a shame, because by adopting this attitude, she forgoes the opportunity to help the field of film studies to acknowledge the implications, for feminism, of Cavell's intuition that comedies of remarriage exemplify not patriarchal ideology but, rather, an Emersonian moral outlook that was ascendant in Hollywood, as it was in America, in the New Deal years. And it's doubly a shame because Glitre is a gifted, astute critic who has original, thought-provoking things to say, in the later chapters of her book, about Hollywood romantic comedies of the 1940s and beyond. If she had acknowledged the fruitfulness of the ideas in *Pursuits of Happiness*, as well as the magnitude of her own indebtedness to those ideas, rather than finding pretexts to distance herself from Cavell's way of thinking, her good book could have been a great one.

9

Viewing the World in Black and White

In *Contesting Tears*, Stanley Cavell identifies a genre of romantic melodrama he calls "the melodrama of the unknown woman" (taking this name from *Letter from an Unknown Woman*, one of the genre's definitive instances). The book devotes chapters to *Stella Dallas*; *Now, Voyager*; *Gaslight*; and *Letter from an Unknown Woman*, but Cavell also considers such films as *Blonde Venus*, *Camille*, and *Show Boat* to belong to the genre.

The starting point of this essay is the intuition that all of these melodramas that are set in America—and innumerable other American melodramas as well—include at least one African American in the cast. Some play minor roles. Some are all but invisible. They are nonetheless present. Starting from the hypothesis that this is not a coincidence, but rather constitutes a significant feature of the genre, "Viewing the World in Black and White" explores some implications of this feature for our understanding of classical Hollywood genres and broaches the question of the roles of gender and race within the American cinema as a whole.

I wish to emphasize the exploratory nature of this essay, which raises more questions than it answers, and barely scratches the surface of complex, and sensitive, matters. In speaking about race in our culture, even more than in speaking about gender, it is wise to proceed with caution and with humility. Who has standing to speak about such matters, and on what grounds, are questions all Americans must take seriously.

Paper presented at the "Twenty-Third Annual Conference on Literature and Film," Florida State University, 1998, and later published in *The "I" of the Camera: Essays in Film Criticism, History and Aesthetics*, 2nd ed. (New York: Cambridge University Press, 2004), 96–109. Reprinted with permission.

Now, Voyager

I begin with *Now, Voyager* (Irving Rapper, 1942), a melodrama with an African American character whose presence seems all but accidental. Blink, and you miss him. He's a man called Samson, and he appears when Charlotte, the Bette Davis character, arrives at Cascade, a school for troubled children, after her mother's death, and for the first time meets Tina, the young daughter of Jerry, the love of Charlotte's life. In the published screenplay, Miss Trask, a teacher at the school, orders Samson to take Charlotte's suitcase, but he never appears on screen. In the film, it is Charlotte who asks Miss Trask whether Samson can get her bags from the car. Miss Trask orders him to do so, and he heads out the door, wordlessly

Irving Rapper, the film's director, handles the moment so as not only to render this black man all but invisible, but to *highlight* his invisibility. Samson is invisible to Charlotte, who keeps staring at little Tina, whom she is seeing for the first time, even as he enters the frame, completely eclipses Tina from view, tips his hat (but without looking at Charlotte), is in turn eclipsed by Charlotte, and then unceremoniously exits the frame.

The next shot, too, seems deliberately designed to highlight Samson's invisibility. It begins as a shot of Charlotte, and only when she moves toward Tina and Samson moves toward the door do we realize that he has been in the frame all the time, eclipsed by Charlotte from our view. As Samson nears the door, the camera reframes with Charlotte, as he unobtrusively exits.

In a film that is all about visibility and invisibility, knownness and unknownness, this carefully choreographed little passage brings home that Samson is invisible to his world, as Charlotte has been to hers. There is a kinship or affinity between the black man and the "unknown woman." And yet there is a crucial difference between them. This passage declares a fact about society within the world of the film, which is also a fact about the real American society of the 1940s—how much has America changed?—that there exist Americans like Samson who are condemned to unknownness by the color of their skin, who are not free to be anything but invisible, who have no say in the matter. And it also declares a fact about melodrama, or about movie melodramas such as this, that in opening our eyes to one woman's heroic quest for selfhood, we risk closing our eyes to others who are not allowed her freedom to change. Charlotte has the power to pass judgment upon the world, to judge the world to be unworthy to judge her. What gives her this power is her freedom to choose to be invisible like Samson if her quest for selfhood calls for that. America does not allow Samson this choice.

Stella Dallas

Stella Dallas (King Vidor, 1937) is another film in which the presence of an African American character, in this case Stella's black maid, Gladys (Lillian Yarbo), can appear merely incidental. Again, though, by virtue both of an inner bond with the heroine and a difference in their horizons of possibilities, the black character plays a crucial role in defining who the "unknown woman" is.

In the pathos-filled birthday party scene, Gladys is a sympathetic coconspirator with Stella. She helps set things up so as to make the best possible impression on the expected guests, and on Stella's daughter Laurel, who marvels that her mother was able to do it all. Gladys senses as quickly as anyone that no guests will actually be arriving, and her sympathy for Laurel, and for Stella, is apparent. At one point, Stella reminds Gladys that when the guests arrive she should refer to Laurel as "Miss Laurel." Gladys replies with an exaggerated, "Yes *Ma'am*." But most of the time, when the two women are alone, neither puts on airs, and Gladys feels free to call Stella "Stel." Crucially, Gladys appreciates Stella's taste. When she first lays eyes on Stella dressed up for the party, she *loves* her outfit. And when Stella, concerned, comments that Laurel is always telling everyone how beautiful her mother is, Gladys says, in all honesty, "Honey, you can sure live up to it!" To this, Stella replies, "If I live through this thing, I'm going to get myself another corset," and leaves the room, and the camera registers Gladys's appreciative amusement.

Gladys and Stella seem such good friends that it comes as a shock, sometime later, when Laurel comes home from a visit with her father and his friend, the newly widowed Helen, calls for Gladys and Stella tells her, matter-of-factly, that Gladys isn't here anymore, that she had let her go, explaining, "What did I need with anybody around?" She adds, "You know what I did? I saved enough money out of her wages to pay a deposit on a fur coat for *you.*" (Earlier, Stella had mused to Gladys that she would give anything to see Laurel in a fur coat.)

Like Samson, Gladys is not a stereotype, like most of the maids played in 1930s films by Hattie McDaniel, Louise Beavers, or Butterfly McQueen (however, these performers, in their vividly different ways, also found ways to transcend these stereotypes) as well as by the less well-known Lillian Yarbo. Gladys is given no demeaning "business" and comes across as an intelligent, well-mannered, and warm human being. Her evident humanity underscores the fact, however, that she hardly so much as exists as a character. We learn nothing about her life. (Where is she from? Is she married? Does she have children? Does she have dreams and aspirations of being something more than a white woman's maid?) We do not learn how she came to be hired, or what becomes of her when, in the dark days of the Depression, Stella fires her.

It seems that the film takes this character for granted—takes for granted that Stella takes her for granted, takes for granted that we will not give a moment's thought to her fate, not let her distract us from our absorption with Stella. But what if the realization does dawn on us that this woman's life matters as much as Stella's? Then we may well feel like rebuking Stella, and the film, and the genre of melodrama it exemplifies, and, perhaps, ourselves, for being so indifferent to this woman's fate. But over the years, I have learned the danger of underestimating this remarkable film. I do not doubt, in fact, that King Vidor's film *means* such a realization to dawn on us, *means* us to feel rebuked, *means* us at some point to recognize that in opening our eyes to Stella's unknownness we were closing our eyes to the unknownness of others. And do we really know, in any case, that Stella is as indifferent as she seems to be? After all, she is putting on an act for Laurel's benefit; she doesn't want her daughter to know how much she really worries about money. That is the film's point, I believe, or part of its point, in including this African American character, acknowledging her humanity, and then dismissing her as if she were disposable.

Within the body of criticism that has grown up around *Stella Dallas*, an impulse has repeatedly surfaced to rebuke Stella, not for being too selfish but for being too selfless, for being so devoted to her daughter's happiness that she is indifferent to her own. And the impulse has repeatedly surfaced to rebuke the film, and the kind of melodrama it exemplifies, for endorsing the idea that women should sacrifice themselves for the sake of others. My own understanding of the film, like the reading Cavell presents in *Contesting Tears*, is that those who view Stella as selfless are assuming that they know something about her they really do not know; they are denying her unknownness, the way society does, and in that respect are denying her selfhood. As Cavell argues, *Stella Dallas* repudiates such denials. At the end of the film, Stella achieves a philosophical perspective that allows her to transcend society's view of her. Stella is outside because she chooses to be, because society as it stands—a society that judges people by their appearance—is not to her taste, does not live up to her standards. Gladys's presence in the film serves to remind us why Stella's world deserves her disapproval.

Blonde Venus

In Josef von Sternberg's 1932 film *Blonde Venus*, the earliest of the "unknown woman" melodramas Cavell identifies, there are two African American characters. One is Viola, whom Helen, the Marlene Dietrich character, hires as a nanny when she first goes on the lam with her son. Viola seems so forgettable that I had, in fact, forgotten her. There's no forgetting the other, Cora, as played by the great Hattie McDaniel in an early screen performance.

Cora is a friend who helps Helen when she is destitute and hiding from the police. A character played by Hattie McDaniel can hardly be invisible, of course, or, for that matter, silent. This is the film in which McDaniel first displayed that nobullshit wit that is so much a part of her screen persona and that makes her a natural friend to Dietrich (who does not at all feel humiliated by being destitute, because, in her judgment, society, not she, is really on trial).

In *Toms, Coons, Mulattos, Mammies, and Bucks*, Donald Bogle, usually so appreciative of Hattie McDaniel, strangely detects in von Sternberg's *Blonde Venus* an attempt "at first to pass her off as a humorless, less jolly version of Louise Beavers." He goes on,

> The film stars Marlene Dietrich as a Depression heroine driven to shame by her poverty. Fleeing her husband who fights for custody of their young son and carrying the boy with her, Dietrich hides out in a small Southern town where she is befriended by a congenial local mammy. Not only does mammy McDaniel supply provisions and moral support, but she also serves as a lookout, quick to warn Dietrich before the detectives close in. The down-and-out heroine has come to rely on the servant as her last friend, and once again the prehumanized black domestic is the true and trusted companion out to aid the white world, not harm it. (Bogle 1973, 83)

But in *Blonde Venus* Dietrich is anything but a "Depression heroine driven to shame by her poverty." As we have noted, she does not regard her poverty as shameful. In her eyes, women driven to poverty are not degraded or fallen; in their outcast state, they are members of what in *Morocco* the Dietrich character calls "the foreign legion of women." She thinks of these women as her sisters. ("You don't look like those other women," the dumb cop who is on her trail says to her. "Give me time," she replies.) Like every member of this sisterhood, Dietrich in *Blonde Venus* is all too aware of the powerful forces the "white world" can bring to bear. But she does not accept that world's claim to possess *moral* authority. It is she who passes judgment on the world, not the world that passes judgment on her. And her power to pass judgment is anchored by her unknownness, her outsideness, a condition that links her with her black sister.

Cora is not a "mammy," by the way, although she does put on a mammy act to determine whether the white man who has shown up in town is a cop or is simply "browsing around." And Cora is not Helen's servant; she is her friend. In aiding

Helen, she is not, as Bogle suggests, acting to aid the white world. She is aiding a woman who accepts her as a sister, a woman she accepts as a sister, a woman who is a fugitive from the white world, which in *Blonde Venus* is synonymous with the patriarchy. Having said that the Dietrich and McDaniel characters are like sisters, however, I must also point out that the film acknowledges a distinction between them. They are sisters under the skin, but one woman's skin is white, the other's black, and, in the judgment of the world, which has the force of the Law behind it, this makes them unequal. In the film, as in the real America of the 1930s, the world as it stands is a man's world as surely as it is a white world. A white woman is free in a way her black sister is not, but Helen is not free the way her husband is; she is not free, for example, to keep her son from lawfully being taken away from her. No woman can realty be free in such a world. Freedom, for Helen, is an illusion. Yet, however illusory her freedom, she does have the power, as her black sister does not, to transform herself in the eyes of the world, to be reborn, to emerge from a gorilla skin to the beat of jungle drums and assume a new identity as "the Blonde Venus." And in the end, she has the power to return to reclaim her son, to tell her story to him the way he wishes her to tell it, to keep the story—the illusion, the world—going.

In a melodrama like *Blonde Venus*, which hinges on the power of an "unknown woman" to judge a world that claims to judge her, the heroine's acceptance of her outsideness is the source of her freedom, her powers of metamorphosis, which are denied to the black woman. Again, an African American character participates in defining the heroine's condition by virtue of their kinship, the fact that they are sisters under the skin, and their difference, which is only skin deep but makes all the difference to the world.

Show Boat

In *Show Boat* (James Whale, 1937) Julie (Helen Morgan) is a tragic mulatto figure. The daughter of a white father and a black mammy, she keeps her "black blood" a secret. But she has inherited her natural gift to be a "leading lady" on the stage, not in real life. Inheriting her gift for singing, Julie also inherits songs that have been handed down from mammy to mammy, songs that revolve around the idea that it is natural for a woman like her to love one man all her life. Young Magnolia (Irene Dunne), daughter of the showboat owner, does not have a drop of "black blood," but she and Julie have a special bond, an affinity both women recognize. Magnolia, like Julie, possesses that unknownness essential for singing "Negro songs," and essential, in general, for success on the stage. (The film, by the way, touches on the idea that the world of theater, like the world of "only make believe," as one of *Show Boat*'s most famous songs puts it, is a world that allows what society otherwise forbids. Like the show business world in *The Jazz Singer*, like the Broadway theater world of the 1930s, the world of James Whale's film is a world capable of reconciling what remained unreconcilable in the real world.)

If one "only makes believe," one's dream can come true—but only in "make-believe." One must also face facts. In America as it stands, in *Show Boat*, the happy ending that is possible for Magnolia is not possible for Julie. For Magnolia to succeed, Julie, more her mother than her biological mother is, has to withdraw, as Stella Dallas withdraws. But there is also an isolation in Julie's temperament—in the temperament of any woman destined for the stage—that makes her *wish* to withdraw, to remain outside.

In addition to the mulatto Julie, who passes as white, *Show Boat* also contains black characters, most notably those played by Paul Robeson and Hattie McDaniel. No less than McDaniel in this film, the Robeson character no doubt seems a stereotype: the shiftless, lazy, good-for-nothing black man. But it is worth noting that when something he cares about is at stake, he does, much to his wife's surprise, put himself out, as he does when Magnolia is in the throes of a dangerous childbirth and he braves the raging Mississippi River to seek help. (In aiding Magnolia, he is not acting to aid the white world; her bond with Julie marks Magnolia as black.) It is not that he is lazy by nature; rather, as a matter of principle, he "suits himself," as he declares in his duet with McDaniel. He has a philosophy of life, in other words—a philosophy he learned from no less an authority than "Ol' Man River" (or "Ribber," as Robeson impeccably enunciates it in his show-stopping song).

In this brilliant production number, the camera films Robeson differently from the way it treats other singers in the film. Irene Dunne and Allan Jones sing to each other, in shot / reverse shot or in profile. Helen Morgan, when she sings her great number "Bill," is so absorbed within the world of the song that she can be framed in an almost frontal close-up without our ever sensing either that she is performing for the camera or that its presence makes her self-conscious.

Filming Robeson, the camera frames him tightly, too, and nearly frontally, as he sings to no one within the world of the film. Unlike Morgan's character, though, it seems to take an effort for him to avoid meeting the camera's gaze. His eyeline repeatedly, and uneasily, crosses the axis. We sense the pleasure Robeson is taking in his performance, his wish to present himself theatrically. We also sense his inhibition in the face of the camera, his unwillingness or inability to ignore the camera or to address it directly.

Donald Bogle writes, in a particularly fine passage, "In all [Robeson's] movies, audiences were aware of his great bulk and presence. His eyes gleamed. His smile was brilliant and infectious, often revealing the complete joy of the actor as he sang, sometimes masking an ambivalent, ironic side of his personality" (Bogle 1973, 97). And yet, when he finishes his knockout performance of "Ol' Man Ribber," Robeson cannot help smiling with satisfaction, but this smile is not addressed to the film's audience, or to any audience within the world of the film. He has no one to whom he can address this smile. It is this condition of isolation, imposed upon him by a world that will not look a black man in the eye, that is declared by the camera's placement.

Imitation of Life

In *The Negro in Films*, a book published in the 1940s, Peter Noble writes that in the 1934 version of Fannie Hurst's novel *Imitation of Life*, "Louise Beavers appeared as the self-effacing, faithful, kind-hearted epitome of the worst type of 'mammy' role." He goes on,

> All she desired, it seemed, was to be able to serve her mistress well, and to have "a big funeral with white horses" when she died. As *Literary Digest* remarked, "Obviously, Peola, Delilah's daughter, played by Fredi Washington, is the most interesting person in the cast. Her drama is the most poignant, but the producers not only confine her to a minor and carefully handled subplot, but appear to regard her with distaste. They appear to be fond of her mother, because she is the meek type of old-fashioned Negro that, as they say, "knows his place," but the daughter is too bitter and lacking in resignation for them. (Noble 1948, 62)

"Peola," Daniel Leab writes in the same vein in *From Sambo to Superspade*,

> is simply an updated version of the tragic mulatto of nineteenth-century melodrama and early silent film. As was the case with her predecessors, mixed blood can bring nothing but sorrow. And the movie delineates Peola in the same terms that had always defined the mulatto stereotype. While Delilah's mammy figure is treated sympathetically if condescendingly, the character of Peola has virtually no redeeming features. (Leab 1976, 108)

Donald Bogle goes further:

> *Imitation of Life*'s great contradiction, its single subversive element, was the character Peola. Originally, Peola had been conceived as a tragic mulatto type, the beautiful girl doomed because she has a "drop of Negra blood." But as played by Fredi Washington, Peola became a character in search of a movie. With eyes light and liquid and almost haunted, Miss Washington made Peola a password for non-passive resistance. "Mama," she cried, "I want the same things in life other people enjoy." The line was the film's great one, its simplest and most heartfelt. To obtain the equality she wants, Peola has to rebel against the system. Peola was the New Negro demanding a real New Deal. But as the *New York Times* pointed out in its review of the film, "The photoplay was content to suggest that the sensitive daughter of the Negro woman is bound to be unhappy if she happens to be able to pass for white." The explanation for Peola's rebellion is simply that she wants to be white, not that she wants white opportunities. Her weeping by her mother's casket was Hollywood's slick way of finally humiliating her, its way of finally making the character who had run away with herself conform to the remorseful mulatto type. (Bogle 1973, 60)

All these writers, in affirming Peola, find a need to rebuke Delilah and indict the film for endorsing her way of thinking. As Bogle puts it, Louise Beavers's Delilah was

> a combination of tom and aunt jemimah magnified and glorified in full-blown Hollywood fashion. But she introduced to the 1930s audience the idea of black Christian stoicism. "Bow your head," she tells daughter Peola. "You got to learn to take it. Your pappy kept beating his fists against life all his days until it eat him through." In its historical perspective, this Christian stoicism—particularly because Beavers was able to make movie patrons believe that she herself believed it—"elevated" the Negro character in films by endowing him with Christian goodness far exceeding that of any other character. Of course, the irony of this stoicism was that it made the Negro character more self-effacing than ever, even more resolutely resigned to accepting his fate of inferiority. (Bogle 1973, 59)

This misses the point of the film. Without question, *Imitation of Life* expects us to love Delilah, as does the film's protagonist Bea, played by Claudette Colbert (in a role that counterpoints her role in *It Happened One Night*, the earliest of the remarriage comedies, also made in 1934). But the film does not expect us to embrace Delilah's way of thinking. Indeed, Delilah is as unfathomable to us as she is to her daughter or, for that matter to Bea. Unlike Delilah, we *do* know what Peola wants, we know why she wants it, we want it too, as does Bea. We do not blame Peola for thinking the way she does. But neither do we blame Delilah for not being able to fathom her daughter's thinking.

At first, Bea thinks she understands Delilah's way of thinking, because she thinks that Delilah simply thinks the way any mother thinks. But in thinking this, Bea does not take into account Delilah's conviction that mammies are different from mothers. As the film goes on, Delilah becomes more and more a mystery to Bea. Bea discovers a wonderful example of the unfathomable difference between them in Delilah's reaction to her offer to give her 20 percent (?!) of the profits from the sale of pancakes made according to Delilah's secret recipe, a recipe handed down to her by her own mammy. Delilah expresses her wish not to own her own home; she would rather continue looking after Bea and Jessie, Bea's daughter. Bea reacts to Delilah's reaction with that sense of affectionate but superior amusement—a mode we see again and again in *It Happened One Night*—so characteristic of Claudette Colbert on screen. To Bea, as to us, Delilah is a woman so innocent that she is terribly vulnerable; she needs to be protected from a world beyond her ken.

In Delilah's view, mothering, like making pancakes (or, in *Show Boat*, singing "Negro songs"), comes naturally to a black woman; the knowledge of how to be a mammy was passed down to her from her own mammy, who learned it from her own mammy before her. But if mothering comes naturally to a black woman, how come her daughter reacts to her the way she does? What mammies know, Delilah believes, is that a mammy's love, like Christ's *love*, is unconditional. Hence Donald Bogle sees her as the embodiment of "Christian stoicism."

And yet, when her daughter "unborns" herself from her, as she puts it, Delilah's stoicism fails her. Believing that mothering comes naturally, not knowing how her daughter can react to her in this unnatural way, she is pushed beyond her capacity to endure. She does not have the spiritual strength to bear such suffering, she says. (The implication is not that a white mother would have the spiritual strength Delilah feels she lacks, but that if a white mother were disavowed by her daughter, that would not constitute the same kind of trial, because a white mother's love is not absolute the way a mammy's love is.) For Peola to pass for white, to reject her own mother, is for her to go against God's wishes, Delilah believes, because God made her black. And yet God also made Peola the way she is, gave her a nature her own mother cannot comprehend. In despairing of life here on earth, in forsaking her worldly existence for the sake of a great funeral, Delilah is asserting her faith in God, but she is also rejecting the world that God created.

Again, *Imitation of Life* does not rebuke Peola for rejecting her mother's way of thinking. After all, the film rejects it, too. And yet Delilah's way of thinking, unfathomable though it may be, profoundly affects everyone in the film. For example, when Peola leaves school and writes to her mother that she never wants to see her again, Bea, knowing how much it means to Delilah, goes to track Peola down and to try to get her to change her mind. It is while Bea is away on this mission that Jessie falls in love with the man who, unbeknownst to her, is the love of her mother's life. And it is after Delilah's funeral that Bea, acting on the lesson she feels the tragedy has taught her, decides to reject this man's proposal or, rather, to defer accepting it until such a time that her daughter falls out of love with him.

It might seem that in making this decision, Bea has come to embrace Delilah's way of thinking, that she is now thinking like a mammy, not like a mother. But that is not so. For one thing, Delilah always thought it unnatural for Bea not to desire to remarry and immediately recognized Bea's Mr. Right when he finally came along. For another, Bea makes her decision in the hope of avoiding Delilah's fate. Unlike Delilah, Bea acts out of a genuine understanding of her daughter's desire, not an inability to understand her. Besides, she acts to satisfy her own desire as well. For Bea takes pleasure in being close to Jessie, and the film ends in anything but a mood of resignation. Bea and Jessie are together, looking forward to a bright future, even as Bea reminisces to her daughter about the very scene between them, now so long ago, that constituted the film's opening. When this scene—so reminiscent of the ending of *Blonde Venus*—now fades out, as several earlier scenes had done, it creates an uncanny sense that the film's opening scene is now about to fade in, as if this were the beginning of the film, not the end—as if the entire film had been a story told, and about to be told again, by this mother to her daughter.

Imitation of Life does not condemn Peola for rejecting her mother's way of thinking. But neither does it condemn Delilah for failing to understand her daughter. Peola loves her mother no less than her mother loves her. And in the end, Peola is not humiliated. Bea remarks, after she witnesses Peola's traumatic break with her mother, that she has witnessed a tragedy. But *Imitation of Life* is not a tragedy. A tragedy has no villain. But in this film, there is a villain. Society, America as it stands, is to blame for Delilah's death and Peola's unhappiness. The film does not advocate that we beat our fists against life, which is what drove Peola's father to his death. But neither does it advocate that we passively accept the world as it is, much less that we abandon the here and now for the sake of the hereafter, as Delilah does. The world must be changed. We must change the world. Otherwise, we are all to blame.

Imitation of Life, for all its sympathy for Delilah, does not endorse "Christian stoicism." The film has a social consciousness it is often thought to lack. That is the import of two remarkable moments we would do well to ponder.

One is the great passage, early in the film, when Delilah rings Bea's doorbell, thinking she has placed a "help wanted" ad for a "girl." Bea's young daughter falls into the bathtub and begins crying, and her mother, alarmed, runs upstairs to see if her baby has been hurt. Delilah waits downstairs, concerned for Bea's baby and also for her own child, because she is in desperate need of a job. John Stahl, the film's director, frames Delilah through the bars of the balustrade, creating a strikingly Hitchcock-like composition.

Surely, this shot is making a statement about racism, the statement that this black woman's lot—any black woman's lot—is to be unfree. Note, however, that at the

very moment the film is declaring Delilah's condition as a black woman to be one of bondage, Delilah is smiling. She is smiling, presumably, because as a mother—or as a mammy—she is happy that baby Jessie is OK. But she is also smiling, I take it, because it is clear to her at this moment that this white woman, herself a mother, will not turn her or her child away. That is, being unfree is a mother's lot, as it is a black person's lot.

The other passage concludes with Delilah pondering the mystery that some people are born white and some black, when there is no real difference between them that justifies their being treated so differently. Because she believes that it can't be the Good Lord's fault that human beings are judged by the color of their skin rather than by the content of their character, who is to blame, Delilah wonders, staring into the camera with a bewildered look that makes me think of Emma (Patricia Collinge) in *Shadow of a Doubt*, unable or unwilling to put two and two together, when she ponders the mystery that for a second time in as many days her daughter narrowly escaped death. Delilah is too innocent, or too oblivious, to point a finger. But the film is not. What we know that Delilah does not is that society is to blame, we are to blame, we are responsible.

10

Cavell's Creation

In the climactic passage of *A Happy Mother's Day* (Richard Leacock and Joyce Chopra, 1963), an early cinéma vérité film, a South Dakota woman who has given birth to quintuplets is stoically enduring a luncheon, ostensibly in her honor. This luncheon is preparatory to the parade that the Chamber of Commerce hopes will successfully kick off its campaign to promote Aberdeen as the place where the epic "blessed event" transpired. From an amateur soprano, singing with a perkiness she obviously mistakes for sophisticated sauciness, Leacock cuts to Mrs. Fischer, the mother for whom this luncheon is supposed to be, as one town booster puts it, "her own fun time." Leacock's camera dwells on Mrs. Fischer's plain face, calling upon us to recognize what the film has already revealed about this woman.

We know, for example, that she knows that this luncheon is a travesty, and that she is going along with it only because she understands that the family needs the town's help to pay the expenses that will be incurred by five new crying and hungry mouths. We know that she knows, as we do, that the local business community and the national media have a vested interest in conspiring to put her family on display. We know that she knows that her husband, while a decent man, is not capable of perceiving the seriousness of the threat to the family's privacy, and hence that it is up to her to draw the line. We know that she must resolutely safeguard her family from the powerful forces that threaten it. And we know that she knows that no one in her world knows her intelligence or her strength. That is, we know that she knows that she stands alone. What we do not know is how she feels about being filmed by Leacock's camera, about being the central subject of this film.

This essay was published in Ted Cohen, Paul Guyer, and Hilary Putnam, eds., *Pursuits of Reason: Essays in Honor of Stanley Cavell* (Lubbock: Texas Tech University Press, 1993). Reprinted with permission. "Stella's Taste" had not yet been published when I wrote "Cavell's Creation." In what follows, page references are to *Contesting Tears*.

104 | The Holiday in His Eye

The camera continues to hold on Mrs. Fischer's face until we may well begin to wonder what, if anything, it could possibly find there that would satisfy it. Leacock pioneered a conception and practice of filmmaking that undertook—by choosing subjects from "real life," by forsaking script and directing—to make filming itself an adventure. But now his camera seems paralyzed, fixated on this woman's face, as if it were up to her to free it to move on to frame other subjects, to resume its life of adventure. But what could it be searching for in this face that could possibly free the camera?

All this time, Mrs. Fischer's eyes are downcast, as if she were veiling the fact that she is not really listening to the singer. As if suddenly sensing that the camera has been attending to her, thus revealing that it is in her thoughts, she shifts her eyes to steal a glance at the camera. Her suspicion confirmed, she furtively shifts her gaze away, as if she thinks she can deceive the camera by pretending she had never been interested in its interest in her. But then, no longer willing or able to continue this pretense, she deliberately meets its gaze with her own. At this moment, we sense that anything can happen, and everything is at stake. What does happen, miraculously, is that as her gaze meets the gaze of the camera the trace of a smile lights up her impassive face.

Then, as if authorized by this woman's acknowledgment of its capacity to acknowledge her, the camera pans from Mrs. Fischer to one person after another in the auditorium, finding obliviousness in the eyes of all the people gathered to honor this woman they do not really know. Mrs. Fischer and Leacock's camera are joined in this summation of her world, as I think of it, which is also a summation of the film. The vision they conspire to create has a nightmarish aspect, but it also contains an affirmation: It is into a world of utter oblivion that this mother's five infants have been born, the film is saying, but this is a world capable of being transfigured.

There is hope for these four little girls and one little boy, hope that they may grow up to really know their mother, hope that they may carry on her spirit, hope that they may one day appreciate this film. Everything is redeemed; even the irrepressible voice of the perky soprano, which a moment before had been maddening, plays its part in animating the film's affirmation, helping to give this moment its absurdly upbeat mood. The capacity to transfigure the world is the secret bond between this mother and the camera. And now this secret is told.

From the fact that such a reading of the film is even possible, it will be clear to any serious reader of Stanley Cavell's writings abut film that *A Happy Mother's Day* bears an intimate relationship to the Hollywood genres he calls "the comedy of remarriage" and "the melodrama of the unknown woman." Yet how could this be, since Leacock and his fellow pioneers in cinéma vérité maintained that their filmmaking represents a complete rejection of the Hollywood tradition?

Actually, I understand the aspiration of documentary filmmakers like Leacock, Donn Pennebaker, and the Maysles brothers to be closely akin to that of the creators of the genres Cavell continues to study so fruitfully. Yet the pioneers of cinéma vérité fervently believed that Hollywood had never produced films that could have served to instruct them. And who at the time said otherwise? What this confirms is that, by the early 1960s, America had lost, repressed, the knowledge that America's movies had once sustained serious conversations with their—our—culture.

In *The "I" of the Camera*, I speculated on the specific mechanisms of this repression, associating it with the rise of suburbia in postwar America and the linked event of television's appropriation of film's position of dominance, and with the Cold War. The question of how it was possible for the remarriage comedy and the melodrama of the unknown woman to have been repressed in the years following their creation turned out to have been a fruitful one. But here I wish to pose and address a new and perhaps more perplexing question: How was it possible for Stanley Cavell to have undone this repression? In part, this is a question as to how anyone could have had so much as an idea, given that repression, that these genres *were* repressed, even that they ever existed. Leacock, for example, had no such idea and, to this day, academic film studies in America does more to reinforce than to undo the repression. My question is also a question as to how a philosopher like Cavell was able to overcome or transcend America's cultural amnesia about the significance, and value, of America's own movies. What kind of philosopher is Stanley Cavell?

Who Is Stanley Cavell?

The Philadelphia Story is about the creation of a woman like Katharine Hepburn. It also posits an ideal man, a man like Cary Grant, but the film presupposes that such a man already exists. In a number of other remarriage comedies, such as *The Lady Eve* and *Adam's Rib*, the man may need a little prodding by the woman before he is ready to play the role Cary Grant plays, as it were, naturally. Yet this genre does not dwell on the man's creation, and neither does *Pursuits of Happiness*.

A corollary feature of the remarriage comedy is likewise not dwelled on by *Pursuits of Happiness*. Cavell speculates on the absence of the woman's mother (an absence reinforced by the crucial role the woman's father plays), but not on the absence of the man's mother (and also the man's father). When the man's parents are present, as in *The Lady Eve*, the film compensates in a way that confirms that their absence is a significant feature of the genre. And while *Pursuits of Happiness* reflects on the ways it makes historical sense that Katharine Hepburn, say, should be a member of her particular generation, reflects in turn on her mother's generation and that of her mother, and so on, the book does not in this way reflect on Cary Grant's "real" identity.

Furthermore, it is a guiding intuition of *Pursuits of Happiness* that the remarriage comedy insists on the identity of the flesh-and-blood actress who incarnates the film's leading woman. In the case of *The Philadelphia Story*, the film's allegory about Tracy's creation as a new woman, a woman worthy of marriage to a man like Dexter, the Cary Grant character, is also, *Pursuits of Happiness* argues, an allegory about the creation of Katharine Hepburn, who incarnates Tracy—about her transfiguration by the medium of film. But *Pursuits of Happiness* does not suggest that *The Philadelphia Story* is in the same way an allegory about Dexter's creation, which happens, offscreen, at some point between the film's comical prologue and the moment he walks into Sidney Kidd's office and sets the narrative in motion. *The Philadelphia Story* calls upon us to envision Katharine Hepburn, as she is projected on the movie screen, as a real woman of flesh and blood, a woman who really exists in the world, but it leaves us free to doubt whether Cary Grant, as he appears before us, is, or could be, in the same way real. In the remarriage comedy there is a mystery to the creation of the leading man. This mystery is a striking feature of the genre, but this feature, too, is not dwelled on by *Pursuits of Happiness*.

Cary Grant did not simply exist in the world; he had to be created, created out of the "stuff" of a working-class Englishman named Archie Leach. Archie Leach did already exist in the world, but can we believe that this Bristol lad was already a man who "holds the holiday in his eyes," a man "fit to stand the gaze of millions," as Cavell, invoking Ralph Waldo Emerson, characterizes him? By what magic was Cary Grant created out of the stuff of Archie Leach, and whom do we envision as the creator? In fact, Archie Leach set out quite deliberately to re-create himself. But was Archie Leach already Cary Grant when he—Archie Leach? Cary Grant?—first presented himself to a Hollywood movie camera? Was the camera the agency of Archie Leach's transfiguration? Was it the medium of film that transformed a man who never stopped being Archie Leach into the Cary Grant we know?

Marian Keane has argued persuasively that John Barrymore was an example, possibly the only example, of a man who presented to the camera a "self" that was definitively his own creation.[1] On the stage, through performing a succession of dramatic roles—some Shakespearean, some written with the actor himself in mind—Barrymore created a unique theatrical identity, an identity *as* theatrical. Keane envisions Barrymore's acting on film not only as the camera's study of Barrymore, but as Barrymore's study of the camera as well, a study he incorporated into his ongoing meditation on his prior identity as an actor, his capacity for theater. Cary Grant's creation was different, insofar as it was not mediated by theater (at least not theater of the "legitimate" persuasion). Yet how his creation was different—what took the place of Barrymore's theatricality in Cary Grant's case, for example, or what made Grant on film but not Barrymore fit to play the male lead in comedies of remarriage—must have been a living question to Howard Hawks and George Cukor, two directors of remarriage comedy who directed both Grant and Barrymore—if one can speak of directing Barrymore at all.

Who Is Cary Grant?

It is a pivotal moment in *Pursuits of Happiness* when, in his reading of *The Philadelphia Story*, Cavell identifies Dexter, the Cary Grant character, as a philosopher. I would add that although Cavell was not yet prepared to say this, Dexter, therapist and Emersonian sage, is Cavell's kind of philosopher. Hence the mystery of Dexter's creation, the mystery of Cary Grant's creation, reflects the mystery of Stanley Cavell's creation, his creation as a philosopher.

---

1. Marian Keane, "Acting About Acting: John Barrymore's Performances on Stage and Screen" (unpublished doctoral dissertation, New York University Department of Cinema Studies, 1991). This dissertation, which takes John Barrymore's self-creation as its subject, contains innumerable formulations that resonate with my own formulations in this present essay. My essay also gained insight as well as inspiration from conversations with Marian Keane during the course of its writing. I am also grateful to Daniel Herwitz for his encouragement and for the insightful comments he made on a draft of the essay.

In his reading of *The Philadelphia Story*, Cavell identifies Dexter, the philosopher, as also a figure for the film's director, George Cukor. This implies that Cavell envisions Cukor, too, as identifying with Dexter's kind of philosopher. And in identifying with Dexter and with Cary Grant, the star who incarnates Dexter, Cavell is also identifying with Cukor, the genius who directed *The Philadelphia Story*, *Adam's Rib*, and *Gaslight*, who straddles the two genres Cavell has studied, yet who remains strikingly unknown.

I cannot help but marvel that such a man as Cukor, who grew up in a far from wealthy New York Jewish household in the Lower East Side and would not have been allowed past the gate of a mainline Philadelphia estate, could possibly have identified with the decidedly upper-class Dexter of *The Philadelphia Story*. Then again, how was it possible for Archie Leach, who had Cary Grant's matinee-idol good looks but not a drop of his blue blood, to identify with the likes of Dexter? To be sure, envisioning Cukor as identifying with Dexter, hence with Cary Grant, does not preclude us from envisioning the director as also identifying with Kittredge, that other George, who is decisively cast out of the community at the end of the film. And it does not preclude our envisioning Cukor as envisioning himself, in his role as director, as the creator of Cary Grant as well. Nor does it preclude envisioning Cukor, whom we know to have been gay, as also desiring Cary Grant, who was, it goes without saying, utterly gorgeous. But I will not speculate here on the question of where, if anywhere, within the role of film director, the boundary between erotic desire and self-love is to be found.

The point I am making is that *Pursuits of Happiness*, which does not dwell on the question of who Cary Grant "really" is, is also silent as to the "real" identity of George Cukor, a film director of remarkable powers—who his parents were, for example, or his teachers, or his lovers. Within the films of the comedy of remarriage, it is a mystery how a movie director is created or creates himself—a mystery this genre does not dwell on, but links with the mystery of the creation of the leading man, which is also the creation of a philosopher. It is the films of the melodrama of the unknown woman, as Cavell understands them, that do take these mysteries as a subject.

"Stella's Taste"

Cavell's reading of *Stella Dallas* begins with an all but explicit declaration that his entire reading of the film is guided by an intuition of his mother's, his intuition of her intuition. He remembers knowing, even as a boy, that she identified with Stella Dallas, or at least did not dissociate herself completely from her.

E. Ann Kaplan and Linda Williams, among other women prominent in film studies, have written influential critiques of *Stella Dallas* from the standpoint of what the field calls "feminist film theory." They envision Stella as oblivious, not self-aware—oblivious, for example, of the impression her clothes make on others. Because they deny even the possibility that there could be an alternative way of envisioning Stella, and deny this in the face of massive evidence to the contrary within the film,

Cavell speaks of these women as being in the grip of a fixation—a fixation that, indeed, afflicts virtually the entire academic field of film studies these days.

Cavell envisions Stella as self-aware, not as oblivious, and presents an impassioned brief that with ironclad logic proves not that Stella *must* be envisioned his way, but that she *can* be. His brief is so impassioned because it is his way of thinking whose legitimacy—indeed, whose possibility—is being denied, his voice that is being excluded, silenced. He has an interest in participating in a conversation about gender with women who feel as strongly about the subject as he does; and he understands that as long as feminist film theorists remain fixated on the idea that Stella must be oblivious, they will have an incentive to reject his invitation to conversation. For this fixation has made it a dogma within film studies that a film like *Stella Dallas* must consign women to oblivion because, as feminist film theory purports to teach us, Hollywood movies are made by the patriarchy to serve patriarchal ends, and philosophy itself is patriarchal and participates actively in "putting women in their place."

Cavell is a philosopher and he is a man, but he has no wish to silence women or force women to speak in his voice. It is their different voices he wishes to hear, and his voice he wishes to be heard. After all, it is his mother's intuition that guides his reading of *Stella Dallas* and moved him to speak about this film in the first place—and to speak at all times in his own voice.

Let us turn to the opening passage of "Stella's Taste," and listen for a moment to Cavell's voice.

> When my mother asked for an opinion from my father and me about a new garment or ornament she had on, a characteristic form she gave her question was, "Too Stella Dallas?" The most frequent scene of the question was our getting ready to leave the apartment for the Friday night movies, by far the most important, and reliable, source of common pleasure for the three of us. I knew even then, so I seem always to have remembered it, that my mother's reference to Stella Dallas was not to a figure from whom she was entirely dissociating herself. Her question was concerned to ward off a certain obviousness of display, not to deny the demand to be noticed. (Cavell 1996, 200)

The scene this passage invokes is not the source or origin of Cavell's intuition about his mother's intuition; that scene is prior, and the essay does not dwell on it. Within the essay, the genesis of his guiding intuition of his mother's intuition remains mysterious. Indeed, an aura of mystery hovers over the entire passage. Cavell's language leaves it ambiguous, for example, whether he envisions his mother as viewing Stella as self-aware, the way he does, or as oblivious, the way the feminist film theorists do.

Riding in a car with Cavell after he read his *Stella Dallas* paper at a symposium on "Women and the Media" at the University of California at San Diego—an occasion on which Tania Modleski, who had become a prominent figure in academic film studies, publicly rejected his invitation to enter into conversation—I posed this question to him point-blank: Does he think his mother envisioned Stella as self-aware or as oblivious? He looked momentarily taken aback at my question, no doubt struck by the intent insistence in my voice. When one asks Stanley Cavell a question that provokes such a look, one knows that one is struggling to give birth to a thought, an idea worth thinking through. (What idea isn't?) But one also knows that one has to think it through before one can formulate it in a way that, as Emerson would put it, pays the tuition for the intuition.

Does the author of "Stella's Taste" identify with his mother, or does he dissociate himself from her (although perhaps not completely)? After pondering my question for a moment, Cavell answered that he supposed his mother must have envisioned Stella as a little of both—a little self-aware, a little oblivious. At that moment, something distracted us—it is hard to sustain philosophy while searching for a parking place—and the conversation strayed.

Cavell's answer suggests that when he wrote "Stella's Taste," he must have envisioned his mother, the way she envisioned Stella, as "a little of both." Was this also the way he had envisioned his mother when he was a boy, or had his vision of her changed? And are we to envision the boy in the essay's opening passage as envisioning Stella as oblivious; or the way the author of "Stella's Taste" did, as self-aware; or the way he came to envision his mother as envisioning Stella, as "somewhere in between"? Are we to envision young Stanley as already the philosopher Stanley Cavell (already possessing his philosophically sophisticated conception of self-knowledge, for example)? Or did this philosopher still have to be created, or create himself, out of the "stuff" of this boy?

I suspect that Cavell would answer each of these questions the way he answered my question in the car. Since he envisions himself as capable of still being guided by his mother's intuition, it follows that he envisions himself, as a boy and as a grown-up, as "a little of both." It is not that the boy was simply not yet the philosopher he was to become, but the philosopher's creation, or self-creation, was not yet completed. No doubt, Cavell's creation as a philosopher was not completed even when he wrote "Stella's Taste"; there is no end to it. But there is no denying that, in the transition from being the boy in the opening passage of "Stella's Taste" to the philosopher capable of invoking such a boy, a transfiguration occurred, although it remains to be specified what role, if any, we are to envision his mother as playing in this transformation of her little boy into her son the philosopher.

One thing is clear: when he wrote "Stella's Taste," Cavell envisioned his relationship to his mother the way he envisioned the relationship between Stella and her daughter Laurel. And he understood in the same terms the relationship between the boy he once was and the philosopher he was to become. Specifically, these relationships all participate in what in his essay he calls the "mutuality of mothering." "When the daughter is motherly to her mother, both may be comforted (they may, for example, do what Laurel calls 'cuddle together'); and mothering may be transmitted so" (Cavell 1996, 16).

Such mutuality is a feature of the grammar of "mothering," Cavell is saying, and internal to its transmission or teaching. The mutuality of mothering is passed on when a daughter is mothering her mother as surely as when her mother is mothering her. When Cavell envisioned his mother as "not entirely dissociating herself" from Stella, in this vision his mother and Stella keep switching places, as it were, oscillate between mothering and being mothered. So do he and his mother. So do the boy remembered and the philosopher remembering. So do Archie Leach and Cary Grant. What Cavell knows as a philosopher, the knowledge that he "seems always to have remembered," is precisely the knowledge that the relationship between self-knowledge and obliviousness, between philosophy and what precedes and motivates philosophy, participates in the "mutuality of mothering."

And so does the art of film. In Cavell's reading of *Stella Dallas*, this emerges as the film's teaching. The teaching of the genre of the melodrama of the unknown woman, the teaching of film itself, is the teaching, hence also the learning, of the mutuality of mothering. The painful part of this teaching and learning is that to become capable of passing it on, one must learn, and learn to be able to teach, that one is separate from one's mother. To know what it means that his mother gave birth to him, to acknowledge that he was born into the world and is fated to die, he must acknowledge his separateness from her; he must suffer separation, he must experience loss.

Film is a medium capable of transmitting this teaching, *Stella Dallas* teaches the author of "Stella's Taste," because the film's subject, as Cavell formulates it, is "the search for the mother's gaze, in view of its loss, or of threatened separation from it" (Cavell 1996, 210). When we gaze upon the world projected on the movie screen, we are searching for the gaze of the mother. Mothering is mutual. Because we envision the screen as possessing a gaze, like a statue of a god or goddess in a Hindu temple, we must be envisioning the screen as gazing back at us—gazing at us in search of the mother's gaze. (For all its undeniable obscurity, I find Cavell's formulation here endlessly suggestive.)

In the remarriage comedy, three male figures—the woman's father, her husband-that-was who is also her husband-to-be, and the film's director—all claim a relationship with the woman that participates in the "mutuality of mothering." Yet in this genre there appears to be something like a literal denial of the primacy of the mother. The absence of the woman's mother is often one form this denial takes. A second is the feature that the woman herself is childless, is not literally a mother. A third is that the man's mother is usually also absent, and beyond this absence, as we have seen, is the implication that there is a mystery to the man's creation, as if he were not "born of woman" but created himself, the way the "unknown woman" in the melodramas creates herself with no help from man. But the melodrama of the unknown woman provides a more persuasive explanation for the absence of the man's mother in the remarriage comedy: He has already learned her teaching, her teaching of the necessity of separation, so he is able to go on, go on as a student and a teacher, go on giving birth to himself, even in his mother's literal absence.

North by Northwest posits Jessie Royce Landis as the Cary Grant character's mother but allows us to imagine that this is only a joke. But it does not follow that we cannot really envision Cary Grant—perhaps I should refer to him here as "Archie Leach"—as having a mother. Would it be a joke to envision his mother as Stella Dallas?

It is no accident that in the preceding sentence I refer to Stella Dallas, rather than Barbara Stanwyck. As I have observed, it is a crucial claim in *Pursuits of Happiness* that *The Philadelphia Story*, say, insists that we view its leading woman as Katharine Hepburn and not simply as Tracy Lord. In thus insisting on the identity of the flesh-and-blood actress who incarnates her character, the remarriage comedy implicitly differentiates the conditions of its leading woman and leading man, as we have seen. Significantly, though, Cavell nowhere claims that the melodrama of the unknown woman likewise insists on the identity of the flesh-and-blood actress who plays the film's protagonist. On the contrary, when he argues that at the end of *Stella Dallas* a woman is created rather than obliterated, as feminist film theorists maintain, Cavell identifies Stella with Barbara Stanwyck but in the same stroke identifies Stanwyck not as the flesh-and-blood actress who inhabited the one existing world—who went to my high school in Brooklyn, in fact—but as a *star*. When Cavell says that the film claims that this woman has a future, what he means is that, like all authentic stars, she is capable of undergoing repeated incarnations on film.

In Cavell's reading, then, *Stella Dallas* emerges as an allegory of the creation of a star out of a flesh-and-blood human being. And nothing in this allegory prevents it from applying to a man as well as to a woman—to the creation of Cary Grant, say, or George Cukor, or Stanley Cavell, for that matter. The melodrama of the unknown woman reads between the lines of the remarriage comedy, in effect, to discover an essential lesson underlying the myth that underwrites, and is underwritten by, that genre. The remarriage comedy is about a man who creates a new woman by teaching her to undergo death and rebirth so as to create herself. What the melodrama of the unknown woman discovers about this story is the condition that the man must satisfy to be such a teacher, such a creator: His mother must have already passed on to him her teaching of the mutuality of mothering, her teaching of being born, of giving birth, of separation and loss, of learning and teaching. Cavell envisions Cary Grant as knowing about himself that he is such a student and such a teacher, I take it, and that is why Dexter claims for himself—why Cavell claims not only for Dexter but for Cary Grant as well—the status of "Emersonian sage."

In his writing about the melodrama of the unknown woman, Cavell learns, and teaches, how to read between the lines of *Pursuits of Happiness* to discover that his writing has, as one level, always been about the creation of philosophy, and about his own creation as a philosopher. Cavell's writing has always known itself to be about the teaching and learning of philosophy, has always taught, and learned, that philosophy is characterized by what he is now prepared to call "the mutuality of mothering." The quest for self-knowledge that is defining for philosophy cannot be separated from knowledge of the necessity of separation; self-knowledge must know itself to be separate from obliviousness, otherwise it would not be self-knowledge at all. And it is always possible for the self-knowledge defining of philosophy to be lost.

Allegorically, the comedy of remarriage envisions no parents, and specifically no mother, for a man like Cary Grant (or for George Cukor, or for Stanley Cavell). Allegorically, the melodrama of the unknown woman attributes to such a man a mother like Stella Dallas, a mother Stanley Cavell's own mother could (at least up to a point) identify with. And the genre, allegorically, attributes to such a mother's teaching, her teaching of mothering, the capacity to give birth to Cavell's kind of philosopher. But what man can have fathered such a philosopher?

Within *Stella Dallas*, Stella's father is a presence only in the early scenes of her family's life, scenes Cavell aptly speaks of as "primitive sketches." And in "Stella's Taste," Cavell's own father is comparably reduced to his presence in the scene of family life with which the essay opens. That scene, too, is a sketch. But it is a sketch of a scene of a real form of human life, not a primitive one. I read the opening passage of "Stella's Taste" as alluding to, even parodying, the opening of Wittgenstein's *Philosophical Investigations*, with its depictions of primitive language games. (Cavell is dissociating himself—although obviously not completely—from Wittgenstein.)

Cavell's opening passage never draws our attention to the figure of his father, whose presence we might even overlook, or think the author overlooks. But the father is there. Stanley and his mother and his father go together to the Friday night movies, which is the threesome's primary source of common pleasure, the passage tells us. And his mother's "Too Stella Dallas?" is posed to Stanley and to his father, whose opinion she is also soliciting, with no indication that she values her son's judgment on such matters more than his father's. This is all Cavell's passage tells us about his father, but it is enough for us to know, for example, that this boy's mother could not have envisioned Stanley's father as a man like Stella's husband, who is unwilling or unable to "read between the lines," unless she also envisioned her—their—son that way. For she appears to identify her son with his father, as if, in her eyes, they equally needed mothering. And Cavell's few words are enough for us to know that we can no more simply identify his own father with Stella's "wooden, shadowy father delivering ugly orders" than we can identify Stella's "monosyllabic, helpless mother" with his own mother.

In differentiating between "mothering" and "fathering," Cavell observes, "when the son is fatherly to his father, the father is transcended" (216). But this remark must not be misconstrued. The idea that fathering, unlike mothering, is *not* a relationship of mutuality is a feature of a conception of fathering that corresponds to a primitive conception of the father (I call this conception "primitive," although Freud elaborated it with unmatched sophistication). This conception is adequate to characterize Stella's father, perhaps, but only because he is a figure who has no real existence apart from scenes in the film that are only primitive sketches. Stella's father is like a builder in one of Wittgenstein's primitive language games. Unless we can imagine an intelligible human context for it, a language game in which nothing can be said but "Brick" or "Pillar" or "Slab" or "Beam" is too primitive to be any part of a real human language, too primitive to participate at all in a human form of life. No real father's relationship to his son can be summed up by primitive sketches. No real father is a primitive father. Manifestly, Stanley Cavell was not a primitive father, and neither was his father. (Who his father was and what role he played in his son's education are, I am convinced, questions that Cavell will surely find himself returning to in his future writings.) To understand how Cavell's conception and practice of fathering transcends the primitive one, it is helpful to turn to *Pursuits of Happiness* and its discussions of the woman's father in remarriage comedy and in Shakespearean romance—the ideal father to have, at least for a daughter. And helpful to reflect on the kind of father, and the kind of son, Stanley Cavell himself is. I have in mind not only his relationships with his children Rachel, Benjamin, and David and with his own father, but also with his students, his readers, and his "philosophical fathers," who are the likes of Shakespeare, Emerson, Thoreau, Freud, Wittgenstein, Heidegger, and Austin. (Freud is a most trying philosophical father for Cavell, both because Freud's work is an elaboration of a primitive conception of the father that Freud never quite transcended, and because he was, in Cavell's view, a philosopher who refused to own up to being a philosopher.)

Reading Cavell, I never have the impression that he wishes to conquer his philosophical fathers, to obliterate them, silence them, or force them to speak in his voice, not their own. I never sense that he feels he could not exist as a philosopher unless he overcame or transcended his philosophical fathers, or that he fears that his students and readers are threatening to overcome or transcend him. On the contrary, Cavell's writing is always patient, always nurturing and being nurtured, teaching and learning, remembering past conversations and inviting future ones. Cavell's way of declaring his separate existence as a philosopher is by acknowledging his bond and continuity with his philosophical fathers, and by calling upon his students and his readers to acknowledge their philosophical fathers—including Cavell, of course, but fair's fair—yet always to think for themselves, as I, personally, have always aspired to do.

Clearly, Cavell's relationships with his students, his readers and his philosophical fathers all aspire to the mutuality exemplified by the relationship of Stella Dallas and her daughter. They are guided by the teaching of mothering. Yet we must not conclude from this that Cavell's philosophical fathers are really philosophical mothers, as it were, nor that he is a philosophical mother, not a philosophical father, to his students and readers. He is a father who speaks in a mothering voice; the language of mothering is this father's mother tongue. A human being has a mother and a father. For conception, both are necessary. But conception completes the father's biological role, while it is the mother alone who gestates, labors, and gives birth. Originally, every human being is inseparable only from the mother, not from the father. Thus, from birth, mothering is a given, is internal to human experience, in a way fathering is not.

Stanley Cavell was born into the world. He had one and only one mother, from whom he was separated when she gave birth to him. In his creation as a philosopher, too, he had one and only one mother, metaphorically speaking. But this mother, unlike his biological mother, remained inseparable from him, the way, as *The World Viewed* points out, in a photograph, unlike a mold, the original is as present as it ever was. Stanley Cavell alone can give voice to his intuitions, give birth to his thoughts. Only within him can his thoughts gestate; only through his labor can they be born; only he can experience the pain of separation when his expressions of his thoughts are born into the world. But allegorically, when Cavell stakes his identity on a thought he voices, when he claims it as his own, he declares himself to be that thought's father as well as its mother. This does not imply, however, that the thought grew from a seed that he alone planted. What transpired at the moment of conception, what prior thought or thoughts were needed for this thought to germinate, cannot fully be known. There is no limit to the number of "fathers" a thought can have, no limit to the number of "philosophical fathers" a philosopher can have.

None of Cavell's "philosophical fathers" labored and gave birth in order for him to be born, created, as a philosopher. None of his "philosophical fathers" was his "philosophical mother." Cavell himself was the "philosophical mother" who had to give birth for this philosopher to be born. (None of this, of course, in any way denies that a woman who is a mother can be a philosopher. I am not even denying that Cavell's own mother may have been a philosopher, indeed one of her son's philosophical fathers. Actually, this strikes me as an extremely appealing possibility.) Yet in fulfilling his aspiration to be a "philosophical father," to be a father to philosophy, Cavell embraces a conception of fathering that aspires to the mutuality of mothering and thus acknowledges the primacy of his mother's teaching.

Mothering, thus understood, is unconditional. The mutuality of Cavell's relationships with his "philosophical fathers" (and students and readers) is unconditional, too—but only on the condition that they keep faith with the kind of philosophy that is their bond. When Freud asserts that his own work is science, not philosophy, for example, Cavell dissociates himself from him (but not completely), constructs arguments to disprove him. But this does not mean that Cavell is, after all, only in the grip of Freud's primitive conception of the father. For Cavell does not argue against Freud in order to overcome or transcend a primitive father whose existence threatens to obliterate his own. The claim Cavell is entering—entering in his own voice—is that philosophy can—and must—free itself from the grip of the primitive conception of the father.

Cavell understands his own understanding and practice of philosophy to be an alternative to a conception and practice that he takes to have dominated the modern history of philosophy, one that, as I put it in "Cavell's Philosophy and What Film Studies Calls 'Theory,'" is "fixated on a vision of philosophy as locked in a kill-or-be-killed conflict, as it were, with the skeptic who denies that we can ever really know anything" (62). That a father's capacity to doubt that his child is his is a paradigm of skeptical doubt underscores that there is a parallel between the skeptical problematic and Freud's conception of the oedipal complex, the male child's fixation on the idea that to achieve manhood he has to vanquish his father—a conception that hinges, indeed, on a primitive conception of the father.

Cavell's philosophical practice is everywhere guided by his intuition that philosophy cannot "cure" this fixation by refuting the skeptic, but only by overcoming or transcending the primitive idea that lack of certainty is philosophy's mortal enemy. To again quote from "Cavell's Philosophy and What Film Studies Calls 'Theory'":

> Cavell's philosophical practice is everywhere guided by the intuition that philosophy cannot "cure" its fixation by silencing the skeptic but only by transcending the primitive notion that skepticism is a mortal threat to philosophy. The war of words between philosophy and skepticism has been going on for centuries, but the "mother of all battles" has yet to be fought between them because—and this is one of Cavell's leading intuitions—each depends on the other for its existence and its very identity: Skepticism is "other" to philosophy, yet its voice is also internal to philosophy. Philosophy's true interest is not in silencing skepticism but in acknowledging its voice, acknowledging the ways this voice motivates, and is motivated by, philosophy. Acknowledging "the truth of skepticism," as he sometimes calls it, does not make Cavell a skeptic. (63)

The skeptic's voice is not to be silenced but listened to, no less than we are to listen to the voice of "reason" that is intent on refuting skepticism. On philosophical principle, Cavell unfailingly listens to these voices, takes their motivations seriously, attends to them with an "understanding heart," to borrow a term from the Katharine Hepburn character's father in *The Philadelphia Story*—the way Cavell attends to everyone who is willing to enter into conversation with him. These voices are internal to philosophy, Cavell learned, and teaches, not separable from who he was, not separable from what philosophy is.

A philosopher fixated on refuting skepticism, no less than a film theorist who is fixated on the idea that Hollywood movies are really instruments of patriarchal ideology, will hear Cavell's voice, in *Pursuits of Happiness*, as threatening. So, too, will a man fixated on the idea that he must vanquish his father if he is fully to achieve manhood. To a man fixated on the primitive conception of the father that underpins the oedipal complex, a melodrama like *Stella Dallas*, too, will seem threatening. To be in the grip of the oedipal complex is to reduce one's mother to an object, the object of a conflict with one's father. It is to deny her separate existence, hence the mutuality that is her teaching. A melodrama like *Stella Dallas*, as Cavell reads it, like a comedy of remarriage, affirms the primacy of the mutuality of mothering. A film theorist fixated on the idea that Hollywood movies are instruments of patriarchal ideology will likewise have a motive to avoid acknowledging the teaching of a melodrama like *Stella Dallas*, no less than the teaching of a remarriage comedy. For *Stella Dallas* calls upon the viewer, male or female, to acknowledge that the "unknown woman" projected on the screen, like the viewer's own mother, is a separate human being. At the same time, *Stella Dallas* calls upon each viewer to identify with this "unknown woman"—to acknowledge that he or she is an "unknown woman," too. To avoid acknowledging the teaching of these Hollywood genres is to avoid awakening from what I think of as American culture's collective amnesia about its glorious cinematic past—about its value, and about the value of the philosophical outlook, ascendant in the New Deal years, that enabled so many Hollywood movies of the period to be at once popular and artistically serious. It is to participate in their repression.

In an analogous way, a philosopher fixated on refuting skepticism has a motive to avoid acknowledging Cavell's teaching and that of his philosophical fathers. The almost total avoidance of *The World Viewed* within the field of philosophy, as well as within the fledgling field of film studies, must have tempted him at times to let himself become fixated on the idea that academic philosophy itself was his mortal enemy. He had a motive for repudiating philosophy, for wishing the field of philosophy to be consigned to oblivion. Instead, he committed himself to staking a claim *within* philosophy—the claim that philosophy, to be true to itself, had to acknowledge *as philosophy* what Cavell values most about philosophy, which is what I've been calling "the teaching of the mutuality of mothering"—Cavell's own teaching, with which he continues to keep faith, and that of his philosophical fathers. In staking this claim, he gave voice to his experience, declared this voice to be his own, and gave birth to the philosopher he has become.

The history of the repression of the genres Cavell has written about cannot be separated from the history of the repression, within philosophy, of Cavell's teaching and that of his philosophical fathers. The repression of the remarriage comedy and the melodrama of the unknown woman must have been engendered, historically, by specific mechanisms that can be studied, as I have argued in *The "I" of the Camera*. And yet, there must never have been a moment when these genres were not repressed, even when they were at the height of their popularity. Their teaching is the teaching of Emerson and Thoreau, which was, as they understood, an undoing of a prior repression. America gave birth to this teaching, yet has never stopped repressing it. When Stanley Cavell stepped forward with *Pursuits of Happiness* and "Stella's Taste," he knew that he was undoing a repression—a repression of the philosophical outlook—I've been calling it the *teaching*—that he found to underwrite the Hollywood genres he was writing about. This teaching was always already known in America—by Emerson and Thoreau, for example, and by the directors of the definitive members of the genres, who knew what they were doing the way serious artists do. When Cavell published *Pursuits of Happiness* and "Stella's Taste," he knew what he was doing, too. He knew that in undertaking to undo our culture's repression of the philosophical outlook that underwrote the films he was writing about, he was taking on a role that had already been created. Yet he also knew that this was a role he was born to play.

This is what it means for a philosopher like Stanley Cavell to perform his own *cogito ergo sum*. To claim his birthright, all he had to do was give voice to his experience and claim this voice as his own. To make his own the role his "philosophical fathers" played before him, the role his mother gave birth to for him to play, all he had to do was create himself.

11

Nostalgia Ain't What It Used to Be

> I'm going back someday
> Come what may
> To Blue Bayou
> Where the folks are fine
> And the world is mine
> On Blue Bayou
> Where those fishing boats
> With their sails afloat
> If I could only see
> That familiar sunrise
> Through sleepy eyes
> How happy I'd be.
>
> —"Blue Bayou," by Roy Orbison
> and Joe Nelson

Nostalgia is a state of mind, a feeling or mood—Charles Foster Kane's mood when he whispered his last word, "Rosebud." Dictionary.com defines the word as a "wistful desire to return in thought or in fact to a former time in one's life, to one's home or homeland, or to one's family and friends; a sentimental yearning for the happiness of a former place or time" (and defines "sentimental," in turn, as "expressive of or appealing to sentiment, especially the tender emotions and feelings, as love, pity, or nostalgia").

Such films of the 1940s as *How Green Was My Valley* (John Ford, 1941), *My Vines Have Tender Grapes* (Roy Rowland, 1945), *Life with Father* (Michael Curtiz,

---

Adapted from an essay published in Matthew Leggatt, ed., *Was It Yesterday? Nostalgia in Contemporary Film and Television* (Albany: State University of New York Press, 2021). Reprinted with permission.

1947), and *I Remember Mama* (George Stevens, 1948), among others, are "overtly nostalgic"; virtually all contemporary American movies, especially blockbusters, are too frenetic, too hopped-up, to "elicit or display nostalgia" or to appeal to the "tender emotions or feelings." They lack nostalgia's requisite wistful yearning, its longing for a happier, freer time that has, like childhood, slipped into the past and is now accessible only in memory. Indeed, I don't think it's possible to experience nostalgia without knowing, in one's heart, that one's childhood *is* past, that one is no longer entitled to the privileges and responsibilities or, rather, irresponsibilities, we grant to children. (I first knew that my own childhood was over one night in my junior year of high school when I watched a performance of *The Cherry Orchard* on WNET's *Play of the Week*, with my sister out on a date and my parents hosting a New Year's Eve party in the living room. Anya's recognition that she was no longer a child so moved me and, to be honest, I so lusted after the young Susan Strasberg, who played her with such passion, that it hit me like a ton of bricks that I, too, was no longer a child. Remembering this makes me nostalgic, but at the time, the tears I wept were bitter, not bittersweet.)

When Roy Orbison sings "I'm going back someday, come what may, to Blue Bayou," we hear in his voice that he knows there's no going back, no way of bringing back those happy times. (When it's Linda Ronstadt singing, we hear this, too.) To know that our childhood is over is to know, really know, that we are mortal, fated to die, and that it is impossible to turn back the clock or stop time in its tracks. Being human, knowledge of our mortality can make us feel, in dark moods, as if we have been sentenced to imprisonment for life, without hope of parole, behind an impassable barrier. But a barrier that is impossible to cross—the speed of light, for example, or the screen that separates our world from the projected world—is not a real barrier, not really a barrier, however natural it may be for us to imagine that it is.

In the opening voiceover of *How Green Was My Valley*, Huw, the film's protagonist (Roddy McDowall in the body of the film; Irving Pichel speaks the narration), now grown up, speaks a truth about the reality of being human:

> There is no fence nor hedge around time that is gone. You can go back and have what you like of it, if you can remember. So, I can close my eyes on my valley as it is today, and it is gone, and I see it as it was when I was a boy. Green it was, and possessed of the plenty of the Earth. In all Wales, there was none so beautiful.

Huw speaks another truth about human reality when he says, "Strange that the mind will forget so much of what only this moment has passed, and yet hold clear and bright the memory of what happened years ago—of men and women long since dead." But then he adds, "Yet who shall say what is real and what is not?" In saying this, Huw is expressing skeptical doubt about what we ordinarily assume are further truths about human reality: you cannot make the past the present again; the present is real in a way the past not; the living are alive and the dead not, our allotted time on this mortal coil has, to use Huw's own metaphor, a fence or hedge around it. Then again, the world of *How Green Was My Valley*, like the world of any film, is not reality; it is reality transfigured by the medium of film. And the world on film, that transfigured reality, is "a moving image of skepticism," as Stanley Cavell puts it in "More of *The World Viewed*." In the world on film, the separateness of past and present, inviolable in the one existing world, is overcome or transcended. Once *How Green Was My Valley* puts its nostalgic prologue behind it, the past is indistinguishable from the present. Is it that the past has become the present? Or has the present become the past, as Cavell more or less suggests when he observes that as we experience movies, our powerlessness to affect the events unfolding within the projected world makes those events akin (he adds, "mythically") to the past, not the present?

When we're feeling nostalgic, the past reveals itself to possess a precious beauty that we feel is missing from our lives in the present. But what makes the past appear so precious cannot be separated from the warm glow with which our nostalgia infuses it, nor from our knowledge that it *is* the past, that it is unreachable except in memory. We are powerless to alter the past, just as we are powerless to intervene in the events of a film. When we are in a nostalgic mood, what we most cherish about our memories is the sense they fleetingly allow us—is this illusory?—of being transported to a time when a world of possibilities for the future that have since become closed off were still open to us, as if we had regained the lost freedom of childhood. But this glimpse of freedom comes at a price. When the nostalgic mood itself slips into the past, it brings home to us that the past cannot become the present again. The freedom of childhood is gone forever. Nostalgia cannot bring it back. We cannot become free by living in the past, if only because the past is fixed; unalterable. It permits us no freedom. The only way to become free of the past is to acknowledge that it *is* past.

Knowledge of the irrecoverable loss of something precious to us is what makes nostalgia possible. Then how can nostalgia be pleasurable? That there's nothing we can do to make the past the present, nor anything we can do to keep the present from slipping into the past, is a key to the fact that nostalgia gives us pleasure—a bittersweet pleasure akin to what the Japanese call *mono no aware*, the exquisite sense of the fleetingness of all beauty. What separates the past from the present is only time itself, the inevitability of change, the condition of our finitude as human beings—a condition for which no one is to blame. When we are feeling nostalgic, we look back at our past freed from the shame, guilt, and rancor that haunts so much of our lives that we are often fearful of remembering the past.

Most recent American movies are addressed, rhetorically, to viewers who assume—as do nearly all my students these days, and I don't doubt they are more or less representative of the film industry's target audience—that there *is* no past that is "relatable" (a word my students favor); that being "relatable," like being "engaging" (another word they favor), is an attribute or quality some films simply possess and others do not (as if establishing a meaningful relationship with a film were entirely up to the film, in no way up to the viewer); and that only movies they call "modern," not ones they call "old," can be "relatable"; that "modern" movies are more *advanced*, ideologically as well as technologically, than "old" movies; that "modern" viewers (as so many moviegoers now assume they are) are likewise more advanced, in their ways of thinking, than viewers could possibly have been in the era of "old" movies. What gives young people today so much as the idea that they are justified in making such assumptions? How has it come about that they think this way?—I will return to these questions.

"Modern" movies assert their *presentness* (to use a term from *The World Viewed* in a way slightly different from Cavell's use of it), deny any connection or indebtedness to the past. This is what distinguishes them from "old" movies, in my students' estimation—what *makes* them "modern," what locates them in the present, not the past. Because the latest version of *A Star Is Born* (Bradley Cooper, 2018), for example, is a "modern" movie—if in doubt, experience it in buttocks-battering Dolby—my students assume that it is "relatable" and that the 1937, 1954, and 1976 versions—"old" movies all—are not. I, too, find the 2018 version, elevated by a performance by Lady Gaga that is beyond praise, as was Judy Garland's performance in George Cukor's 1954 version, to be the pick of the litter. But, in my experience, the recent film's "modernness," its assertion of its presentness, weakens as well as strengthens the film, which goes to excessive lengths to provide the Bradley Cooper character with a backstory that is meant to make him "relatable" by providing a psychological explanation for his behavior, an explanation of how his troubled past caused him to become the way he is in the present, caused him to be vulnerable to becoming a victim of addiction (understood, in present-day terms, as a disease, not a character flaw or moral failing)—a backstory that serves to deny him any blame, any responsibility for his actions, any moral agency. (That's what makes him "relatable," I suppose.)

A Disney "reboot" like *Frozen* (2013) asserts its presentness by its CGI technology, which deprives the film of the visual beauty that cel animation enabled "old" Disney films, like *Bambi* (1942), to achieve—a beauty that appeals to "the tender emotions and feelings." It also asserts its own presentness by declaring its political correctness. I am thinking, above all, of the moment Kristoff, handsome but a lowly ice seller, kisses Princess Anna and his kiss fails to save her, although in the film's world true love is supposed to have the power to melt a frozen heart. As it turns out, the love of Elsa, Anna's sister, possesses that power. Evidently, her love is stronger, truer, than Kristoff's, even though we are given no reason to believe that there is anything lacking in Kristoff's love, or that his love is in some way untrue. Kristoff is not a fairy tale Prince Charming, which is what villainous Hans appears to be; he's a regular guy whose actions, not his looks or class, prove him a worthy suitor. It is only the film's need to assert its presentness that anoints the sisterly Elsa, not the sincere suitor Kristoff, with the power to save Anna.

Perhaps it takes the wisdom of King Solomon—rarer than ever these days, it seems—to know that if two people's love is true, one's love can't be truer, or stronger, than that of the other. The movie ends with Anna and Kristoff together. But if their love for each other is somehow lesser than the love between Anna and Elsa, their relationship must fall short of a real marriage, as judged by the standard of what Cavell, in *Pursuits of Happiness*, dubbed "comedies of remarriage"—or by *my* standard. Ideologically, *Frozen* is not more advanced than "old" movies. It's hogwash—politically correct, but hogwash nonetheless. And, while I'm feeling churlish—or am I just feeling nostalgic?—I will add that I would say the same about more than a few of the most critically acclaimed recent movies. (*Get Out*, I'm thinking of you.)

In Terrence Malick's *The Tree of Life* (2011), a rare "modern" film that is steeped in nostalgia and utterly devoid of false "nostalgia," some of the protagonist's memories reflect experiences common to any number of American boys of his (and Malick's) generation, such as doing unspeakable things to frogs or chasing DDT trucks. Yet even these collective memories, the film makes clear, are ultimately personal, particular to this one individual (and perhaps to Malick). I can feel nostalgia only for my own past—the only past I can look back on, the past only I can look back on. Nostalgia is *always* personal, although in some incidents it makes me nostalgic to think about the companions I was with at the time. Reminiscing together can be a special pleasure. (These days, my sister Judy is the only person left with whom I can reminisce about childhood.)

As Cavell put it in the opening sentence of *The World Viewed*, memories of movies are strand over strand with memories of our lives. Or at least they *were*. It makes me nostalgic to remember the first time I watched *Casablanca* with Jerry and Richie, my two best friends in high school, on the television in Jerry's family's basement. But when my students, fifty years from now, reminisce about the past—if the practice of reminiscing, one of the perks of being human, hasn't died out by then—will memories of *Tron Legacy*, say, or of any of the metastasizing mass of Marvel films (the politically correct *Black Panther* is not really more advanced than the others), be strand over strand with memories of their lives? I don't see how they could be. In asserting their presentness, such blockbusters may be "relatable" to impersonal media clichés, but not to the human reality of their viewers' lives. As I've said, most of my students assume that their experience of watching "modern" films has nothing to do with "living in the past." Too often, it also has nothing to do with living in the present.

∽

Watching home movies my father shot a lifetime ago makes me feel nostalgic—even those taken before I was born—because it was my father who took them, enabling them to be a link to my memories of him. But Hollywood movies, past or present, are different. No matter how strongly I may identify with their characters—whatever exactly that means—their experiences are not my experiences. Hollywood movies do not address their viewers *personally*. The events in the world projected on the screen, however analogous they may be to incidents in my own life, are not *my* past. Our outsideness to the film's world, our powerlessness to intervene in the events unfolding before our eyes, makes those events, as I've said, akin to the past, not the present. But insofar as the events projected on the screen are unfolding before our eyes, they aren't really *anyone's* past. They're our present. Then how can we be nostalgic when we're watching these events?

To be nostalgic is to look back at the past from a position in the present, with a bittersweet awareness of the barrier-that-is-no-real-barrier that keeps past and present apart, keeps the past from becoming the present again, makes the past unreachable except in memory. But the medium of film makes the impossible not only possible, but *necessary*. The projected world fuses past and present, in effect, overcoming or transcending their separation. When I'm watching a movie, I can't feel nostalgia for the events in the film's world for two reasons. First, these events are unfolding before my eyes and are thus, temporally, akin to the present, not the past, to me. Second, my outsideness to the film's world, my powerlessness to alter events in that world, makes those events, temporally, akin to the past to me—but it is not *my* past, and nostalgia is always personal.

When we're watching a movie of any period, it thus can't be nostalgia as such that we feel. But because it is through no fault of our own that we are outside the film's world, just as it is no fault of our own that we are outside the world of the past, we can watch movies, as we can think of the past when we're feeling nostalgic, freed from shame, guilt, and rancor. Movies can engender a pleasure analogous or comparable to nostalgia—a wistful longing, a bittersweet awareness that something we wish were possible—to be free of responsibility for our lives in the world—is in reality impossible. We cannot escape from our lives by seeking asylum within the world of a film, just as we cannot escape our responsibilities in the one existing world by living in the past.

∽

It was in the 1940s, it would seem, that nostalgia became prominent in Hollywood movies. Not coincidentally, it was in the 1940s, too, that flashbacks became prevalent. Innumerable Hollywood movies of the 1940s and early 1950s begin with a voiceover spoken by the film's protagonist, who begins to tell the story—before a flashback takes over—of the events in his life that led him to the crossroads at which he now finds himself. In *Double Indemnity* (Billy Wilder, 1944), and in the innumerable postwar film noirs for which it served as a prototype, the mood cast by the protagonist's opening voiceover is anything but nostalgic. He is unburdening himself of memories that are painful, not pleasurable, to him. In *How Green Was My Valley*, nostalgia enters the picture not through its setting in the past—although a recent television dramatic series like *The Americans*, for example, may be set in the 1980s, it never permits us even a moment of nostalgia for the period—but by mediating our experience of the events of the film by Huw's nostalgic voiceover. Nostalgia isn't contagious. Huw's nostalgia doesn't make us long for the lost past he longs for. His once green valley isn't our valley. (My Brooklyn has no valleys, much less green ones.) But his nostalgic mood casts a lingering spell over us, a spell sustained and deepened by Arthur Miller's luminous cinematography, which accords the film's world a precious visual beauty—as if it were bathed in nostalgia's warm glow.

Because the events in a film's world don't in themselves make us nostalgic, and because nostalgia is always personal, nostalgia only enters even "overtly nostalgic" movies by way of the mood cast by *someone's* nostalgia. Hence it was common for movies of the 1940s and early 1950s, even those that didn't incorporate a nostalgic voiceover or embed the body of the narrative within a flashback, to dwell empathetically on the nostalgia of characters whose longing for the past, longing for the present to be like the past, colors our experience of the film as a whole. It is possible for the "someone" whose nostalgia bathes a film in a warm glow to be not a character but, rather, the film's director. Watching *The Quiet Man* (John Ford, 1952), for example, it is John Ford's wistful longing for Ireland—a mythical Ireland, to be sure, not the world of his own childhood—not that of the John Wayne character, that colors our mood as we watch the film.

Is Hollywood of the 1940s and early 1950s my once green Welsh valley? No. For me, Hollywood's "Golden Age" was the period between 1934, the year of *It Happened One Night*, and the entrance of the United States into World War II—the New Deal era in which what Cavell in later writings calls "Emersonian perfectionism" was ascendant in Hollywood, as it was in America. In *The "I" of the Camera*, I sketched a view of the history of the popular American cinema that envisions the shift from prewar to postwar Hollywood less as a liberation from constricting generic formulas than as an intensifying repression of the philosophical and moral outlook that had granted American movies their combination of extreme popularity and extreme seriousness. What Emerson called "the wonderful way of *life*" is a matter of looking ahead, taking steps to create a more perfect future, not looking back and longing to return to the past; the past needs to be acknowledged so that we can move on, walking in the direction of what Emerson calls "the unattained but attainable self" and moving America a step closer to becoming the "more perfect union" that was—is—its promise. Thus, it was no accident, I believe, that the repression of the Emersonian outlook of prewar Hollywood coincided with Hollywood's turn toward nostalgia. Increasingly, in the 1940s and early 1950s, nostalgia in Hollywood movies was a manifestation Hollywood's willful forgetfulness, its self-imposed amnesia, about its own past.

More than today, remakes were a staple of Hollywood production in the 1940s and early 1950s. Almost without exception—Douglas Sirk's 1950s remakes of fine John Stahl melodramas of the 1930s are exceptions, as is Hitchcock's 1956 remake of his own *The Man Who Knew Too Much*—these remakes are, aesthetically and intellectually, glaringly inferior to the originals. *In the Good Old Summertime* (Peter Fitzgerald, 1949), a musical remake of Ernst Lubitsch's great *The Shop Around the Corner* (1940), is a case in point. Judy Garland throws herself into her role, as always, and belts out the mediocre songs she was given as if they were worthy of her, but the screenplay (by the husband-and-wife team of Albert Hackett and Frances Goodrich, whose credits include the utterly brilliant screenplays for *The Thin*

Man [W. S. Van Dyke, 1934] and three of its sequels) censors out every bit of the seriousness, the dark undertones, in Samson Raphaelson's original screenplay. For example, the remake replaces the emotionally profound subplot in the original, which climaxes in the shattering suicide attempt by Mr. Matuschek (Frank Morgan) with an aggressively silly—no, *stupid*—storyline revolving around the boss's Stradivarius violin. And in shifting the setting from (what was then) present-day Budapest, at the historical moment Europe as we knew it was facing an existential threat from Nazi aggression, to a conventionally "nostalgic" turn-of-the-century, post-Exposition Chicago, the remake loses the original's palpable conviction that something great and important was at stake in the fate of its characters; lost, in short, is the original film's Emersonian philosophical and moral outlook. And the way *In the Good Old Summertime* trivializes *Shop Around the Corner* is all too typical of remakes of the 1940s and early 1950s. As befits a musical of the period, *In the Good Old Summertime* is in color and, in that respect, it declares its newness—but it does not, in the fashion of *La La Land*, say, assert a presentness, a "modern-ness," that claims a complete break with the past. Because all its departures from *Shop Around the Corner* so obviously weaken *In the Good Old Summertime*, its commercial success was contingent on the public not remembering, or not knowing, or not appreciating, the original's aesthetic and moral achievement.

The same can be said of such other musicals of the period as *One Sunday Afternoon* (Raoul Walsh, 1948), a vastly inferior remake of *The Strawberry Blonde* (1941), also directed by Walsh, which, like *The Philadelphia Story*, feels more like a 1930s film than a 1940s film. *The Strawberry Blonde* was itself a remake—a remake superior to the 1933 original, also called "One Sunday Afternoon" (Stephen Roberts, 1933), a fine film but a box-office flop, early 1930s audiences evidently not being receptive to its brand of nostalgia. Another example is *High Society* (Charles Walters, 1956), a disposable remake—even with Grace Kelly and a turn by Louis Armstrong—of *The Philadelphia Story*. None of these inferior remakes would have had a chance to be hits—indeed, they wouldn't have been made—if it weren't for America's inability or unwillingness to acknowledge the value—or the values—of prewar Hollywood movies underwritten by what Cavell calls "Emersonian perfectionism." Such remakes not only exploited that amnesia; they actively reinforced it.

So did the genre that Kathrina Glitre, in *Hollywood Romantic Comedy: States of the Union, 1934–1965* (2006) dubbed the "career woman comedies" that effectively shoved prewar-style comedies of remarriage off American screens during the wartime and postwar years. Films such as *Woman of the Year* (1942), *Take a Letter, Darling* (1942), *She Wouldn't Say Yes* (1945), and *Without Reservations* (1946), among numerous others, share many of the features of comedies of remarriage, but with a glaring ideological difference. The "career woman," in learning to embrace her nature as a woman, embraces domesticity and motherhood. Even *Woman of the Year*, the best of these films, humiliates its "leading lady"—played by Katharine Hepburn, no less—and does so not to help her open her eyes to her longing to become more fully human, as in *The Philadelphia Story*, but to shame her into conforming to an essentialist view as to which forms of life are, and which are not, appropriate for women, as if for a woman to pursue a career is for her to deny her true nature, to deny what makes a woman a woman. A woman's nature is best expressed, these films assert, by marrying a man and embracing the life of domesticity and motherhood that "naturally" follows marriage. Comedies of remarriage revolve around a woman's quest for selfhood. Career woman comedies mock that quest. And they promote a fake nostalgia for a prewar America that never existed—a place where women knew and happily embraced their God-given roles. To find these films funny, audiences had to forget that prewar America was *not* such a place, as Hollywood movies of the period make clear.

Postwar film noirs reinforced that collective amnesia in a different way—not by turning toward nostalgia, but by turning away from it. The typical film noir protagonist has no past, at least no past in any way relevant to his present identity—or to the film. When he begins to relate, in voiceover, the events that led him to his present dire situation, it is as if, apart from the particular events he is remembering, his past doesn't exist for him—or for us. Remembering these events doesn't make him feel nostalgic; it causes him pain, not pleasure. Although *Double Indemnity* served in many ways as a prototype for postwar film noirs, it is different in this regard, in that its protagonist Walter Neff (Fred MacMurray) has a past very much relevant to his present identity—and to the film. Walter has worked for so many years at the same insurance company, with Barton Keyes (Edward G. Robinson) his boss and mentor, that his past is his present, his present his past. He doesn't long nostalgically for a past when his life was better; he dreams of a better future. His is a romantic dream, a dream of romance—or is it sex?—he has in common with his fellow film noir protagonists—a dream of a future he tries to make real by betraying his past, in the person of Keyes.

Keyes no more feels nostalgia for the past than Walter does. Rather than longing for a lost past, he is committed in his work to keeping alive, in the present, what he values about the past, a time when insurance companies were run by men for whom insurance was not a business but a calling, as it still is for Keyes. And he believes that Walter feels the same way and will keep alive his dream for the future. But when Keyes reveals to Walter that he had overheard the confession he had recorded—illustrated by the flashback that makes up the body of the film—Walter knows that his dream of a better future is dead. And Keyes knows, from Walter's confession, that his own dream for the future is dead, too.

Meet Me in St. Louis (Vincent Minnelli, 1944) is set in a turn-of-the-century St. Louis in the year leading up to the World's Fair that epitomized an America embracing the changes the new century was ringing in. But the film used its nostalgic setting to make a point about the (then) present—the moment in the Second World when the outcome was no longer seriously in doubt. Esther (Judy Garland), fearful of the family's impending move to New York City, wants her life to stay as it is. Like the daughter played by the great Setsuko Hara in Yasujiro Ozu's *Late Spring* (1949), another film about a society in the throes of change, Esther is, as we might put it, nostalgic for the present. She doesn't want her life to change. But life *is* change. In the end, the family stays in St. Louis but, as the film's ending at the

World's Fair affirms, Esther now accepts the necessity of change and looks to the future in a spirit of adventure. So, too, must America, the film is saying, when the Second World War is over, as it soon will be, and we are faced with the challenges of making America a more perfect union and helping to create a better world.

Double Indemnity was made the same year as *Meet Me in St. Louis*, and is also mindful of the time soon to come when America will no longer be at war. But unlike *Meet Me in St. Louis* and Minnelli's 1953 musical *The Band Wagon*, which find no real conflict between looking toward the future and acknowledging the past, and tap into the spirit of prewar Hollywood movies, Wilder's film is less hopeful. At the end of *Double Indemnity*, the future doesn't belong either to Walter or to Keyes, who are both dreamers. The future belongs to young Lola and her boyfriend, neither one a dreamer, who have a shot at a decent life together, and to the "heartless so-and-so's," to borrow a term from *Sunset Blvd.*, like Keyes's boss, representative of a new breed of insurance company executive for whom the corporation's bottom line and his own ego are the only things that matter and who will be running the new America, an America unfit for dreamers.

Meet Me in St. Louis makes it clear where Minnelli stands, but in *Double Indemnity* Wilder is more ambivalent. He does not take a stand, as Minnelli does, against forgetting—repressing—the philosophical and moral outlook of prewar Hollywood. And to not take a stand is to participate in that repression, whether one likes it or not. In prophesying a postwar America in which dreamers have no place and "heartless so-and-so's" hold the power, Wilder holds back from casting his lot with the dreamers.

Double Indemnity focuses on the insurance business, in which men like Keyes, who have actuarial tables running through their veins, were giving way to corporate types for whom insurance is a commodity like any other. But Wilder's *Sunset Blvd.* (1950) is explicitly about Hollywood, as are a number of other Hollywood movies of the period, the most famous of which is *Singin' in the Rain* (Stanley Donen and Gene Kelly, 1951).

Singin' in the Rain is another film whose popularity depended on audiences not knowing, or remembering, or appreciating, what prewar Hollywood movies, or the America to which they gave expression, was really like. Set in Hollywood during the transition from silent films to talkies, the film looks back at the period with affection, but not with nostalgia. It encourages viewers to feel that they would rather live in the present than live in such a past, even if they could. *Singin' in the Rain* depicts American movies of that period, and the men who made them and their audiences, as hopelessly naïve, childlike at best and childish at worst, granting license to the film's viewers to believe—indeed, to take for granted—that they are superior to viewers of that period and entitled to look down on them.

In a direct way, then, *Singin' in the Rain* at once exploits, promotes, and furthers America's deepening repression of the Emersonian worldview that had been ascendant in prewar Hollywood. In a more indirect and complex way, so does *Sunset Blvd.*, Wilder's most brilliant film, in which a clash between Hollywood's present and its past has tragic consequences. One might have expected Wilder to depict the film business the way *Double Indemnity* depicted the insurance business, focusing on the parallels between them. After all, the moguls who built and ran the Hollywood studios lived and breathed movies, not crunching numbers, but they were, like Keyes, representatives of a dying breed, inevitably to be replaced—as has largely really happened—by corporate types for whom movies were no different from any other product.

But *Sunset Blvd.* refrains from implying that present-day Hollywood is run by "heartless so-and-so's," reserving that category for reporters and paparazzi, who are also the target of Wilder's scorn in *Ace in the Hole* (1951). When Norma (Gloria Swanson) has Max (Erich von Stroheim), her chauffeur and driver (and, as he later confides to Joe, her first husband and the once-famous film director whose films made her the great star of the silent screen that she was), drives her to Paramount so she can have a face-to-face conversation with Cecil B. DeMille, many of the older studio hands warmly welcome her back. And DeMille himself, depicted as a bridge spanning the chasm between Norma's Hollywood and present-day Hollywood, treats Norma with kindness and respect. To be sure, the film makes clear that there are people at Hollywood studios like Cole, who keeps phoning Norma not because the studio is interested in the script that Joe (William Holden) is writing with her but because the studio wants to rent her luxurious car, a rare antique. But as long as there are still dreamers like DeMille in Hollywood, *Sunset Blvd.* implies, the film business isn't heartless. It's the newspapers, magazines, radio, and the new medium, television, that have made America forget Norma; Hollywood hasn't forgotten her. But that doesn't mean that Hollywood would produce her comeback film.

Key to the film's depiction of present-day Hollywood is the character of Betty Schaefer (Nancy Olson), a young script reader for Paramount, whose harsh critique of one of Joe's scripts dooms it at the studio. She is looking for scripts that have something to say, not slick, derivative rehashes of material that was never meaningful to begin with. Later, though, she finds "potential" in a scene in another of Joe's scripts. He is being "kept" by Norma and working with her on what he knows is a hopelessly bad, old-fashioned screenplay that she is deluding herself into believing will secure her comeback as a star. At the same time, Joe is secretly meeting with Betty, who helps him to complete a screenplay that develops what she sees as his potential as a writer—and who falls in love with him, even though she is engaged to another man.

Sunset Blvd. gives us no reason to question Betty's acuity as a script reader, hence no reason to doubt that, judged by Hollywood's criteria at the time, the screenplay Joe writes under her tutelage would make a successful film. But if that screenplay were to be produced, the resulting film would not—could not—be a film like *Sunset Blvd.*, which has at its heart Joe's perverse, conflicted, tormented relationship with Norma, a relationship that ultimately dooms him—a relationship that is utterly beyond Betty's ken. Like young Lola in *Double Indemnity*, Betty is not a dreamer, but in the world of *Sunset Blvd.*, she has a future in the film business. Joe does not. He is doomed.

We cannot simply assume that Wilder's film is asserting its superiority to the kind of movie Betty believes in, the kind *Hollywood* believed in at the time, as *Sunset Blvd.* would have it, since Betty's boss evidently respects her judgment as a reader. Betty believes that films should have something to say, but she wouldn't know what to make of a film that says what *Sunset Blvd.* has to say. In any case, there's a major discrepancy between 1950s Hollywood as it really was and Hollywood as *Sunset Blvd.* depicts it. In the real Hollywood, *Sunset Blvd.* was a smash hit that won three Academy Awards and was nominated for eight more. In the film's America, audiences of the time wouldn't have loved *Sunset Blvd.* And in the film's Hollywood, Paramount wouldn't have made a film like *Sunset Blvd.* Betty would have nixed it.

And there's an even more telling discrepancy between Hollywood's glorious past and Hollywood's past as the film invokes it. Start with Erich von Stroheim, who was nominated for a "Best Supporting Actor" Oscar for his performance as Max. True, we learn that Max was the director whose movies made Norma a star, but that knowledge doesn't keep us from seeing him as almost as delusional, almost as pathetic, as Norma. The film offers no sense of von Stroheim's stature within film history. For the vast majority of viewers in 1950, von Stroheim would be, at most, a famous name, but no more. *Sunset Blvd.* doesn't help this great artist to be remembered; it helps him and his art to be forgotten.

The same is true of Gloria Swanson, also nominated for an Oscar. She certainly threw herself into her performance, mugging and grimacing and chewing up the scenery in ways appropriate for the histrionic character she was playing, but which convey no sense of the down-to-earth quality and delicate comic touch that were Swanson's calling cards as a star in the silent cinema and beyond. Rather, the film turns the fifty-one-year-old actress, still possessing star quality, into a grotesque and demented old hag, anticipating the way *What Ever Happened to Baby Jane* (Robert Aldrich, 1962) was to treat Bette Davis and Joan Crawford, both then only in their mid-fifties.

There is one passage in *Sunset Blvd.* that allows us a glimpse of Swanson at the height of her stardom. It occurs when Norma makes Joe watch one of her old movies and the sequence incorporates four brief shots—glorious, but far from representative of her "screen persona"—from *Queen Kelly* (1929), the ill-fated, never completed von Stroheim film in which Swanson was cast—or miscast—against type as an innocent convent girl, which she definitely was not.

These shots are followed by a shot of Norma in the present, backlit by the projector beam and framed as if this, too, were a shot from the silent film. Clearly, this shot isn't meant to suggest that Norma—or Swanson—is as radiant as ever. Rather, it underscores how pathetic Norma has become—and how monstrous. This effect is enhanced by the fact that in this shot she is screaming hysterically, like an angry and bitter madwoman, a grotesque contrast with her eloquent silence in the shots from the film-within-the-film. In what kind of world could such a woman ever have been a beloved movie star?

When in their initial awkward encounter Joe first recognizes Norma and says, "You used to be big," she replies, in one of the film's most famous lines, "I *am* big; it's the pictures that got small." To viewers who know the silent cinema at its glorious best, most movies of 1950—even those "with something to say" that Betty would have greenlighted—*are* small. But *Sunset Blvd.* is addressed primarily to viewers who, thanks to what I have been calling America's collective amnesia about Hollywood's past, an amnesia increasingly exploited and reinforced by Hollywood movies themselves, do not know, or do not remember, or do not appreciate, how "big," in Norma's sense, Hollywood pictures once were. And Wilder's film forgoes the opportunity to help awaken America from this amnesia. Rather, like *Singin' in the Rain*, it reinforces the assumption, endorsed in innumerable ways at the time by American culture as a whole, that the film's viewers are superior to viewers of the past and entitled to look down on them.

How "big," then, is *Sunset Blvd.*? "Bigger" than most—not all—movies of the period, I would say. But not as "big" as the most glorious silent films, numerous films of the prewar years, or any of the films Cavell writes about in *Pursuits of Happiness*, *Contesting Tears*, and *Cities of Words*. At the climactic moment of *Sunset Blvd.*, the film fails a crucial test. To quote the fine synopsis of the film on the Internet Movie Database, written by an anonymous contributor:

> The scene returns to the opening. Still narrating, Joe expresses fear over how Norma will be unable to cope with the disgrace, and the discovery of how forgotten she truly is. By the time the police arrive, however, she has completely broken with reality and slipped into a delusional state of mind, thinking the news cameras are set up for a film shoot. To help the police coax her down the stairs, Max plays along with her hallucination that she is on the set of her new film. He verbally sets up the scene for her, and cries, "Action!" Norma dramatically descends her grand staircase. Joe, in voiceover, remarks that life has decided to spare her the pain of that discovery, and that "the dream she had clung to so desperately had enfolded her." Norma makes a short speech declaring how happy she is to be back making a film, and delivers the film's most famous line: "All right, Mr. DeMille, I'm ready for my close-up."

As if taking pity on Norma, Wilder withholds, rather than presents, the pathetic close-up we imagine the newsreel cameras to be "really" capturing, thus distancing itself from the "heartless so-and-so's" taking photos for the sensational news story about the once great movie star's emotional breakdown. But Wilder also withholds, rather than presents, the glorious close-up that Norma, in her madness, imagines Max's camera to be capturing—a transcendent close-up with the power to restore her to stardom and assure her immortality. In so doing, Wilder is renouncing, or forgoing, his own camera's capacity for revelation. Unwilling or unable to reveal Gloria Swanson, who is Norma Desmond incarnate—older but still capable of being radiant onscreen—to be, in the words of Muggsy in *The Lady Eve*, "positively the

same dame" as the camera revealed her to be in her silent movies, Wilder's camera symbolically obliterates her image.

I will close these rather rambling remarks by returning, as promised, to the questions: What gives young people today so much as an idea that they are justified in making such pejorative assumptions about the moviegoers who came before them? How has it come about that they think this way?

In lieu of anything like a full answer to these questions, I will simply suggest that the 1940s and early 1950s was the period in which the idea took shape within American popular culture, and began to be cultivated by Hollywood movies themselves, that present-day moviegoers, and the movies made for them, are incomparably more advanced than they used to be—the assumption that is almost universal among my students today. It may be a long way from *Singin' in the Rain* to today's box office hits, but it's down a slippery slope.

12

Cavell on Film, Television, and Opera (excerpts)

Writing about movies has been strand over strand with Stanley Cavell's philosophical life, from *The World Viewed*, published between *Must We Mean What We Say?* and *The Senses of Walden*, to *Pursuits of Happiness: The Hollywood Comedy of Remarriage*, a companion piece to *The Claim of Reason*, to *Contesting Tears: Hollywood Melodramas of the Unknown Woman*, his most recent book about film. Film has also figured importantly in numerous other essays and occasional pieces. And he has also reflected, philosophically, on other artistic media, such as television and opera, which bear an intimate relationship to film.

Cavell is the only major philosopher in the English-speaking world who has made the subject of film a central part of his work. Yet to many philosophers, the relation of his writings on film to his explicitly philosophical writings remains perplexing; and within the field of film study, the potential usefulness of philosophy—as he understands and practices it—remains generally unrecognized. It has long been one of Cavell's guiding intuitions that a marriage between philosophy and film is not only possible but also necessary. Over the years, his vision of such a marriage has been an unfailing source of inspiration for me, and for the authors whose writings about film I find most fruitful. What follows is an account, at times unavoidably sketchy, of some of the leading thoughts in Cavell's three books about film, in "The Fact of Television," and in "Opera and the Lease of Voice" (chapter 3 of his 1994 book *A Pitch of Philosophy*) and the recent "Opera in and as Film." By providing such an account, I hope to illuminate, above all, why Cavell aspires to a marriage between philosophy and film, and how he achieves it.

This essay was published in Richard Eldridge, ed., *Stanley Cavell* (Cambridge: Cambridge University Press, 2003), 218–38. Reprinted with permission. For the present volume, I have omitted the sections on film, which substantially overlap with several other essays in the book.

"The Fact of Television"

In 1981, the year in which *Pursuits of Happiness* was published, Cavell was asked to contribute to an issue of *Daedalus* devoted to television. The resulting essay, "The Fact of Television,"[1] begins by observing that television, like the electric light, the automobile, and the telephone, has "conquered." Yet there has been a lack of critical attention to television too complete to be a simple lack of interest; it is a refusal of interest. The disapproval of television evinced in educated circles suggests a fear of television for which Cavell has heard no credible explanation.

Although he, too, has sometimes felt such disapproval of television, Cavell cannot accept the view that the medium has not yet come of age, or that it is inherently impoverished. He argues that television's "poverty" lies in our failure to grasp "what the medium is for, what constitutes its powers and its treasures" (Cavell 1990, 2).

It is a guiding thesis of *The World Viewed* that major films are those in which the medium is most richly or deeply revealed. In the case of television, however, revelation of the medium is not primarily the business of the individual work, this episode of *I Love Lucy*, but of *I Love Lucy* itself, the program as such, the *format*.

Most film critics think of a genre as a category whose criteria for membership are as unproblematic as the exemplification of a serial in its episodes. Cavell calls this way of thinking about genre "genre-as-cycle" and contrasts it with *Pursuits of Happiness*'s way of thinking about genre, which he here calls "genre-as-medium."

When a remarriage comedy diverges from the other members of the genre, it compensates for this divergence. The genre undergoes revision as new members introduce new points of compensation. When other films negate a feature shared by a genre's members, those films comprise an "adjacent" genre. Compensation and negation, however, are not pertinent to genre-as-cycle, or to the serial–episode relationship. The episodes of a sitcom exemplify a format that can unproblematically be called a formula. But in a film genre like the remarriage comedy, "what you might call the formula, or what in *Pursuits of Happiness* I call the myth, is itself under investigation, or generation, by the instances" (Cavell 1984, 248).

If film as an artistic medium is primarily revealed by a genre-member mode of composition, and television primarily by a serial-episode mode, this difference must reflect a difference between their material bases. *The World Viewed* characterizes film's material basis—what it is apart from which there would be nothing to call a movie, as without color on a delimited two-dimensional support there would be

---

1. "The Fact of Television" was first published in *Daedalus* in the fall of 1982, republished in *Themes Out of School: Events and Causes* (San Francisco: North Point Press, 1984), and later reprinted in William Rothman, ed., *Cavell on Film* (Albany: State University of New York Press, 2005). Of course, in this age of digital technologies, television, as it was when Cavell wrote the piece, has undergone such drastic changes that we might say that it no longer exists. Nonetheless, as I hope my discussion here shows, Cavell's brilliant essay retains its relevance and contains much food for thought.

nothing to call a painting—as a "succession of automatic world projections" (Cavell 1979b, 72). "The Fact of Television" characterizes television's material basis as a "current of simultaneous event receptions" (Cavell 1984, 251). The intimacy of the difference between these formulations registers Cavell's sense of the intimacy of the difference, hence affinity, between film and television. This intimacy is reflected, as well, in the difference, and affinity, between viewing, the mode of perception that film calls for, and "monitoring," the mode that television calls for. ("The mysterious sets or visual fields, in our houses, for our private lives, are to be seen not as receivers, but as monitors" [Cavell 1984, 252].) Television's successful formats—the sitcoms, game shows, sports, talk shows, news, weather reports, specials, and so on—are, he argues, "revelations (acknowledgments) of the conditions of monitoring" (Cavell 1984, 252).

A notable feature of such formats, Cavell notes, is the amount of talk they incorporate.

> This is an important reason . . . for the . . . descriptions of television as providing "company." But what does this talk signify, how does it in particular signify that one is not alone; or anyway, that being alone is not unbearable? Partly . . . this is a function of the simultaneity of the medium, or of the fact that at any time it might be live and that there is no sensuous distinction between the live and the repeat, or the replay; the others are there, if not shut in this room, still caught at this time. One is receiving or monitoring them, like callers. (Cavell 1984, 253)

Each format for talk incorporates opportunities for improvisation, hence preserves the quality of the live that seemed threatened when television switched to primarily taped production. The exchanges of pleasantries that have become common on news shows, for example, demonstrate that "our news is still something that can humanly be responded to, in particular, responded to by the human power of improvisation." But, Cavell wonders, what news "may be so terrible that we will accept such mediocre evidence of this power as reassuring?" (Cavell 1984, 256).

Before answering this question, Cavell ponders the fact that television monitors the uneventful (the repeated, the repetitive, the utterly familiar) as readily as it monitors events. Each television format can be thought of as "the establishing of a stable condition punctuated by repeated crises or events that are not developments of the situation requiring a single resolution, but intrusions or emergencies . . . each of which runs a natural course and thereupon rejoins the realm of the uneventful" (Cavell 1984, 258). A tree branch, viewed on a movie screen, is in the world, *The World Viewed* argues; the world is in the viewed branch, in "that thing now, in the frame of nature" (Cavell 1979b, 200). But the world is not in a monitored branch, "whose movement is now either an event (if, say, you are watching for a sign of wind) or a mark of the uneventful (a sign that the change has not yet come)" (Cavell 1984, 259). But, again, what change would be so fearful that we turn to television for reassurance that it has not yet happened?

Television's "conquering" began just after the Second World War, Cavell reminds us—just after "the discovery of concentration camps and the atomic bomb," the discovery of "the literal possibility that human life . . . is willing to destroy itself." And it continued with "the decline of our cities and the increasing fear of walking out at night, producing the present world of shut-ins." What television monitors is often a setting of the shut-in, "a reference line of normality or banality so insistent as to suggest that what is shut out, that suspicion whose entry we would at all costs guard against, must be as monstrous as . . . the death of the normal, of the familiar as such" (Cavell 1984, 266–67).

Cavell's guiding hypothesis, then, is that we seek the "company" of television to "overcome the anxiety of the intuition the medium embodies" (Cavell 1984, 267). The fear large or pervasive enough to account for our fear of television, according to his hypothesis, is the fear that what television monitors is "the growing uninhabitability of the world, the irreversible pollution of the earth, a fear displaced from the world onto its monitor." This is a hypothesis the concluding paragraph of *The World Viewed* prepares for by intimating that the breaking of our "natural relation" to movies may spell the end of film's ability to reassure us that nature will survive our turning away from nature, from our own nature.

The real possibility that nature will not survive us, hence that our anxiety may well have a fitting object, in Cavell's view, does not rule out a "psychological etiology for our anxiety, say in guilt, toward that same object." And he ends "The Fact of Television" with an expression of guarded optimism.

> Who knows?—if the monitor picked up on better talk, and probed for intelligible connections and for beauty among its events, it might alleviate our paralysis, our pride in adaptation, our addiction to a solemn destiny, sufficiently to help us allow ourselves to do something intelligent about its cause. (Cavell 1984, 268)

That would mean, to paraphrase the ending of *The World Viewed*, that the present judgment upon us is not yet the last.

Contesting Tears

"Is it true in movies that virtue is always rewarded and vice vanquished?" Cavell asks in *The World Viewed* (1979b, 48). Someone who draws the morals of movies too hastily might assume that movies condemn the "woman outside" for luring men to stray. Yet such a woman is "outside" because she rejects a marriage that would deny her nature, not because she is unworthy. It is a crucial datum in pondering the morals of movies that in films it is a moral imperative to pursue happiness.

What Cavell discovered, in discovering this, is the depth of film's commitment to what his later writings call "moral perfectionism," and "Emersonian perfectionism" in particular. In *The World Viewed*, it is already a central theme that there is a serious moral philosophy internal to the stories that movies are forever telling. In *Pursuits of Happiness*, Cavell does not yet use the term "perfectionism," but that way of thinking about morality is an implicit subject throughout. It becomes an explicit (if still unnamed) subject when he invokes Matthew Arnold's idea of the "best self" existing in each of us.

> More natures are curious about their best self than one might imagine, and this curiosity Arnold calls the pursuit of perfection. "Natures with this bent," Arnold says, "emerge in all classes . . . and this bent tends to take them out of their class, and to make their distinguishing characteristic not their Barbarianism or their Philistinism, but their humanity." (Cavell 1982, 157–58)

Cavell understands perfectionism not as a theory of morality but as "a dimension or tradition of the moral life." His goal is to develop what he calls "an open-ended thematics" of perfectionism, not a theory or a definition of the idea. "That there is no closed list of features that constitute perfectionism follows from conceiving of perfectionism as . . . embodied in a set of texts spanning the range of Western culture" (Cavell 1990, 4).

Henrik Ibsen's *A Doll's House* is one. Nora's "imagination of her future, in leaving, turns on her sense of her need for education whose power of transformation presents itself to her as the chance to become human. In Emerson's terms, this is moving to claim one's humanness . . . , to follow the unattained" (Cavell 1990, 115). Moral perfectionism is as internal to comedies of remarriage as it is to Shakespeare's late romances, Emerson's and Thoreau's writings, *A Doll's House*, and to *Pursuits of Happiness* itself.

Cavell most fully develops the theme of a woman's rejecting marriage in order to "follow the unattained" in *Contesting Tears: The Hollywood Melodrama of the Unknown Woman*. In the films that the book "reads"—*Gaslight*, *Letter from an Unknown Woman*, *Stella Dallas*, and *Now, Voyager*—the woman seeks fulfillment outside marriage. Marriage is not reconceived and provisionally affirmed; marriage is overcome or transcended. In comedies of remarriage, it is the man who claims the woman; he needs only prodding, while she needs to undergo a metamorphosis; and the woman's mother is absent, her absence underscored both by her father's role and by the fact that the woman herself is not a mother. In short, the creation of the woman is the business of men, even though the creation is that of the so-called new woman, the woman of equality—as if there were a taint of villainy inherent in maleness.

"This so to speak prepares the genre for its inner relation to melodrama," Cavell remarks in the introduction to *Contesting Tears*, where he points out that *Pursuits of Happiness* predicted the discovery of a genre of melodrama adjacent to the comedy of remarriage in which that genre's themes are negated in a way that hinges on the threats of misunderstanding and violence that dog the happiness of the comedies (Cavell 1996, 5).

> It is a claim central to *Contesting Tears* that the genre therein called the Melodrama of the Unknown Woman is derived from the remarriage comedy by the mechanism of negation. For example, in these melodramas the woman's father, or another older man (it may be her husband), is not on the side of her desire but on the side of law, and her mother is always present (or her search for or loss of or competition with a mother is always present), and she is always shown as a mother (or her relation to a child is explicit). In the comedies the past is open, shared, a recurring topic of fun, no doubt somewhat ambiguous; but in melodramas the past is frozen, mysterious, with topics forbidden and isolating. Again, whereas in remarriage comedy the action of the narration moves from a setting in a big city to conclude in a place outside the city, a place of perspective, in melodramas of unknownness the action returns to and concludes in a place from which it began or in which it has climaxed, a place of abandonment or transcendence. (Cavell 1996, 5–6)

In both genres, the woman's goal is creation. But in the melodramas, she "achieves existence (or fails to), apart from or beyond satisfaction by marriage (of a certain kind)" (Cavell 1996, 5–6). The "something" in her language that negates the conversation of the pair in remarriage comedy is irony. Irony isolates the woman. That is a reason Cavell characterizes the genre as studying the unknownness of the woman.

The World Viewed claims that the most significant films are those that most significantly reveal the medium of film. *Pursuits of Happiness* develops this claim by arguing that comedies of remarriage reveal film's power of transfiguration, as expressed in the woman's suffering creation, where this refers both to the character's metamorphosis and to the transfiguration of the flesh-and-blood actress into projections of herself on a screen.

Contesting Tears develops the claim further by reflecting on the fact that the melodrama of the unknown woman registers the woman's transfiguration less by revealing her body than by tracing its changes of costume and circumstance. Whatever role such a woman chooses to play at a given moment, in playing that role she declares that her identity is not fixed. And she declares that in this role she is, and is not, herself, with that "flair for theater, that theater of flair, exaggeration it may be thought, call it melodrama," that these films require of their leading women. Their star quality resides not in their beauty but in their "dangerous wish for perfect expressiveness," their flair for declaring their distinctness, their freedom, their human existence (Cavell 1996, 128).

This last point registers Cavell's intuition that these women emblematize the fact about human identity that "every single description of the self that is true is false, is, in a word, or a name, ironic" (Cavell 1996, 134). So "one may take the subject of the genre of the unknown woman as the irony of human identity as such" (134–35).

In his introduction to *Contesting Tears*, Cavell describes both the remarriage comedies and the melodramas of unknownness as "working out the problematic of self-reliance and conformity as established in the founding American thinking of Emerson and of Thoreau" (Cavell 1996, 9). In an earlier essay—"Being Odd, Getting Even"—Cavell linked Emerson's idea of self-reliance with the self-consciousness demanded in the Cartesian *cogito ergo sum* ("I think, therefore I am"), Descartes's answer to philosophical skepticism (Cavell 1988, 10). Emerson's essays, "Being Odd, Getting Even" suggests, propose a new proof of human existence. And Cavell's essay linked Emerson's revision of Descartes's *cogito* to melodramas like *Now, Voyager*.

The melodrama of the unknown woman, *Contesting Tears* argues, is an expression of a stage in the development of the skeptical problematic at which the theatricalization of the self becomes the main proof of the self's existence. And the book develops this suggestion further by linking the invention of film with the simultaneous emergence of psychoanalysis. While men in movies primarily appear in contexts of mutual competition and of uniform or communal efforts, as *The World Viewed* had argued, it is individual women who have given film its depth. It is as if the role of women in originating both psychoanalysis and film—in psychoanalysis as suffering subjects, in film as subjects of the camera—reveals that by the turn of the twentieth century, psychic reality—the existence of minds—had become believable primarily in its feminine aspect.

A melodramatic star such as Bette Davis reveals the affinity between film's interest in the "difference of women" and that of psychoanalysis, insofar as she "taps a genius" for that expressiveness

> in which Breuer and Freud, in their *Studies in Hysteria*, first encountered the reality of the unconscious, the reality of the human mind as what is unconscious to itself, and encountered first in the suffering of women; a reality whose expression they determined as essentially theatrical, a theatricality of the body as such. (Cavell 1996, 105)

In remarriage comedies, the woman's happiness depends on her choosing the right man to educate her. The melodrama of the unknown woman, too, presses the question of the woman's interest in knowledge, but "within their mood of heavy irony, since her knowledge becomes the object—as prize or as victim—of the man's fantasy, who seeks to share its secrets (*Now, Voyager*), to be ratified by it (*Letter from an Unknown Woman*), to escape it (*Stella Dallas*), or to destroy it (*Gaslight*), where each objective is (generically) reflected in the others" (Cavell 1996, 13–14).

In remarriage comedies, the "war between the sexes" is a struggle for mutual recognition. In the melodrama of the unknown woman, the man struggles against recognizing the woman. The woman's struggle, as Cavell puts it, "is to understand why recognition by the man has not happened or has been denied or has become irrelevant, hence may be thought of as a struggle or argument (with herself) over her gender" (Cavell 1996, 30). In each melodrama, the woman, unrecognized, isolated, is torn not simply over the conflicting desires or demands between being a mother and being a woman, say, but over questions "as to what a mother does and what a woman is, what a mother has to teach, what a woman has to learn, whether her talent is for work or rather for the appreciation of work, whether romance is agreeable or marriage is refusable, how far idiosyncrasy is manageable" (Cavell 1996, 198).

Early and late in "Stella's Taste," the final essay in *Contesting Tears*, there are moments of autobiography, as we might put it, that construct a bridge to *A Pitch of Philosophy*, Cavell's next book, where he takes autobiographical expression further than ever before in his work. In the first of these moments in "Stella's Taste," he writes, "When my mother asked for an opinion from my father and me about a new garment or ornament she had on, a characteristic form she gave her question was, 'Too Stella Dallas?'" He adds, "I knew even then, so I seem always to have remembered it, that my mother's reference to Stella Dallas was not to a figure from whom she was entirely dissociating herself" (Cavell 1996, 200).

In this passage, Cavell all but explicitly declares that his reading is guided by an intuition of his mother's, by his intuition of her intuition, his recollection of knowing, even as a boy, that she identified with Stella. The (male) voice that "speaks" in this writing is attuned to his mother's way of thinking—and to Stella's.

Thus, this moment of autobiography is pertinent to what Cavell calls a "presiding question" in his writing about film melodramas and comedies: whether a male voice such as his is "well taken into a conversation with women" on the issues he finds raised in such films (Cavell 1996, 200). This question of the pertinence of the male voice, as it emerges in "Stella's Taste," is a way of articulating the subject of *Stella Dallas* (and hence of each of the melodramas of the unknown woman).

In his reading of *Now, Voyager* in *Contesting Tears*, Cavell anticipates—and contests—the charge that he appropriates, or wishes to appropriate, Charlotte Vale's voice. But why is it only now, writing the book's final chapter, that he finds himself "willing to confront more systematically the provenance and pertinence" of his own voice in these matters? (Cavell 1996, 200). He attributes this willingness, or links it, to his "willingness for taking further steps in autobiographical expression"—the mode in which, he is increasingly convinced, his "encounter with feminism must take place."

It is in the context of his questioning of the pertinence of his own (male) voice in thinking about *Stella Dallas* and his linking of this question to the question of autobiography's pertinence to philosophy, that Cavell mounts a devastating brief against the theory—it is all but a dogma within academic film study—that "film seems to be the perfect agent for generalizing the Freudian fetishistic process, extending it to the masculine gender as such—a generalizing ratified somehow by taking on at the same time a Marxian development of the idea of the universal commodification (in capitalist society) of women" (Cavell 1996, 207–08).

According to this theory, Freud's concept of fetishism explains Stella's victimization and utter lack of self-knowledge and confirms an essentially male stake in viewing a film such as *Stella Dallas*. Cavell contests this fashionable theory, first, because the film itself contests a fixed view of the woman's victimization, and second, because "the details of Freud's description of fetishization do not account for what becomes of things and persons on film" (Cavell 1996, 209).

The second of Cavell's arguments amounts to the idea that film assaults human perception at a more primitive level than the work of fetishizing suggests; that film's enforcement of passiveness, or say victimization, together with its animation of the world, entertains a region not of invitation or fascination primarily to the masculine nor even, yet perhaps closer, to the feminine, but primarily to the infantile, before the establishment of human gender (Cavell 1996, 209).

Up to this point in *Contesting Tears*, Cavell has formulated the subject of the melodrama of the unknown woman as the irony of human identity, and alternatively, as the question of the pertinence of the male voice. Having now insisted on the dimension of infantilization in the viewing of film, and in light of *Stella Dallas*'s closing (Stella looks through the lit window behind which her daughter's wedding is taking place, then turns away from that window and jauntily walks toward us), Cavell further articulates the genre's subject: "Stella's gaze before the window, as the camera gives it to us, is the mother's, backed by mothers; and as Stella turns to walk toward us, her gaze, transforming itself, looms toward us, as if the screen is looming, its gaze just turned away, always to be searched for (For what it grants; for what it wants.)" (Cavell 1996, 216). Thus, Cavell formulates the field of feminine communication effected by the film screen, as allegorized in *Stella Dallas* by the screen-within-the-screen of the lit window, as "the search for the mother's gaze—the responsiveness of her face—in view of its loss, or of threatened separation from it" (Cavell 1996, 214–15).

The ratifying of Stella's reliance on her own judgment, her own taste—of her "taking on the thinking of her own existence, the announcing of her *cogito ergo sum*"—happens without her yet knowing who this thinker is who is proving her existence (as in Descartes's presenting of the *cogito*, which happens without his yet knowing who he is). This woman's "walk toward us, as if the screen becomes her gaze, is allegorized as the presenting or creating of a star." As an interpretation of stardom, it "is the negation, in advance so to speak, of a theory of the star as fetish. This star, call her Barbara Stanwyck, is without obvious beauty or glamour/ But she has a future." Not only do we now know that this woman was to become the star of *The Lady Eve*, "she is presented here as a star (the camera showing her that particular insatiable interest in her every action and reaction), which entails the promise of return, of unpredictable incarnation" (two features of stardom singled out in *The World Viewed*) (Cavell 1996, 219).

What is Cavell's stake in insisting that Stella is self-knowing, that she puts herself in the way of a transfiguration that he associates with the teachings of Emerson and Thoreau? "The Emersonianism of the films I have written about as genres," Cavell writes, "depict human beings as on a kind of journey . . . from what he means by conformity to what he means by self-reliance; which comes to saying (so I have claimed) a journey, or path, or step, from haunting the world to existing in it; which may be expressed as the asserting of one's *cogito ergo sum* . . . , call it the power to think for oneself, to judge the world, to acquire—as Nora puts it at the end of *A Doll's House*—one's own experience of the world." For Cavell, acceptance of this woman's transfiguration would provide "a certain verification of this philosophy, hence, of philosophy as such," as he cares about it most (Cavell 1996, 220).

Cavell's publication of this reading, in the company of the other readings in *Contesting Tears*, can thus be seen as part of his effort "to preserve that philosophy, or rather to show that it is preserved, is in existence, in effect, in works of lasting public power—world-famous, world-favored films—while the Emerson text itself, so to speak, is repressed in the public it helped to found" (Cavell 1996, 220). Yet these films too are repressed in that public. For all their popularity, their thinking remains unhonored and unsung (if hardly unwept).

> I assume that movies have played a role in American culture different from their role in other cultures, and more particularly that this difference is a function of the absence in America of the European edifice of philosophy. And since I assume further that American culture has been no less ambitious, craved no less to think about itself, than the most ambitious European culture, I assume further still that . . . . American film at its best participates in this Western cultural ambition of self-thought or self-invention that presents itself in the absence of the Western edifice of philosophy, so that on these shores film has the following peculiar economy: it has the space, and the cultural pressure, to satisfy the craving for thought, the ambition of a talented culture to examine itself publicly; but its public lacks the means to grasp this thought as such for the very reason that it naturally or historically lacks that edifice of philosophy within which to grasp it. (Cavell 1996, 72)

Like the difficulty of grasping a remarriage comedy, the difficulty of grasping a melodrama of the unknown woman, the difficulty of assessing its thought, is the same as the difficulty of assessing everyday experience. Again, this difficulty calls for philosophy's capacity to receive inspiration for taking thought from the conditions that oppose thought. "Nothing much to me would be worth trying to understand" about a melodrama like *Now, Voyager*, Cavell writes, "unless one cares for it, cares to find words for it that seem to capture its power of feeling and intelligence, in such a way as to understand why we who have caused it (for whom it was made) have also rejected it, why we wish it both into and out of existence" (Cavell 1996, 117–18).

In the introduction to *Contesting Tears*, Cavell observes that despite most critics' condescension, *Stella Dallas*, *Gaslight*, *Letter from an Unknown Woman*, and *Now, Voyager* are worthy companions of the remarriage comedies. "They are of course less ingratiating," he adds. Indeed, they "are so often the reverse of ingratiating that it becomes painful to go on studying them. A compensating profit of instruction must be high for the experience to be justified" (Cavell 1996, 7). The readings in *Contesting Tears* are worthy companions of those in *Pursuits of Happiness*, too, although they are less ingratiating, are indeed at times painful to go on studying. In each melodrama, the woman suffers an isolation so extreme "as to portray and partake of madness," as Cavell puts it, "a state of utter incommunicability, as before the possession of speech" (Cavell 1996, 16).

A woman like Stella has a capacity to judge the world as a place fit to live in or not, a power that comes from the extremity of her isolation. But isolation so extreme is painful to think about. Less painful is to deny this woman's power of judgment and fixate on the idea that she is pathetically oblivious to her own inadequacy. Not shrinking from the pain of thinking about Stella's thinking, and calling on us too to face that pain, Cavell's writing seeks to undo that fixation, to understand what is of value in such a woman, in such a film. What, then, is the "compensating profit of instruction" in the understanding, the pain, that is to be exchanged in the writing, and reading, of *Contesting Tears*? This is a question that guides Cavell's reading of *Stella Dallas* and, indeed, the book as a whole.

In *Contesting Tears*, Cavell writes about these melodramas "as though the woman's demand for a voice, for a language, for attention to, and the power to enforce attention to, her own subjectivity, say to her difference of existence, is expressible as a response to an Emersonian demand for thinking" (Cavell 1996, 220). What authorizes this supposition is his interpretation of Emerson's authorship "as itself responding to his sense of the right to such a demand as already voiced on the feminine side, requiring a sense of thinking as reception . . . , and as a bearing of pain, which the masculine in philosophy would avoid. To overcome this avoidance is essential to Emerson's hopes for bringing an American difference to philosophy" (Cavell 1996, 221). Overcoming this avoidance, bearing the pain, is no less essential to Cavell's hope to inherit philosophy, as received, and founded, in America by Emerson's (and Thoreau's) writings—essential to his hope to preserve that philosophy, or rather to show that it is preserved, that it does exist.

Cavell ends the body of his reading of *Stella Dallas* by posing three questions. Does Emerson's idea of the feminine philosophical demand serve to prefigure the "difference of women" that film lives on? Does it articulate or blur the difference between the denial to women of political expression and a man's melancholy sense of his own inexpressiveness? And is the relation of the Emersonian and the feminine demand for a language of one's own a topic for a serious conversation between women and men? "It is . . . the logic of human intimacy, or separateness," Cavell writes, "that to exchange understanding with another is to share pain with that other, and that to take pleasure from another is to extend that pleasure. And what reason is there to enter this logic in a particular case?" (Cavell 1996, 221).

"No reason," Cavell concludes, with an echo of Wittgenstein. ("Reasons come to an end somewhere.") This invocation of Wittgenstein is followed by a typographical break and, in turn, by a page-long coda, another autobiographical moment, which brings *Contesting Tears* to a close with a haunting image of isolation and pain. (*The World Viewed*, too, ends with an invocation of Wittgenstein, a typographical break, and a haunting image of isolation and pain.)

> Now I am recognizing another of my mother's moods, somehow associated with the demand to be noticed (perhaps with its explicit failure, perhaps with the implicit failure of having to demand it). She named this state migraine—definable, I assumed, assume, through her therapy for it, which was to play the piano, in a darkened room (her eyes were

evidently affected), alone. (I am interpreting the mood, after the fact, from the few times I came home from school late in the afternoon to enter such a scene.) What music she would play then (mostly Chopin, her favorite composer), and how she became a prominent pianist in Atlanta, then largely a culturally unprominent part of the country, and hence what her relation was to a certain stardom, and to her refusal of the chance for more, are pertinent matters. They must concern the relation between searching for the mother's gaze and being subjected to her moods. Hence, they concern the question of what her moods are subjected to, to what scenes of inheritance. Was the music filling the loss or impoverishment of a self-abandoned ego (so speaking to melancholia), or was it remembering, say recounting, the origins, hence losses, of her reception of her glamorous talent for the world of music (so speaking of dispossession and nostalgia)? Music, moods, worlds, abandonment, subjection, dispossession—of course, we are speaking of melodrama. (Cavell 1996, 222)

Suffering the pain that she called "migraine," Cavell's mother was playing the piano, alone, in a dark room, on the occasions when her son happened to "enter" such a scene. Are we to think of the writing of *Contesting Tears* as comparable to her piano playing on those occasions? No less than hers, the extremity of his isolation can be glimpsed in these words. But so can the way, in all his writings, philosophy overcomes or transcends that isolation, finds its way to locate its author within the world, enables him to suffer creation, to perform his own *cogito ergo sum*.

"Opera and the Lease of Voice"

In the melodrama of the unknown woman, *Contesting Tears* argues, the woman's flair for theater declares her dangerous wish for perfect expressiveness. Chapter 4 ("Postscript") stresses the condition that, Cavell finds, grounds the desire to express all, "the terror of absolute inexpressiveness, suffocation, which at the same time reveals itself as a terror of absolute expressiveness, unconditioned exposure." These extreme states of voicelessness, he observes, "are the polar states expressed in the woman's voice in opera" (Cavell 1994, 43). With such remarks, *Contesting Tears* provides another bridge to *A Pitch of Philosophy*, in whose culminating third chapter ("Opera and the Lease of Voice") opera joins film as a central subject of Cavell's philosophical reflections.

Early in "Opera and the Lease of Voice," as in "Stella's Taste," Cavell introduces a moment of autobiography. ("Twice I remember asking my mother, 'Why are operas always sad?' She tried no answer, but she was someone to whom I could direct such a perplexity" [Cavell 1994, 132]). Cavell goes on, responding continuously to the answer that another woman, Catherine Clément, gives in her book *Opera, or the Undoing of Women*. Her answer is, in effect, that "opera is about the death of women, and about the singing of women, and can be seen to be about the fact that women die because they sing" (112). In "Opera and the Lease of Voice," Cavell puts together what he characterizes as "jigsaw shapes of intuition" about what it is that singing in opera betokens, about what operas have revealed about the powers, and limitations, of the human capacity to raise the voice (155).

As Cavell had argued in *The World Viewed*, the medium of film reverses the priority that theater gives to character over actor. On film, as he puts it in "Opera and the Lease of Voice," the actor is the subject of the camera, emphasizing that this actor could (have) become other characters (that is, emphasizing the potentiality in human existence, the self's journeying), as opposed to theater's emphasizing that this character could (will) accept other actors (that is, emphasizing the fatedness in human existence, the self's finality or typicality at each step of the journey). In opera the relative emphasis of singer and role seems undecidable in these terms, indeed unimportant beside the fact of the new conception it introduces of the relation between voice and body, a relation in which not this character and this actor are embodied in each other but in which this voice is located in—one might say disembodied within—this figure, this double, this person, this persona, this singer, whose voice is essentially unaffected by the role (Cavell 1994, 137).

The fact that Claudio Monteverdi's *Orfeo*, the first masterpiece of the new medium, is a rendering of the story of Orpheus and Eurydice "is almost too good to be true," Cavell writes, "in establishing the myth of opera, of its origins—the story of the power of music, epitomized as the act of singing" (Cavell 1994, 139). That Orpheus ultimately looks back and fails to redeem Eurydice for their everyday life together also makes this a story of the limitations of the powers of the voice. The question of whether this story, transformed by the medium of opera, is to end happily or sadly—a bone of contention between Monteverdi and Alessandro Striggio, his librettist—provides us with two interpretations of the expressive capacity of singing: "ecstasy over the absolute success of its expressiveness in recalling the world, as if bringing it back to life; melancholia over its inability to sustain the world, which may be put as an expression of the absolute inexpressiveness of the voice, of its failure to make itself heard, to become intelligible—evidently a mad state" (Cavell 1994, 140).

The first operas, contemporaneous with Shakespeare's major tragedies, marked the crisis of expression engendered by the traumatic discovery that human language no longer assured connection with reality, a discovery that Descartes articulated philosophically in the radical skepticism that heralds modern philosophy. As Cavell observes, a "Cartesian intuition of the absolute metaphysical difference between mind and body, together with the twin Cartesian intuition of an undefined intimacy between just this body and only this spirit, appears to describe conditions of the possibility of opera" (Cavell 1994, 138).

The significance of the fact that assaults on marriage are narrative figures for skepticism, Cavell adds, has been a central theme of his own writings since his studies of film and Shakespearean theater prepared him to recognize marriage, in "its idea of mutual, diurnal devotion," as a "figure for the ordinary" (Cavell 1994, 141). Before going on to consider instances of such marriage, or their avoidance, in opera, Cavell develops further the concept or condition of the voice raised in song by relating the duality of the singer—the figure of the human as both necessarily and accidentally body and spirit—to the Orpheus myth, which pictures this doubleness as the spanning of two worlds. "I am counting here on an intuition of opera which . . . I imagine as widely shared," Cavell writes, as the "intervention or supervening of music into the world as revelatory of a realm of significance that either transcends our ordinary realm of experience or reveals ours under transfiguration" (142).

In Kant, the passage from one realm to the other—perfectionism's upward path of education—takes place in every moral judgment, "every time you stop to think, to ask yourself your way." Perfectionism's journey "has been cut short—to a half-step—you see how to take it, where it lies, or you do not." Emerson's contribution to perfectionism, which Cavell finds decisive, is that "the moral constraint upon the human can be expressed not, as for Kant, as an obligation, but as an attraction. . . . Attraction as the basis of commitment—as paradoxical as taking narcissism as the basis of altruism" (Cavell 1994, 143).

These "Kantian/Emersonian modifications of perfectionism," Cavell suggests, help to explain why in most operas—*The Magic Flute* is exceptional—there is little elaboration of perfectionist journeys. "Rather we may leap," he writes in one of his inimitable sweeping summations,

> from a judgment of the world as unreal, or alien, to an encompassing sense of another realm flush with this one, into which there is no good reason we do not or cannot step, unless opera works out the reasons. Such a view will take singing to express the sense of being pressed or stretched between worlds—one in which to be seen, the roughly familiar world of the philosophers, and one from which to be heard, one to which one releases or abandons one's spirit (perhaps to call upon it, as Donna Anna and Donna Elvira do; perhaps to forgo it, as the Marschallin and as Violetta do; perhaps to prepare for it, as Desdemona and Brünhilde do; perhaps to identify it with this one, as Carmen does), and which recedes when the breath of the song ends. (Cavell 1994, 144)

Cavell's image of singing as abandonment draws on Emerson's use of the concept of abandonment "to name a spiritual achievement (of, let us say, neutrality) expressed as a willingness to depart from all settled habitation, all conformity of meaning" (Cavell 1994, 144). Cavell's passage also draws on Thoreau's idea that being beside oneself in a sane sense—the dictionary definition of ecstasy—is that which proves one's humanity. Thus, singing is to be understood "as an irrupting of a new perspective of the self to itself," an "ecstatic response whose self-reflectiveness suggests the structure of narcissism" (145).

In bringing the concept of narcissism into play in order to articulate a double intuition of singing as ecstasy and as abandonment, Cavell is registering the sense that singing is at once primitive (the "spectacular vocality of opera in its aspect as orality") and sophisticated ("in its aspect as exposure or display, sometimes named seductiveness") (Cavell 1994, 144–45).

With regard to singing's "sophisticated" aspect, Cavell argues that if we reformulate Clément's "women die because they sing" to say that "women's singing exposes them to death, the use of the voice to the stopping of the voice," we have also to ask what the woman's singing exposes (Cavell 1994, 145–46). Cavell's answer: It exposes her as thinking, as performing the *cogito*, the thinking that confirms existence. Thus, it exposes her to "the power of those who do not want her to think," do not "want autonomous proof of her existence." He cites, as opera's "most precise, appropriately defiant, announcement of the fact of thinking as narcissism, of its exposure in or as defiant seduction," Carmen's "Seguidilla" ("Don José: I forbid you to speak to me; Carmen: I didn't speak to you . . . I sing for my own pleasure / And I'm thinking . . . It's surely not forbidden to think") (146).

On the "primitive" side, too, Cavell argues, the woman's singing reveals her intellectual agency, her autonomous existence. Cavell cites Freud's claim that judgment has an oral, primitive basis in the original process by which the ego took things in or expelled them, which "amounts to the judgment of the world, as affirmation or negation in each utterance or outcry." In the fact that singing, in its breaths, "incessantly draws in and lets out the world as such," Cavell suggests, lies a hint as to why opera "so attunes itself to moments of separation, as if this is the founding trauma of human experience" (Cavell 1994, 148).

According to Kant, ideas that assure us of a moral universe (for example, the moral law and freedom of the will), like concepts that assure us of a world (substance and causation, for example), are grounded in the a priori conditions of reason or of understanding. Aesthetic judgments, by contrast, claim universal assent upon no more than subjective grounds. "The feeling," as Cavell puts it, "comes first (Emerson calls it 'Intuition'), and its putative grounded concepts (the reasons for the judgment) await determination in . . . acts of criticism (Emerson calls them 'Tuitions')" (Cavell 1994, 149).

Inverting Kant's formulation that aesthetic judgments rest on "the predication of pleasure without a concept," Cavell proposes, in one of his own most elegant—and provocative—formulations, that "we think of the voice in opera as a judgment of the world on the basis of, called forth by, pain beyond a concept." Opera cannot demand that we "take events as hard, and as far, as Desdemona, Aida, Verdi's Leonora, Carmen, Brünhilde, the Marschallin, and Melisande do." But opera can make it irresistible for us "to listen and to understand beyond explanation" (Cavell 1994, 149).

In the remainder of the chapter, Cavell provides sketches—each a gem of criticism—of moments from five masterpieces of opera: Mozart's *Marriage of Figaro*, Verdi's *Il Trovatore* (and the Marx Brothers' grand burlesque and homage of *Il Trovatore* in *A Night at the Opera*) and *La Traviata*, Wagner's *Gotterdammerung*, and Debussy's *Pelléas and Mélisande*). In each of these instances, Cavell finds that the woman, in singing, is, like Carmen, performing the thinking that confirms existence. Not coincidentally, each woman is thinking specifically about "how to manage a marriage, that is, how to keep its idea intact; or how to avoid one" (Cavell 1994, 151–52). Cavell's task, in these critical sketches, is not to explain the woman's thinking, to enable us to know what she knows; it is to listen to her voice, and to his own voice, in order to enable a certain kind of understanding—an understanding beyond explanation—to take place.

Cavell concludes "Opera and the Lease of Voice," and with it *A Pitch of Philosophy*, by posing questions that seamlessly join his concerns with the powers and limitations of the human voice, with philosophy's capacity to receive inspiration for taking thought from the conditions that oppose thought, and with the provenance and pertinence of his own voice.

> Am I ready to vow . . . that I know my mother's mother tongue of music to be also mine? The hills are different ones now, but the world is, I'm glad to say, the same when I have to catch my breath at such promises. Are they mine? Have I, throughout these pages, been asking anything else? (Cavell 1994, 169)

As in his reading of *Stella Dallas*, Cavell stakes this writing's right to exist on his own claim to a double inheritance—the inheritance of Emerson's (and Thoreau's) thinking, which itself claimed to inherit philosophy for America, and the inheritance of his own mother's powers of thought—whether they be called, as they are here, her "mother tongue of music" or, as in "Stella's Taste," "migraine."

"Opera in and as Film"

When Cavell proposes, in "Opera and the Lease of Voice," that we think of the voice in opera as a judgment of the world on the basis of, called forth by, pain beyond a concept, the question of what is comic in opera briefly comes up. "Perhaps it lies in affirming the thought that whatever causes happiness does not occur in the absence of pain, or the thought that the world may for a moment be found to escape judgment altogether," Cavell observes (1994, 149). Marking a region for future exploration, he adds, "Such thoughts would suggest the affinity of Shakespearean romance with opera." Hence, they would also suggest opera's affinity with the comedy of remarriage, as well as with the melodrama of the unknown woman. That is, they would suggest opera's affinity with film itself—an affinity so intimate, Cavell testifies, that it has led him in recent years to experiment with the thought that what has happened to opera, as an institution, is that it has "transformed itself into film, that film is, or was, our opera" (136).

As I was in the midst of composing the present remarks, Stanley Cavell sent me his as-yet-unpublished "Opera in and as Film." This latest of his ongoing reflections on film, on opera, and on the thought-provoking intimacy of their relationship, does indeed explore this region of the affinity between opera and film.

This relatively brief piece begins by considering a moment in Frank Capra's *Mr. Deeds Goes to Town* (1936) that Cavell reads as confessing "film's sense of affinity with opera, often expressed in an impulse of competition with opera." Assaulted by proposals for ways to spend his newly inherited fortune, Mr. Deeds (Gary Cooper) is informed that he has been elected to replace his uncle as president of the Friends of the Opera, "an immediate privilege of which is for him to continue his uncle's annual subsidy of the opera's productions." Told that ticket sales alone cannot support opera productions, he replies, "Well, maybe you're putting on the wrong kind of shows."

Clearly, Cavell remarks, "the film is proposing that the right kind of shows for them to put on are movies, and that it is offering itself as an example." And, he adds, "I read the moment of Mr. Deeds refusing a use of his inheritance to support opera as an argument of film with opera generally about its claims to inherit from opera the flame that preserves the human need, on pain of madness of melancholy, for conviction in its expressions of passion."

It is, Cavell observes, an old argument. During the silent era, Cecil B. DeMille made a film of the opera *Carmen*—one of several silent *Carmens*, in fact—"as if to declare that the expressive powers of silent film are equal to those of music." Evidently, DeMille believed in film "to the extent that he would measure its power of, let's say, the magnification of gesture against music's intensification of speech in making human expression lucid." (Already in *Pursuits of Happiness*, Cavell drew a connection between film and opera by suggesting that the camera's powers of transfiguration, and music's, are in some sense comparable.)

Tracing some of the vicissitudes of the old argument, Cavell distinguishes three principal ways, citing several instances of each category, in which "opera and film have intervened in one another." Films can (1) realize the full performance of an opera, or (2) incorporate an opera essentially within the film's structure, or (3) briefly or intermittently allude to an opera. Cavell dwells, in particular, on two instances of the second of these categories: *Moonstruck* (1989, directed by Norman Jewison) in connection with *La Bohème*, and *Meeting Venus* (1991, by the Hungarian director Istvan Szabo) in connection with *Tannhäuser*. In these instances, as Cavell puts it, "the competition between an opera and the attention given it in the film becomes an essential part of the film's subject, or, to say it otherwise, to understand the relation between the film and the opera to which it weds itself sets the primary task of the understanding of the film."

We will not trace here the sublime details of Cavell's accounts of these films but will only note one salient point that repeatedly resurfaces: the tendency for film, when it incorporates an opera into its narrative, to seek to divert death—as if, by providing "a happier, anyway less fatal, ending," the film is declaring its own powers in opposition to those of opera.

Cavell develops this point further when he concludes "Opera in and as Film" by remarking on a reference to *Tannhäuser* that occurs near the end of Preston Sturges's *The Lady Eve*, one of the definitive remarriage comedies.

If we may say that *Tannhäuser* is about two women who are opposite aspects of a woman's powers of love, where each promises redemption and each proves to be lethal, then we may say that *The Lady Eve* is about one woman who plays two opposite women, each of whom pretends, and cons the man into believing, that she is not someone she is. Sturges's insertion of a "Wagnerian air of profundity," which has become so famous that it "inevitably risks banality," is designed, Cavell suggests, to shock us into posing necessary and banal questions, such as how this man can fail to recognize the woman he has married as the woman he loves, or loved. One answer is that while she has not disguised her appearance, she has altered her voice. But what about that voice does the man not want to hear? Presumably, that he has placed his desire where he loves and that this singular woman is prepared to become an object for him in whom the currents of passion and tenderness can flow together. Such is this woman's proposal of the reality that prolongs life, or say, that diverts death. It is frightening, but the man allows himself foolishness and bewilderment and persistence enough perhaps to welcome it. But why is it through film that such a proposal becomes credible? Cavell answers this last question, or draws its moral, by responding to Mr. Deeds's dismissal of opera in favor of film.

> Even when what were called movie palaces increasingly put on what he implied were the right shows, those picture shows more often than perhaps they knew demanded an inheritance from opera's transcendent powers of communication. And some of us find that movies have proven to deserve that inheritance. To think about the conditions of the inheritance, principally about how film's reflections provide further chapters of opera's life, has afforded me pleasures to which, while strength lasts, I see no end. (Cavell and Rothman 2005, 318)

Viewed from *The Lady Eve*'s philosophical perspective, the old argument between film and opera, like the far older "war between the sexes," takes on the aspect of the "meet and happy" conversation in a marriage worth having. Film's proposal of the reality that prolongs life, or diverts death, is frightening, but Cavell allows himself enough "foolishness and bewilderment and persistence" to welcome it. Affirming the thought that whatever causes happiness does not occur in the absence of pain, and the kindred thought that the world may for a moment be found to escape judgment altogether, Cavell expresses his passionate belief in opera's, and film's, transcendent powers of communication, and in philosophy's expressive powers as well. This happy session of thought about opera and film and philosophy ends not with a haunting image of isolation and pain, but with a tribute to the pleasure—and the promise of pleasure—that makes philosophy so humanly attractive.

13

Cavell on Film

Introduction

As Stanley Cavell observes in the preface to *Contesting Tears: The Hollywood Melodrama of the Unknown Woman*, Cavell's thinking about film has for four decades been bound up with his thinking "about most of whatever else I have been thinking about in what may be called philosophy or literature" (Cavell 1996, xi, xii). *Contesting Tears*, which follows *The World Viewed: Reflections on the Ontology of Film* and *Pursuits of Happiness: The Hollywood Comedy of Remarriage*, is his third book devoted to the subject of film—or third and a half, if we include the four essays on film (and one on television and its relation to film) in his 1984 collection of essays, *Themes Out of School: Events and Causes*. In addition to these books, he has also written a substantial number of other pieces on film, in a diversity of formats—some ambitious theoretical statements, others apparently slight "occasional pieces"—originally presented to a diversity of audiences, on a diversity of occasions, and published, if at all, in a diversity of journals and anthologies.

In "The World as Things: Collecting Thoughts on Collecting," one of the writings in *Cavell on Film*, Cavell remarks that "every collection requires an idea," and that this "seems to presage the fact that collections carry narratives with them, ones presumably telling the point of the gathering, the source and adventure of it" (Cavell and Rothman 2005, 243). The idea of *Cavell on Film* is, quite simply, to gather under one cover all of Cavell's writings on film—including the material from *Themes Out of School*—other than *The World Viewed*, *Pursuits of Happiness*, and *Contesting Tears*.

From William Rothman, ed., *Cavell on Film* (Albany: State University of New York Press, 2005), ix–xxvii. Reprinted with permission.

The idea of such a collection is mine, not Cavell's. He has never chosen to isolate his writings on film in this way. Nor is it my wish, in putting together this collection, to suggest that the writings it contains, or Cavell's writings on film in general, stand apart in their concerns, or in their status as philosophy, from his other writings.

In his preface to *Themes Out of School*, Cavell finds value in the fact that it is a collection of writings that address a wide range of topics. By focusing on only one topic, film *Cavell on Film* may seem to be denying that value. But that is not really the case. The pieces in this volume address "classical" Hollywood movies, such as *Mr. Deeds Goes to Town*, *North by Northwest*, *Now, Voyager*, and the films of Fred Astaire and the Marx Brothers; European "art" films, such as Ingmar Bergman's *Smiles of a Summer Night* and Luis Buñuel's *Belle de Jour*; documentaries, such as Robert Gardner's *Forest of Bliss*; iconoclastic modernist films, such as Dušan Makavejev's *Sweet Movie* and Jean-Luc Godard's *Hail Mary*; postmodernist films, such as Andy Warhol's *Sleep* and *Empire*; and popular movies as current, or nearly current, as, among others, *The Matrix*, *American Beauty*, and *Being John Malkovich*. The writings gathered in this collection also address film's relation to other media, such as television, opera, and the novels of Jane Austen and George Eliot. They address the ideas and intellectual procedures of such major thinkers as Nietzsche, Freud, Heidegger, Wittgenstein, Austin, and, on this side of the Atlantic, Emerson and Thoreau. And they address, philosophically, such diverse concepts as medium, art, language, reading, collecting, and America, to name only a few. Taken together, these writings reflect, and illuminate, the major developments that have marked Cavell's thinking over the years. These include the emergence, as central themes, of such matters as the problematic of skepticism (which links the beginning of modern philosophy in Descartes with Shakespearean tragedy and romance); voice; the ways skepticism and voice are inflected by gender; and the outlook on morality—embraced both by Cavell and by the films he cares most about—that he calls moral perfectionism or Emersonian perfectionism.

In all the writings collected in this volume, in other words, Cavell is thinking about film, but he is also thinking about topics no less diverse and wide-ranging than those addressed in the essays that comprise *Themes Out of School*, or, for that matter, in the totality of his work. Indeed, the writings collected in this volume are noteworthy not only for the range and diversity of the topics they address, but also for the range and diversity of the audiences that attended their original presentations, the range and diversity of the institutions that have invited this American philosopher to share his thoughts on the subject of film.

And yet all of these writings are also of a piece. Every one participates, in its own way, in furthering Cavell's philosophical enterprise as a whole. It is, indeed, a defining feature of that body of work that it aspires to be a whole, an oeuvre in the fullest sense of the word, even as all his individual writings undertake to acknowledge, as he puts it in *Themes Out of School*, "the autonomy of their separate causes" (Cavell 1984, xi).

Cavell is the only major American philosopher who has made the subject of film a central part of his work. Yet to many philosophers, the relation of Cavell's writings on film to his explicitly philosophical writings remains perplexing. And, within the field of film studies, the potential usefulness of Cavell's writings—the potential usefulness of philosophy, as he understands and practices it—remains generally unrecognized. It has long been one of Cavell's guiding intuitions that a marriage between philosophy and film is not only possible but also necessary. To illuminate why Cavell's work aspires to such a marriage, and how it achieves it, is the "point," the "source and adventure," of the present collection.

When Marian Keane and I published *Reading Cavell's "The World Viewed": A Philosophical Perspective on Film*, our book promised a companion volume, a retrospective of Cavell's previously unpublished and uncollected writings on film. Such a collection, we argued, would help readers grasp the trajectory of Cavell's writing about film in the thirty years subsequent to *The World Viewed*, all of it marked by that book's initial articulation of film's philosophical importance. It would also illuminate the relation of his writings on film, as they developed in those years, to the development of his philosophical enterprise as a whole. At the same time, it would illuminate the relation of Cavell's practice of philosophy, as it developed in the same years, to the institution and development of film studies as an academic field in America and throughout the world.

The academic study of film had reached a point, Marian and I felt as we were writing our book on *The World Viewed*, at which the field could no longer move forward without revisiting its own history. Looking back on that history from the philosophical perspective exemplified by *The World Viewed*, it became clear to us that at each stage of the field's development there were alternative paths that were not taken, paths of discovery that have remained unexplored. Thus, we felt, together with a reading of *The World Viewed* that undertook to introduce or reintroduce that book to the field of film studies (and to introduce or reintroduce it to the field of philosophy, as well), a complete retrospective of Cavell's writings on film—including material unknown even to most readers of his books on the subject—could help the field to achieve a new perspective on its own origins and development, hence a new understanding of the possibilities, and challenges, that remain for those who are committed to thinking seriously about film, about our experience of film.

Cavell on Film is that promised retrospective. It contains the four essays on film and the essay on television—all written between 1978 and 1983—that were reprinted in *Themes Out of School*, as well as six additional pieces from the 1980s, and sixteen written since the early 1990s. As luck would have it, however, the present volume is also something different, something much more, than the retrospective Marian and I envisioned when we began composing our book on *The World Viewed*. In the past several years, Cavell has been enjoying a period of remarkable productivity, and film has been looming more prominently than ever in his thoughts. As it turns out, more than half of this collection consists of recent writings, many of them previously unpublished. This new material includes "Nothing Goes without Saying:

Reading the Marx Brothers"; "Seasons of Love: Bergman's *Smiles of a Summer Night* and *The Winter's Tale*"; "Something Out of the Ordinary"; "The World as Things: Collecting Thoughts on Collecting"; his remarks presented at the Paris Colloquium occasioned by the publication of *The World Viewed* in French translation; his remarks on psychoanalysis and film presented at the Freud Museum Festival; "Opera in and as Film"; "Philosophy the Day After Tomorrow"; "The Good of Film"; "Moral Reasoning: Teaching from the Core"; "After Half a Century," his epilogue to a new edition of Robert Warshow's *The Immediate Experience*; and "Crossing Paths," a version of a paper he presented at a colloquium on the work of Arthur Danto.

The fact that so much of this volume is "all new," as television networks like to put it, gives it a quite unanticipated richness and contemporaneity. That it gathers Cavell's current thoughts even more than his thoughts from earlier periods, however, might seem to make my task all the more daunting in penning a narrative that tells the "point" of this collection. In truth, however, it makes it easier for me to introduce this volume to its potential audience, or audiences. For Cavell has already done most of the hard part in the most recent of the writings on film gathered in this collection. With that lucidity that is the wonder of so many late works by great authors, those recent writings, even as they blaze new paths, look back on his own lifetime of writing on film, speak to its "point," its "source," its "adventure."

In looking back in order to move forward, Cavell's recent writings on film bear the mark of his turning to autobiography—and to autobiography's relation to philosophy—in his recent book *A Pitch of Philosophy*. This turning was already adumbrated in *Contesting Tears*, whose final chapter, "Stella's Taste," begins and ends with moments of autobiography. Then again, it is an idea that has always figured prominently in Cavell's work that in philosophy it is necessary to look back if one is to move forward. As early as the introduction to *Must We Mean What We Say?*, he had argued that innovation in philosophy has traditionally gone together with a repudiation of most of the history of the subject, but that in a modernist situation, the repudiation of the past has a transformed significance, "as though containing the consciousness that history will not go away except through our perfect acknowledgment of it (in particular, our acknowledgment that it is not past), and that one's own practice and ambition can be identified only against the continuous experience of the past" (Cavell 2002, 19).

In innumerable ways, the writings gathered in this volume illuminate, and are illuminated by, Cavell's books on film and thereby help clarify the overall trajectory of his thinking. It will be helpful to recount a few of those ways.

—Cavell can quite accurately say, as he does in one of the most recent pieces in *Cavell on Film* (remarks he presented in Paris at a colloquium occasioned by the publication of *The World Viewed* in French translation),

> The theoretical concepts put in play in *The World Viewed* have seen me ... through two further books about film, the one on comedy and a companion volume on Hollywood melodrama ... and a number of further essays on the subject.

And yet in those "two further books," references to *The World Viewed* are few and far between. In *Pursuits of Happiness* and *Contesting Tears* it goes almost without saying, whether in their introductions or in the readings that make up the body of each book, the extent to which the theoretical concepts put in play in *The World Viewed* indeed "see those readings through," to use Cavell's terms.

Then, too, although it is the central thrust of *The World Viewed* that it is not possible to think seriously about film apart from the perspective of self-reflection only philosophy is capable of providing, and that philosophy for its part cannot avoid the subject of film, the kinds of remarks about philosophy that are everywhere to be found in *Must We Mean What We Say?* are absent in Cavell's first book on film. In *The World Viewed*, it goes almost without saying the extent to which his reflections on the ontology of film derive philosophically from the "theoretical concepts put in play" in *Must We Mean What We Say?*

Must We Mean What We Say? is curiously submerged within *The World Viewed*, in other words, even as *The World Viewed* is curiously submerged within Cavell's later books about film. *The World Viewed* is not comparably submerged, however, in the writings gathered in *Cavell on Film*. Just as Wittgenstein's writings from the period between the *Tractatus* and *Philosophical Investigations* illuminate both books by helping readers to trace the paths between them, an essay like "What Becomes of Things on Film?," for example—written more or less simultaneously with "More of *The World Viewed*" and the foreword to the enlarged edition of *The World Viewed*—is a transitional work that illuminates the continuities between *The World Viewed* and *Pursuits of Happiness* and *Contesting Tears*.

In the little introduction to "What Becomes of Things on Film?" that he composed for its reprinting in *Themes Out of School*, Cavell observes that this piece played a role in his further thinking about film "out of proportion to its small size. A principal place these thoughts are picked up explicitly is in the *Adam's Rib* chapter of . . . *Pursuits of Happiness*, where I read the presence of its film-within-the film (fictionally a home movie) as a demonstration" that "no event within a film (say no gesture of framing or editing) is as significant (as 'cinematic') as the event of film itself" (Cavell and Rothman 2005, 1).

"What Becomes of Things on Film?" anticipates *Pursuits of Happiness* and *Contesting Tears* in other ways, as well. For one, those books take the form of readings of individual members of the genres Cavell names the "comedy of remarriage" and "the melodrama of the unknown woman," respectively (the latter derived from the former, in his view), while "What Becomes of Things on Film?" raises the question of what "any reading of a film must do" if it is to count as a serious act of film criticism. And it anticipates those books by the twin answers it gives to this question: A reading of a film must "account for the frames of the film being what they are, in the order they are in," and it must accurately state the film's subject. It also anticipates *Pursuits of Happiness* and *Contesting Tears* by its linking of philosophical skepticism and Shakespearean Romance (which *Pursuits of Happiness* finds a crucial source of remarriage comedies, hence the melodramas that, according to *Contesting Tears*, are derived from them). And by its discovery that such masterpieces of film as *Belle de*

Jour, Persona, Ugetsu, Vertigo, and *It's a Wonderful Life* share, as a common subject, "the meaning, or limits, or conditions, of female identity, hence . . . of human identity." At the same time, "What Becomes of Things on Film?" emphatically declares its continuity with *The World Viewed*. It does so, for example, by its suggestion that what it is about film that lends itself to such a subject as female identity or human identity is a question that demands "so solemn a topic as 'the ontology of film.'"

—When *Pursuits of Happiness* was first published, sympathetic readers were struck by Cavell's vision of a constellation of Hollywood genres logically related to the remarriage comedy, and to each other. Yet we were at a loss to identify groups of films that constituted other comparable genres. Once the essays that were to comprise *Contesting Tears* began to appear, we had, thanks to Cavell, a second genre to think about. Comprised of films such as *Stella Dallas, Gaslight, Letter from an Unknown Woman,* and *Now, Voyager* the "melodrama of the unknown woman," as Cavell names the genre, is, he claims, derived from the remarriage comedy by an operation of negation (as opposed to the operation by which members of a genre "compensate" for the apparent lack of a particular feature; for example, *It Happened One Night* appears to lack a place that functions—like Connecticut in *The Lady Eve*—as the equivalent of the "Green World" in Shakespearean Romance, but it compensates for this by taking place on the road).

Even attentive readers of *Pursuits of Happiness* and *Contesting Tears* may find these operations perplexing, though. They may also find it a perplexing question what other genres there may be that are comparable to the two that proved so fruitful as subjects for Cavell's readings. The essay in the present volume called simply "*North by Northwest*," written between *Pursuits of Happiness* and *Contesting Tears*, finds Hitchcock's great film to exemplify a kind of romantic thriller intimately related to the romantic comedies of remarriage, yet essentially different from them in structure. Cavell elegantly sums up the difference:

> The goal of the comedies requires what I call the creation of the woman, a new creation of a new woman. This takes the form in the comedies of something like the woman's death and revival, and it goes with the camera's insistence on the flesh-and-blood reality of the female actor. When this happens in Hitchcock, as it did in *Vertigo*, the Hitchcock film preceding *North by Northwest*, it is shown to produce catastrophe: the woman's falling to her death, precisely the fate *averted* in *North by Northwest*. Here, accordingly, it is the man who undergoes death and revival (at least twice, both times at the hands of the woman) *and* whose physical identity is insisted upon by the camera. Hitchcock is thus investigating the point that the comedies of remarriage are least certain about, namely, what it is about the man that fits him to educate and hence rescue the woman, that is, to be chosen by the woman to educate her and thereby to achieve happiness for them both. (Cavell and Rothman 2005, 57)

By studying in considerable detail a third instance of a film genre, Cavell's reading of *North by Northwest* complements *Pursuits of Happiness* and *Contesting Tears*, enabling readers to achieve a perspective on the remarriage comedy and the melodrama of the unknown woman that those two books, alone, cannot provide.

—*The World Viewed*, *Pursuits of Happiness*, and *Contesting Tears* all reflect on ways film is different from other artistic media (for example, still photography, painting, poetry, music). In "The Fact of Television," Cavell considers a medium whose relationship with film is especially intimate. This important essay illuminates both *The World Viewed* and *Pursuits of Happiness*, and their relation to each other, by explicitly addressing the ways television's ontological conditions differ from those of film, and by considering television's leading genres in light of those differences.

Similarly, "Opera in and as Film," one of the recent pieces in the present collection, illuminates the relation between film and opera. "Seasons of Love: Bergman's *Smiles of a Summer Night* and *The Winter's Tale*" and "Eric Rohmer's *A Tale of Winter*," two other recent pieces, further illuminate the relation—ontological, historical—between Shakespearean theater and the Hollywood comedies and melodramas Cavell studies in *Pursuits of Happiness* and *Contesting Tears*. And "Philosophy the Day After Tomorrow," yet another recent piece, explores the relation between those genres of film and the novels of Jane Austen and George Eliot. In Cavell's writing, it had long been a guiding intuition that film has special affinities with opera and with Shakespearean theater. It had largely gone without saying, however, that film has comparable affinities with the nineteenth-century English novel, affinities it promises to be equally fruitful to explore. Although it is only occasionally that "Philosophy the Day After Tomorrow" explicitly raises the subject of film, film is everywhere in its thoughts.

—*The World Viewed* was written long before most of today's college students were born. It can leave contemporary readers quite in the dark as to what, if anything, its author might have to say about more recent films. So can Cavell's subsequent books on film, which focus on genres of "classical" Hollywood movies of the 1930s and 1940s.

In this regard, an essay like "On Makavejev on Bergman" (1979), which contains an extended reading of Dušan Makavejev's *Sweet Movie* (1974), a major modernist film made more than a decade after the latest films referred to in *The World Viewed*, is instructive. Written during the period Cavell was composing the readings of remarriage comedies that were to comprise *Pursuits of Happiness*, "On Makavejev on Bergman" is illuminating, among other reasons, for affirming—at a moment when Cavell's readers might have thought he had turned his back on current films—that works such as Makavejev's, which he accepts as a significant present in the history of the art of film, were still being made. And for reaffirming that such works constitute a place in which the future of filmmaking, hence of significant film theory and of film studies generally, will have to work itself out.

In "*Prénom*: Marie," his foreword to Jean-Luc Godard's *"Hail Mary": Women and the Sacred in Film*, an anthology of essays edited by Charles Warren and Maryel

Locke, Cavell is led by his experience of *Hail Mary*—an even more recent film whose claim to seriousness he finds himself prepared to accept—to revise his perhaps too harsh judgment of Godard in *The World Viewed*. Godard's films of the mid-1960s, Cavell had charged, criticized our culture for treating people as if they had no souls, yet that seems to be precisely how the filmmaker himself treated his subjects—and his viewers. From so compromised a position, how can an artist achieve an authentically radical critique of our culture? How is the world's dehumanizing of its inhabitants to be distinguished from Godard's depersonalizing of them? Those inclined to side with Godard's earlier Marxist politics, Cavell observes in "*Prénom*: Marie," are "apt to sense a falling off, or backing off," in Godard's late films. Yet Cavell thinks of *Hail Mary* "not as an evasion of politics, but as a critique of politics, of what he had once named politics." And he thinks of Godard's self-criticism, in this film, "as a continuation of a mode of criticism internal to his work from the beginning" (Cavell and Rothman 2005, 176). Godard is thinking about film and about films, about their origins, the conditions of their possibility. Wasn't he always?

And in "Eric Rohmer's *A Tale of Winter*" (1992) Cavell addresses a yet more recent film he accepts as a "significant present in the history of the art of film," taking seriously the film's invocations of Shakespeare's *The Winter's Tale*, which *Pursuits of Happiness* identifies as a source for the Hollywood remarriage comedies of the 1930s and 1940s. If the Shakespeare play is about "an art / which does mend nature—change it rather—but / The art itself is nature" (act 4, scene 4), Rohmer's film, in Cavell's view, is in part a meditation on the fact that Shakespeare's words, when applied to film—"writing in light and motion"—"take on an uncanny literalness" (Cavell and Rothman 2005, 287).

No less illuminating are the pieces that incorporate Cavell's thoughts on recent American movies and their relation to "classical" Hollywood genres. These range from his tiny piece on *Groundhog Day* (Harold Ramis, 1993), which in sixty-two words suggests that this "small film that lives off its wits and tells a deeply wonderful story of love" poses the question—deeply resonant in the context of Cavell's work—"how, surrounded by conventions we do not exactly believe in, we sometimes find it in ourselves to enter into what Emerson thought of as a new day" (Cavell and Rothman 2005, 222) to "The Good of Film," one of the most recent of the essays in *Cavell on Film* and among the most ambitious. In the course of its extended meditation on film's affinity with Emersonian perfectionism, "The Good of Film" considers a wide range of recent movies (among them: *As Good as It Gets, Clueless, Groundhog Day, The Savage Heart, Inventing the Abbotts, Four Weddings and a Funeral, My Best Friend's Wedding, Everyone Says I Love You, Cookie's Fortune, Say Anything, Grosse Point Blank, Good Will Hunting, The Matrix, Fight Club, Being John Malkovich, Dogma, Waking the Dead, American Beauty, The Sixth Sense*, and *The Cider House Rules*). These films differ from remarriage comedies of the 1930s and 1940s in a number of ways the essay explores (for example, the couples in the recent films tend to be, or to seem, much younger than their counterparts). How could today's films not differ from those of the 1930s and 1940s, Cavell observes, since "the fear of divorce has changed, the threat of pregnancy has changed, the male and female stars and the directors and writers who put them in action are gone?" Nonetheless, he argues, "there do seem to me a remarkable number of new films (within my limited experience)" that have something of the "feel" of classical remarriage comedies, provide interpretations of some of their features, and, like them,

> concern a quest for transcendence, a step into an opposite or transformed mood, not so much by becoming another person, or taking a further step in attaining an unattained self, or becoming who you are, as by being recognized as the one you are by having, or giving, access to another world. (Cavell and Rothman 2005, xxi)

—In "*North by Northwest*," Cavell writes,

> What I found in turning to think consecutively about film a dozen or so years ago was a medium which seemed simultaneously to be free of the imperative to philosophy and at the same time inevitably to reflect upon itself—as though the condition of philosophy were its natural condition. (Cavell and Rothman 2005, 41)

In almost every one of the writings in *Cavell on Film*, as in all three of his books on film, Cavell reflects on the affinity he finds between film and philosophy, an affinity that makes the marriage between them, exemplified by his own writings on film, possible—and necessary. In "The Thought of Movies," for example, he poses the question: What does it reveal about movies, and what does it reveal about philosophy, that "the same sensibility that is drawn to and perplexed about philosophy is drawn to and perplexed about movies"? (Cavell and Rothman 2005, 92). Cavell's thoughts on this affinity and its implications, both for philosophy and for the serious study of film, become deeper and more complex as he ponders, in the writings collected in this volume, the role movies played in his own philosophical education.

During the period he was writing *The World Viewed*, it had not yet fully dawned on Cavell the extent to which the combination of popularity and artistic seriousness of American movies, especially of the 1930s and 1940s, was a function of their inheritance of the concerns of American transcendentalism. Not coincidentally, during the period he was writing *The World Viewed*, the extent to which Cavell's own way of thinking inherited Emerson's understanding and practice of philosophy also had not yet fully dawned on him. In the writings collected in *Cavell on Film*, however, Cavell's intuition that Hollywood movies have inherited the philosophical concerns of American transcendentalism, conjoined with his intuition that he has inherited these concerns, too, led him, as Marian Keane and I put it in the introduction to *Reading Cavell's "The World Viewed*,*"* "to the astonishing further intuition that his own philosophical procedures are underwritten by the ways American movies think about society, human relationships, and their own condition as films" (Rothman and Keane 2000, 27).

By comparison with *The World Viewed*, *Pursuits of Happiness*, and *Contesting Tears*, some of the writings contained in the present volume may, as we have suggested, appear to be relatively slight, mere occasional pieces. Yet Cavell's occasional pieces bring home, with special vividness, a crucial feature of his aspiration and achievement as a writer, namely, that every one of his writings is an occasional piece. Every one of Cavell's writings responds to, acknowledges, its particular occasion, an occasion inseparable from the writing's "cause." This brings home, in turn, that any and every occasion may be found to call for philosophy. And it is in itself an occasion whenever philosophy finds itself answering to its calling. Some of those occasions—the writing of *Claim of Reason*, for example—are of extraordinary importance within Cavell's career as a whole. Others are more . . . everyday or ordinary. Cavell, like Emerson, is capable of finding something out of the ordinary in the most ordinary of occasions. Philosophy, for Cavell, is not a realm of abstract thought. It is an activity performed by human beings *in* the world, an activity best performed in a spirit of adventure. Philosophy is a way of rising to its occasion.

Even when in a particular piece of writing Cavell may seem only to be reiterating an idea or argument he has already articulated elsewhere, his recounting on this new occasion always constitutes a new accounting, a revision that creates a new thought from the old, enables a new aspect to dawn. Every piece of his writing questions every other, acknowledges every other, is as capable as any other of revealing something about philosophy as Cavell understands and practices it. Attentive readers of this collection can expect the pleasure of discovering, or rediscovering, that every one of Cavell's writings, even those that may seem the slightest, contains at least one new idea or thought, an idea or thought so astonishing that it illuminates the entirety of his work, and that he expresses, puts into words, more fully there, on that occasion, than anywhere else in his writings.

The remarks by Cavell at the Paris colloquium that we have already had occasion to cite, for example, are studded with such revelatory ideas or thoughts. One is his intuition that it was thinking about film that moved him to recognize the need for prose capable of evoking the evanescence of the world on film, the ever-shifting moods of "faces and motions and settings" capable of capturing, as well, what remains inflexible, fixed, in the physiognomy of the world on film (what in *The World Viewed* he calls the "reality of the unsayable," the "unmoving ground" that makes film capable of exhibiting the world) (Cavell and Rothman 2005, xiii). Then the double existence—the transience and permanence—that is automatically possessed by the world on film, vouchsafed by the ontological conditions of the medium, became an aspiration of Cavell's philosophical prose.

Part of what this means can be registered by saying that each of Cavell's writings (this Paris talk, for example) aspires to permanence (it lives on in these pages). Yet it also aspires to acknowledge, to rise to, the transient occasion that gave rise to it. But the point is also, I take it, that "the moods of faces and motions and settings, in their double existence as transient and permanent," are the stuff of philosophy, as Cavell aspires to practice it, no less than the stuff of film (Cavell and Rothman 2005, xiii). The originality and power of Cavell's view of skepticism, for example, resides in the way he envisions the onset of skeptical doubt as a scene—not a scene from a stage play, but a scene that happens in the world, like a scene from a movie. For Cavell, writing philosophical prose that is capable of achieving conviction, like writing about film that is capable of achieving conviction, requires the ability, and willingness, to be evocative.

Thus, it is quite characteristic and instructive that Cavell's way of contesting the philosophical position staked out by Saul Kripke, in his influential book *Wittgenstein on Rules and Private Language*, is by taking issue with the way Kripke "reads" a particular "scene" from Wittgenstein's *Philosophical Investigations*. (From *PI*, section 217: "If I have exhausted the justifications [for following the rules of mathematics or of ordinary language as I do] I have reached bedrock, and my spade is turned. Then I am inclined to say, 'This is simply what I do.'") Hence the following passage from "Philosophy the Day After Tomorrow" (yet another of the recent pieces in the present collection), which provides a perfect illustration of the way Cavell's thinking about film has empowered his prose, freed it to be evocative, helped liberate it from the "guarded rhythms" that keep most philosophical writing from swinging, or soaring. (Writing powerful, evocative prose like this is simply what Cavell does.)

> Kripke . . . takes the teacher's (or speaker's) gesture of showing what he does to be meant as a show of power. . . . I have taken the gesture oppositely, as acknowledging a necessary weakness, I might call it a creative limitation, in teaching (or socialization), stressing that the arrival at an impasse between teacher and pupil also threatens, and may enlighten, the teacher. This difference of interpretation demands a long story (which I undertake to tell in *Conditions Handsome and Unhandsome*). At the moment I wish to be as uncontroversial as possible and draw a moral from the fact that, whichever way you take the scene of instruction, when the teacher recognizes that she or he has exhausted the justifications, he becomes silent and waits. Satisfaction eludes him, but more words are pointless. Wittgenstein anticipates this inevitable moment of silence in teaching—that the student must at some point go on alone—in the very opening section of the *Investigations*, where he notes, casually but fatefully, "Explanations come to an end somewhere." The moral I draw for Wittgenstein is that an utterance must have a point, whether to inform, amuse, promise, question, insist, beseech—in that sense must be worth saying; and that the point will exceed the saying, is inherently vulnerable, as human action is, to misfortune. . . . And the moral of silence in teaching at the same time implies a task of teaching, namely to demonstrate that informing, amusing, promising, questioning, insisting, beseeching, etc., must themselves be seen to be worth doing. Quite as if teaching must, as it were, provide a reason for speaking at all. As if we might become appalled by the gift of language, the fatedness to speech, the condition Wittgenstein describes as the life form of talkers, of us. (Cavell and Rothman 2005, 321)

Within academic film studies, it is sometimes supposed that Cavell's writing is impressionistic, unrigorous, self-indulgent. Cavell's writing is, to be sure, unsystematic.

That is, Cavell—like Kierkegaard, like Emerson, like Thoreau, like Nietzsche, like Wittgenstein—is not a philosopher who strives to construct a *system* of thought. As a consequence, his writing, like theirs, can be difficult. Insisting on the difficulty can make it seem—and sometimes it can seem—that reading Cavell is a painful matter. There are occasions when Cavell's writing is painful. For example, *Contesting Tears* dwells on films, such as *Gaslight*, which in their own ways are as great as the comedies of remarriage Cavell writes about in *Pursuits of Happiness*, but which are at times not pleasurable, are even painful, to watch. Cavell's writing does not shrink from this pain. *Pursuits of Happiness* itself, however, is altogether pleasurable to read and to savor. Most of the pieces in the present collection are closer to *Pursuits of Happiness*, in this regard, than to *Contesting Tears*. In them, Cavell generously shares pleasures movies in his experience have given him, as well as pleasures philosophy alone is capable of providing. (Are they the same pleasures?)

Another way to put this is to say that there is poetry to Cavell's writing. In his writings on film, as in the films that move him to write this way about them, art and philosophy cannot be separated. "Unlike the prose of comic theatrical dialogue after Shakespeare," Cavell writes,

> film has a natural equivalent for the medium of Shakespeare's dramatic poetry. I think of it as the poetry of film itself, what it is that happens to figures and objects and places as they are variously molded and displaced by a motion-picture camera and then projected and screened. Every art, every worthwhile human enterprise, has its poetry, ways of doing things that perfect the possibilities of the enterprise itself, make it the one it is. . . . You may think of it as the unteachable point in any worthwhile enterprise. I understand it to be, let me say, a natural vision of film that every motion and station, in particular every human posture and gesture, however glancing, has its poetry, or you may say its lucidity. . . . Any of the arts will be drawn to this knowledge, this perception of the poetry of the ordinary, but film, I would like to say, democratizes the knowledge, hence at once blesses and curses us with it. It says that the perception of poetry is as open to all, regardless as it were of birth or talent, as the ability is to hold a camera on a subject, so that a failure so to perceive, to persist in missing the subject, which may amount to missing the evanescence of the subject, is ascribable only to ourselves . . . , as if to . . . fail to trace the implications of things . . . requires that we persistently coarsen and stupefy ourselves. (Cavell and Rothman 2005, xxvi)

We "coarsen and stupefy" ourselves insofar as we think about film, write about film, in ways that miss the poetry of the subject. The study of film cannot be a worthwhile human enterprise insofar as it isolates itself from the kind of criticism Walter Benjamin had in mind when he argued, as Cavell paraphrases him, that "what establishes a work as art is its ability to inspire and sustain criticism of a certain sort, criticism that seeks to articulate the work's idea; what cannot be so criticized is not art" (Cavell and Rothman 2005, 283). And yet, as Cavell reminds us, Benjamin himself developed "his famous speculations concerning the technological medium of film . . . without consulting a film's idea of itself, or undertaking to suppose that one or another may have such a thing." Contrast *Pursuits of Happiness*, say, in which Cavell treats "the seven films principally studied in that book both as representative of the best work of Hollywood's classical period and (hence) as works capable of reflecting critically on the cultural conditions that make them possible" (Cavell and Rothman 2005, 283).

Marrying film and philosophy, the writings gathered in *Cavell on Film* do not miss the poetry of either subject, and thinking about film emerges as a worthwhile human enterprise, indeed. In these writings, the study of film achieves its own poetry, its own "ways of doing things that perfect the possibilities of the enterprise itself, make it the one it is." That is the "unteachable point" of this collection, the lesson it above all aspires to teach.

14

The Same Again, Only a Little Different

Cavell's Two Takes on *The Philadelphia Story*

In an August 2004 entry in his philosophical memoir *Little Did I Know*, Stanley Cavell cites a complaint, by someone who had valued his earlier work, that in his just-published book *Cities of Words* he was "just going over the same old films." Cavell felt provoked to write, "I never take up a film again that I care about unless I feel that I have something new to convey in considering it, which is part of my claim that the films I have studied are inexhaustible" (Cavell 2010, 494). So I thought it would be an appropriate contribution to this wonderful colloquium for me to identify, and assess, what *Cities of Words* does convey about "the same old films" that goes beyond *Pursuits of Happiness*; I imagined that such a paper would almost write itself. If only! For *Pursuits of Happiness* and *Cities of Words*, too, are inexhaustible. As I soon discovered, so was the task I had set for myself.

In 1978, the year Cavell completed *The Claim of Reason*, he wrote "Thinking of Emerson." It wasn't until almost a decade later, though, with *In Quest of the Ordinary*, *This New Yet Unapproachable America*, *Conditions Handsome and Unhandsome*, and the Harvard core curriculum course he called Moral Reasoning on which he later based *Cities of Words*, that Emerson's full impact on Cavell became manifest. *Pursuits of Happiness* was published in 1981, but as Cavell writes in the introduction, "Thoughts of remarriage as generating a genre of film began presenting themselves to me during a course on film comedy I gave in 1974 at Harvard's Carpenter Center" (Cavell 1981b, 275). In 1975 Cavell first presented his reading of *Bringing Up Baby*. In

---

Keynote address, conference on "Cavell and Film" at the Sorbonne, 2019.

1976, he gave a version of the film comedy course designed to "test out those ideas as rigorously as I knew how." By 1978, he had also written the *Lady Eve* chapter and had worked out the structure and argument of the book that became *Pursuits of Happiness*. Surely, thinking about the distinctly American movie genre he named "the comedy of remarriage" was instrumental in moving him to return to Emerson, only a little differently this time, and in enabling him to read Emerson's essays in a way he'd never been able, or willing, to do.

In *The Claim of Reason*, Emerson's name appears once, in passing, as it does in *Must We Mean What We Say?* In *The World Viewed* Emerson's name appears never; in *The Senses of Walden*, rarely. In *Pursuits of Happiness*, Emerson is invoked more than a few times, notably in the caption for the book's frontispiece, that glorious frame from *The Awful Truth* of Cary Grant, who manifestly *does* "carry the holiday in his eye" and *is* "fit to stand the gaze of millions." But if Cavell had written "Thinking of Emerson" *before* beginning *Pursuits of Happiness*, Emerson would surely have played a more prominent role in the book, as was already the case in Cavell's 1983 essays "The Thought of Movies" and "A Capra Moment." Even in those essays, though, Cavell didn't have a name for the way of thinking he was coming to recognize as his own, no less than Emerson's.

The Hollywood comedy of remarriage, *Pursuits of Happiness* argues, is born full-blown in its first instance, *It Happened One Night*, and has no history, in the sense that there is no necessity to the order in which the members are created. "But if the genre emerges full-blown," Cavell asks in his introduction, "how can later members of the genre *add* anything to it?" He goes on, "This question is prompted by a picture of a genre as a form characterized by features, as an object by its properties; accordingly, to emerge full-blown must mean to emerge possessing all its features. The answer to the question is that later members can 'add' something to the genre because there is no such thing as 'all its features.' It will be natural in what follows, even irresistible, to speak of individual characteristics of a genre as 'features' of it; but the picture of an object with its properties is a bad one" (Cavell 1981b, 238). Indeed, the chapters that follow do repeatedly refer to the genre's "features." But the introduction to *Pursuits of Happiness* exemplifies Cavell's regular practice of prefacing each book with an introductory essay, written last, that addresses the book as a whole from a perspective that only completing the chapters that follow enabled him to achieve. Thus, the introduction offers an alternative picture of a genre's "characteristics," which is that

> the members of a genre share the inheritance of certain conditions, procedures and subjects and goals of composition, and that each member of such a genre represents a study of these conditions, something I think of as bearing the responsibility of the inheritance. There is, on this picture, nothing one is tempted to call *the* features of a genre which all its members have in common. (Cavell 1981b, 28)

What Cavell is proposing here is that we think of the "common inheritance" of the members of a genre as a story or myth. "The members of a genre will be interpretations of the myth," he writes, "or to use Thoreau's word, revisions of it, which will also make them interpretations of one another" (Cavell 1981b, 31).

In *Pursuits of Happiness*, the chapter on *The Philadelphia Story*, like every chapter, takes the form of what Cavell calls a "reading" of a definitive member of the remarriage comedy genre—an account of the film that, viewed from the perspective articulated in the introduction, undertakes to discover that film's particular *way* of exemplifying the genre, its particular *way* of interpreting, revising, the genre's story or myth. Each such reading is an act of criticism that takes the film it "reads" as its subject. But given the conception of genre Cavell is working with, each reading is also philosophy. Taking the film as its subject is the reading's way of taking the film's genre as its subject. The comedy of remarriage—hence genre in film in general, hence film itself—is what every chapter of *Pursuits of Happiness* is about, what the book as a whole is about, the subject of the book's philosophical investigation.

The chapter on *The Philadelphia Story* in *Cities of Words* doesn't in the same way perform a reading of the film. It continually refers to, and defers to, the reading of the film performed in *Pursuits of Happiness*, which it mines for evidence it puts in the service of the book's philosophical investigation of its own subject, which is moral perfectionism, and in particular Emersonian perfectionism—the version of perfectionism that *Cities of Words* is *defending*, as the first sentence of the *Philadelphia Story* chapter declares—Cavell's acknowledgment that Emerson's way of thinking was also his own.

In *Cities of Words*, Cavell observes in *Little Did I Know*, "the sets of comedies and melodramas I have devoted a book each to are cast systematically in a new light, namely, as embodying a specific register of the moral life, a register running, if largely unheralded, throughout Western philosophy and literature, from Plato and Aristotle through Dante and Montaigne and Jane Austen and Emerson and George Eliot and Nietzsche and Mill to Heidegger and Wittgenstein" (Cavell 2010, 259)—and, of course, Cavell. The "new light" *Cities of Words* casts on these films reflects back on, and illuminates, the "register of the moral life" that is both the subject the book illuminates and the way of thinking its writing exemplifies—the "light" the book casts on its subject. In this way, *Cities of Words* exemplifies the view Cavell articulated in a 1989 interview, during the period of his Moral Reasoning course, that it is *defining* of philosophy that it is "at every moment answerable to itself," indeed, that *any* place in which the human spirit allows itself to be under its own question *is* philosophy" (Conant and Cavell 1989, 59).

What does *Cities of Words* enable us to *know* about *The Philadelphia Story*, for example, that goes beyond *Pursuits of Happiness*? Next to nothing. *Pursuits of Happiness* already brought into plain view virtually everything within the film that *Cities of Words* "casts a new light" on. But this isn't a flaw or weakness of the book. In *Cities of Words*, Cavell writes, "Wittgenstein, in *Philosophical Investigations*, declares it to be 'of the essence of our investigation that we do not seek to learn anything new by it. We want to *understand* something that is already in plain view, something that the human being cannot simply fail to know." This formulation captures the familiar fact that "philosophers seem perpetually to be going back over something, something most sane people would feel had already been discussed to death. A more familiar formulation is to say that philosophy does not progress." Cavell adds, flashing his underappreciated gift for delivering mordantly witty comebacks without ruffling his Georgia-born decorum, "This depends on who is doing the measuring" (Cavell 2005a, 14).

It is Cavell himself doing the measuring when, in the preface for the 2002 edition of *Must We Mean What We Say?*, he cites "something specific about the way, or space within which, I work, which I can put negatively as occurring within the knowledge that I never get things right, or let's rather say, see them through, the first time, causing my efforts perpetually to leave things so that they can be, and ask to be, returned to. Put positively, it is the knowledge that philosophical ideas reveal their good only in stages" (Cavell 2002, xvii).

For Cavell, *Cities of Words* was doubly a return in that he adapted it from lectures for a course he first offered almost twenty years earlier, and because in this book he returned to movies he'd already written about, continuing his earlier thinking from a changed perspective. In reflecting back on, and illuminating, the book's subject, the "new light" *Cities of Words* casts on these films enables it to convey a new understanding of philosophy's origins and history—philosophy's public life, we might say—and on *itself*, on its own writing, the private dimension of Cavell's philosophical life.

Cities of Words accepts its own place within an intellectual and artistic tradition as old as philosophy itself. At the same time, its writing manifests, indeed *validates*, the late turn to autobiography that led to *Little Did I Know*, Cavell's final book, in which he tells the story of his life up to the completion of *The Claim of Reason*, the work in which he declared his existence as the only kind of philosopher who could have written such a book or could have wanted to. In this story, his own story, as *Little Did I Know* tells it—and this, for Cavell, is its philosophical *point*—the public and the private, the philosophical and the personal, philosophy and life, are inextricably intertwined, as they are—this is the guiding intuition in *Cities of Words*—both in Emersonian perfectionism and in the lives of the characters in the genres it inspired.

To be sure, Cavell's late turn to autobiography, motivated by and motivating *Cities of Words*, was anticipated in his earlier writings. *Little Did I Know* is itself a return, a continuation from a changed perspective of thinking that can be traced back—*he* traces it back—to *Must We Mean What We Say?*, in which the guiding intuition is that philosophical appeals to ordinary language have a private, personal, dimension. But it is only from the changed perspective of his late writings, *Cities of Words* among then, that Cavell came to recognize as an inescapable subject for philosophy the intimacy of philosophy's relation to autobiography, an intimacy rooted both in philosophy's historical origins, its public history, and in its origins, in the private life of the human individual, within the realm of the ordinary, the everyday, what Emerson called the "near" and the "low."

I said earlier that *Cities of Words* enables us to know next to nothing about *The Philadelphia Story*, say, that *Pursuits of Happiness* hadn't already placed in plain view. There's one telling exception. In the introduction to *Contesting Tears*, written during the period he was teaching the Moral Reasoning course, Cavell puts together a passage from Genesis with a moment in *The Philadelphia Story* that when he was writing *Pursuits of Happiness* he "had passed over as obvious filler, even boring" (Cavell 1996, 27). Near the end of the film, Dexter invites Liz for a morning swim, but she declines, saying she'll wait to take that pleasure with Mike. When Dexter asks her whether she isn't running a risk in waiting so long for him, she replies that Mike still had something to learn. What had Mike to learn?

In revisiting this passage from *Contesting Tears* in *Cities of Words*, Cavell writes, "I have elsewhere described the thought of Mike's not being ready to put aside his intactness by recurring to the moment—the 'detour'—in Genesis where, just before God creates woman as a helpmeet for the single man, he allows Adam to give names to the animals." Adam's—Mike's—"detour" accomplishes two things, Cavell suggests. First, it creates time for the man, a sense of the reality of life as irreversible, consequential, time to come into his own words (Mike is said to be a writer), giving himself language, his names for things, making the shared world his. Second, it allows him to survey the world of living things and to learn that "none but the woman will make him feel other than alone in the world, will be a companion, reciprocal." Mike's "not being ready" thus means that, as Cavell puts it, "he is not ready to recognize Liz as his other, not Liz as opposed to all others, but as another to his separateness, to what Emerson calls 'the recognition that he exists,' the fact Emerson identifies as the Fall of Man in his wonderful essay 'Experience.'" By the end of *The Philadelphia Story*, Cavell concludes, "Tracy has learned that Dexter is ready, that he is her company, that they exist" (Cavell 2005a, 47).

When he was writing *Pursuits of Happiness*, Cavell wasn't ready to recognize the significance of this moment. He too, still had something to learn. Perhaps we can say that, like Mike, he wasn't yet fully ready to "put aside his intactness," or, as Emerson put it in "Self-Reliance," to "accept the place the divine providence has found for you, the society of your contemporaries, the connection of events." What was it that Cavell did in the "detour" between *Pursuits of Happiness* and the Moral Reasoning course that made *Cities of Words* possible? What enabled him to achieve the perspective articulated in his late work cannot be separated, I suggest, from his act of giving this perspective, *his* perspective, a name.

What's in a name? For Cavell, this, too, was an inescapable philosophical question. In pondering this question, I find myself drawn to the account, in *Little Did I Know*, of his decision as a young man, made entirely on his own, to change his last name from Goldstein to Cavell in the hope that giving himself a name would free him—in a sense, it did—to be reborn, to find a place for himself in a world that didn't yet know him. Giving the name "Emersonian perfectionism" to his way of thinking enabled Cavell to put aside his intactness, in effect, and acknowledge that he existed, in and out of philosophy, within both a private and a public world.

Within *Little Did I Know* as a whole, the significance of this incident is that the lengthy, arduous, process he had to endure to change his name *legally*, to make his private change take effect in the public world, was young Stanley's traumatic introduction to the vexing tensions and conflicts that are inevitable consequences of the reality that we human beings inhabit two worlds—a theme central to all versions of moral perfectionism and to the comedies and melodramas that in *Cities of Words* the not-so-young Stanley understood Emersonian perfectionism to have inspired.

When writing *Must We Mean What We Say?*, Cavell, like Wittgenstein, found himself in a modernist situation in relation to the tradition of philosophy in which he had received his professional training, the essential fact of modernism being, as he put it, that the relation between the present practice of an enterprise and the history of that enterprise has become problematic. His recognition of his reciprocity with Emerson, as we might think of it, opened his eyes to the fact that, to invoke again a passage to which I keep returning, he had also inherited, without being aware of it, an alternative philosophical tradition founded in America by Emerson, embraced by Emerson's great readers Thoreau and, in Europe, by his devoted reader Nietzsche (and, through Nietzsche, Heidegger), and kept alive in American culture and in *himself* by the films he watched in the years going to the movies was a normal part of his week. Cavell didn't find himself in a modernist situation in relation to *that* tradition. And unlike Groucho Marx, he was happy to belong to a club that accepted him as a member.

As I put it in "Cavell Reading Cavell," in finding Emerson, Cavell found himself. And in the Moral Reasoning course, hence in *Cities of Words*, he went beyond this by placing Emersonian perfectionism, foundational for "the American event in philosophy," within a broad and deep tradition of moral perfectionism he traces back to Plato and Aristotle and forward, from there, to the major modern thinkers and artists he considers in this remarkably ambitious book.

By placing his chapter on Emerson first, and pairing it with *The Philadelphia Story*, *Cities of Words* looks back over the history of philosophy from the perspective of that American rebeginning. From this perspective, *Cavell's* perspective, that history looks very different from the way it appears to philosophers who, in his words, "begin their sense of philosophy's re-beginning in the modern era with the response, in Bacon and in Descartes and in Locke, to the traumatic event of the New Science of Copernicus and Galileo and Newton, for which the basis of human knowledge of the world, rather than of human conduct in that world, is primary among philosophical preoccupations" (Cavell 2005a, 2).

Cavell writes, "Each of the thinkers and artists we will encounter in the following pages may be said to respond to some insight of a split in the human self, of human nature as divided or double." Each provides a position "from which the present state of human existence can be judged and a future state achieved, or else the present judged to be better than the cost of changing it" (Cavell 2005a, 2). Cavell understands *Emersonian* perfectionism to propose that one's quarrel with the world need not be settled, nor cynically set aside as unsettleable. It is a condition in which you can at once want the world and want it to change—even change it, as the apple changes the earth, though we say the apple falls. In demonstrating our lack of *given* means of making ourselves intelligible (to ourselves, to others), Emerson's writing at once "details the difficulties in the way of possessing those means, and demonstrates that they are at hand" (Cavell 2005a, 18).

Emerson expresses two dominating themes of perfectionism. "The first theme is that the human self—confined by itself, aspiring toward itself, dissatisfied with its present condition—is always becoming, as on a journey, always partially in a further state." The second is that the other to whom I can use the words I discover in which to express myself is the Friend—a figure that may occur as the goal of the journey but also as its instigation and accompaniment" (Cavell 2005a, 2).

The questions couples in remarriage comedies address in their witty conversations, *Cities of Words* argues, are *moral* questions, questions about how they should live their lives, what kind of persons they wish to be. But how are we to *know* what we truly desire? To know our true desires, we must know our true feelings. In comedies of remarriage, the moral questions are also philosophical questions. As Cavell writes, "Film, the latest of the great arts, shows philosophy to be the often-invisible accompaniment of the ordinary lives that film is so apt to capture" (Cavell 2005a, 6)—but only if we understand philosophy, as moral perfectionism does, to be a moral calling; only if we understand the ancient imperative "know thyself" to be *defining* for philosophy.

In *Must We Mean What We Say?*, Cavell argues that Austin's and Wittgenstein's appeals to ordinary language are procedures for achieving self-knowledge, for rendering perspicuous to us our words, our concepts, the ways we really think. In *Cities of Words*, Cavell argues, in a similar spirit, that Emersonian perfectionism and the movies it inspired are equally concerned with the achievement of self-knowledge—not knowledge of our thinking but, rather, knowledge of our desires, our passions. One difference, of course, is that the procedures of ordinary language philosophy can be employed by a solitary individual, but to achieve the kind of self-knowledge Tracy achieves in *The Philadelphia Story*, it helps to be in a conversation of a certain kind with a true friend.

Conversation is the form moral reasoning takes in Emersonian perfectionism and the genres it inspired. The conversations between the women and men in comedies of remarriage aren't just pleasurable in themselves, to us as well as to them. And they don't just lead to mutual forgiveness. Being in conversation with Dexter moves Tracy to open her eyes to the kind of person she desires to be, the kind of life she desires to live, and with whom, if anyone, she desires to share her life. Such claims are argued as clearly in *Pursuits of Happiness* as in *Cities of Words*. But *Cities of Words*, viewing these matters in the light of Emersonian perfectionism, makes the further claim that insofar as Tracy's conversation with Dexter empowers her to achieve self-knowledge, their conversation has a philosophical dimension. To be sure, in *Pursuits of Happiness* Cavell anticipates this claim when he writes, "Dexter's demand to determine for himself what is truly important and what is not is a claim to the status of a philosopher" (Cavell 1981b, 150). But Cavell wasn't yet ready to add that Dexter is Emerson's kind of philosopher—or that he is Emerson's kind of philosopher, too.

In *Pursuits of Happiness*, Cavell doesn't unambiguously *defend* Dexter, the way he defends Emerson in *Cities of Words*. When in *Pursuits of Happiness* Cavell goes on to ask whether the acceptance of individual desire, Dexter's form of self-knowledge, is of "national importance," he uses this question to help set up the chapter's wonderful closing pages. But those pages do not *answer* the question. Instead of affirming that Dexter's form of self-knowledge *is* of national importance, Cavell defers to Matthew Arnold's distinction between "the two historical forces still impelling us on the quest for perfection or salvation" (Cavell 1981b, 158). (By the way, this is the first time in Cavell's writings that he had ever invoked the idea of perfectionism.)

In *Pursuits of Happiness*, Cavell claims that these two "sources of authority—"Hellenism," that is, "spontaneity of consciousness," and "Hebraism," "strictness of conscience"—are exemplified by Dexter and Tracy, respectively, and that "what the marriage in *The Philadelphia Story* comes to" is "a proposed marriage or balance between Western culture's two forces of authority, so that American mankind can refind its object, its dedication to a more perfect union, toward the perfected human community, its right to the pursuit of happiness" (Cavell 1981b, 159).

From the standpoint of Emersonian perfectionism, however, this formulation, as eloquent as it is, doesn't quite "get things right." But it does "leave things so that they can be, and ask to be, returned to"—as in *Cities of Words* Cavell would go on to do. For although it is accurate to say that Tracy Hebraizes to a fault—especially to other people's faults—and has to learn to balance her Hebraizing with Hellenizing, Dexter, therapist and Emersonian sage, had already learned what he needed to know in order to become a philosopher of Emerson's, and Cavell's, stripe. But when he was writing *Pursuits of Happiness*, Cavell wasn't yet ready to say this. Philosophical ideas reveal their good only in stages. Then again, *Cities of Words*, too, would "leave things so that they can be, and ask to be, returned to." For Cavell, the next stage—the *last* stage—would be *Little Did I Know*.

The Philadelphia Story is about Tracy's creation, not Dexter's—about the way the "conversation of marriage" enables her to open her eyes. Dexter opens *his* eyes off camera, in the "detour" between the film's comical prologue and the time he walks into Sidney Kidd's office and sets the narrative in motion. During that "detour," he tells Mike, he did a lot of reading, including Mike's own book, which didn't help him get his eyes opened. Whether anything he read did help, Dexter doesn't say, although I suspect that *Cities of Words* might well have done the trick. Dexter's creation, how he becomes a philosopher, isn't part of the story the film tells. It is by consigning to silence Cavell's own creation as a philosopher, in other words, that *Cities of Words* "leaves things so that they can be, and asks to be, returned to." This is what Cavell did by writing *Little Did I Know*, which tells the story of how Stanley Goldstein became Stanley Cavell, the philosopher whose work, and life, this essay is celebrating.

15

Cavell, Emerson, Hitchcock

Reflections Inspired by Stanley Cavell's *Cities of Words*

Several years ago, at an earlier Sorbonne colloquium organized by Sandra Laugier, this one occasioned by the publication in French translation of *The World Viewed*, Stanley Cavell remarked that thinking about film had taught him the "necessity to become evocative in capturing the moods of faces and motions and settings, in their double existence as transient and as permanent" (Cavell and Rothman 2005, xxiii). In *Hitchcock—The Murderous Gaze*, my first book, I characterized my own aspiration as "putting into words the thinking inscribed in a film's succession of frames."

As this pair of quotations suggests, in writing about film, my way of doing things is very different from Cavell's. *The Murderous Gaze* has over six hundred frame enlargements; *Pursuits of Happiness* and *Contesting Tears*, a handful; *Cities of Words*, none. And yet, if it is by "moods of faces and motions and settings" that films express themselves, and if to put into words what a film is saying it is necessary to evoke those moods, then following the film's thinking and capturing its moods cannot be separated. Nor can a film's moods be separated from the ways the camera frames its "faces and motions and settings," the ways they appear, projected on the screen, "in their double existence as transient and as permanent." Cavell's writings

---

Adapted from a paper presented at "Cinéma et éducation morale," a colloquium at the Sorbonne organized by Sandra Laugier in 2011 on the occasion of the publication of *Cities of Words* in French translation. The essay focuses more on Emerson's writings than Cavell's, but insofar as Cavell's embrace of—indeed, identification with—Emersonian perfectionism is a major theme in *The Holiday in His Eye*, everything said here about Emerson illuminates—and was meant to illuminate—Cavell's philosophical perspective as well.

about film and mine are anchored by a common critical practice. We both call this practice "reading."

The Murderous Gaze was published in 1982. During the years I was writing the book, I was teaching at Harvard and in almost daily conversation with Cavell, who a few years earlier had been my doctoral advisor (and who never stopped being my friend and my teacher). Those were the days! He was then at work on two of his most important books: *The Claim of Reason*, his philosophical masterwork, and *Pursuits of Happiness: The Hollywood Comedy of Remarriage*, published two years later, his seminal study of the genre of romantic comedy whose members include *It Happened One Night*, *The Awful Truth*, *Bringing Up Baby*, *His Girl Friday*, *The Philadelphia Story*, *The Lady Eve*, and *Adam's Rib*. In the profound vision *Pursuits of Happiness* presents, all the leading Hollywood genres of the 1930s and 1940s found stories to tell, and ways of telling those stories, that enabled them to tap into the remarriage comedy's commitment to channeling film's awesome power to help America become a more perfect union by helping Americans take a step toward what Emerson, in his essay "History," calls the "unattained but attainable self" (Emerson and Porte 1983, 239).

In the mid-1980s, Cavell broadened and deepened this vision in a Harvard lecture course on moral reasoning (that itself broadened and deepened a course on Great Ideas of the Western World he had taught twenty years earlier, taking in stride the obstacle of having a very naïve young me as one of his teaching assistants). And twenty years after inaugurating the moral reasoning course, he made its lectures the basis of *Cities of Words*, the remarkable book whose publication in French translation we are celebrating today in its author's presence.

In his moral reasoning course, Cavell drew a new circle, in Emerson's sense, by explicitly acknowledging that the philosophical way of thinking Hollywood comedies of remarriage exemplify was also his own. By characterizing this way of thinking as a form of moral perfectionism, he acknowledged that philosophy, as he practices it, is a *moral* enterprise. And he took the momentous step of giving that enterprise— *his* enterprise—a name. In naming it "Emersonian perfectionism," Cavell declared himself to be an *Emersonian* perfectionist.

Cities of Words, whose subtitle is "Pedagogical Letters on a Register of the Moral Life," is Cavell's only work that explicitly declares his abiding commitment to teaching. Within the book, Emerson plays a privileged role insofar as his writing, and only his, is used as both an object and as a "*means, or touchstone,*" of interpretation—as a tool for reading, and for *teaching* reading. With breathtaking intellectual assurance, the book pairs chapters on thinkers of the magnitude of Aristotle, Plato, Locke, Hume, Kant, Nietzsche, Freud, and Cavell's Harvard colleague John Rawls—as well as Shakespeare, Ibsen, Henry James, and George Bernard Shaw, who are treated, in this context, as the significant thinkers these artists also were—with chapters on individual films, all classic Hollywood comedies and melodramas except for Eric Rohmer's *Tale of Winter* (1992), which in its cultivated way is as grand an entertainment as its American cousins.

Every chapter on a thinker presents a powerful, utterly original interpretation of that thinker's work, an interpretation that makes clear why it is illuminating to pair the thinker with the particular film Cavell has chosen as a match—given, in each case, his powerful, utterly original interpretation of the corresponding film. Taken together, these pairs of chapters make the case that although America has not inherited the European edifice of philosophy, America's movies have engaged in conversations with its culture that are, philosophically, fully serious. And Emerson is the linchpin that clinches Cavell's case.

As Cavell has elsewhere observed, Emerson is a thinker, with the "accuracy and consequentiality one expects of a mind worth following with that attention necessary to decipher one's own" (Cavell 1990, 1). Perhaps the same can be said about every major thinker *Cities of Words* addresses. However, the idea that without following our own thinking we cannot know the minds of others, and that without knowing the minds of others we cannot know our own mind—the idea that it is by reading and by writing, by conversation understood broadly, that we come to know our own minds as well as the minds of others—is purest Emerson. And purest Cavell.

"People wish to be settled," Emerson writes, but "only so far as they are unsettled is there any hope for them" (Emerson and Porte 1983, 413). *Cities of Words* unsettled my thinking about Hitchcock, or helped me to recognize how unsettled my thoughts had become since the publication of *The Murderous Gaze* thirty years earlier. In that book, I argued that in Hitchcock thrillers murder and marriage are both metaphors for their author's relationship with viewers, and that being suspended between two incompatible pictures of his own art was Hitchcock's principled position. In effect, *The Murderous Gaze* pictured Hitchcock as choosing, on principle, not to choose. Between what alternatives? Between an art committed to walking in the direction of the unattained but attainable self, and an art that equates itself with murder. But no principle can justify choosing not to choose between being principled and being unprincipled. As I put it in the introduction to *Must We Kill the Thing We Love?*, "Not to choose is to *be* unprincipled."

In *Little Did I Know*, his philosophical memoir, Cavell discerns a kind of necessity in contingent moments of his past. They could have been different, but then he would be different. Our futures are not yet written, and we do not have to let others write them for us. Nor, to paraphrase Emerson, are we bound to write our futures in foolish consistency with our pasts. That is Cavell's faith, as it was Emerson's. The Hitchcock who emerges in the pages of *The Murderous Gaze*, however, is split between embracing and resisting such a faith. *Cities of Words* helped open my eyes to this fact, and also to the more unsettling fact that in writing my book I was split no less than Hitchcock. This split manifested itself in a conflict or tension between my practice of reading, which was, without my realizing it, underwritten by Emersonian perfectionism, and certain conclusions I drew from my readings, which were incompatible with Emerson's—and Cavell's—way of thinking.

To be sure, I had my reasons for drawing those conclusions. But I no longer wished to be the kind of person who would be satisfied by such reasons. Thus, I found myself moved to write a new book about Hitchcock. This new book pictures Hitchcock as profoundly attracted to the Emersonian perfectionism exemplified by the Hollywood genres Cavell studied. *The 39 Steps* followed the lead of *It Happened*

One Night, for example, by ending with the union of a man and woman that holds hope of being a relationship worth having. But Hitchcock also never tired of quoting Oscar Wilde's line, "Yet each man kills the thing he loves." Hence the book's title: *Must We Kill the Thing We Love? Emersonian Perfectionism and the Films of Alfred Hitchcock*.

It is a defining feature of the Hitchcock thriller that a murderous villain dwells within its world. As I argued in *The Murderous Gaze*, the Hitchcock villain, master of the art of murder, is also a stand-in for the film's author, Hitchcock, master of what he called the "art of pure cinema." Hitchcock's villains are his accomplices in artistic creation. And Hitchcock is their accomplice—or they are his—in murder. This is one reason Hitchcock thrillers call for the stylistic signatures (the "tunnel shots," the "////"s, curtain raisings, eclipses, white flashes, circles, frames-within-frames, profile shots, and symbolically charged colors, sounds, and objects, such as staircases, curtains, lamps, and hands), which *The Murderous Gaze* catalogues. These "signature motifs," as I call them, function as a means by which Hitchcock declares his authorship and links his role as author with that of the murderous villain. That his own art has a murderous aspect is a—at the time I wrote *The Murderous Gaze*, I believed it was *the*—quintessentially Hitchcockian idea.

In comedies of remarriage, the outcome of a failed marriage is divorce or, at worst, a lifetime of unhappiness. In Hitchcock thrillers, the worst case is murder. Divorced couples can remarry, but murder—divorce Hitchcock style—is final. (*The Trouble with Harry* [1955], in which the Shirley MacLaine character's dead husband keeps turning up like a bad penny, is the exception that proves this rule). Remarriage comedies conclude with their couples achieving mutual forgiveness. But within a world on film, it is impossible for murderers to be forgiven. The victim is in no condition to forgive his or her murderer, and no living person has the standing to offer forgiveness on the victim's behalf. Hitchcock, a churchgoing Catholic, may have believed in the existence of a God with the power to absolve even mortal sins like murder. As author, however, Hitchcock wielded godlike powers over his characters, but not the power to grant himself the authority to absolve murderers; he could play God, but he could not make himself God, thank God. Murderers terminate their victims' cycles of death and rebirth that make it possible, in Emerson's view, for human beings to walk in the direction of the unattained but attainable self. By irrevocably depriving their victims of the freedom to change that is a defining feature of being human, murderers, in Hitchcock thrillers, forfeit their own freedom to change, hence their own humanity. They are condemned never to become other than the murderers their own acts have made them.

Must We Kill the Thing We Love? argues that Hitchcock's ambivalence toward Emersonian perfectionism, as reflected in the defining features of the Hitchcock thriller, was the driving force of his work. In tracing the trajectory of his career, the book discerns, in the vicissitudes of his relationship to Emersonian perfectionism, a complicated progression from his British thrillers of the 1930s, like *The 39 Steps, Secret Agent*, and *Sabotage*; to his earliest American films, such as *Rebecca, Mr. and Mrs. Smith*, and *Suspicion* (made when the Emersonian moral outlook that was in the ascendancy in Hollywood from the release of *It Happened One Night* in 1934 to the end of the decade was beginning to suffer repression); to his wartime films, such as *Shadow of a Doubt* and its companion piece, *Lifeboat*; to postwar films like *Notorious* and *Rope*; to his masterpieces of the 1950s, culminating in *The Wrong Man*, *Vertigo*, and *North by Northwest*; to *Psycho*; to *The Birds*; and ultimately to *Marnie*, in which the Emersonian side of Hitchcock's split artistic personality definitively prevailed.

In *Must We Kill the Thing We Love?*, I argue that despite the resistance to Emersonian perfectionism that Hitchcock definitively overcame only late in his career, he and Emerson, *as authors*, have surprisingly deep affinities. One significant feature that Hitchcock's films have in common with Emerson's essays is that they are meant to offer something to everyone—they were meant to be, and were, *popular*—and yet the more closely we attend to them, the deeper they reveal themselves to be, the more they instruct us as to the kind and degree of attention necessary to follow their thinking, to *read* them. Another is that every Hitchcock film and Emerson essay "draws a circle" encompassing the circles the preceding ones have drawn. Yet another is that what Cavell calls "self-images" are everywhere to be found in their works—and Cavell's own. Hitchcock's signature motifs, which declare his authorship, serve as invocations of the movie screen, the film frame, the camera lens, and so on, and are precisely analogous to Emerson's "master tones," as Cavell calls them—philosophically charged words that recur in Emerson's writings—and in Cavell's writings, to be sure—within each essay and from essay to essay, their occurrences meant to resonate with each other, and that at one level refer to the writing itself.

Hitchcock was powerfully drawn to the idea that we live out our lives in private traps within which, in the words of Norman Bates, "for all we scratch and claw, we never budge an inch." Norman is no Emersonian. Nor was Emerson a Batesian (unless this means a follower not of Norman Bates, but the late (and sorely missed) philosopher Stanley Bates). Yet Emerson could write, in an oft-quoted passage, "Every man beholds his human condition with a degree of melancholy. As a ship aground is battered by the waves, so man, imprisoned in mortal life, lies open to the mercy of coming events" (Emerson and Porte 1983, 418). If the human condition is to be "imprisoned in mortal life," is our humanness not a trap in which we are born—a trap we can never escape for all we "scratch and claw," as Norman puts it, or for all we "clutch at things," to use Emerson's virtually identical metaphor?

"Clutching" is one of Emerson's "master tones." Objects "slip through our fingers . . . when we clutch hardest at them," he writes in his great essay "Experience." "I take this evanescence and lubricity of all objects, which lets them slip through our finger's then when we clutch hardest, to be the most unhandsome part of our condition" (Emerson and Porte 1983, 473). Cavell takes Emerson to mean that what is most unattractive about us, most "unhandsome" about our human condition, is not that "objects for us, to which we seek attachment, are, as it were, in themselves evanescent and lubricious." Rather, it is "what happens when we seek to deny the standoffishness of objects by clutching at them, which is to say, when we conceive thinking, say the application of concepts in judgments, as grasping something, say synthesizing" (Cavell and Hodge 2003, 117). What is "unhandsome" is not that we are finite, limited in our powers, that our concepts and judgments lack unity, that we are creatures of moods. In Cavell's view, the idea that what is "unhandsome" is our "clutching at things" in our human effort to escape our humanness is central to the philosophical enterprise Emerson took himself to be founding, which in the New World was to replace the European edifice of philosophy. Indeed, Cavell characterizes Emerson's enterprise—which Cavell takes himself to be inheriting—as the "overcoming of thinking as clutching."

In favor of what?

In writing about "Experience," Cavell gives the name "indirection" to something Emerson's essay refrains from naming: the opposite of "clutching," that which would be the "most handsome," the "most attractive," part of our condition. "The idea of indirection," Cavell specifies, "is not to invite us to strike glancingly, as if to take a sideswipe; it is instead to invite us, where called for, to be struck, impressed." The opposite of "clutching" is, as he puts it, "the specifically human form of attractiveness—attraction naming the rightful call we have upon one another, and that I and the world make upon one another . . . (Heidegger's term for the opposite of grasping the world is that of being *drawn* to things.)" (Cavell and Hodge 2003, 135).

Just as "clutching" is one of Emerson's "master tones," images of a hand clutching or clutching at or losing its grip on something constitute one of Hitchcock's "signature motifs." Such images appear at crucial moments in every Hitchcock thriller. Think of Scottie in the opening of *Vertigo* desperately clutching at the falling policeman's hand and watching in horror as the man plummets to his death. Or Alicia, in *Notorious*, clutching the key to the wine cellar. Or Bruno, in *Strangers on a Train*, desperately reaching through the grating for the lighter that seems just beyond his reach. Or the dying Bruno involuntarily unclenching his hand, revealing to the police the lighter he had been holding in his clutches. Or Marion, in *Psycho*'s shower murder sequence, her body slowly sliding down the wall, looking with glazed eyes in the direction of the camera as she reaches out to something she cannot see, something whose presence she senses—as if she were trying to reach the camera, or reach the screen, or, rather, to reach through the screen to our world on the "other side."

At this moment in *Psycho*, the camera pulls slowly away, precisely reversing the movement by which it had earlier allowed the shower curtain to engulf the movie screen—as if the "safety curtain" that separates us from the projected world, and the shower curtain Marion's murderer tears asunder, were one and the same. Now, Marion's hand, framed in extreme close-up, continues its movement until it grasps the shower curtain in the foreground of the frame. She is holding on for dear life. But her grip is so strong, so fierce, that it bears an aspect of violence, as if she were struggling less to hold herself up than to pull the curtain down with her as she falls, dying.

As this shot in *Psycho* makes explicit, Hitchcock's recurring images of a hand clutching or clutching at or losing its grip on something can be viewed as having a self-referential dimension, as can all his "signature motifs." Like Emerson's "master tones," they are "self-images," in Cavell's sense. That is, they participate in the films'

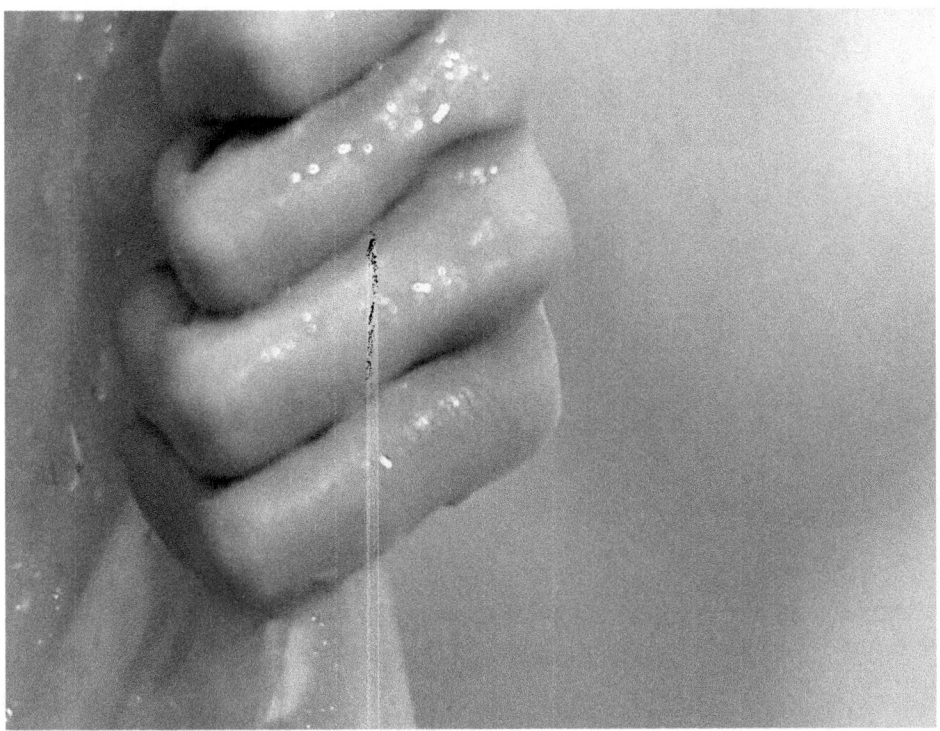

thinking—at one level, their thinking about their own way of thinking, about *film's* way of thinking. They invite—or provoke—us to open our eyes to the fact that films do not think by "clutching at things." The "art of pure cinema," as Hitchcock liked to call it, is an art of "indirection." If Hitchcock had consciously sought a way to express cinematically Emerson's thought that what is most "unhandsome" about us is our effort to escape our real condition by "clutching at things," he could not have come up with a more perfect illustration than the moment—a crucial turning point in the film—when Marnie, having unlocked the office safe, reaches out toward the stacks of twenty dollar bills inside, but, unaware that Mark is watching, finds her hand unable, or unwilling, to grasp the money, however desperately she clutches at it. This is the moment Marnie knows in her heart, if not yet consciously, that she really wishes to change, to abandon the way of thinking that has for so long imprisoned her, a way of thinking that Hitchcock, no less than Emerson, envisions, metaphorically, as "clutching at" things.

Marnie's mood is very different from Marion's. In taking a step, however unconsciously, toward the unattained but attainable self, she is, to paraphrase that great Emersonian Bob Dylan, busy being born, not busy dying. But this shot, even more emphatically than the one in *Psycho*, invites or provokes us to recognize that films think by "indirection," not by "clutching at things." By equating, visually, Marnie's clutching at the money with the gesture of reaching toward the camera, the close, frontal framing conveys the impression that what makes the money

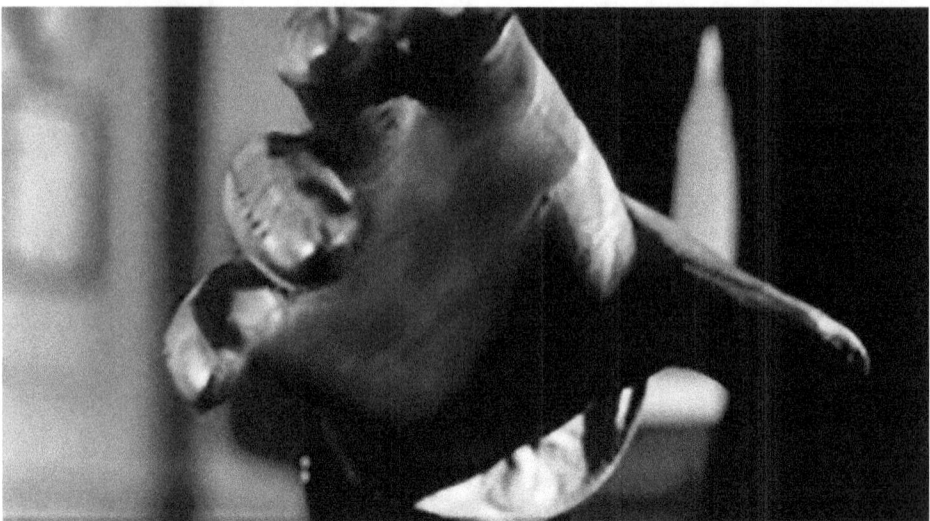

unreachable by her is what makes the camera unreachable by her, what makes the screen unreachable by her, what makes our world unreachable by her, what makes her world unreachable by us.

At the end of the film, with Mark standing by her, Marnie *is* changed. No longer believing that she is fated always to kill the thing she loves, she is finally free, has finally freed herself, from her "private trap." She has not escaped from her mortal life, her humanness. She has come to feel, as Tracy puts it at the end of *The Philadelphia Story*, "like a human, like a human being." And by creating *Marnie*, I wish to believe and I do believe, Hitchcock, too, freed himself from his own "private trap"—his belief that his own art, metaphorically, is the moral equivalent of murder. Overcoming the Hitchcock thriller's murderous aspect, which had always seemed to define his identity as an artist, he finally abandoned his ambivalence toward the Emersonian perfectionism he had longed to embrace for the sake of humanity, but believed he had to resist for the sake of his art.

How "unhandsome" is the notion, which for so long was dogma within American film studies, that to think seriously about films we must break our attachment to them, stop letting them move us, so we can hold them in our clutches! For if we keep ourselves from being struck by films, keep them from making impressions on us, we cannot think about their value, why we seek our attachments to them, how they attract us, what rightful call they make upon us. That is, we cannot think seriously about films at all.

Equally "unhandsome" is the notion, once dogma within film studies as well, that in classical movies the camera is an instrument of "the male gaze"—as if there were only one thing men's eyes are forever doing, and as if the camera is forever doing this same one thing, that thing being "clutching at" women, treating female subjects as objects to be seized, held, kept, interrogated, controlled. But if the camera's way of capturing "faces and motions and settings" were really by "clutching at" them, their moods would slip through its fingers, figuratively speaking, and films couldn't attract us, strike us, make impressions on us, express themselves with indirection, the way they do.

In truth, there *is* only one thing movie cameras do: they film whatever is in front of them. Cameras are machines. They have no subjectivity, no moods in whose hues they paint the world. As Hitchcock knew full well, cameras are not capable of "clutching at" people, but they have no need to do so in order to capture the moods human bodies express. This is because human bodies possess what Emerson calls "wonderful expressiveness." In his late essay "Behavior," he writes, "If [the human body] were made of glass, or of air, and the thoughts were written on steel tablets within, it could not publish more truly its meaning than now. The whole economy of nature is bent on expression. The tell-tale body is all tongues" (Emerson 1911, 236). And this leads to a brilliant passage that shows, by citing some of the amazing variety of things that it can do and express, how the eye is exemplary of the "wonderful expressiveness" of the human body.

Our bodies *express* our moods, make us readable by others, as they make others readable by us. "Men are like Geneva watches with crystal faces which expose the whole movement," Emerson writes. "They carry the liquor of life flowing up and down in these beautiful bottles, and announcing to the curious how it is with them. . . . We look into the eyes to know if this other form is another self, and the eyes will not lie, but make a faithful confession what inhabitant is there. When we look into another's eyes, both our eyes and the eyes we behold testify that this "other form" *is* "another self," that the "liquor of life" that flows in us flows in the other as well. "'Tis remarkable, too," Emerson adds, "that the spirit that appears at the windows of the house does at once invest himself in a new form of his own to the mind of the beholder." We are not alone. When our eyes communicate, an "inundation of life and thought" that "moves all the springs of wonder" is "discharged from one soul into another." It is "natural magic" (Emerson 1911, 285). But if "communication by the glance" is the "bodily symbol of identity of nature," as Emerson asserts, this other "self" is identical to us *in nature*.

The "forms" that appear in the "window" that is the movie screen, too, appear to us as beings whose nature is no different from our own. In an Emersonian spirit, comedies of remarriage express the idea that these "beautiful bottles" are other selves, that they carry the "liquor of life." Hitchcock was drawn to this idea. But he was no less drawn to the idea that film is a medium of taxidermy—as if the "forms" projected on the movie screen have no more life than Norman Bates's stuffed birds; as if film has an *unnatural* magic—the power to breathe into these "forms," these "spirits," only an imitation of life. This may seem a way of thinking alien to Emerson.

And yet, it resonates with the metaphorical language he employs to characterize the action of what he calls "the intellect." When the intellect casts on a "fact in our life" the "certain, wandering light" of a "lantern," it transforms it into a "thought," a "truth," which is an object "impersonal and immortal. It is the past restored, but embalmed. A better art than that of Egypt has taken fear and corruption out of it" (Emerson 1903, 327). The projector is literally a lantern. Metaphorically, the camera is a lantern, too. Should we find it surprising that André Bazin, a century later, used the identical metaphor to characterize the film image?

In "Intellect," Emerson writes, "Every man, in the degree in which he has wit and culture, finds his curiosity inflamed concerning the modes of living and thinking of other men." These are, as he elsewhere remarks, the very stuff of novels—and, of course, films. In our everyday lives, we "aggregate" such "facts in our life," as he calls them. In an inspired gloss on Plato's allegory of the cave, Emerson writes, "The walls of rude minds are scrawled all over with facts" (Emerson 1903, 330).

These "facts" are traces of past experiences. "In common hours, we have the same facts as in the uncommon or inspired, but they do not sit for their portraits; they are not detached, but lie in a web" (Emerson 1903, 7). To isolate a "fact in our life" from "the web of our unconsciousness" is, metaphorically, to shine a lantern on an object and make it sit for its portrait—as if we were pointing a camera at it, isolating it in a close-up, and projecting its image on a movie screen. In illuminating a "fact of our life," the intellect/lantern enables us to read its inscription. Indeed, given the nature of the object the lantern illuminates, and the nature of the lantern itself, there is no difference between seeing the object and reading what the lantern's light reveals to be inscribed on it. The light reveals the object to *be* an inscription. And to see it in this light *is* to read it.

By "making a fact the subject of thought," the intellect raises it above the "considerations of time and place, of you and me, of profit and hurt" that "tyrannize over" men's minds. Because the mind's vision "is not like the vision of the eye, but is union with the things known," the intellect has the power to dissolve the difference between seeing and reading. Here, too, Emerson's metaphorical language pictures the "action of the mind" (Emerson and Porte 1983, 417–18) in terms that make it irresistible to draw parallels with film. No director understood more fully than Hitchcock that film, too, can dissolve the difference between seeing and reading. Given that films make their thoughts knowable indirectly, by capturing and casting "moods of faces and motions and settings," how could such a medium not have this power? To read Cary Grant's expression in the close-up Hitchcock presents to us at the moment in *North by Northwest* at which Roger learns that Eve is a double agent, all we have to do is see it.

Emerson understood the "facts in our life" the intellect "raises" to be traces of past experiences—traces that our mind's eye beholds in a "state of rapture" when a lantern appears, as if by magic, and isolates a "fact" from the "web of our unconsciousness" by shining its "certain, wandering light" upon it. Film images, too, are traces of the past. The "faces and motions and settings" projected on the screen were once present to the camera that filmed them. In turn, our experiences of films become "facts in our life" that we "aggregate," like all the "facts" woven into the "web of our unconsciousness." This is precisely what makes it possible for Cavell to open *The World Viewed* with the haunting sentence, "Memories of movies are strand over strand with memories of my life."

When a lantern shines its "certain, wandering light" on a "fact in our life," an intuition dawns in us; a thought is born. We behold the "fact" as illustrating a principle, a truth. Because the vision of the mind is "union with the thing known," the thought *is* the lantern. But it once was the lowly "fact" the lantern illuminates. Facts beget thoughts; thoughts beget further thoughts. Hence Emerson's formulation: "Every intellection is mainly prospective" (Emerson 1903, 332).

Our thoughts could not beget further thoughts, however, if the intellect were not "constructive," as he puts it, as well as "receptive." It is futile to try to "clutch at" an intuition in an effort to keep it from falling back into the "web of our unconsciousness." We must "pay the tuition" for the intuition by expressing it, making it available to ourselves and others. We have to "bethink us where we have been, what we have seen, and report, as truly as we can, what we have beheld." To "revisit the day" in this way, Emerson proclaims, "is what is called Truth" (Emerson 1903, 329). What more perfect description could there be of the act of "reading" a film as both Cavell and I have aspired to perform it?

The constructive intellect "produces thoughts, sentences, poems, plans, designs, systems"—and films, not to mention books about films. For a thought to be "reported," *published*, it needs "a vehicle of art by which it is conveyed." It "must become picture or sensible object," Emerson writes. "The most wonderful inspirations die with their subject, if he has no hand to paint them to the senses. As all men have some access to primary truth, so all have some art or power of communication in their head, but only in the artist does it descend into the hand." He concludes: "We must learn the language of facts" (Emerson 1903, 335). But film images are not made by hand, as *The World Viewed* reminds us. Godard defined film as "truth twenty-four times a second" to register that the camera is a machine that can do nothing but capture whatever takes place in front of it, as the projector can do nothing but "report" whatever the camera captures. This is what makes it possible for film to manifest the astonishing facility it shares with what Emerson, in a marvelous passage, calls the "mystic pencil" with which we "draw" our dreams.

> As soon as we let our will go, and let the unconscious states ensue, see what cunning draftsmen we are! We entertain ourselves with wonderful forms of men, of women, of animals, of gardens, of woods, and of monsters, and the mystic pencil wherewith we then draw has no awkwardness or inexperience, no meagerness or poverty; . . . the whole canvas which it paints is life-like, and apt to touch us with terror, with tenderness, with desire, and with grief. (Emerson 1903, 337)

Having no will to let go, the "mystic pencil" that draws films likewise "has no awkwardness or inexperience, no meagerness or poverty." Because the whole canvas it paints is reality, although reality re-created in its own image, the world on film is life itself, and our experiences of films become "facts in our life" like any other. The "language of facts" is film's mother tongue. In a film such as *North by Northwest*, every framing, every cut, every camera movement, at once inscribes an intuition and "pays the tuition" for that intuition. Thus, it dissolves the difference, in a way only films can, between the "receptive" and the "constructive" intellect. But films do not *automatically* express thoughts. It is possible for a camera to isolate a face in a close-up without "raising" that expression, the way Hitchcock's camera unfailingly does—without illuminating it, revealing it to be a legible inscription of the *film's* thought.

Nor do films *automatically* "touch us with terror, with tenderness, with desire, or with grief" any more than novels do. "Society is the stage on which manners are shown," Emerson writes in his essay "Manners." "Novels can be as useful as Bibles if they teach you the secret that the best of life is conversation and the greatest success is perfect understanding between sincere people" (Emerson 1919, 244). This is the gospel Emerson's essays preach in the hope of achieving "perfect understanding" with their readers. "Experience," like every Emerson essay, aspires to take a step toward reconciling the "discrepance" between the "world I converse with in the city and in the farms" and the world "I think" (Emerson 2000, 326). This requires at once "raising" the world of the everyday and bringing down to earth our thoughts of a more perfect world, acknowledging what we value in what is near to us, embracing what is "handsome" in our condition. "Why not realize your world?" is the challenge Emerson poses to his readers—and to himself.

Teaching that "the best of life is conversation and the greatest success is perfect understanding between sincere people" is the aspiration of comedies of remarriage, too. A novel can assert that a man's eyes "have no mud at the bottom of them," but cannot show such a man. Because the world projected on the screen does not stand in need of being "realized," films are, in a sense, better equipped than novels to preach the Emersonian gospel that we can, and must, "realize" the world we "think."

As my moment on this stage is transient, and as *Cities of Words* is permanent, I must draw these reflections to a close with a final thought.

A shadow of a doubt darkened the Hitchcock thriller. We can think of this shadow as the thought, or we might say the suspicion, that we are fated always to kill the thing we love. Or that we are all in private traps from which we can never be freed. Or that we all have "mud at the bottom of our eyes," hence that insofar as it is his own thoughts that Hitchcock thrillers make knowable, insofar as the camera is the instrument of a merely human author, it, too, has "mud at the bottom of its eye," as it were. Or that the art of pure cinema is itself corrupt, and corrupting. How this shadow came to be lifted, how this doubt came to be overcome or transcended, how Hitchcock came to abandon the ambivalence that seemed to define his identity as an artist, how he finally came to embrace what Emerson calls the wonderful "way of life," is the story I have told in *Must We Kill the Thing We Love?* Had Stanley Cavell not taught his course on moral reasoning, such a story would not have become mine to tell. How *Cities of Words* helped teach me to overcome or transcend my own doubt, to abandon my ambivalence to the Emersonian perfectionism my new book wholeheartedly embraces, is the story I have told here.

16

On Richard Allen's "Hitchcock and Cavell"

My mother may not always have practiced what she preached, but she inculcated in me the principle that if you can't say anything nice about someone, don't say anything at all. Thus, I will begin by saying, in all sincerity, that Richard Allen is a gifted, serious writer whose critical writings I respect and admire. I think of him as a friend, so it doesn't give me pleasure to say what I will be saying here. But Stanley Cavell's work means too much to me to allow Allen's claim to have refuted his philosophy—a claim seconded by Malcolm Turvey, co-editor of their anthology *Wittgenstein, Theory and the Arts*—to go unchallenged. And it is my further hope that showing, point by point, how Allen's essay fails to acknowledge—in effect, *erases*—Cavell's thought will cast light on his way of thinking philosophically. So, for the remainder of this piece, no more Mr. Nice Guy. (Mom, wherever you are, I hope you understand.)

In *The Talk of the Town* (George Stevens, 1942), Jean Arthur, cooing at the Cary Grant character, amorously repeats his name, "Oh Theodore, Theodore..." until Grant abruptly stops her cooing by saying, "You can't do that with a name like Theodore." From its opening paragraph on, Allen's essay continually characterizes

---

In 2000, I presented a response to an earlier version of Richard Allen's essay. The essay that follows—that most recent of the (uneasy) polemical pieces I've decided to include in the present volume—was written in response to the publication in 2006 of "Hitchcock and Cavell" in "Thinking through Cinema: Film as Philosophy," special issue, *Journal of Aesthetics and Art Criticism* 64, no. 1 (Winter 2006): 43–53. It incorporates material from my remarks at that occasion. I presented this paper, in its present form, at the conference "Perfectionism in Literature, Philosophy and Film: A Tribute to Stanley Cavell," University of New Mexico, Philosophy Department, Albuquerque, 2019. Many thanks to the organizer, Russell Goodman.

what he calls "Cavell's philosophy" by summarizing or paraphrasing, only occasionally quoting, his actual words. You can't do that with a writer like Cavell. Allen often gets Cavell almost right. But with Cavell's writing, or Emerson's before him, getting him almost right means getting him completely wrong.

In a 1989 interview, Cavell observed that if you give up traditional routes to conviction in philosophy—proceeding systematically by formal arguments, for example, as both Wittgenstein and Heidegger felt it necessary to do, then "conviction must be achieved by the writing itself, by nothing other than this prose just here, as it's passing before our eyes" (Conant and Cavell 1989, 59). It is characteristic of a Cavell sentence, like an Emerson sentence, that it pointedly does *not* say what we might take it to say if we fail to attend to its words with the kind and degree of attention required, as Cavell liked to put it, to follow our own thinking, to know our own minds. One summarizes or paraphrases Cavell at one's peril.

Take the essay's opening paragraph. (The Henny Youngman in me is tempted to add, "Please!") Every sentence of this paragraph gets Cavell wrong. These are the paragraph's first two sentences:

> Stanley Cavell's philosophy and Alfred Hitchcock's films share a distinctive feature: they are both concerned with the relationship between doubt and romance. Cavell is a thinker who has forcefully articulated the idea that the narrative of heterosexual romance is a place where philosophical doubt or skepticism enters into the everyday or the ordinary. (Allen 2006, 43)

I don't think of Hitchcock's films as primarily concerned with the relationship between doubt and romance; Hitchcock had other fish to fry. But I recognize that Allen, in his critical writings, has made an honest case for that view. As a characterization of a position Cavell "forcefully articulates," though, it doesn't hold water.

First, it is clear from the rest of the paragraph that when he refers here to "doubt," he means the radical doubt Allen calls "philosophical doubt." Allen's language here is un-Cavellian, however, insofar as it implies that the terms "philosophical doubt" and "skepticism" are simply interchangeable for Cavell. This is a point—I think of it as the essay's fatal flaw—that we will return to more than once.

Second, it is not un-Cavellian to call the films he writes about in *Pursuits of Happiness*, say, or the relationships of their protagonists, "romances"—but only if we keep in mind, as Allen fails to do, that "romance," for Cavell, is a concept that his readings of the films, and the films themselves as he reads them, are engaged in revising—revising our understanding of what romances *are*, what romance *is*.

Third, Allen's formulation "the narrative of heterosexual romance" *is* un-Cavellian in its implication that there is such a thing—*one* such thing—as "the narrative of heterosexual romance." It is a main thrust of *Pursuits of Happiness*, after all, that the comedy of remarriage is one genre of the classical Hollywood cinema, one kind of narrative, distinguishable from others (such as "the melodrama of the unknown woman," as *Contesting Tears* calls it) that incorporates a couple's achieving, or failing to achieve, a kind of relationship (intimate, yes, but also public, "capable of withstanding, and returning" society's gaze, as Cavell puts it in *Contesting Tears*) that constitutes a true marriage—a new kind of marriage these films teach us to think of as possible—"marriage," like "romance," being a concept Cavell takes these films, and his writings about them, to be thinking through and revising.

Already by the end sentence of his first paragraph, Allen's tendency to overlook the diversity of what we call "romances" comes back to bite him when he commits the quite egregious error of saying that Cavell's 1981 essay on *North by Northwest* claims that the film is "an exemplification of what Cavell calls 'Comedies of Remarriage'"—altogether ignoring what Cavell actually says in his essay, the main thrust of which is to elucidate the features of Hitchcock's film that *exclude* it from the remarriage comedy genre (Cavell 1981a, passim).

Fourth, although these Hollywood genres have sources, among them Ibsen's *A Doll's House* and Shakespeare's *The Winter's Tale*, the comedy of remarriage, and by extension the melodrama of the unknown woman (a genre Cavell takes to be "derived" from it) distinguish themselves from classical "narratives of heterosexual romance"—both so-called Old Comedy and New Comedy, for example—precisely by their commitment to rethinking such concepts as "romance" and "marriage."

Fifth, in Allen's formulation "the narrative of heterosexual romance," the word "heterosexual" has no function other than to intimate that Cavell's writings not only are tainted with patriarchal ideology, as some have falsely charged, but also tainted with what in today's academic parlance is called "heteronormativity"—an equally groundless charge.

Sixth, when Allen invokes what he takes to be Cavell's idea of "a place where philosophical doubt or skepticism enters into the everyday or the ordinary," his wording again implies that the terms "philosophical doubt" and "skepticism" are interchangeable for Cavell. Actually, "philosophical doubt" is not a term Cavell never used, if for no other reason than that it wrongly suggests that the word "doubt," as philosophers use it, refers to a special *kind* of doubt. Doubt is doubt. A term that Cavell did find useful is "philosophical skepticism," precisely because it suggests that skepticism manifests itself in forms other than the form it has taken in modern philosophy since Descartes. It isn't radical doubt as to the existence of the "external world" that "enters into the everyday or the ordinary" in the genres of comedy and melodrama Cavell wrote books about—or in our lives in the world. It is skepticism with respect to the knowledge of others—the only kind of skepticism it is possible for human beings to *live*.

In his late book *Cities of Words*, Cavell writes,

> Continental philosophizing, from Hegel to Heidegger and to Lévinas, takes up inescapably our encounter with the other, but as a perpetual struggle, not as posing a further skeptical issue within epistemology that might conceivably find a resolution. In Anglo-American philosophizing, the presence of the other has only since the middle of the twentieth century, in Wittgenstein's *Investigations*, become a featured topic of

philosophical investigation. The problem of the existence of other minds is the formulation given in the Anglo-American tradition of philosophy to the skeptical question whether I can know of the existence (not, as primarily in Descartes and in Hume, of myself and of God and of the external world, but) of human creatures other than myself, know them to be, as it were, like myself. (Cavell 2005a, 110)

It is a central claim of *The Claim of Reason* that what philosophy knows as skepticism is what Shakespearean theater knows as tragedy. Cavell's claim is that both are responses to the same thing—to the reality that our condition is to exist, as separate, embodied, talking, finite human beings, in a world in which we are not alone. In part 4 of *The Claim of Reason*, Cavell argues that Othello's story is a tragedy because as painful as it is for him to believe that he doesn't know with certainty that Desdemona, who means the world to him, is faithful, doubting her love is less painful than acknowledging her love would be, for that would require acknowledging that she is real, a creature of flesh and blood separate from him, hence that he, too, is finite, mortal, fated to die. For Cavell, in other words, Othello's tragedy isn't that he doubts; it's that he fails to acknowledge something he knows, something he cannot simply fail to know, something he *refuses* to recognize that he knows.

Allen's essay does at times register the fact that Cavell understands skepticism to manifest itself in a variety of forms, not solely as Cartesian doubt. Thus, he quotes this fine passage from *In Quest of the Ordinary*, published a decade after *The Claim of Reason*: "Skepticism is a place, perhaps the central secular place, in which the human wish to deny the condition of human existence is expressed" (Cavell 1988, 5). But as Allen repeatedly does in his essay, he slips back into using the word "skepticism" as if it were interchangeable with radical doubt as Descartes conceived of it. Thus, Allen commits what academic philosophers call a "howler" when he follows this quote—Cavell's own words can always be counted on to say what he means, to "pay the tuition" for each intuition, as Emerson would put it—with a sentence of his own that begins, "By skepticism, [Cavell] means the familiar philosophical argument"—here he quotes from *The Claim of Reason*—"that we can never know with certainty of the existence of something; call it the external world, and call it other minds" (Cavell 1979b, 37).

That is pointedly what the word "skepticism" does *not* mean in the passage from *In Quest of the Ordinary*. Allen's inattentiveness to Cavell's words—to "this prose, just here"—leads him doubly astray because, in context, the words from *The Claim of Reason* that he quotes actually mean the exact *opposite* of what Allen takes them to mean. The quote is from a passage that *contests* the view—and those who take Wittgenstein to hold this view—that skepticism is defined by what Allen calls that "familiar philosophical argument"—what in *The Claim of Reason* Cavell calls "the concluding thesis of skepticism" (Cavell 1979b, 37).

Allen continues. "What is 'the condition of human existence' that human beings wish to deny and why do they wish to deny it?" His answer to the first question: "Broadly speaking, by 'the condition of human existence' Cavell seems to mean"—the "seems" is gratuitous; Cavell's language about this is perfectly clear—"human mortality or 'finitude.'" Apropos of his second question, Allen writes: "The wish or impulse to deny human mortality seems"—that word again; the "seams" of his argument are showing—"to arise out of the very fact that to be human is to be aware of one's mortality" (Allen 2006, 44). Why wouldn't it seem so to Cavell? Doesn't it seem so to you? And I suspect that it also seems to you, as it did to Cavell, that, as Allen paraphrases him, "Human beings are inevitably drawn to conceive of their embodied nature as a constraint or limitation that they seek to overcome or deny"—although the words "inevitably" and "seek" are too strong to catch Cavell's drift, which is that for human beings skepticism is inescapably a threat, a *possibility*, not that skepticism is our inescapable *fate*.

Allen writes, "Although Cavell admits that"—here he quotes from another fine passage from *In Quest of the Ordinary*—"'there is no (single) motive' underlying 'the human denial of the conditions of humanity,' he requires a quite general explanation to support his theory" (Allen 2006, 46). Allen's language deceptively suggests that it is *Cavell* who is asserting that the human impulse to skepticism, understood as a response to a sense of disappointment or dissatisfaction with the human condition, is a "theory" that stands in need of a general explanation. Why should it? It is no more a "theory" than it is a "theory" that human beings wish to live, to be free, to pursue happiness. For Cavell, as for Wittgenstein, explanations come to an end somewhere.

Allen gets Cavell almost right—that is, completely wrong—when he writes, "Cavell uses the term 'skepticism' to describe the isolation from or overidentification with the other," where "'skepticism' is interpreted as a failure of 'acknowledgment,' a failure to attain a realistic sense of shared finitude that issues from a deluded quest for certainty" (Allen 2006, 51). For Cavell, failures of acknowledgment are *not* failures to attain "a realistic sense of shared finitude"; they are failures to *respond*, to *act*, in a way that acknowledges a particular claim that another person's separate existence makes on one. Achieving a "sense of shared finitude," no matter how "realistic," is not enough.

When in *It Happened One Night* Peter smooths the hay for Ellie to lie down on it, there's a moment when they *almost* kiss, but Peter pulls away. Framed in a luminous close-up, Ellie asks him what he's thinking about. He answers that he was wondering "what makes dames like you so dizzy." Clearly, in implying that Ellie's mind—the mind of any "dame"?—is too "dizzy," too irrational, for him—for any man?—to comprehend, Peter is denying what he is really thinking about, the feelings his attraction to Ellie has stirred up in him. Is he in the grip of "philosophical doubt" as to whether other minds exist?

And when Capra ends the sequence with his camera lingering on Ellie *thinking*, is *she* gripped by "philosophical doubt as to the existence of other minds"? Not if we picture doubt the way Descartes did. But it is part of Cavell's understanding of the comedy of remarriage that a film like *It Happened One Night* addresses, *and aspires to resolve*, what philosophers call "the problem of other minds" by reconceiving it, we might say by envisioning it as the problem, for a woman and a man, of becoming human to one another.

When Ellie later walks around the "Walls of Jericho" to declare that she is the woman Peter has been dreaming of finding, he fails to declare his feelings for her not because of what he doubts, but because of what he knows (in his heart, as we say). Cavell writes, in a memorable passage,

> Why can he not allow the woman of his dreams to enter his dream? But just that must be the answer. . . . To acknowledge her as this woman would be to acknowledge that she is "somebody that's real, somebody that's alive," flesh and blood, someone separate from his dream who therefore has, if she is to be in it, to enter it; and this feels to him to be a threat to the dream, and hence a threat to him. To walk in the direction of one's dream is necessarily to risk the dream. (Cavell 1981b, 100).

Cavell does *not* take failures of acknowledgment, such as Othello's or Peter's, to "issue from a deluded quest for certainty." In Othello's case, it's precisely the other way around. His deluded quest for certainty "issues from" his failure to respond to the claim—to respond in a way that acknowledges the claim—that Desdemona's separate existence makes on him. And Peter, who is not deluded, isn't on a "quest for certainty" at all. In walking around the blanket, Ellie makes a *claim* on Peter, calls for a response that acknowledges the claim—a response Peter isn't yet ready to give. His failure, like Othello's, isn't a failure to attain certainty; it's a failure to act in a way that acknowledges something he knows. Knowledge is not enough. As Cavell puts it in another memorable passage,

> The form [Peter] attempts to give acknowledgment is to tell their story. [*It Happened One Night*] can be said to describe the failure of this attempt as a last attempt to substitute knowledge for acknowledgment. As finite, you cannot achieve reciprocity with the one in view by telling your story to the whole rest of the world. You have to act in order to make things happen, night and day; and to act from within the world, within your connection with others, forgoing the wish for a place outside from which to view and to direct your fate. (Cavell 1981b, 90)

Allen presumes to identify what he takes to be the "two interrelated claims" on which "Cavell's philosophy" is based.

> First, our relationship to other people and the world is not one of knowing. This is what Cavell calls "the truth of skepticism." Second, romantic love and, in particular, marriage, is the place where we best learn to live with "the truth of skepticism," where we overcome or succumb to its corrosive effects. (Allen 2006, 43)

For a start, it is distinctly un-Cavellian to refer to "Cavell's philosophy," as Allen repeatedly does. In *Must We Mean What We Say?*, Cavell takes issue with critics who interpret Hamlet's line "There are more things in heaven and earth, Horatio, than are dreamt of in your philosophy" to be referring to something we might call "Horatio's philosophy," rather than referring to philosophy itself. For Cavell, philosophy is philosophy, just as doubt is doubt. To speak *as* a philosopher is to speak *for* philosophy, but it is not to claim philosophy as one's own. Cavell's way of thinking philosophically cannot be reduced to a single "theory" or thesis.

And Allen's assertion that what he calls "Cavell's philosophy" is "based on" these two "claims" is doubly un-Cavellian insofar as it implies that these "claims" are his philosophical starting points—axioms or premises from which all his other claims follow. Actually, the second of these supposed "claims" bears virtually no resemblance to anything Cavell ever said or would have said. And "the truth of skepticism" is not where Cavell's thinking begins; in *The Claim of Reason*, it's his elegant formulation for summing of a conclusion he arrives at only after literally hundreds of pages of examples, counterexamples, and precisely reasoned arguments. To think of "the truth of skepticism" as an axiom or premise is to erase the serious thought that makes *The Claim of Reason* a major work of philosophy that needs to be reckoned with.

And although it is not exactly wrong to say that for Cavell the "truth of skepticism" is that "our relationship to other people and the world is not one of knowing," this formulation, by itself, conveys nothing of the richness and complexity of the thinking that stands behind Cavell's term "the truth of skepticism," or the diversity of the ways he understands what the term means. (In his late book *Philosophy the Day After Tomorrow*, for example, he writes, "Philosophy's disparagement of, or its disappointment with, the ordinary, is something I have called the truth of skepticism" [Cavell 2006, 11–12].)

I can't help wondering what gives Allen so much as the idea that in acknowledging "the truth of skepticism," Cavell is denying that we sometimes do know, and sometimes know with certainty, the thoughts and feelings of people other than ourselves. In his philosophical memoir *Little Did I Know*, there's a wonderful passage in which Cavell reflects on his response as a child to his father's rages and identifies it as a source of his coming to understand, as the philosopher his young self was to become, not that knowledge of other minds is unattainable, but that it is not enough.

> How could I have failed to be suspicious, no matter how many years later, when I found philosophers asking such questions as "Do I know your pain the way you do?" My principal problem was not that of doubting my knowledge of the feelings of others, but rather of standing apart from them, or failing to. Not to know them would require exorcism. (Cavell 2010, 20)

When in *North by Northwest* the Professor informs Roger that Eve is a double agent, the camera captures the moment he acquires this knowledge—it is also self-knowledge. (In *Notorious*, Devlin, another Cary Grant character, is offscreen when he acquires such knowledge about Alicia—and about himself.) Knowledge—even self-knowledge—isn't enough for Roger or Devlin, either, as it isn't enough for Peter in *It Happened One Night*.

Nor is it enough to have a sense of "attunement" with the woman he loves. The claim this woman's separate existence makes on him cannot be acknowledged without *acting* on his knowledge. If Peter ultimately failed to act, Ellie would have been trapped in a loveless marriage with a man unworthy of her. Roger and Devlin, being Cary Grant, heroically risk life and limb to act; in each case, to fail to act would condemn the woman he loves to death, and the blood would be on his hands.

In "What Is the Scandal of Skepticism?" Cavell writes,

> If I sought a solution to the skeptical problem of the acknowledgment of the other, in the form, say, of an answer to the question "How can I trust the basis upon which I grant the existence of the other?" I feel I could not do better than to respond "You shall not kill." But in the everyday ways in which denial occurs in my life with the other—in a momentary irritation, or a recurrent grudge, in an unexpected rush of resentment, in a hard glance, in a dishonest attestation, in the telling of a tale, in the believing of a tale, in a false silence, in a fear of engulfment, in a fantasy of solitude or of self-destruction—the problem is to recognize myself as denying another, to understand that I carry chaos in myself. (Cavell 2006, 151)

For Cavell, skepticism with respect to other minds is not an *intellectual* lack. It is, as I've said, a failure to acknowledge other people—a stance it is all too possible for us to take in the face of the nontransparency of the other and the demands the other's existence places upon me. It is the denial or annihilation of the other, thus the denial or annihilation of the self. In a case as extreme as that of Othello or *Vertigo*'s Scottie, its consequence is tragedy. But skepticism, signified by failures to acknowledge claims that other people, in their difference, make on us, manifests itself in less extreme, more ordinary ways as well. In yet another memorable passage, Cavell writes, "In our slights of one another, in an unexpressed or disguised meanness of thought, in a hardness of glance, a willful misconstrual, a shading of loyalty, a dismissal of intention, a casual indiscriminateness of praise or blame"—in an inattentiveness to a serious writer's words, to "this prose, just here," I would add—"in any of the countless signs of skepticism with respect to the reality, the separateness, of another—we run the risk of suffering, or dealing, little deaths every day" (Cavell and Rothman 2005, 340).

In repeatedly slipping back to the notion that for Cavell "the truth of skepticism" is simply that "the concluding thesis of skepticism" is true, Allen is in lockstep with Malcolm Turvey's essay in *Wittgenstein, Theory and the Arts*, the anthology they jointly edited. Turvey's piece, contentiously titled "Is Skepticism a 'Natural Possibility' of Language: Reasons to Be Skeptical of Cavell's Wittgenstein," provides ample reasons to be skeptical of Turvey's Cavell.

Here's one. Turvey quotes this fine passage from *The Claim of Reason*:

> Wittgenstein does not negate the concluding thesis of skepticism, that we do not know with certainty of the existence of the external world (or of other minds). On the contrary, Wittgenstein, as I read him, rather affirms that thesis, or rather takes it as *undeniable*, and so shifts its weight. (Cavell 1979a, 45)

In this passage, Cavell is clearly *not* saying that Wittgenstein *affirms* the "concluding thesis of skepticism." As is his wont, he is registering an *impulse* to say such a thing but, as his "rather" unambiguously indicates, he rejects that impulse in favor of saying that Wittgenstein takes the thesis to be *undeniable*. When Turvey follows Cavell's words with a sentence that begins "For Cavell, the philosophical motivation behind Wittgenstein's affirmation of the 'concluding thesis of skepticism,'" he assumes that what Cavell means is that Wittgenstein takes the thesis to be undeniably *true*. That cannot be right, for then Cavell would have felt no need to override his impulse to say that Wittgenstein affirms the thesis. Clearly, what Cavell *does* mean is that, to put it crudely, there is no ordinary "language game" in which we do, or can, deny the thesis, but neither is there an ordinary language game in which we do, or can, affirm it. For Cavell's Wittgenstein and (more importantly to me) for Cavell himself, the "concluding thesis of skepticism" is neither affirmable nor deniable. Wittgenstein's teaching, as *Contesting Tears* puts it, is that

> skepticism is (not exactly true, but not exactly false either; it is the name of) a standing threat to, or temptation of, the human mind— that our ordinary language and its representation of the world can be philosophically repudiated and that it is essential to our inheritance and mutual possession of language, as well as to what inspires philosophy, that this should be so. (Cavell 1996, 89)

This realization frees Cavell and his attentive reader to achieve greater clarity— always Cavell's goal, no less than Wittgenstein's—as to what skepticism is, "shifting the weight," as he puts it, so that the "concluding thesis of skepticism" no longer does, and no longer *can*, bear the full burden of defining skepticism, as it had been understood within modern philosophy since Descartes. To acknowledge "the truth of skepticism," as Cavell understands himself and Wittgenstein to be doing, is precisely *not* to assert that "the concluding thesis of skepticism" is true.

Infuriatingly, Turvey announces that he feels the need to warn readers in advance that "Cavell's writing is" notoriously opaque and, according to some, "'self-indulgent,' something which even his defenders acknowledge"; that the obscurity of his prose "often makes for difficulty in identifying precisely what Cavell is arguing"; and thus that he is attributing to him arguments that Cavell *seems* to be making, "in the full knowledge that some of his defenders and interpreters may dispute whether

Cavell is actually making such arguments"—as if his own failures to follow Cavell's thoughts, to acknowledge "this prose, just here," were failures of writing, not his own failures of reading (Allen and Turvey 2011, 120).

Acknowledging "the truth of skepticism" did *not* make Cavell a skeptic, as both Turvey and Allen claim. And that claim is the linchpin that holds together the arguments they both bring to bear against Cavell. That this claim is demonstrably false makes their entire case against Cavell collapse like a house of cards, to borrow Wittgenstein's metaphor, or, worse, like the final season of the series *House of Cards*.

Wittgenstein, Theory and the Arts is committed to the implausible proposition that for the humanities, the sole legitimate way of using Wittgenstein's thought is propaedeutically—a tool to be used exclusively as a preliminary *to* criticism, never as a tool *for* criticism. Turvey recognizes that their whole book is called into question if "it is true, as Cavell argues, that 'the truth of skepticism' is the underlying principle"—*principle*?!—"of not only Wittgenstein's later philosophy in its entirety but almost every human phenomenon imaginable" (Allen and Turvey 2001, 120). Cavell doesn't actually argue anything like this, of course, but Turvey is the book's designated hit man tasked with the job—someone had to do it, and neither Bill Barr nor Rudy Giuliani were available—of discrediting Cavell's thought in general and, in particular, "disproving" his interpretation of Wittgenstein.

In a nutshell, Turvey's argument, in his contribution to *Wittgenstein, Theory and the Arts*, is that Cavell is a skeptic and Wittgenstein is not. In "Hitchcock and Cavell," Allen's argument is that Cavell is a skeptic and Hitchcock is not. And my argument, I have the impulse to say, is that by virtue of their efforts to erase Cavell's thought, Allen and Turvey are skeptics and Cavell is not. I have to qualify that, though, because the idea that some people *are* skeptics and others *not* is un-Cavellian. Cavell's idea, rather, is that no human beings are exempt from "the risk of suffering, or dealing, little deaths every day"; no human beings are immune to failures to acknowledge the claims that others, in their separateness, make on them. But no human beings are *fated* to skepticism, either.

"Although in Hitchcock's cinema, doubt, duplicity, and deception infect human relationships," Allen writes,

> Hitchcock's films do not demonstrate the "truth of skepticism." On the contrary, often there is a point at which the protagonist of a Hitchcock film and the spectator alongside him or her arrives at a state of certainty that may support either the affirmation of romance or disillusionment with it. The affirmation of romance or romantic disillusionment in Hitchcock's works does not mean that the characters have learned to live with their skepticism or succumbed to it, but that doubt or uncertainty has been overcome. (Allen 2006, 52)

All it takes to refute "Cavell's philosophy," Allen believes, is to point out that (1) Cavell held that in "the narrative of heterosexual romance," skepticism, in the form of radical doubt, is the central "problem"; (2) although the relation between romance and doubt was a central concern for Hitchcock as it was for Cavell, the characters in his films ultimately acquire the knowledge they had lacked, achieve a certainty that puts their doubts to rest; (3) thus, it is implausible to conceive the success of romance in Hitchcock as an exemplification of the overcoming of skepticism.

Note that Allen had just attributed to Cavell the clam that in "the narrative of heterosexual romance," the characters learn to "live with their skepticism" or succumb to it. Now he is implying that Cavell's "theory" is, rather, that "the success of romance" exemplifies the *overcoming* of skepticism. Which is it?

In any case, all it takes to refute Allen is to point out that Cavell does *not* claim that radical doubt is the central "problem" in all the diverse kinds of "narratives of heterosexual romance." It follows that even if it were the case, as Allen claims, that the romances in Hitchcock's films cannot plausibly be seen as exemplifying success or failure in either overcoming skepticism or learning to live with it, that wouldn't make these films "counterexamples" that prove that "Cavell's philosophy" is false. Q.E.D.

But I don't want to leave it at that.

First, Allen is wrong to assert, as if it were a universal rule, that the romances in Hitchcock's films do not "demonstrate the truth of skepticism" (that is, as Cavell, not Allen, understands it). Cavell observes in *Contesting Tears* that "the overcoming of skeptical doubt can be found in all remarriage comedy," but in no two of the films addressed in *Pursuits of Happiness* does "skeptical doubt," or its overcoming, manifest itself in the same way. *It Happened One Night*, in Cavell's words, "dramatizes the problem of unknownness as one of splitting the other, as between outside and inside, say between perception and imagination." Can't the same thing be said about Hitchcock's *Notorious*? In *The Lady Eve*, as Cavell puts it, "The man's not knowing the recurrence of the same woman is shown as the cause of his more or less comic, hence more or less forgivable, idiocy" (Cavell 1996, 90). Doesn't Scottie's noncomic, more or less unforgivable "idiocy" in the second half of *Vertigo* result from the same cause? Isn't it as true of *Rear Window* as it is of *The Awful Truth* that "the woman shows the all-knowing man what he does not know about her?" And so on.

In comedies of remarriage, as Cavell understands them, skepticism enters the picture not in the form of radical Cartesian doubt, but primarily in the form of failures to acknowledge others in their difference, signified by the inflicting of "little deaths." In Hitchcock films, as in *Gaslight* and *Letter from an Unknown Woman*, the consequence of skepticism is death itself. In *Cities of Words*, Cavell observes that

> the angle of incidence at which skepticism strikes the film melodramas is different from that at which it manifested itself in Shakespearean tragedy. In the Shakespearean cases I adduce in my book *The Claim of Reason*, the collapse of confidence in our knowledge of others is precipitated by the collapse of confidence in what I call a best case of knowledge, or rather of acknowledgment. Desdemona is the world for Othello, his loss of her is the loss of interest for him in whatever else the world has to offer. (Cavell 2005a, 110)

Paula in *Gaslight*, by contrast, seems to be of no interest in herself to Gregory, who marries her to gain admittance to the house in which he believes her aunt's jewels—which are the world to him—must be hidden. However, Cavell adds, "Unless, perhaps, he has . . . become fascinated by this woman's manifestation not of radical Cartesian self-doubt, but of Emerson's perception of mankind as ashamed, too timid to declare its existence as revealed in its power of thinking, so that it attempts to abandon thinking, to suspend the power of judgment, so as to haunt itself. As Paula enters her house, she becomes its ghost." Or, as Uncle Charles in *Shadow of a Doubt* might put it, she becomes "a sleepwalker; blind."

Second, it is at least arguably the case that in some Hitchcock films—perhaps in all the films he made in England before relocating to Hollywood—the romance resists being interpreted as a demonstration of "the truth of skepticism." But Hitchcock films have ways other than their romances of "demonstrating the truth of skepticism." In a footnote, Allen justifies not addressing my book *Hitchcock—The Murderous Gaze* on the ground that I use "the inspiration of Cavell to reflect not on the relationship between doubt and romance in Hitchcock's work, but on the idea of authorship in film." But my book's reflections on authorship bear directly on Allen's central thesis that Hitchcock films are counterexamples to "the truth of skepticism," hence to "Cavell's philosophy." "Film, in Hitchcock's work," I wrote in the postscript to *The Murderous Gaze*, "is the medium by which Hitchcock made himself known, or at least knowable—the bridge between himself and us. But it is also a barrier that stands between Hitchcock and us. It stands for everything that separates Hitchcock from his audience, and indeed for everything that separates any one human being from all others" (Rothman 2012, 247). Without reflecting on authorship in film, and on *Hitchcock's* reflections on his own authorship, it is impossible to understand how, and why, the "problem of other minds" was central to Hitchcock's art.

In *The Murderous Gaze* I argue that when the camera calls attention to itself in a Hitchcock film, as it often does, the film's author is showing his hand, declaring that he possesses the godlike power to preside over "accidents" within the projected world—the power to grant wishes, to make characters' dreams (or nightmares) come true. Hitchcock was famous for planning every detail of his films, storyboarding every shot, and in general striving to minimize the accidents of filming so as to exercise as complete control as possible over the production—and over our experience of the projected film.

As I argue in *The Murderous Gaze*, the fundamental difference between a Hitchcock villain and a Hitchcock protagonist is the villain's hubris, his presumption in attempting to arrogate to himself the author's godlike power to preside over the film's world, in contrast to the protagonist who, to paraphrase Cavell, forgoes the wish for a place outside from which to view and to direct his fate, and ultimately accept that once he does what it is in his power to do, his fate is in the hands of a higher power. And yet, Hitchcock himself resisted ceding control, resisted acknowledging limits to his own powers as author. The Hitchcock villain, master of the art of murder, is a human being who dwells, along with the film's other characters, within the world of the film. But the villain is also a stand-in for Hitchcock, master of what he liked to call "the art of pure cinema."

As I argue in *Must We Kill the Thing We Love?*, "Metaphorically or allegorically, Hitchcock's villains are his accomplices in artistic creation, and Hitchcock is their accomplice in murder. That his own art has a murderous aspect is a—at the time I wrote *The Murderous Gaze*, I thought *the*—quintessentially Hitchcockian idea" (Rothman 2014, 6). I have come to understand, though, that as much as he enjoyed quoting Oscar Wilde's line "Yet each man kills the thing he loves," and as much as he was drawn to the skepticism it expresses, the idea that human existence is inescapably tragic, Hitchcock was no less drawn to the Emersonian moral outlook, as Cavell's later writings have taught me to think of it, of the comedy of remarriage and the melodrama of the unknown woman. *Must We Kill the Thing We Love?* argues that the driving force of Hitchcock's art was his aspiration to transcend or resolve the tension or conflict between these incompatible worldviews—between denying and affirming "the truth of skepticism," we can say—culminating in his embrace of Emersonian perfectionism in *Marnie*.

In arguing that Hitchcock's films disprove the theory or thesis he calls "Cavell's philosophy," Allen hopes, as he puts it, "to establish the broader point that Cavell's interpretations of the works of popular culture fail to provide 'evidence' for the truth of his philosophy." He adds, "Of course, I do not expect Cavell or his followers to be persuaded by the putative counterexample to his philosophy provided by Hitchcock's films" (Allen 2006, 44).

No one *should* have such an expectation, for it would surely be as obvious to Cavell and his "followers" as it is to this one of Cavell's "followers" that Allen's "putative counterexample" is bogus. But why does Allen feel entitled to add the condescending "of course"? Perhaps for the same reason he calls me, in a footnote, "Cavell's disciple"—as if my book *Hitchcock—The Murderous Gaze* were devoted to proselytizing the Gospel of Cavell, not to thinking for myself, "paying the tuition" for intuitions of my own. And perhaps for the same reason he refers to Cavell's "followers," implying not that we read his words with the kind and degree of attention required to follow his thinking and our own but, rather, that we are cult members mindlessly following the cult leader—a leader who is himself bewitched by an idea that has taken possession of his mind. Once more in lockstep with Turvey, Allen writes,

> For it seems to me that Cavell's assumption that "the truth of skepticism" is portrayed in the vicissitudes of romance is probably an intellectual presupposition of the kind that Ludwig Wittgenstein after Goethe called an *Urphänomen*, a preconceived idea that takes possession of us. By captivating the mind of the person who adopts it, the *Urphänomen* is claimed to underlie all phenomena, regardless of anything that might count as evidence against it. Cavell implicitly presupposes that the explicit representation of doubt and its resolution in texts, such as those of

Hitchcock, are secondary to the radical doubt or "the truth of skepticism" that he perceives to underlie the human condition and that is dramatized in the romance. (Allen 2006, 44)

Cavell does *not* presuppose, implicitly or otherwise, what Allen is claiming he does—a claim rendered moot, in any case, by his once again slipping back to equating "the truth of skepticism" with Cartesian doubt. And note that Allen's word "implicitly" here—like his word "probably" earlier in the passage—all but confesses that his assertion that for Cavell "the explicit representation of doubt and its resolution in texts" is "secondary" to "the truth of skepticism" is itself a claim not based on evidence subject to objective verification. Allen offers a putative counterexample, if a bogus one, to "the truth of skepticism" as he (mis)understands it. But he doesn't deign to cite, much less contest, anything Cavell actually *says* about any film.

Allen's claim is, or is based on, his *interpretation* of Cavell's writings—an interpretation that "implicitly presupposes" that for Cavell all the claims he is moved to make about the films he writes about are "secondary" to proving that "the truth of skepticism" really is true. And yet, as far as I recall, the term "the truth of skepticism" never even appears in *Pursuits of Happiness*, *Contesting Tears*, *Cities of Words*, or the essays collected in *Cavell on Film*, all works published after *The Claim of Reason*. And the term appears rarely—in most cases not at all—in his other post–*Claim of Reason* writings.

In "Cavell Reading Cavell," "The Same, Only a Little Different," "Cavell in Transition," and "Cavell, Emerson, Hitchcock," I sketch a picture of the trajectory of Cavell's authorship that envisions the publication of *The Claim of Reason* as a decisive event in his philosophical life because it made his doctoral dissertation a work he could stand behind, and—perhaps even more consequentially—because it enabled him to put his dissertation behind him, freeing him for the new departures represented by *Pursuits of Happiness*, his discovery of Emerson, and the momentous step of giving a name—"Emersonian perfectionism"—to his own way of thinking philosophically as well as Emerson's. Concepts that figured prominently in his earlier writings, such as "modernism" and, yes, "skepticism," all but dropped out of his lexicon. And, as I put it in "The Same Again, Only a Little Different,"

> In *Cities of Words*, Cavell observes in *Little Did I Know*, "the sets of comedies and melodramas I have devoted a book each to are cast systematically in a new light, namely, as embodying a specific register of the moral life, a register running, if largely unheralded, throughout Western philosophy and literature, from Plato and Aristotle through Dante and Montaigne and Jane Austen and Emerson and George Eliot and Nietzsche and Mill to Heidegger and Wittgenstein"—and, of course, Cavell. (169, this volume)

In Cavell's post–*Claim of Reason* writings, where the impact of his discovery of Emerson increasingly manifests itself, the view, never plausible, that the totality of his thought can be reduced to the single theory or thesis that Allen calls "Cavell's philosophy" becomes impossible to sustain—or so one would think. That Allen nonetheless takes "the truth of skepticism" to be an *Urphänomen* for Cavell, the "principle" underlying all of his writings, makes it all too obvious that it is he, not Cavell, who is possessed by an *Urphänomen*. I can't resist adding that within academic film studies, the Freudian concept of the fetish became fetishized. And that Lacan's theory of the mirror phase came to serve the same function within the field that, according to the theory, the mirror image serves for the infant: enabling the field to imagine itself as a unified subject. In Allen's essay—and Turvey's as well—the concept of the *Urphänomen* becomes an *Urphänomen* and makes a strong bid to be added to this list.

Throughout Allen's essay, as I've said, there's a slippage in his language between acknowledging and denying that Cavell understands radical doubt to be only one of the forms that skepticism has assumed. When Allen writes, "The grounds of the truth of Cavell's philosophy cannot be convincingly based on the interpretation of texts if nothing could qualify as a counterexample to those interpretations," there is a comparable slippage in his language between the word "philosophy" and the word "interpretations"—between asserting that counterexamples won't shake the conviction of Cavell and his "followers" in the truth of Cavell's *philosophy*, and asserting that nothing would count, for Cavell and his "followers," as counterexamples to his *interpretations*—as if refuting "Cavell's philosophy" would in the same stroke disprove all his interpretations.

As Cavell observes in the introduction to *Pursuits of Happiness*, however, interpretations, unlike theories or theses, can be valid or invalid, but not true or false. To be valid, an interpretation has to be consistent with what is objectively "there" in the work. But an interpretation also has a subjective dimension. Whether it is *meant* and whether it is accountable to the critic's *experience* of the work are *not* objectively verifiable. I do not doubt that Cavell meant every interpretation of a film or film moment he advanced in his writings, that it is an expression of his existence as a human being, just as Hitchcock's films are expressions of who he was.

Every interpretation Cavell was moved to advance makes a claim on us, calls for a response that acknowledges that claim. This doesn't mean we have to *accept* Cavell's interpretation. But we *are* called upon to check it against our own experience and, if we find it unconvincing, to seek a competing interpretation, as Cavell puts it—one that, for us, *does* carry conviction. A competing interpretation is not a *counterexample*; both interpretations can be equally valid. An interpretation can be invalidated only by showing that it cannot be reconciled with what is objectively there in the work.

In all his writings about film, Cavell hewed rigorously to the discipline of backing up his interpretations with evidence from the films themselves—as, for example, in his reading of *Stella Dallas* where he contests the conventional interpretation of Stella as oblivious of the way others see her by citing, among other features of the film, the objectively verifiable fact that Stella makes her daughter's fashionable clothes. In the concluding section of "More of *The World Viewed*," Cavell, writing from memory, misdescribed a moment in *The Rules of the Game* (an error he acknowledged, corrected, and pondered in the foreword to the 1979 enlarged edition of *The World Viewed*) (Cavell 1979b, xi–xiii, 219–30). As far as I am aware, however, once he had access to video cassettes or DVDs, he never again misdescribed a film moment. If he had committed such an error and it had been pointed out to him, on philosophical principle he would have acknowledged it, of course, and revised his interpretation accordingly. In "implicitly presupposing" otherwise, and doing so solely on the basis of an *Urphänomen*, Allen fails to acknowledge the claims Cavell's writings make on him. In succumbing to skepticism, he deals "little deaths" to his readers—and to the field of film studies.

17

Introduction to *Must We Kill the Thing We Love? Emersonian Perfectionism and the Films of Alfred Hitchcock*

When I wrote *Hitchcock—The Murderous Gaze* thirty years ago, my stated goal was to achieve an understanding of Hitchcock's authorship and at the same time to investigate, philosophically, the conditions of authorship in the medium of film. *The Murderous Gaze* looked closely at five characteristic Hitchcock films (*The Lodger* [1926], *Murder!* [1930], *The 39 Steps* [1935], *Shadow of a Doubt* [1943], *Psycho* [1960]); the second edition added a sixth, *Marnie* (1964). My method was simply to follow these films, and the experience of viewing them, as they unfold, moment by moment, from beginning to end, putting into words, as I put it, "the thinking inscribed in their successions of frames" (Rothman 2012, 1).

It was at once a premise and a conclusion of *The Murderous Gaze* that Hitchcock's films *are* thinking. They *have* thoughts "inscribed in their successions of frames." (Perhaps some films do not.) And those thoughts have a *philosophical* dimension. As I put it: "Within the world of a Hitchcock film, the nature and relationships of love, murder, sexuality, marriage, and theater are at issue; these are among Hitchcock's constant themes. His treatment of these themes, however, and his understanding of the reasons film keeps returning to them, cannot be separated

---

William Rothman, *Must We Kill the Thing We Love? Emersonian Perfectionism and the Films of Alfred Hitchcock* (New York: Columbia University Press, 2014), 1–30. Reprinted with permission. Like "Cavell, Emerson, Hitchcock," this introduction focuses more on Emerson's writings than Cavell's but, again, everything said here about Emerson illuminates—and was meant to illuminate—Cavell's philosophical perspective as well.

from his constant concern with the nature of the camera, the act of viewing a film, and filmmaking as a calling. In demonstrating something about the 'art of pure cinema,' as he called it, Hitchcock's films are asserting, *declaring*, something about themselves, something about their medium, as well as something about our existence as human beings within the world" (Rothman 2012, xi). His films also declare, I would add, something fundamental about Hitchcock's authorship; about the conditions of authorship in film; and about the kind of thinking—and writing—serious films call for if their seriousness is to be acknowledged.

During the time I was writing *The Murderous Gaze*, I was teaching at Harvard and in almost daily conversation with Stanley Cavell, who was then completing *Pursuits of Happiness*, his seminal study of the Hollywood genre he calls the "comedy of remarriage." *Pursuits of Happiness* presents a profound vision of this genre as exemplifying a singularly American philosophical perspective—in particular, a way of thinking about morality. The book's guiding intuition is that the popular American cinema's inheritance of concerns of American Transcendentalism is what enabled Hollywood to reach its artistic high-water mark. Although *The Murderous Gaze* approached Hitchcock films primarily through the prism of authorship, it noted that the "Hitchcock thriller" could also be viewed as a genre comparable to the comedy of remarriage or the genre Cavell calls the "melodrama of the unknown woman," four exemplary members of which he went on to study in *Contesting Tears* (*Stella Dallas* [King Vidor, 1937], *Now, Voyager* [Irving Rapper, 1942], and *Gaslight* [George Cukor, 1944], in addition to *Letter from an Unknown Woman* [Max Ophuls, 1948], whose title he appropriates for the genre).

In comedies of remarriage, a woman and man pursue happiness not by overcoming societal obstacles to their marriage, as in classical comedies, but by overcoming obstacles internal to their relationship, obstacles that are between and within themselves, obstacles they cannot overcome without achieving a radically changed perspective. These Hollywood movies present women and men as equals, as having an equal right to pursue happiness and as being equal spiritually or, we might say, morally—equal in their powers of imagination and thinking and in their capacity to cultivate the better angels of their nature. What is at issue in such films is not simply whether the leading woman and man will marry or remarry, but whether the kind of marriage they create together will be a relationship worth having, one that enables them, as individuals and as a couple, to embrace every day and every night in a spirit of adventure—a kind of marriage exemplified by Nick and Nora (William Powell and Myrna Loy) in *The Thin Man*, another landmark film made in 1934 (W. S. Van Dyke). Hence comedies of remarriage pose, and address, a philosophical question about marriage itself. What is a marriage? What, if anything, validates or legitimates a marriage, if a couple can be married according to the church and the laws of the state, and yet, by the higher standards of the comedy of remarriage, not have a true marriage?

The Philadelphia Story renders it explicit that this question about marriage is also a question about what it is to be human, a question about human relationships in general, a question about community and, as such, a question for, and about, America. Implicitly advocating America's joining the war against fascism already raging in Europe, *The Philadelphia Story* is a summary statement as to what makes America worth fighting for, what is worth preserving in its heritage. In a comedy of remarriage, a woman and man seek, and achieve, a conversation of equals—a relationship with each other, at once private and public, based on mutual trust—that can serve as a model of community and thus as an inspiration for America in its own quest to form a more perfect union.

What is worth fighting for, *The Philadelphia Story* declares, is not America as it is (as the wartime documentary series *Why We Fight* was later to assert, whitewashing reality in a way that Hollywood romantic comedies of the 1930s refrained from doing). America as it is, *The Philadelphia Story* asserts (as do all the romantic comedies Cavell studies), is a place where the likes of George Kittredge—the phony "man of the people" trumpeted by cynical Sidney Kidd's media empire—passes for a great American. America's promise has not yet been fully realized. America has not yet become America. And yet, these romantic comedies affirm, that "unattained America," as Ralph Waldo Emerson calls it, is still attainable. The dream of a more perfect union was still alive, though imperiled, in 1930s America, as it was in Emerson's time when, as he wrote, the moral scourge of slavery was keeping America from taking a step toward becoming America. (The dream is still alive today. And still in peril.)

The remarriage comedies Cavell celebrates are grand entertainments that gave pleasure to viewers living through dark times, but they also entered into a serious conversation with their culture that set a high standard of moral purpose. That their commitment to channeling the awesome power of film to help America and Americans to awaken, to change, was not confined to a single genre is a point Cavell fleshes out in *Contesting Tears*. In Cavell's inspiring vision, indeed, all the leading Hollywood genres during this period found stories to tell, and ways of telling their stories, that enabled them to share in the remarriage comedy's way of thinking about morality. In *Cities of Words*, Cavell characterizes this way of thinking as a species of moral perfectionism he names "Emersonian perfectionism."

Cavell does not view Emersonian perfectionism as a theory of moral philosophy comparable to Kant's deontological view that there is a universal moral law (the Categorical Imperative) by which we can rationally determine whether an action is right or wrong, or Mill's utilitarian view that the good action is that which will cause the least harm, or the greatest good for the greatest number. Instead, moral perfectionism in general is an outlook or register of thought, a way of thinking about morality expressed thematically in certain works of philosophy, literature, and film, that takes our task as human beings—at once our deepest wish, whether or not we know this about ourselves, and our moral obligation—to become more fully human, to realize our humanity in our lives in the world, which always requires the simultaneous acknowledgment of the humanity of others (our acknowledgment of them, and theirs of us). The moral questions couples in remarriage comedies address in their witty give-and-take, for example, are, as Cavell puts it in *Cities of Words*, "formulated less well by questions concerning what they ought to do, what it would be best or right for them to do, than by the question how they shall live their lives, what kind of persons they aspire to be" (Cavell 2005a, 11).

In *Bringing Up Baby*, for example, Susan (Katharine Hepburn) teaches David (Cary Grant) that every day and every night is to be lived in a festive spirit, a spirit of adventure. That is, she helps open his eyes to the reality that this is, and always has been, his goal, no less than hers. When the brontosaurus skeleton that he had thought meant the world to him collapses in a heap, he knows that Susan has helped him discover what it is that he really seeks. What is sought, and achieved, in comedies of remarriage is a new perspective. It is a *philosophical* perspective insofar as the knowledge it makes possible is self-knowledge, the self's awakening to its own condition, the reality that it is in the process of becoming, that it stands in need of creation. To become oneself, one must abandon oneself, for there is always a new perspective one must achieve, a new step one must take—and then another step, and then a step after that, and then . . .

The knowledge to which David awakens, with Susan's help, is that he had let others dictate to him what and how to think. In Susan's view, as in Emerson's, letting others do the thinking for you is not thinking badly, not thinking in a bad way; it is not thinking at all. In discovering what he thinks, what he seeks, what really matters to him, David discovers who he has been, who he is, how and why he wishes to change. Discovering what we really think, achieving a new perspective on who we are, who we have been, *is* thinking, in Emerson's view. The moment David thinks, he discovers what makes thinking necessary. He also discovers that it is necessary for him to *act*. Since David's awakening thought is that being with Susan is what really means the world to him, it is to Susan, within their ongoing conversation, that he finds it necessary to express this thought, to marry thinking and action.

The witty but profound conversations between women and men in the comedies of remarriage Cavell studies are among the glories of world cinema precisely because they manifest, and declare, the possibility, and the necessity, of thinking and of giving expression to our thoughts, of marrying thinking and purposeful action, as David learns to do. For Susan as for Emerson, thinking has a *moral* dimension. What she helps David discover is that he *should* think, he *must* think, *must* give expression to his thoughts, *must* marry thought and action. The thought that we *must* walk in the direction of the unattained but attainable self, that this is the path toward freedom, is the heart and soul of Emersonian perfectionism.

Hitchcock was profoundly attracted to the worldview that underwrote classical American genres such as the comedy of remarriage. *The 39 Steps* followed the lead of *It Happened One Night*, the monster hit that marked the beginning of the period when Emersonian perfectionism was in the ascendancy in Hollywood, by concluding with the union of a man and woman that holds a hope of being a relationship worth having. In turn, *Secret Agent* (1936), *Sabotage* (1936), *Young and Innocent* (1937), and *The Lady Vanishes* (1938), the brilliant films Hitchcock made in the few years remaining before his departure for Hollywood, all followed the lead of *The 39 Steps* by aligning the Hitchcock thriller, up to a point, with the Hollywood comedy of remarriage. As these films show, however, he found himself unwilling, or unable, simply to abandon himself to the American genre's Emersonian outlook. He was no less powerfully drawn to an incompatible vision. No doubt affected by a Catholic upbringing that impressed on his young imagination a strong and abiding sense of original sin, he never tired of quoting Oscar Wilde's line from "The Ballad of Reading Gaol," "Yet each man kills the thing he loves." A central thesis of *Must We Kill the Thing We Love?* is that the tension or conflict between these two incompatible worldviews is the driving force of Hitchcock's work.

In the introduction to the first edition of *The Murderous Gaze*, I observed that I could "imagine a reader coming to the end of the book and suddenly being overcome by the magnitude of all that separates *Psycho* from *The Lodger*. "What separates these films," I wrote, "is also what joins them: a body of work that movingly stands in for an entire human life, even as it traverses and sums up the history of an art." But I also observed that I could "imagine the book engendering in the reader the sense that Hitchcock's work ends where it began." I believed I had conclusively demonstrated that "*Psycho's* position was already declared, indeed already worked out, in *The Lodger*" (Rothman 2012, 2).

I no longer believe this.

In recounting the vicissitudes of Hitchcock's shifting and ambivalent relationship to Emersonian perfectionism, *Must We Kill the Thing We Love?* discovers a progression from British thrillers like *The 39 Steps*, *Secret Agent*, and *Sabotage*; to his earliest American films, such as *Rebecca* (1940), *Mr. and Mrs. Smith* (1940), and *Suspicion* (1941); to his wartime films, such as *Shadow of a Doubt* (1943) and its companion piece, *Lifeboat* (1944); to postwar films like *Notorious* (1946) and *Rope* (1948); to his great masterpieces of the 1950s, culminating in *The Wrong Man* (1956), *Vertigo* (1958), and *North by Northwest* (1959); to *Psycho*; and ultimately to *The Birds* (1963) and *Marnie* (1964), in which, I propose, Hitchcock overcame or transcended his ambivalence and embraced the Emersonian perfectionism he had always resisted.

After *Vertigo*, his most devastating illustration of the principle that "each man kills the thing he loves," Hitchcock no longer wished to be the kind of artist for whom artistic creation was the metaphorical equivalent of murder. But how was he to create a film that bore his authorial signature, yet in which his role as author overcame or transcended the murderous aspect that was a defining feature of the Hitchcock thriller, the genre he had staked out as his own? Hitchcock picked himself up, dusted himself off, and started all over again, to paraphrase Fred Astaire, by making *North by Northwest*, which concludes with a couple achieving a marriage fully worthy of a 1930s remarriage comedy. In effect, by creating *North by Northwest* Hitchcock vowed that he would never again make a film that equated its own creation with murder. But then why did he next make *Psycho*, a film in which, allegorically, he killed the thing he loved most in the world: the "art of pure cinema" itself? And how did *Psycho* free him to make *The Birds* and *Marnie*? In creating these last two masterpieces, Hitchcock definitively overcame or transcended his ambivalence toward the Emersonian way of thinking he had longed to embrace for the sake of humanity, but resisted embracing for the sake of his art.

To embrace Emersonian perfectionism means, in part, to abandon oneself to the view that, as Emerson puts it in "Circles," "Every action admits of being outdone," that "our life is an apprenticeship to the truth, that around every circle another can be drawn; that there is no end in nature, but every end is a beginning" (Emerson and Porte 1983, 403). In the creation of *Marnie*, Hitchcock drew a new circle. Looking back from the perspective *Marnie* achieves, it is possible to perceive the Hitchcock thrillers that precede it as leading up to it, as constituting a series whose order has a certain necessity to it—as if with each film Hitchcock drew a new circle, took a step toward what Emerson, in his essay "History," calls the "unattained but attainable self" (Emerson and Porte 1983, 239). Emerson's writings, too, can be understood to constitute such a series. A progression can be discerned from his early writings (such as his "Divinity School Address," "The American Scholar," and *Nature*); to *Essays: First Series* (which includes, among others, "History," "Circles," and "Intellect," as well as the famous "Self-Reliance"); to *Essays: Second Series* (which includes "Experience," perhaps his greatest masterwork); to the later writings (including the essays in *The Conduct of Life*, such as "Fate" and "Behavior"). It is, indeed, a defining feature of the Emerson essay that it draws a circle around which another circle can be drawn (by another essay that succeeds it). *Must We Kill the Thing We Love?* claims that this is a defining feature of the Hitchcock thriller as well. And the essays in *The Holiday in His Eye*, collectively, demonstrate that the same can be said of Cavell's writing.

I am not claiming that Hitchcock consciously planned the trajectory his films turned out to follow, as if he were acting out a scenario he had scripted (the way, I argue in my chapter on *Vertigo*, the woman we know as Judy can be seen to do in the second part of the film). "The one thing which we seek with insatiable desire," the passage from "Circles" goes on, "is to forget ourselves, to be surprised out of our propriety, to lose our sempiternal [i.e., everlasting (having infinite temporal duration) as opposed to eternal (outside time and thus lacking temporal duration)] memory, and to do something without knowing how or why; in short, to draw a new circle" (Emerson and Porte 1983, 414). To draw a new circle, in Emerson's understanding, requires us to awaken to powers we had not been conscious of possessing, to open our eyes to the reality that we are not who we had believed ourselves to be, that our being is not limited to who we have been. It requires us to abandon an old self, to acknowledge that this self is now as dead to us as a heap of brontosaurus bones, so as to give birth to a new self. This is what Emerson calls the "way of life."

Emerson writes, "The way of life is wonderful: it is by abandonment," In prefacing this with the sentence "Nothing great was ever achieved without enthusiasm," his wording is implying, first, that anything a human being can achieve that is worthy of being called "great"—the creation of a work like *Vertigo*, "Experience," or *The Claim of Reason*, for example—is an instance of drawing a new circle, of being born anew, hence of abandoning a self, a habitation, that once had been new (Emerson and Porte 1983, 414.). Second, that without enthusiasm, it is not possible to draw a new circle; to draw a new circle, we must do so *with abandon*. Thus, the sentence "The way of life is wonderful: it is by abandonment" is playing, quite characteristically for Emerson, on two senses of the word "abandonment." It is also playing on two senses of the word "enthusiasm." In today's parlance, the word means possession by an intense interest in an activity, whatever the provenance of that interest. But Emerson is also invoking the word's original implication of being divinely inspired.

In creating *Marnie*, *Must We Kill the Thing We Love?* argues, Hitchcock finally abandoned himself to the wonderful "way of life." The Emersonian side of his split artistic identity decisively prevailed. But for Hitchcock, personally, this was a pyrrhic victory. *Marnie* achieved a philosophical perspective from which he could see that his way was clear, as an artist, to go on in a spirit of self-reliance, to take further steps, to draw ever larger circles. But *Marnie*'s critical and commercial failure was a catastrophe from which Hitchcock's career never recovered. It hardened Universal's resolve to prevent him from making *Mary Rose*, which would surely have been another masterpiece, but which the studio believed—probably not wrongly—would have further diminished the dollar value of the Hitchcock "brand." These reversals precipitated a crisis so traumatic that the films he did go on to make (*Torn Curtain*, *Topaz*, *Frenzy*, and *Family Plot*), for all their brilliant, beautiful, and profound passages, moved him no closer to the "unattained but attainable self." *Marnie* drew Hitchcock's largest circle.

Must We Kill the Thing We Love? invokes the names "Emerson" and "Cavell" only occasionally, and most often in the context of reflecting on the Hitchcock thriller's relationship to the Hollywood genres Cavell has shown to be exemplary of Emersonian perfectionism. Viewed in this light, Hitchcock thrillers may well seem—in a sense they *are*—much further removed from Cavell's and Emerson's way of thinking than comedies of remarriage, for example, which manifest none of Hitchcock's ambivalence toward it. And yet, for all their obvious differences, *as authors* Hitchcock has profound affinities with Cavell and Emerson—affinities not fully shared by Frank Capra, Howard Hawks, Leo McCarey, George Cukor, or Preston Sturges, major artists in their own right, who directed the remarriage comedies Cavell studied. This is an intuition that fully dawned in me only in the course of writing *Must We Kill the Thing We Love?* Such is the case, as well, with the intuition that my own practice of reading, as the writing in this book and *The Murderous Gaze* exemplify it, is itself underwritten, philosophically, by Cavell's way, which was Emerson's way, of thinking about reading and writing.

Only after I completed the body of *Must We Kill the Thing We Love?* did I realize that the book would be incomplete unless I "paid the tuition" for both intuitions, to borrow one of Emerson's felicitous terms. To that end, I composed an afterword that complements this introduction by looking closely at passages from several of Emerson's essays and tracing some of the implications, for the study of film, of the quite astonishing fact that the terms in which he speaks about reality, about our "flux of moods," about what it is within us that never changes, about freedom, about reading, about writing, and about thinking, are remarkably pertinent—almost uncannily so—to "reading" films, to writing about them, and to thinking about their medium, and about the art this medium makes possible.

Consider, for example, this oft-quoted sentence from Emerson's great essay "Experience": "Life is a train of moods like a string of beads, and as we pass through them they prove to be many-colored lenses which paint the world their own hue, and each shows only what lies in its focus" (Emerson and Porte 1983, 473). Insofar as films express themselves by their successions of moods (moods they capture; moods those moods cast over us), a film is a "train of moods," too.

When Emerson adds, "Temperament is the iron wire on which the beads are strung," his formulation invites us to understand that our "temperament" is also the "iron wire"—the iron rail—that enables our "train of moods" to run smoothly, even as at every moment it limits us to moving in a predetermined direction—as if, for all their "flux," our moods run along a single track" (Emerson and Porte 1983, 473). A film's "train of moods" runs along an "iron wire," too, figuratively speaking. We can think of it as the strip of celluloid, or as the succession of frames it bears, which assures that every time the film is screened, its "train of moods" keeps to the same track. Every film is its own "train of moods." It runs along its own track—the track laid down by its succession of frames. And every master of the art of pure cinema, such as Hitchcock, inscribes his or her own thinking in those frames. Hence, we can also think of the "iron wire" on which a Hitchcock film's "colored beads" are strung as its author's own temperament—the temperament, particular to Hitchcock, to which the film's succession of frames gives expression.

Emerson observes, later in the essay, that our "flux of moods" only "plays about the surface" and never "introduces [us] into the reality, contact with which we would even pay the costly price of sons and lovers," but that "there is something in us that never changes." This irresistibly reminds me of the fact that, in Cavell's words, a film's "faces and motions and settings" (or is it their moods?) have a "double existence as transient and as permanent" (Emerson and Porte 1983, 472). Every human being has his or her own temperament, particular to that individual. But we have in common the mind's power—a power that is itself baffling to the mind—to "raise" a "fact in our life" from the "web of our unconsciousness," as Emerson puts it in "Intellect," as if by illuminating it with the "certain, wandering light" of a "lantern," we transform it into a "thought," a "truth," an object "impersonal and immortal. It is the past restored, but embalmed. A better art than that of Egypt has taken fear and corruption out of it" Emerson and Porte 1983, 418). Perhaps it should not surprise us that André Bazin, a century later, was to employ the identical metaphor in characterizing the film image. For the film projector is literally a lantern. Metaphorically, the camera is a lantern, too.

In *North by Northwest*'s art auction sequence, Roger Thornhill, the Cary Grant character, harps on his knowledge that Eve Kendall (Eva Marie Saint) throws her whole body into her job, deliberately arousing the jealousy of the villainous Phillip Vandamm (James Mason) and placing Eve in dire jeopardy. Roger is so angry and hurt that he *wishes* her to die. But Roger is no Vandamm. The difference between them, in Hitchcock's eyes, is revealed at the moment the Professor (Leo G. Carroll) tells Roger that Eve is a double agent, and the camera moves in to frame Grant in a medium close-up, his expression underscored by the headlights of a taxiing plane.

This shot powerfully conveys the anguish Roger feels, the mood his face expresses, at this moment. Beyond this, Hitchcock designs the shot to communicate to us that Roger's pain is engendered by his onset of knowledge that is also self-knowledge. To convey the pain of Roger's enlightenment, Hitchcock creates a shot

that perfectly illustrates the point Emerson makes when he writes, "The eye obeys exactly the action of the mind. When a thought strikes us, the eyes fix, and remain gazing at a distance" (Emerson and Porte 1983, 418).

What Hitchcock's camera captures is the dawning of an intuition in Roger at this moment, the birth of a thought. What is particularly striking here is the way the shot underscores the fact that a thought is striking him by having a harsh light momentarily illuminate Grant's face. Had Hitchcock deliberately sought a way of illustrating, in the medium of film, Emerson's picture of the way the mind works, he could not have come up with a more perfect example. Within the world of the film, this light is cast by the headlights of a taxiing airplane. Metaphorically, it is the light—at times painful, at times blinding—of what Emerson calls "the intellect." By choosing to frame Grant frontally as well as closely, not only does Hitchcock enable the camera to capture the birth of this man's thought; he designs the shot in a way that identifies the camera—enables the camera to identify itself—with the intellect. The shot at once captures Roger's mood and inscribes his thought—his awakening to the knowledge that it is necessary for him to change. In inscribing Roger's thought, the shot also inscribes—we might say it realizes—*Hitchcock's* thought. I have in mind not only Hitchcock's thought about Roger, but his thought that, in Emerson's terms, the camera is a "lantern" whose "certain, wandering light" has the power to "raise" a "fact" in our life from the "web of our unconsciousness," transforming it into a "thought," a "truth," an object "impersonal and immortal."

Hitchcock dissolves from this shot to a view of the Mount Rushmore Monument. The dissolve is so slow that for a long, lingering moment Roger—Cary Grant—shares the screen with these American presidents—heroes all, as our nation's mythology would have it—chiseled permanently into the rock, their human faces "raised" into objects "impersonal and immortal."

The monumental visages, rendered small by being superimposed over Grant's larger-than-life face, convey an impression that these American heroes are standing guard over Roger, "having his back," as characters in today's action movies are wont to put it. But it is also as if these figures are projections of Roger's own imagination, what he is seeing in his "mind's eye" at this moment—the moment this man has opened his eyes, for the first time, to the reality that he longs to change, to become a man of true character, a worthy inheritor of the legacy of the likes of George Washington and Abraham Lincoln.

By this dissolve, in other words, Hitchcock again expresses his own thought, or thoughts, about Roger. And in thinking about Roger, Hitchcock is thinking about Cary Grant as well. "A man is but a little thing in the midst of the objects of nature," Emerson observes in his essay "Manners." "Yet, by the moral quality radiating from his countenance, he may abolish all considerations of magnitude, and in his manners equal the majesty of the world" (Emerson and Porte 1983, 529). This is the kind of person Roger at this moment is wishing he could become. It is the kind of person Hitchcock's camera reveals Cary Grant to be, as Cavell puts it in *Pursuits of Happiness*, a man "with the holiday in his eye" who is "fit to stand the gaze of millions."

These shots, and those that immediately follow, make it evident that in thinking about Roger and about the great star who incarnates him, and in thinking more generally about myth and reality, about heroism, about America, Hitchcock in this sequence is also thinking about the camera, about the medium of film, about the art of pure cinema, about change, about transience, about permanence, about the double temporal existence of the world on film. Films express themselves in the "flux of moods" they capture, and the "flux of moods" those moods cast over us. But there is something in them that remains fixed, unchanging—an unmoving ground that makes films capable of realizing a world at all. Writing about D. A. Pennebaker's classic documentary *Don't Look Back* (1967), I put the point this way:

> In the world on film, everything is forever turning, turning, turning again. Film is a medium of the ephemeral, the never-to-be-repeated, a medium of the rain and the wind. That the world is forever changing is the only thing that never changes about the world, part of what makes the world a world. Hence film is also a medium of the unchanging. *Don't Look Back* enables us to return to this moment, fall under its spell, experience its moods, every time we view the film. (Rothman 1997, 168)

And this double temporal existence of the projected world, vouchsafed by the ontological conditions of the film medium, is a key to thinking about the work of the director known as "the Master of Suspense."

∽

"The Moving Finger writes; and, having writ, moves on: nor all thy Piety nor Wit shall lure it back to cancel half a Line, nor all thy Tears wash out a Word of it." Our lives inexorably move on, every moment succeeded by the next, until our time runs out. At every moment, our future becomes the present; our present, the past. Is our future, like Scottie's, already written? Are we fated, as he is? Or are our powers of thought capable, as Emerson believed, of freeing us—but also making it our responsibility—to write our own future, to realize our world? There are no accidents, no contingencies, within the world on film; nothing that is not real is possible. But our world abounds in unrealized possibilities. And our lives are woven of contingencies. I was not fated to write *The Murderous Gaze*. And I am not fated to be writing these words now. And yet, I can now discern permanent marks the writing of *The Murderous Gaze* left on me, and not only on my writing. Every moment of our lives is transient, yet leaves permanent marks. Had I not written *The Murderous Gaze* then, my temperament would still be what it was, what it is. But I would not be writing *Must We Kill the Thing We Love?* now. I would not have become the writer, the person, I am. In this sense, it becomes possible, looking back on our pasts, to discern a kind of necessity in the contingent moments of our lives. They could have been different. But if they had been different, we would now be different. Our futures are not yet written. And we do not have to let others write them for us. Nor do we have to write our futures in foolish consistency with our pasts. It is by acknowledging the past—acknowledging that it *is* past, abandoning it, yet mourning its passing—that we free ourselves to move on. This was Emerson's faith, as it was Cavell's—a faith that Hitchcock was torn between embracing and resisting, between wishing to embrace and wishing to resist. As I have said, at the time I was writing *The Murderous Gaze*, I was teaching film at Harvard and in almost daily conversation with Cavell, who only a few years before had been my doctoral advisor (and who never stopped being my teacher as well as my friend).

And yet, when I read *The Murderous Gaze* now, I can see clearly, as I could not when I was writing the book, that I, like Hitchcock, was torn between embracing, and resisting, this faith. *The Murderous Gaze* argues that in Hitchcock thrillers both murder and marriage are metaphors for their author's relationship, made possible by the art of pure cinema, with viewers. And that being suspended between these incompatible pictures of his art—and the incompatible worldviews they underwrite, and are underwritten by—was Hitchcock's principled position, as if he understood it to be the truth, the reality of our condition, that choosing between these two pictures, or even knowing whether we have to choose, is an impossibility. But for this to be his principled position, Hitchcock had to have chosen it over at least one other option. In effect, then, *The Murderous Gaze* pictures Hitchcock as deciding, on principle, not to decide. Not deciding between what alternatives? Between acts of creation committed to walking in the direction of the unattained but attainable self, and acts of creation that are, metaphorically, acts of murder. That is tantamount to choosing between art that is principled and art that is unprincipled. What principle could possibly justify choosing not to choose between being principled and being unprincipled? Not to choose is to be unprincipled. (It is not possible to decide to be fated, I might add.)

In the process of writing *Must We Kill the Thing We Love?*, I was relieved to discover that I love Hitchcock's cinema no less than I did, or knew I did, when I wrote *The Murderous Gaze*. If each man kills the thing he loves, I am happy to have botched it with Hitchcock. Of course, "killing" Hitchcock's cinema, or anyone's love for it, is not my goal—nor, I trust, the outcome—in writing *The Murderous Gaze*. Neither is it my goal, in writing *Must We Kill the Thing We Love?*, to "kill" *The Murderous Gaze*, which I also have not stopped loving. No one had ever written such a book before, about Hitchcock or any other director. It does not say everything there is to say about Hitchcock's films. Far from it. But what it does say is said nowhere else. And it says it in a singular way and in a distinctive voice I still embrace as my own.

In the decades since the publication of *The Murderous Gaze*, Hitchcock's films have been the subject of dozens of books and essays, many of them substantial, informative, and illuminating.[1] Thanks to this impressive body of literature, we know far more about Hitchcock's working methods, the circumstances of the production of his films, their reception, and so on. We also have the benefit of illuminating insights into the films themselves gleaned by a wide range of critical approaches. The discoveries that scholars and critics have since made about Hitchcock's work reinforce, rather than call into question, my book's claims and arguments. Nor do they cast doubt on the practice of reading that underwrites my book, or the philosophical perspective that practice exemplifies. How could they?

---

1. To name just a few of the writers from whose work on Hitchcock I, personally, have benefited (with apologies to those I have inadvertently omitted, and others whose writings I have not yet discovered): Richard Allen, Dan Auiler, Charles Barr, Raymond Bellour, Lesley Brill, Paula Marantz Cohen, Tom Cohen, Robert Corber, Sidney Gottlieb, Nicholas Haeffner, Sam Ishii-Gonzáles, Steven Jacobs, Robert Kapsis, Marian Keane, Bill Krohn, Leonard Leff, Thomas Leitch, Frank Meola, Tania Modleski, Tony Lee Moral, Christopher Morris, John Orr, Dennis Perry, Leland Poague, Murray Pomerance, Stefan Sharff, Irving Singer, Susan Smith, David Sterritt, George Toles, James Vest, Michael Walker, Robin Wood, Slavoj Žižek.

Nonetheless, there will be more than a few instances, in the pages that follow, in which I part with my young self. For example, the emotionally charged and densely argued reading of *Vertigo* that plays a pivotal role in *Must We Kill the Thing We Love?* hinges on two intuitions that had not yet dawned on me—or on any other commentator on the film, for that matter—when I wrote "*Vertigo*: The Unknown Woman in Hitchcock," an essay published several years after *The Murderous Gaze*. How could I not have known what I now know about *Vertigo*? How could I have come to see what once I could not see?

"Everybody wants to be settled," Emerson writes, "but only insofar as they are unsettled is there any hope for them" (Emerson and Porte 1983, 529). I unsettle all things," one more oft-quoted Emerson sentence, along with a portrait of the Sage of Concord, is emblazoned on one of my tee shirts, now more than a bit the worse for wear. (Another bears the cherubic visage of the Master of Suspense.) Writing *Must We Kill the Things We Love?* has, indeed, unsettled my thinking about Hitchcock, or revealed to me how unsettled my thoughts had become in the years since I wrote *The Murderous Gaze*. "Our life is an apprenticeship to the truth that around every circle another can be drawn" is another inspiring Emerson sentence, too long, unfortunately, for a tee shirt (Emerson and Porte 1983, 403). In writing this book, I have drawn a new circle.

When I was writing *The Murderous Gaze*, I believed I was giving equal weight to the two pictures of Hitchcock's authorship I discerned in the films I was studying. I can see now how much I favored the darker picture. I wasn't then conscious of doing so. And yet, after I had finished the chapters on *The Lodger*, *Murder!*, *Shadow of a Doubt*, and *Psycho*, I thought at first that the book was complete, but then I decided to add a chapter on *The 39 Steps* because I didn't want my book to give the misleading impression that I failed to value the matchless pleasures, the sheer enjoyment, that Hitchcock films, like Hollywood comedies of remarriage, are capable of giving us. Nonetheless, in *The Murderous Gaze* dark moods predominate. They keep intensifying until they climax in the last pages of the *Psycho* chapter and the melancholy postscript I began writing when I heard the news that Hitchcock had died.

Dwelling largely on films *The Murderous Gaze* passes over, *Must We Kill the Thing We Love?* retraces the trajectory of Hitchcock's career—with several detours along the way—in a manner intended to balance the scales. Happily, the Moving Finger, having writ again, has tilted the scales in favor of the Emersonian philosophy I find myself no longer resisting.

18

On Stanley Cavell's *Band Wagon*

Although Stanley Cavell's *Philosophy the Day After Tomorrow* is not a book about film, it contains two essays, "Something Out of the Ordinary" (the main focus of my remarks in this essay) and "Fred Astaire Asserts the Right to Praise," in which the reading of a passage from a film plays a central role. Specifically, these essays reflect on the first two Fred Astaire routines from *The Band Wagon*, a critically admired 1953 MGM musical produced by Arthur Freed and directed by Vincente Minnelli, with songs by Howard Dietz and Arthur Schwartz. Some of the songs in the film, but not "By Myself" and "A Shine on Your Shoes," the songs Astaire sings in the passages Cavell considers, are from the 1931 musical revue also called *The Band Wagon*, the last time Fred Astaire and sister Adele danced together on a Broadway stage.

I have written extensively about Cavell's work, mainly about his writings on film. But "Something Out of the Ordinary" is different from those books and essays. For one thing, Cavell keeps deferring a reading of the film passage, although he repeatedly informs us of the kinds of things he *will* be saying once he gets to the reading. Evidently, he felt the need to prepare his audience—he originally presented it as his Presidential Address at the ninety-third annual meeting of the Eastern Division of the American Philosophical Association—for the discoveries his reading was to present by doing what he calls "philosophical table-setting," as if to keep the philosophical bearing of those discoveries from being lost on his audience of professional philosophers—and on himself.

Before Cavell gets to the reading itself, he invokes so many of the twists and turns of the long path of philosophy on which he, like the Astaire character

---

Paper presented at the conference on *Philosophy the Day After Tomorrow*, organized by Sandra Laugier, at the Sorbonne, 2013. Published online in *Film-Philosophy*, 2014.

in the film, has gone his way by himself over his long career that the essay is like a passport stamped with visas to its author's favorite philosophical ports of call, among them the writings of Kant, Wittgenstein, and Austin, as well as his own earlier writings. In this way, the essay participates—as does *Philosophy the Day After Tomorrow* as a whole—in the turn to autobiography that is characteristic of his late writing in general. But in looking back, in returning to the origins of his way of thinking philosophically, "Something Out of the Ordinary," like all the essays in the book, explicitly aligns itself with philosophy's future, as the title "Philosophy the Day After Tomorrow" attests.

Surprisingly, in "Something Out of the Ordinary" (and in "Fred Astaire Asserts the Right to Praise" as well) references to Cavell's own writings about *film* are all but completely absent. Absent as well is the kind of evocative, eloquent, often sprightly prose that makes *Pursuits of Happiness* such an unending source of pleasure to me, as to so many readers. Although Cavell began his Presidential Address with the observation that he was speaking only a few miles from the Atlanta neighborhood where he spent the first seven years of his life, absent, too, is the equally evocative, eloquent, at times devastatingly moving prose of *Contesting Tears* and the turn to autobiography adumbrated by *A Pitch of Philosophy* and brought to completion, philosophically and personally, by *Little Did I Know: Excerpts from Memory*. It is with a retracing of the trajectory of its author's philosophical life, not his personal life (might we call this his "ordinary life"?), that "Something Out of the Ordinary" "sets the table," philosophically, for his reading of the Astaire routine.

As a consequence, in the philosophical table setting that precedes the reading, the concept of the ordinary, upon which the essay hinges, receives much less intimate specification and thus comes across, in relation to Cavell's personal life, as more of an abstraction than in *The World Viewed*. In "Something Out of the Ordinary," the Astaire routine itself, in which his manner of walking is essential to his delivery of the song, bears the full burden of "emblematizing" the ordinary (Cavell 2006, 7–27).

In "The Acknowledgment of Silence," the final chapter of *The World Viewed*, Cavell presents a list—obscure, to be sure—of instances of what he means by "the unsayable."

> The pulsing air of incommunicability which may nudge the edge of any experience and placement: the curve of fingers that day, a mouth, the sudden rise of the body's frame as it is caught by the color and scent of flowers, laughing all afternoon mostly about nothing, the friend gone but somewhere now which starts from here—spools of history that have unwound only to me now, occasions which will not reach words for me now, and if not now, never. (Cavell 1979b, 148)

After *The World Viewed*, the word "unsayable" altogether dropped out of Cavell's lexicon—until its reappearance in "Fred Astaire Asserts the Right to Praise," where Cavell takes the extraordinary—and unprecedented—step of explicitly equating "the unsayable" and "the ordinary." By implication, he takes his characterization of "the unsayable," in one of the most obscure but thought-provoking passages in *The World Viewed*, to apply to "the ordinary" as well: The "reality of the unsayable is the unmoving ground upon which I cannot but move" (Cavell 1979b, 148)—the solid ground we must have beneath our feet if our need for horizons, for uprightness and frontedness, is to be satisfied, if we are to walk in the gait that is natural for human beings on earth.

"Two Cheers for Romance," an early version of Cavell's reading of *Now, Voyager* (Irving Rapper, 1942), which he adapted to turn it into a chapter of *Contesting Tears*, begins, "Film is an interest of mine, or say a love, not separate from my interest in, or love of, philosophy. So when I am drawn to think through a film, I do not regard the reading that results as over, even provisionally, until I have said how it bears on the nature of film generally"—until he has said how the reading furthers his philosophical investigation of film's ontology—"and on the commitment to philosophy"—until he has also said how the reading casts light on the value of such an investigation, the value of philosophy (Cavell and Rothman 2005, 153). Cavell doesn't just finish "Something Out of the Ordinary" by saying how his reading of the Astaire routine bears on the commitment to philosophy. Rather, saying this is *the* task of the essay.

In *Reading Cavell's "The World Viewed,"* Marian Keane and I undertook simply to read that profound, beautiful, but famously difficult little book. In so doing, we hoped to demonstrate that, and how, it can be read. Even for readers who accord it the kind and degree of attention it calls for, however, *The World Viewed* remains difficult. The difficulty of the book is inseparable from what Cavell calls "the obscurity of its promptings." "Something Out of the Ordinary" is not in the same way obscure. All one has to do is read it to see that, and how, it reads itself. Aye, there's the rub. It is possible, if difficult, for readers without academic training in philosophy to follow Cavell's thinking in *The World Viewed*. Indeed, such training can be more hindrance than help if it encourages the tendency to see other thinkers as opponents whose arguments—and egos—are to be crushed.

Cities of Words, Cavell's only overtly pedagogical book, explicitly undertakes to provide the education in philosophy that a reader requires to follow its thinking. But "Something Out of the Ordinary," like many of the essays that comprise *Philosophy the Day After Tomorrow*, originally an address to professional philosophers, was written for an audience Cavell counted on—his generosity in offering the benefit of the doubt is one of his most endearing attributes—to possess not only philosophical training, without which it would be all but unreadable, but also the commitment to philosophy, without which it would be all but impossible to read it with pleasure.

In all honesty, I do not love *The Band Wagon* unreservedly, the way I love some of the Astaire/Rogers musicals of the 1930s, especially *Top Hat* (Sandrich, 1935). Nor do I love this Cavell essay, or its companion piece "Fred Astaire Asserts the Right to Praise," the way I love *The World Viewed* and *Pursuits of Happiness*, among others of his writings. Those books give me a kind of pleasure that a shared love of movies makes possible. "Something Out of the Ordinary" gives me less of that kind of pleasure. But the kind of pleasure that only a shared commitment to philosophy makes possible is not foreign to me. And far be it from me to underestimate its value. In what follows, simply reading "Something Out of the Ordinary" will be my main task, although I will add an epilogue in which I will offer my own complementary reading of the Astaire routine, which I am inclined to see, as is my wont, as a cinematic sequence bearing the stamp of the authorship of the film's director, Vincente Minnelli.

∼

"Something Out of the Ordinary" begins with two quotations, one from John Dewey and one from Friedrich Nietzsche, which lead Cavell to remark that in his early essay "Aesthetic Problems of Modern Philosophy," included in *Must We Mean What We Say?*, he had observed that "Kant's characterization of the aesthetic judgment models the claim of so-called ordinary language philosophers to voice what we would ordinarily say when, and what we should mean in saying it" (Cavell 2006, 9). But he has since come to understand that there is a feature of the aesthetic claim, which Kant described as a kind of compulsion to share a pleasure, that Cavell did not acknowledge in this early essay: the fact that an aesthetic pleasure I feel compelled to share is tinged with an anxiety that the claim might stand to be rebuked. And it is tinged with another, related, anxiety, which is that "something I know and cannot make intelligible stands to be lost by me" (Cavell 2006, 9).

This "fact or fantasy of experience passing me by," Cavell writes, "is also explicitly a way I have wished to word my interest in Austin and the later Wittgenstein, especially I think when their procedures present themselves as *returning* us to the ordinary . . ." (Cavell 2006, 9). In ending this sentence by adding "a place we have never been," he marks a difference between his own way of thinking and theirs—a difference that aligns Cavell with Ralph Waldo Emerson who, observing the "discrepance" between the world we "converse with in the cities and in the farms" and the world we *think*, admonishes us, in his great essay "Experience," to take steps to "realize" our world—to return to a place we have never been, in effect, by at once transfiguring the ordinary and bringing our thinking down to earth (Cavell 2006, 9–10).

"Experience missed, in certain of the forms in which philosophy has interested itself in this condition," this important passage goes on, "is a theme developing itself in recent years in various of my intellectual turns" (Cavell 2006, 10), among them his "turning" toward film and opera. And this leads Cavell to his first characterization of the reading of the Astaire routine he will be presenting later in the essay.

> To epitomize the surprising extensions of the theme and as an experiment highlighting the difficulties in the way of showing and sharing the pleasures in its discoveries . . . , I am going toward the end of this chapter to discuss a brief film sequence, chosen also so as to allow some chance . . . of showing a difference in my approach to aesthetic matters from that of most, of course not all, work in aesthetics in the Anglo-

American ways of philosophy, or for that matter in the practice of Kant. (Cavell 2006, 10)

This "difference" is Cavell's emphasis on the criticism, or what he calls "reading," of individual works of art. And a distinctive feature of his practice of reading is its attention to "letting a work of art have a voice in what philosophy says about it." He adds, "I regard that attention as a way of testing whether the time is past in which taking seriously the philosophical bearing of a particular work of art can be a measure of the seriousness of philosophy" (Cavell 2006, 10).

This quintessentially Cavellian sentence is studded with disorienting twists. It does *not* say, for example, that readings such as the one he will be presenting test whether taking seriously the philosophical bearing of a particular work of art can be a measure of the seriousness of philosophy. What such a reading tests, the sentence says, is whether this is *still* possible. The implication is that it is to be accepted as a fact—a fact about art, about criticism, about philosophy—that there was a time when this *was* possible.

This sentence is uncharacteristically imprecise, however, in that taken literally—which is how all Cavell sentences are at one level meant to be taken—it implies that his readings have always aspired, the way the reading of the Astaire routine in "Something Out of the Ordinary" does, to test whether something that once was possible is *still* possible. But that could hardly have been the aspiration of his pioneering readings of *King Lear* and Samuel Beckett's *Endgame* in *Must We Mean What We Say?*, for example (Cavell 2002, 169). They were unprecedented, within the tradition of Anglo-American aesthetics, for the philosophically serious attention they accorded to the "philosophical bearing" of particular works of art.

What those readings tested, rather, was whether something that had never before been done was possible at all. Had the time finally arrived for what Henry James, half a century earlier, had called "the criticism of the future"? In "Something Out of the Ordinary," Cavell's question is whether that time has come and gone, whether that future is now past. He has a personal stake in this question, of course, for what is at issue is the continuing viability of his own approach to aesthetic matters. If philosophy were no longer to allow a particular work of art to have a voice in what it says about aesthetic matters, it would be consigning Cavell's voice to the past as well.

When Cavell speaks of the "philosophical bearing" of particular works of art, his choice of the word "bearing" is meant, I take it, to highlight a certain ambiguity or doubleness. A work's "philosophical bearing" is the way it bears on philosophy—its capacity to influence philosophy, to invite or demand a response from philosophy, one that pushes philosophy forward or alters its course. But a work's "philosophical bearing" is also its orientation—how it takes its own bearings, philosophically, how it locates the conditions of its own art, acknowledges what (and, metaphorically, where) it finds itself.

In any case, the "philosophical bearing" of a work of art is not something the work *says* or, rather, it is something the work says precisely by not saying it. To take seriously the "philosophical bearing" of a work of art is thus a matter of saying, *in a way that makes philosophy*, what goes without saying by, or within, the work itself. Indeed, I would go so far as to suggest—this is my thought, not Cavell's—that giving voice to what a work of art consigns to silence is philosophy's *way* of allowing the work to have a voice in what philosophy says about it. If philosophy no longer regarded taking seriously the "philosophical bearing" of particular works of art to be a measure of its own seriousness, how would philosophy find anything serious to say about art, anything to say that justified the commitment to philosophy?

In this context, Cavell turns again, not surprisingly, to Kant's characterization of the aesthetic judgment. Kant's location of the aesthetic judgment, as claiming to record the presence of pleasure without a concept, makes room for a particular form of criticism, one capable of supplying the concepts that, after the fact of pleasure, articulate the grounds of this experience in particular objects. The work of such criticism is to reveal its object as having yet to achieve its due effect. Something there, despite being fully opened to the senses, has been missed (Cavell 2006, 11).

Here, Cavell offers a further description, one that resonates with this passage, of the reading to come: "The fragment of film I have chosen readily allows itself to be dismissed as inconsequential, but to my mind that precisely fits it to be a memorable enactment of the ordinary as what is missable" (Cavell 2006, 11). His reading will aspire to discover, and take seriously, the "philosophical bearing" of this feature of the Astaire routine, that by virtue of its "missability" it is able to serve—is meant to serve—as a "memorable enactment" of the unmemorable in our experience, which simply is the ordinary, as Wittgenstein conceptualized it in *Philosophical Investigations* (published posthumously, in G. E. M. Anscombe's English translation, in 1953, the same year *The Band Wagon* was released).

More than once in "Something Out of the Ordinary," as we shall see, Cavell calls the Astaire routine "a touchstone of experience," a formulation that at first perplexed me. I kept thinking that Cavell would have better expressed what he meant had he called it "a touchstone of our experience of the ordinary" or "a touchstone of the ordinary in our experience," or had found some other way of specifying the particular experience, or kind of experience, that he finds the routine to be a touchstone *of*. Finally, it dawned on me that Cavell's point is that what is paradigmatically unmemorable in our experience—and here, the word "in" is misleading; "about" would be no less so—is our experience itself. (I have an impulse to add something like "as we ordinarily experience it," but isn't that a distinction without a difference?)

Before presenting the reading itself, Cavell finds it necessary to do some more philosophical table setting to enable us, he says, to appreciate the role that missability plays in enabling Astaire's routine to give us pleasure and thereby a reason to value it. The reading that the essay is leading up to will claim, Cavell now tells us, that "while it is not a fact that the Astaire routine is trivial, the sequence can be seen to be *about* triviality," and that showing this "will require showing how its pleasure derives from its location of formal conditions of its art"—how it takes its "philosophical bearings," in effect (Cavell 2006, 11).

In writing *Pursuits of Happiness*, Cavell felt no need to perform much philosophical table setting for his readings of films like *The Awful Truth* (Leo McCarey, 1937) and *The Philadelphia Story* (George Cukor, 1940) to show how they bear on philosophy. He could approach those films directly, in part, because as soon as he began attending seriously to them, they revealed themselves to be self-evidently consequential. Comedies of remarriage have no reason to present themselves as if they were trivial, because unlike the Astaire routine, as Cavell will read it, they are not *about* triviality.

Cavell's next act of philosophical table setting refers to yet another passage that invokes his own philosophical past.

> A further variation in the relation of the ordinary to what may be seen as the aesthetic . . . goes back to my having responded to Wittgenstein's *Investigations* as written, however else, in recurrent response to skepticism but not as a refutation of it; rather on the contrary, as a task to discover the causes of philosophy's disparagement of, or its disappointment with, the ordinary, something I have called the truth of skepticism. (Cavell 2006, 11)

In his early essay "Knowing and Acknowledging" (Cavell 2002, 238–66), Cavell characterized the ordinary not as what is perceptibly missable, but as what is intellectually *dismissible*, what *must* be set aside if philosophy's aspirations to knowledge are to be satisfied. He writes, "There I articulated my sense of what happens to philosophy's aspirations by saying that skepticism is not the discovery of an incapacity in human knowing, but an insufficiency of acknowledging what in my world I think of as beyond me, or my senses" (Cavell 2006, 12).

This early insight was to lead Cavell to his seminal intuition, for which *The Claim of Reason* paid the tuition, that Shakespeare's tragedies can be seen to be about (what philosophy conceptualizes as) skepticism.

In "Something Out of the Ordinary," Cavell proposes, more generally, that the arts may variously be seen, and claimed, as chapters of the history, or development, of philosophy and, indeed, as present manifestations of philosophy. He writes, "I am going in a little while, as said, to extend this thought to a polar relation of tragedy, a Hollywood musical" (Cavell 2006, 14)—a Hollywood musical, I cannot resist adding, that explicitly presents itself *as* a polar relation to tragedy. Astaire plays an aging star of stage and screen musicals whose career is in decline in the changed world of postwar America. He signs on to play the lead in a lighthearted Broadway show his good friends have written for his comeback, only to find that the show's A-list director wants to turn it into an allegory of the Faust story, a further irony being that the 1943 all-black musical *Cabin in the Sky* (1943), also produced by Arthur Freed and directed by Vincente Minnelli (it was his debut as a film director), is *literally* an allegorical version of *Faust*.

In any case, the claim that a "lowly" Hollywood musical like *The Band Wagon* can be seen to be about what the most advanced philosophy of its time was conceptualizing as the ordinary—in the work of Wittgenstein and Austin—gains plausibility from two of Cavell's convictions, both of which he had originally argued for in *The World Viewed*. First, that the great arts, together with their criticism, increasingly take on the self-reflective condition of philosophy (teaching us, let us say, that *King Lear* is about theater as catharsis, that *Macbeth* is about theater as apparition, *Othello* is about the treacherous theater of optical proof, *Hamlet* about what surpasses theatrical show). Second, that the medium of film is such that it could take on the seriousness of the modern, hence the self-reflective condition of philosophy, without splitting its audience between high and low (Cavell 2006, 14).

Given these two convictions, it should come as no surprise that Cavell finds a routine in a Hollywood musical to be capable of orienting itself by locating the formal conditions of its own art, and capable as well of serving as a touchstone of experience. But Cavell is still not ready to present the reading. He feels the need first to invoke certain of the themes he developed in a course he gave on the aesthetics of film and opera. The idea Cavell developed in that course "is that words and actions suffer transfiguration in opera (the art which replaces speaking by singing) that bears comparison with the transformation in film (the art which replaces living human beings by photographic shadows of themselves" (Cavell 2006, 15). His interest in opera, he observes, is tied to yet a further way he has formulated an interest in the work of Austin and the later work of Wittgenstein.

> Their sense of returning words from their metaphysical to their everyday use is driven by a sense of a human dissatisfaction with words in which an effort to transcend or to purify speech ends by depriving the human speaker of a voice in what becomes his (or, differently, her) fantasy of knowledge, a characterization I have given of what happens in skepticism. If we provisionally characterize the medium of opera as music's exploration of its affinities with expressive or passionate utterance, then the specific response it invites from the recent present of philosophy, as represented in Austin's work, is to determine how his theory of speech as action may be extended, in a sense re-begun, in order to articulate a theory of speech as passion that can propose an orderly study of the effects of the voice raised in opera, but this must in return allow the study of opera to inspire philosophy's interest in passionate speech. (Cavell 2006, 15)

One reason I have quoted this passage at length is that it provides so clear an example of a mutually beneficial relationship between an art and philosophy. What Cavell is saying is that his provisional characterization of the medium of opera—and in the course on film and opera he derived this characterization not in the abstract but by taking seriously the "philosophical bearing" of particular operas—reveals how opera invites a response from philosophy (inviting a response from philosophy being a way that works of art can have a philosophical bearing). (I admire the adeptness—and the audacity—with which Cavell sidesteps the question as to whether Austin's writings represent philosophy's past or its present by locating them in philosophy's "recent present." For opera as for philosophy, but decidedly not for film, a half a century ago can count as recent.)

Opera, as Cavell provisionally characterizes it, invites philosophy to extend Austin's theory of speech acts so as to articulate a theory of passionate utterances. Cavell accepts this invitation, staking out a claim for philosophy by working out such a theory in impressive detail in "Performative and Passionate Utterance," a companion essay in *Philosophy the Day After Tomorrow*. The study of passionate utterances that he envisions in this essay at once looks to the future and rethinks the relationship between his own philosophical enterprise and that of Austin, one of his major early influences. In "Something Out of the Ordinary," he begins sketching such a study, which he would value for its potential to underwrite an "orderly study" of opera—a study he would value, in turn, for its potential to inspire further interest in passionate utterance on the part of philosophy.

A critical study of the medium and the art of opera, grounded in serious attention to particular operas, would thus provide a justification for "the commitment to philosophy." And the commitment to philosophy, in turn, would provide a justification for such a study. That the same is true for the serious study of film was the guiding intuition—at once premise and conclusion—of all of Cavell's writings on the subject. What is the response that the Astaire routine, as "Something Out of the Ordinary" will go on to interpret it, invites from philosophy? It is the essay itself.

A crucial point Cavell draws from his meditation on opera as music's exploration of its affinity with passionate utterance is that, as Wittgenstein as well as Freud recognized, "what happens when creatures of a certain species fall into the possession of language and become humans is that they become victims of expression—readable—their every word and gesture ready to betray their meaning" (Cavell 2006, 20). With this point in mind, and invoking concepts the essay has already introduced, Cavell offers a last preliminary characterization of the claim his reading will stake out: "In the conjunction of Austin's appeal to the ordinary, and specifically its power to reveal the action of speech, with the passion of abandonment in the raised speech of opera, I can provisionally locate the pertinence I attach to the scene of Astaire singing and dancing" (Cavell 2006, 20).

Cavell also locates the Astaire routine's "pertinence"—its "philosophical bearing," its invitation to philosophy to respond to it—in the conjunction of Austin's (and Wittgenstein's) appeals to the ordinary and Kant's conception of the aesthetic judgment. So much is implied by Cavell's addition of the sentence "The judgment I make in discussing the sequence here expresses my pleasure and sense of value in it and awaits your agreement upon this" (Cavell 2006, 20).

With the philosophical table at long last set, Cavell is finally ready, as I surely am, to present his reading of the Astaire routine.

∽

First, Cavell explains what he calls the "occasion of the number" by describing the passage in the film that immediately precedes and motivates it.

The occasion of the number is that the character played by Astaire—a song-and-dance man whose star has faded in Hollywood and who is returning apprehensively to New York to try a comeback on Broadway—exits from the train that has returned him, mistakenly takes the awaiting reporters and photographers to have come to interview him, and is rudely awakened to reality as a still-vivid star steps out of the adjacent car and the newshounds flock to her (Ava Gardner in a cameo appearance). As our hero walks away ruefully, a porter offers a remark to him on the rigors of publicity to which stardom subjects a person, and upon answering, "Yes, I don't know how they stand it," Astaire arrives at his song, entitled "By Myself." (Cavell 2006, 22)

Next, Cavell begins describing the scene of the routine itself.

From a baggage cart to a gate, the camera leads the man down the length of a train platform in one continuous shot; at the end of the singing, the camera stops as he does and then, as it were, watches him leave through the gate; we then cut to a view from within the station and see the man continue his walk toward us, humming the same tune, then pause, and shift nervously, as if expecting someone. If this were theater, the routine would clearly end with the exit through the gate. As it is a film, the entrance into the station may count as part of the song. Overall it seems as nearly uneventful as a photographed song can be. (Cavell 2006, 22)

Astaire had begun singing with a little self-conscious laugh, magnified by its producing a palpable cloud of cigarette smoke. This is, Cavell observes, "a self-reflexive response"—that is, it participates in the sequence's achieving what he calls "locating the formal conditions of its own art"—to the fact that in this man "thinking (manifest here, classically, as melancholy) is about to become singing." He adds,

I report that when I recall Astaire's delivery of "By Myself," it brings with it a sense of emotional hovering, not so much a feeling of suspense as one of being in suspension, a spiritual bracketing. I cite two pairs of facts to begin to sketch an account of this touchstone of experience, one pair concerning the song, the other concerning the presentation, or representation, of the person Astaire. (Cavell 2006, 22)

About the song, Cavell identifies two features (features, I might add, not dependent on the fact that this is a song in a movie, not a stage musical) that would be impractical for him to try to verify in the essay.
(1) Like certain arias in Italian grand opera and in the basic form of song in the so-called Golden Age of the American musical from the 1920s through the 1940s, it uses a quatrain form—the phrases occurring in the pattern AABA, with the emotional crescendo peaking in the third, or B phrase.

(2) The song's melodic and harmonic organization contributes to the experience of hovering. Here Cavell simply notes that harmonically its opening chord progression can be said to allude to the opening harmonic progression of *Tristan*. He writes that "if the sound of music can ever sensibly be said to represent suspended animation, I suppose *Tristan and Isolde* is the crucial case" (Cavell 2006, 23).

Cavell now turns to a pair of facts concerning the presentation of the person of Astaire, and first of his walking. And here it does make a difference that Astaire is on film, not on stage, although the reading does not explicitly point this out.

> Recall to begin with its jauntiness, the slight but distinct exaggeration of his body swinging from side to side as he paces along the platform. Narratively, he is hoping to cheer himself, letting his body, as William James once suggested, tell him what his emotion is. (Cavell 2006, 23)

Again, Cavell is venturing into the realm in which the sequence may be seen to be "locating the formal conditions of its own art."

> Ontologically, we could say, it is the walk of a man who is known to move in dance exactly like no other man. It is a walk from which, at any step, this man may break into dance—he is known from other contexts to have found dancing called for in the course of driving golf balls, or roller-skating, or while swabbing the deck of a ship. (Cavell 2006, 23)

"Now if his walking does turn into dancing," Cavell continues, "then isn't what we see of his delivery revealed to have been already dancing, a sort of limiting case, or proto-state, of dancing? We should readily agree that it isn't just walking he is exhibiting. Then what is the relation of dancing to walking?" (Cavell 2006, 23).

This last is a philosophical question that Cavell understands the Astaire routine to be asking itself.

> Astaire's song does not continue into unequivocal dancing, as a song-and-dance man's song normally does. That we are for the moment confined, so to speak, to this dance virtuoso's more or less untrained voice, throws the emphasis of interest in this number elsewhere—specifically on his "delivery" of the song (also something for which Astaire is famous); here the walk is part of its delivery. In opera, delivery is essentially a function of voice. What is called "acting" is available to certain opera stars, but apart from the basis of the voice, the operatic presence is ineffective. In American musical theater, the economy is roughly reversed: Unless you are identified as a dancer, or as some kind of clown, your voice may have to be better trained than Astaire's; yet apart from the basis of your delivery (as it were mounting the voice), the theatrical presence will be more or less ineffective. (Cavell 2006, 24)

It is in the film's next routine, which Cavell will read in detail in "Fred Astaire Asserts the Right to Praise," that Astaire does find his way to dance.

> It is on New York's former street of theater, 42nd Street, where, continuing his opening adventures in a space that is now an amusement arcade, he stumbles over the outstretched legs of a preoccupied black shoeshine man, responds by singing a Tin Pan Alley tune called "When There's a Shine on Your Shoes," and, ascending the shoeshine stand and receiving a transfigurative shine, is invited by the black man—so I invite the encounter to be read—to come to earth and join in the dance. There further unfolds one of the most elaborate and stunning in the history of Astaire routines. (Cavell 2006, 24)

"Fred Astaire Asserts the Right to Praise" spells out the details of this second Astaire routine. That essay invites us to see it as a dance of praise, one that provides an occasion for Astaire to acknowledge his indebtedness for his existence as a dancer—his deepest identity, as Cavell suggests—to the genius of black dancers.

Astaire had already achieved stardom in vaudeville partnering with his sister Adele in a ballroom dancing act, when in the early 1920s he sought out the great John Sublett, known professionally as "John Bubbles," whose moves had revolutionized tap dancing. It is said that Astaire paid him $400 a lesson—quite a sum in those days—to help him master tap. In later years, Sublett enjoyed saying that young Astaire had trouble learning some of his moves, but he was also on record as calling Astaire the greatest American dancer. Having been "taught by the best," as Sublett liked to say, Astaire could tap brilliantly, but he was equally masterful at romantic ballroom-style dancing, which blacks were forbidden to perform on the vaudeville stage, and ballet moves as well.

For his part, Astaire regarded "Bubbles" as the greatest of all tap dancers. The year after George Gershwin chose Sublett to create the role of Sportin' Life in the original 1935 production of *Porgy and Bess*, Astaire turned to him again to help him prepare the elaborate "Bojangles of Harlem" number for *Swing Time* (George Stevens, 1936). Ostensibly, the number was a tribute to Bill Robinson, aka Bojangles, who was a generation older than Sublett and a great tap dancer of a very different stripe. But it is Sportin' Life, as Sublett played him, whose image is evoked by Astaire's iconic costume and swagger as he performs the number in blackface. And in this routine, it is Sublett, not Robinson, to whom Astaire's dancing pays the sincerest form of flattery.

The routine begins with Astaire sharing the stage with a chorus line of white women. After they exit, Astaire is a small, solitary figure, except for the three shadows matching him brilliant step by brilliant step. I see these black shadows as stand-ins for the great black dancers in whose footsteps Astaire was literally following. In the America of *Swing Time*, and even the America of *The Band Wagon*, gifted black performers toiled in relative obscurity while whites reaped rewards by "covering" their

work. Even Bill Robinson, who had the talent, the courage, and the self-regard to break the unwritten law of vaudeville that it was taboo for black artists to perform solo acts, died penniless.

The "Bojangles of Harlem" routine was as explicit and sincere an acknowledgment as was allowable in 1950s Hollywood of an unjust reality in which society consigned black dancers to relative anonymity, no matter how worthy they may have been of the fame—and financial rewards—that Astaire had indisputably earned by dint of his hard work and genius. The irony of this tribute to the legion of unrecognized black dancers, of course, is that the spotlight is only on Astaire. The shadows are faceless. Nameless. Indeed, they appear to be *his* shadows. On the other hand, these black shadows dwarf Astaire. And he is dancing in blackface. Are they shadows he casts? Or are they pulling his strings?

In "Fred Astaire Asserts the Right to Praise," Cavell distinguishes between two modes of false praise. One is, as it were, idolatrous: placing someone on a pedestal and praising that person for godlike qualities he or she doesn't really possess. Astaire's "When There's a Shine on Your Shoes" routine, Cavell asserts, "takes up a different aspect of praise, not so much whether it is sufficient or accurate as whether it is earned or acceptable, risking not so much idolatry as blasphemy, this praise is not so much false as vain." In this routine, he goes on, "Astaire can seem to be subject to the latter error of vain, unacceptable, what I am calling blasphemous praise" (Cavell 2006, 66).

Arguably, Astaire's "Bojangles of Harlem" routine in *Swing Time* is vulnerable to such a charge, although I would contest that judgment. But just as Cavell takes the "By Myself" routine, which can seem trivial, to be *about* triviality, in "Fred Astaire

Asserts the Right to Praise" he contends that the "When There's a Shine on Your Shoes" routine is *about* the possibility of its vanity, of lack of authority," a possibility the routine dares to confront head-on (Cavell 2006, 67).

Cavell's reading surmises that Astaire, knowing that he is thereby giving his assent to an America that remains cursed by its history of slavery and racism, and knowing that this curse is a condition, and may be a cost, of his praise, nonetheless asserts his right to praise black dancers, to whom he owes an inestimable debt and who were—and are—unjustly treated by a society that has so lavishly rewarded him. Astaire knows he could be rebuked for exploiting those he wishes to honor by a routine that ends, after all, with his black partner—Leroy Daniels, a real-life Los Angeles "shoeshine boy" and first-time actor, who goes nameless in the film's closing credits—on his knees. And Cavell asserts his right to praise Fred Astaire, to express his gratitude to Astaire for the pleasure the routine gives him, despite knowing that a curse has been a condition, and may be a cost, of his praise, too, and knowing he could be rebuked for it—as, perhaps not surprisingly, he has been in some quarters. (A reader tempted to rebuke Cavell for being naïve about racism, or for being an unwitting racist himself, would do well to read, and take to heart, the ineffably moving sections of *Little Did I Know* in which he recounts two transfiguring experiences—and, decades later, reflects on their "philosophical bearing" and their permanent effect on his life—first, as a high school student in the early 1940s, playing alto saxophone in a nearly all black jazz band (Cavell 2010, 71ff.); then, as part of the so-called Freedom Summer of 1964, joining a group of mostly graduate students from Harvard to teach—and, with John, Rosemary, and Helen Harbison, give classical chamber music recitals—at Tougaloo College outside of Jackson, Mississippi (Cavell 2010, 419, 431). It is also worth mentioning that Cavell played a crucial role in the establishment of Harvard's African American Studies Department, a fact often noted by Cornel West, once one of Cavell's teaching assistants.)

In "Something Out of the Ordinary," Cavell restricts himself to citing a few facts about the "When There's a Shine on Your Shoes" routine.

> From the *pas de deux* of the men, Astaire moves into a trance-like solo, quasi-dancing, quasi-singing, in which his realization that he has found his way (back) to dancing strikes him as having found his feet again, as having re-found his body, and his ecstasy is such that when, in his twirling or reeling through the arcade, he comes across a coin-operated photograph booth, he happily maneuvers his body in it so as to have the picture taken of his feet, or shoes (strictly, of the shine on his shoes). Perhaps out of the experience, or re-experience, of this ode to his feet, we may at some stage remark—after ninety seconds, or as in my case about forty years after having first viewed the film—that the earlier walk we viewed down the train platform is framed in such a way that we never see Astaire's feet, not even when he drops the cigarette that has lasted through the song to the ground and snuffs it out—so we fill in

On Stanley Cavell's *Band Wagon* | 231

the motion—with his foot; he is throughout cut off between the knee and the thigh, giving that conventional Hollywood form of shot a further determinate life. His feet first appear to us as we cut to him walking into the station. (Cavell 2006, 65)

Cavell's assertion that an emphasis on Astaire's feet, or their visible absence, links the two routines is corroborated by a feature of the "When There's a Shine on Your Shoes" number—may I call it a footnote?—that he seems to miss (and what could be stronger evidence of its missability?). In the entire section of the routine that precedes Astaire's tripping over the shoeshine man's legs, with one exception that proves the rule, we are again deprived of the sight of Astaire's feet. Sometimes, they are below the frame line, sometimes other characters "happen" to block our view

of them, and sometimes Minnelli cuts to a new angle the instant that Astaire's feet would otherwise have come into view.

If Astaire were performing this number in a Broadway musical, nothing could correspond to this effect, which is dependent on the agency of the camera. Indeed, in a stage musical, nothing could correspond to the camera's revelation, deferred until a third of the way into the number, that the black shoeshine man had all along been present, but effectively invisible, in the arcade.

These eminently missable effects, which must have taken considerable effort to achieve, can serve as reminders that this musical number can be viewed, as I am inclined to view it, as the work of Vincente Minnelli, the film's director—not without collaborators, of course, the most essential being Fred Astaire—no less than it can be viewed as the work of Astaire himself. If this musical number can be seen the way Cavell sees it, as Astaire's tribute to the genius of black dance, it can no less be seen as Minnelli's tribute to Fred Astaire.

The revelation, deferred until the ending of the number when the black man is on his knees, of a marquee bearing the title "The Proud Land" serves as a very different kind of reminder that the film has a director, whose instrument is the camera, and hence that it *is* a film.

Cavell shrewdly takes the words "The Proud Land," given emphasis by their deferred appearance, as a declaration that this amusement arcade is a symbolic stand-in for America. If so, this is a declaration by Minnelli the director, not Astaire the performer. Followers of Minnelli's work may well recognize "The Proud Land" as (also) an allusion to *The Bad and the Beautiful* (1952), the film Minnelli directed the year before *The Band Wagon*. It is the title of the movie that, within *The Bad and the Beautiful*, the ruthless, cynical Hollywood mogul, played by Kirk Douglas, hopes will revive his career.

At the end of the "By Myself" routine, as Astaire enters the train station and we finally do see his feet, we also hear him repeating or continuing the tune he has just been singing to himself, "not precisely by humming but," as Cavell puts it, with that

> kind of syllabification, or proto-speech, that musicians sometimes use to remind themselves of the exact materialization of a passage of sound, but which can occur, as here, as an unguarded expression of a state of consciousness, in its distraction, disorientation, dispossession: "Da: da, da da; da, da da." That particular consciousness has just been revealed to us (by its delivery along the platform) in concreteness and richness, expressed by whatever is expressed in the song that is still evidently on this fictional figure's mind. Our perception of those syllables (da, da da), we must bear in mind, is what, is essentially all that, the world has so far witnessed of that consciousness; we are alerted to the fact that, or the convention according to which, the opening delivery of the singing was inaudible, and the opening proto-dancing was unnotable, invisible, within its fictional world. (Cavell 2006, 25)

Impishly, Cavell adds, "We should not fail to appropriate this evident triviality for philosophy" (Cavell 2006, 25). Not only does Cavell not fail to do so; he follows this remark with what is up to this point the fullest, most direct statement of his central claim about this routine:

> I take the unremarkableness (the missableness), together with the remarkableness (the unmistakability), of Astaire's musical syllabification, and of the routine that renders it so, to emblematize a way of manifesting the ordinary. That the ordinariness in experience is figured in the image of walking is something I have on several occasions [one of these occasions, as we have noted, being the last chapter of *The World Viewed*] found especially worth taking into account. (Cavell 2006, 26)

I must admit that when I arrive at this point of "Something Out of the Ordinary," I have been known to experience a certain disappointment, as if this moment should feel to me more like a climactic revelation than it does. After all that philosophical table setting, can this really be all Cavell has discovered in the routine—a walk that isn't quite a dance and a "Da da da da da da da" hardly more articulate, and certainly less economically expressed, than a Homer Simpson "D'oh"? As revelations go, aren't these disappointingly—well, ordinary? But perhaps that is precisely Cavell's point. Don't these discoveries have to be experienced as disappointing if they are to serve as touchstones of the ordinary, of what is missable in experience, given Cavell's conviction that a certain disappointment with the ordinary is what he calls "the truth of skepticism"?

"Let me sketch how we got here another way," Cavell writes, preparing to recount what he has shown about the Astaire routine in terms that make clear the philosophical stakes. Let us allow Cavell the last word.

> It seems right to emphasize that Kant's aesthetic judgment (in radical contrast with his moral judgment) is a form, yet to be specified, of passionate utterance: One person, risking exposure to rebuff, singles out another, through the expression of an emotion and a claim of value, to respond in kind, that is, with appropriate emotion and action (if mainly of speech), here and now. And it seems plausible to assume that if tragedy is the working out of a scene of skepticism, then comedy in contrast works out a festive abatement of skepticism, call it an affirmation of existence. Now the utterance or delivery of Astaire's song and proto-dance has singled me out for a response of pleasure which I propose to read in terms of the concepts of psychic hovering, of dissociation from the body, within a state of ordinary invisibility, which (though you have to take my word for it now) subsequently finds resolution in an acknowledgment of origins which reinstates a relation to an intact body and causes a state of ecstasy. In my wish to share this pleasure I judge a scene of walking and of melodic syllabification as appropriate expressions of the ordinary, as the missable, and the taking of a portrait of a shod foot as an ecstatic attestation of existence. (Cavell 2006, 26)

Epilogue

As promised, before concluding my remarks, I would like to look at the "By Myself" routine from a different angle. Reading this number, like the "There's a Shine on Your Shoes" number, as Fred Astaire's passionate utterance, Cavell correctly describes it as "about as uneventful as a photographed song can be" (Cavell 2006, 22). In his view, the routine's philosophical bearing resides in its achievement of "emblematizing" the ordinary; making uneventfulness manifest is the remarkable event it makes manifest. (Shades of Henry James's *The Beast in the Jungle*.) But if we pay close attention to the fact that Astaire delivers his song and "proto-dance" on film, rather than on stage, we can see that this paradigmatically uneventful "photographed song" is, *cinematically*, remarkably eventful. Discovering its eminently missable way of being eventful requires attending to what the camera is doing—what the director is doing with the camera—at each moment, seeing Astaire's delivery of the song as also Vincente Minnelli's "delivery" of this sequence of shots, the passionate utterance by which he presents to us the star's passionate utterance.

A black porter is unobtrusively serving drinks to several white businessmen on a train that is about to pull into Penn Station in New York City. Ironically, we will momentarily discover that the porter, who is effectively invisible to these men, is blocking the camera's view of Fred Astaire, rendering him invisible to us. The men are talking about—what else?—movies. When his name happens to come up

On Stanley Cavell's *Band Wagon* | 235

and the men agree that the guy is a has-been, Astaire reveals his presence to them, and to us, by putting down the newspaper that, after the departure of the porter, had been obstructing our view of his face.

Not rushing to leave the compartment when the businessmen get off the train, Astaire has a conversation with the porter, who is not at all invisible to him, as he was to the businessmen. When Astaire expresses his wish to be able to remain in the compartment instead of venturing into the world outside, the porter tells him that he can't make up his berth—birth?—here, then leaves the compartment, as his work requires. Alone, Astaire begins humming the melody of the song he is about to begin singing, then picks himself up, dusts himself off, and exits. There is a continuity cut to the station, where the camera will momentarily find him slouching against what seems a tall pile of suitcases, joined with the camera in watching the reporters gathered around Ava Gardner, who had been on the same train.

There is a cut to a new angle as the black porter exits the car and has the exchange with Astaire, cited by Cavell, about how tough it must be to endure the kind of red-carpet treatment movies stars receive. As the porter exits the frame and seemingly the film, the camera reframes slightly, just enough for us to recognize, for the first time, that the pile of suitcases on which Astaire is leaning his arm is sitting on a cart, not on the ground.

236 | The Holiday in His Eye

Looking off screen at nothing in particular, Astaire starts singing, with a self-conscious laugh, "I'll go my way by myself, like walking under a cloud. I'll go my way by myself, all alone in a crowd." As Astaire is singing these words to the melody he had been humming on the train, a shadow crosses the frame, then the porter reappears in the background. It is his job to wheel the impossibly heavy cart, laden with suitcases, to the station. He lifts the cart, against which Astaire has been leaning, by its handles, causing it to lurch.

The moment the cart begins to move, Astaire tips his hat respectfully to the porter, plants it on his head, and starts walking in the direction of the camera. His momentary annoyance at being forced to move barely puts a dent in his mood, perhaps because it provides him with such an apt illustration of his point about going his way by himself as if walking under a cloud. His walking seems both to be animated by the bittersweet mood of his singing, and to be motivating that mood.

Astaire begins to walk at the precise moment the porter starts pushing the cart, and they are both moving in the same general direction—that is, toward the camera. At the same moment, the camera begins moving as well, receding from Astaire, or perhaps "leading him," as Cavell puts it. The camera's movement, matching Astaire's, keeps him at a constant distance as he sings.

Although Astaire's first few steps are toward the camera as it recedes from him, he then slightly changes direction. So does the camera. And so does the porter pushing the cart. Momentarily, we realize that this change of direction is caused by their wish to walk down the red carpet—"red-carpet treatment," indeed!—that runs the length of the platform a couple of yards from the stationary train. Singing, "I'll try to apply myself, and teach my heart how to sing," Astaire passes two more black porters, who are walking in the opposite direction.

Next, Astaire comes to a magazine rack, which momentarily eclipses him in the frame. The camera stops moving as Astaire, singing, "I'll go my way by myself, like a bird on the wing," stops walking. The porter with the cart catches up with Astaire, passes him through the narrow space between the red carpet and the train, and exits the frame. Another porter crosses the foreground of the frame, entering and exiting in a split second.

When Astaire puts the book back and resumes walking, the camera again recedes before him, keeping pace. The slow, smooth movement of the camera allows us a long moment to register that the name of the railroad car he is passing is "General Grant." Yet another black porter walks behind him in the opposite direction, but stays in the frame for a while, as Astaire sings, "I'll face the unknown. I'll build a world of my own . . ." Two white conductors walk by. "No one knows better than I myself . . ." A black porter, this one pushing another heavy cart, enters the frame, passes behind Astaire, who momentarily blocks our view of him.

We briefly glimpse two workmen on the tracks before the porter and his cart eclipses them from view. By the time Astaire comes to the end of the train, the porter has exited the frame, restoring our view of the two workmen down on the tracks, beautifully lit by the steam, tending to the train. It is at this moment that Astaire, who has stopped walking, drops his cigarette and stamps it out with his unseen shoe.

Resuming his walk, Astaire sings the last line of the song, "I'm by myself, alone." As he is approaching the song's last word, Astaire is a solitary, harshly lit figure framed against a flat, almost black background. When he reaches the word "alone," the frame suddenly opens up. For the first time in the sequence, there is nothing blocking the camera from seeing into a space with palpable depth. The effect of this sudden opening into depth is rendered uncanny by the backlit steam

238 | The Holiday in His Eye

and smoke emanating from the locomotive at the left of the frame, and the redcaps, going about their business, scurrying toward and away from the camera.

For the first time, the camera follows Astaire's movement as he walks toward the door to the station, not by moving in space to keep pace with his walk, but only by panning, so that by the time he arrives at the door we are looking at his back, not his face. And when he passes through that door and out of the frame, the camera stays behind.

Visually, this door has the aspect of a forbidding barrier the camera cannot, or will not, cross. Astaire is alone, indeed, when he steps through that door and enters the world of the station. Even we no longer accompany him. Our sense of his solitude is underscored when, momentarily, we see Astaire, as if through prison bars, in the brightly lit reality on the other side of the door, framed in the frame-within-the-frame of a small window we hadn't known was a window. And it is at this moment that we begin to hear him "singing" with that strange syllabification whose "philosophical bearing" Cavell so brilliantly articulates.

When the camera nonetheless crosses that barrier and picks up Astaire in the space of the train station, it is, and is not, a continuation of the routine. Astaire's "suspension," like ours, is, and is not, suspended. What we see in this shot is a redcap surrounded by suitcases, sailors, and a woman on the opposite side of the frame, as Astaire strides in. And yes, for the first time we see his feet.

The pleasure Cavell expresses by his reading of the Astaire routine manifests the commitment to philosophy he expects his audience of professional philosophers to share. Having been taught by the best, commitment to philosophy is not foreign to me, as I have said, but my wish to express my pleasure in the remarkably intimate give and take between camera and subject that this "uneventful photographed song" exemplifies—or emblematizes, to borrow Cavell's term—is no doubt more a manifestation of my commitment to the art of cinema, and to the art of film criticism. Nonetheless, viewing this Astaire routine as a Minnelli sequence has provided further evidence in support of Cavell's claim as to its bearing on philosophy. This is because the cinematic events I have pointed out are so unmistakable, but at the same time so missable, so ordinary. And, I might add, the fact that black men play missable yet unmistakable roles in these events lends strong support to Cavell's claim that the "There's a Shine on Your Shoes" routine is a continuation of the "By Myself" routine.

In both "Something Out of the Ordinary" and "Fred Astaire Asserts the Right to Praise," Cavell presents a reading of an Astaire routine as an example, on a small scale, of the kind of criticism he practices, which he characterizes, as he puts it in the latter essay, in "the terms in which [Henry] James calls for a criticism of the future—one that gets into the right relation to an object by finding the idea of it to which one may pay tribute" (Cavell 2006, 67). In this light, criticism becomes "a conduct of gratitude"—the word "conduct" suggesting both that criticism is a conductor, a medium through which gratitude can freely flow, and that it is a mode of conduct in Emerson's sense: a form of behavior, a way of doing something with words—"one could say, a specification and test of tribute, a test in which I am inherently exposed to rebuke. (As Kant roughly puts matters: The ground of my universal voice in aesthetic judgment remains no other than subjective.)" (Cavell 2006, 67).

These Astaire routines are the aesthetic "things" that are the "objects" of Cavell's readings, "objects" that leave room, as the readings show, for the form of criticism they require to achieve their "due effect"—criticism that "supplies the grounds of (the concepts shaping) pleasure and value in the working of the object" (Cavell 2006, 67). The fact that these readings or, rather, the essays that contain them, supply their own grounds, their own concepts, undertake to say what is unsayable about themselves, makes these works of criticism also works of philosophy. And if these works of philosophy are also aesthetic "things," as they surely are, what form of criticism, if any, do they leave room for? What response, if any, is called for by such works—works that set their own table, philosophically?

As I have said, all one has to do is read "Something Out of the Ordinary" to discover that, and how, it reads itself. That is why simply reading Cavell's essay, with gratitude, is the main part of what I set out to accomplish by my remarks here. To read "Something Out of the Ordinary" is to discover the praiseworthy idea Cavell invites us to see Astaire's passionate utterance as expressing. The same can be said of "Fred Astaire Asserts the Right to Praise," which at once exemplifies and articulates the idea of criticism as a form of gratitude, or of gratitude as a form of criticism that aesthetic objects can move us passionately to express. That idea and the kindred idea that there is room for praise within philosophy—and, I would add, within film studies—are among Cavell's most praiseworthy contributions, worthy of gratitude, to philosophy today, tomorrow, and the day after tomorrow.

19

"Excerpts from Memory"

Autobiography, Film, and the Double Existence of Cavell's Philosophical Prose

When I published my first books in the 1980s, academic film studies in America was in the grip of the doctrine that its legitimacy could only be established by the "higher authority" field called "theory." Students were taught that to think seriously about film they had to break their attachment to the movies that were meaningful to them. Happily, the reign of theoretical systematizing over film studies has ended. Yet it remains the case that most of the criticism presented as exemplary to undergraduate and graduate film students applies theoretical systems *to* films. That is not how Stanley Cavell writes about film. He writes in more adventurous ways, ways far more open and responsive to how films themselves think and to our ways of experiencing them. Insofar as Cavell's ambition, like Ralph Waldo Emerson's, was ultimately to be known as a writer, his prose is the measure of his philosophical achievement.

In my own writing about film, I have always aspired to align myself, philosophically, with Cavell's understanding that we cannot acknowledge a film's worth, or its meaning, without finding words we can stand behind, words that give voice to our experience even as they acknowledge the film's own ways of expressing themselves. I have been inspired—and challenged—by Cavell's writings to develop my own idiosyncratic strategies, thematic concerns, and stylistic devices.

Paper presented at a conference on Stanley Cavell and literary criticism organized by Elise Domenach and Sandra Laugier, École normale supérieure de Lyon, 2010. "Excerpts from Memory" appeared in *Critical Inquiry* 32, no. 4 (Summer 2006). It was a first installment of the not-yet-completed "philosophical memoir" Cavell would publish in 2010 under the title *Little Did I Know: Excerpts from Memory*. In what follows, page references are to *Little Did I Know*.

I have in mind, for example, the particular ways I use frame enlargements, and my particular reasons for using them in those ways. My first book, *Hitchcock—The Murderous Gaze*, was written at a time when capturing a frame from a film was a labor-intensive operation. Nonetheless, I felt the need to incorporate over six hundred frame enlargements into my accounts of five Hitchcock films. In writing about Hitchcock's films, I was moved to create a literary form or format that I have made my own over the years. Each chapter takes the form of a "reading" that follows one film from first shot to last.

Such a reading can be thought of as an interpretation or even a kind of performance of the film, in the sense that a pianist performs or interprets a Beethoven sonata by making his or her own sense of the notes as written. In the readings that make up the book, description and interpretation cannot be separated. As this suggests, what it is that is being "read"—described, interpreted—at any given moment is what is taking place *within* the film (what the characters are doing, what the camera is doing), but it is also my *experience* of that moment, how that moment moves me. And when I am motivated, as I am throughout the book, not only to describe and interpret moments but also to think through their implications, my thinking is at once about the film and about my experience. It is also about film itself and what it takes to think, and write, seriously about a film.

For myself, and for the writers about film whose work I most admire, Cavell's aspiration—and achievement—in fashioning prose that succeeds in evoking, as he put it, "the moods of faces and motions and settings, in their double existence as transient and as permanent," has been a basis of freedom from the guarded—no, stultifying—rhythms of so much academic writing about film (Cavell and Rothman 2005, xiii). Thinking about Cavell's prose has had an effect on my aspirations for my own prose and has left permanent marks on the way I write.

"Excerpts from Memory," the installment of Cavell's autobiography published in *Critical Inquiry*, confirms that his achievement as a philosopher cannot be separated from his literary achievement in fashioning prose that captures, in *un*guarded rhythms (and with perfect pitch) the "moods of faces and motions and settings, in their double existence as transient and permanent." Since "memories of movies are strand over strand with memories of his life," as the opening sentence of *The World Viewed*'s preface puts it, telling the story of his life calls for precisely the same powers of evocation as writing about movies. In turn, it is Cavell's hope, and faith, that in writing his autobiography he will find that, to this date, the life he has achieved and his philosophical achievement are one.

∼

"Excerpts from Memory" begins with this sobering passage, which is dated July 2, 2003:

> The catheterization of my heart will no longer be postponed. My cardiologist announces that he has lost confidence in his understanding of my condition, so far based on reports of what I surmise as symptoms

of angina and of the noninvasive monitoring allowed by X-rays and by the angiograms produced in stress tests. We must actually look at what is going on inside the heart. (Cavell 2010, 1)

And, I want to add, the autobiography these words are inaugurating, itself a "look at what is going on inside the heart," is a philosophical procedure, not without its own scary risks, that will no longer be postponed.

"In a previous such period of awaiting surgery, a dozen years ago," Cavell goes on, "I controlled or harnessed my anxiety by reading." At that time,

> I had found that I resisted the efforts of a novel to attract me from my world; I needed the absorption of labor rather than that of narrative. I discovered that reading a book by Vladimir Jankélévitch on the music of Debussy that I had discovered in Paris and brought back a few months earlier, meaning to read it at once (I was planning a set of three lectures, in the last of which the Debussy-Maeterlinck *Pelléas and Mélisande* would play a pivotal role), effectively concentrated my attention. (Cavell 2010, 2)

This time, he is not inclined, as he puts it, "to house my anxiety"—"house" is a thematically significant word throughout "Excerpts from Memory"—"as a secondary gain of reading, but rather by a departure in my writing" (Cavell 2010, 2). The point of this departure is to begin learning whether he can write his way into and through the anxiety by telling the story of his life. Cavell likes to think of philosophy as the education of grownups.

By the philosophical procedure he is undertaking, which he describes as writing himself into and hopefully through his anxiety, he hopes to learn something, to further his own education. What his anxiety *is* constitutes part of what he hopes to learn. The only way to test whether he *can* write his way into and through his anxiety by telling the story of his life is *by* telling it. By writing his way into his anxiety, he hopes to write his way through it—that is what catheterization is for, after all—hopefully without finding that more invasive procedures are necessary. As in all his writing, his wish, his faith, is that the outcome will be a freer, more open future.

Parenthetically—and, as usual, his parenthetical remarks are like riffs in jazz—Cavell adds,

> Or is it the other way around—that I am using the mortal threat of the procedure, and of what it may reveal, to justify my right to tell my story, in the way in which I wish to tell it? What could this mean—my story is surely mine to tell or not to tell according to my desire? But of course the story is not mine alone but eventually includes the lives of all who have been incorporated in mine. (Cavell 2010, 2)

Whose lives have been incorporated in Cavell's? Those who are to figure as characters in the story he is telling (in this first installment, his mother and father above all). And the sundry readers who may come to find themselves in his story.

Yet although this writer's story is not his alone, it is his alone to tell. But who is this "he"? This, too, he hopes to learn by telling his story.

Cavell observes that in recent years he had formed the intention many times to compose a consecutive memoir that tells the story of his life. "There have been autobiographical moments in my writing from the beginning of the first essays I still use," he writes, "and from the time of the book I called *A Pitch of Philosophy* I have sought explicitly to consider why philosophy, of a certain ambition, tends perpetually to intersect the autobiographical." But he has "until now been unwilling, or uninterested," he goes on, "to tell a story that begins with my birth on the south side of Atlanta, Georgia . . ." (Cavell 2010, 2).

He still has no interest in telling the story of his life the way he begins to rehearse it in this passage. For such a narrative strikes him "as leading fairly directly to death, without clearly enough implying the singularity of this life, in distinction from the singularity of all others, all headed in that direction." Rather, his interest in telling the story of his life is "to see how what Freud calls the detours on the human path to death—accidents avoided or embraced, strangers taken to heart or neglected, talents imposed or transfigured, malice insufficiently rebuked, love inadequately acknowledged—mark out for me recognizable efforts to achieve my own death. That, then, is what I have wanted authorization to speak of, which includes the right to assume that something has been achieved on the paths I have taken, obscure to me as that achievement, as I begin this story, may be" (Cavell 2010, 4).

What has now given him the "authorization" he was wanting, or emboldened him to begin without it? What made him feel he has the right to assume that "something has been achieved" on the paths he has taken, obscure to him as that achievement, as he begins this story, may be—where the "something" he must assume he has achieved can be seen as "recognizable efforts" to achieve his own death? The only way to test whether the paths his life has taken do "mark out" for him such recognizable efforts is to learn, by telling the story of his life, whether he *can* recognize such markers on those paths. And what if he finds that he cannot? Is this, then, the anxiety he hopes to write himself into, and through—the terrible possibility that he will discover no such markers, no such achievement, on the paths his life has taken?

And so we come to this writing's "departure," which is dated, appropriate enough, July 4th. "Trying to fall asleep last night," the day's entry begins, "I realized that if I had wished to construct an autobiography in which to disperse the bulk of the terrible things I know about myself and the shameful things I have seen in others, I would have tried writing novels in which to disguise them" (Cavell 2010, 5).

Cavell's aspiration in telling the story of his life is not to "disperse"—the surgical metaphor surfaces again—the monstrousness he knows in himself and the shameful things he has seen in others (both horrifyingly in evidence, for example, in certain of the scenes he evokes between himself and his father). An autobiography courts monstrousness, shamefulness, if it refuses some equitable balance—but what balance?—between "forgetting and remembering the suffering of injustice, the monstrousness of tyranny" that is an inalienable part of its writer's life, as it is of any human life.

Cavell suggests that his aspiration, at least in part, is to compose "a philosopher's or writer's autobiography, which, like Wordsworth's *Prelude* (quality aside), tells the writer's story of the life out of which he came to be a (his kind of) writer."

> But Wordsworth showed that that story had to be told in poetry—or rather showed that the telling of that story was the making of poetry (Emerson calls something of the sort a meter-making argument), keeping the promise of poetry. To do something analogous to that work I would have to show that telling the accidental, anonymous, in a sense posthumous, days of my life is the making of philosophy, however minor or marginal or impure, which means to show that those days can be written, in some sense are called to be written, philosophically. (Cavell 2010, 5)

Cavell is the kind of writer who hopes to achieve a freer, more open future by writing himself into, and through, the anxiety that the paths his life has taken have brought him no closer to achieving his own death. To tell the story of the life out of which he has come to be the kind of writer he is, his autobiography has to evoke the "accidental, anonymous, in a sense posthumous, days" of his life (Cavell 2010, 5). "Accidental," because his writing seeks significance in the "detours" exemplified by "accidents avoided or embraced, strangers taken to heart or neglected, talents imposed or transfigured, malice insufficiently rebuked, love inadequately acknowledged." "Anonymous," because its writer is testing his representativeness. And "posthumous" because, well, this writing aspires to recognize, in the days it evokes, efforts to achieve his own death.

And he must write his autobiography not in poetry but in prose, a kind of prose that makes philosophy. Not that philosophical prose cannot have its own kind of poetry. "Every art, every worthwhile human enterprise, has its poetry"—what Cavell's mother would call its "secrets"—"ways of doing things that perfect the possibilities of the enterprise itself, make it the one it is" (Cavell and Rothman 2005, 96).

To make philosophy, this writing must *show* that it makes philosophy. It must *show* that his life's "accidental, anonymous, in a sense posthumous, days" can be written, in some sense are called to be written, philosophically. And to show that it makes philosophy, it has to stake its claim to *be* philosophy. For it to exist as philosophy, to have that further life in the world, is for this claim to be acknowledged, accepted, where "acceptance does not mean that it is agreed with, only that disagreement with it must claim for itself the standing of philosophy" (Cavell 2010, 6).

"I might say that I am already halfway there," Cavell observes, since Wittgenstein, more to my mind than any philosopher of the century just past, has shown that, or shown how it happens that, a certain strain of philosophy inescapably takes on autobiography, or perhaps I should say an abstraction of autobiography." He goes on,

> This is how I have understood Wittgenstein's *Philosophical Investigations* and Austin's procedures in their appeals to the language of everyday, or ordinary language, namely, that I speak philosophically for others when they recognize what I say as what they would say, recognize that their language is mine, or put otherwise, that language is ours, that we are speakers. . . . As in Emerson, and in Thoreau, this turns out to mean that the philosopher entrusts himself or herself to write, however limitedly, the autobiography of a species—if not of humanity as a whole, then representative of anyone who finds himself or herself in it. (Cavell 2010, 6)

Wittgenstein and Austin may have shown that, and how it happens that, a certain strain of philosophy inescapably takes on an abstraction of autobiography. Yet neither found it inescapable to write an autobiography, much less one that aspires to show that, and how, the "accidental, anonymous, in a sense posthumous, days" of his life call for, are called to, being written philosophically. As we have said, in telling the story of his life, Cavell is *testing* his representativeness. And he is doing this, as he puts it, "from a posture in which I may discern the identities compacted in my existence, a matter of attaching significance to insignificance, and insignificance to significance" (Cavell 2010, 7).

For the identities compacted in the writer's existence to be incorporated in the story he tells, the telling—the prose itself—must "discern" its own influences, its own sources. It's not enough for the writer simply to *assert* that he learned the importance of posture from his mother, say, or that he inherited, as it were, his father's talent for improvisation as well as what his mother calls his father's "seriousness." In "Excerpts from Memory," Cavell's writing, his prose, must show the influences it discerns, must discern the influences it shows. (Whenever my own writing precisely clinches an argument with crystalline logic—I wish this happened more often—I discern an inheritance from my own father. And whenever my own writing makes me choke up or even brings a tear to my eye, I know this is a gift from my mother, who loved to sing songs to me, when I was a child, that begin with such lines as "She was a Rabbi's daughter" or end with words like "I wish that I could, was the man's sad reply, but she's dead in the coach ahead.")

∼

The World Viewed opens with the wonderful sentences,

> Memories of movies are strand over strand with memories of my life. During the quarter of a century (roughly from 1935 to 1960) in which going to the movies was a normal part of my week, it would no more have occurred to me to write a study of movies than to write my autobiography. Having completed the pages that follow, I feel that I have been composing

a kind of metaphysical memoir—not the story of a period of my life but an account of the conditions it has satisfied. (Cavell 1979b, xix)

Because the writing of *The World Viewed* is prompted by memories of movies that are strand over strand with memories of his life, hence private, particular to him, Cavell finds himself feeling, upon completing the body of the book, that he has written a kind of memoir. *The World Viewed* does not tell the *story* of the period of his life in which he enjoyed what he calls a "natural relation" to movies. That story escapes him. The memoir he feels he has composed is an account of the conditions that were satisfied by movies and moviegoing for all who enjoyed the relation to movies he enjoyed. What broke his natural relation to movies? What was that relation, that its loss seemed to demand repairing, or commemorating, by taking thought? Addressing these questions is the business of *The World Viewed* as a whole. The book's writing cannot be separated from what the writing is about. *The World Viewed* is a *metaphysical* memoir.

The autobiography of which "Excerpts from Memory" is the first installment is a metaphysical memoir as well. But it *does* tell the story of its writer's life (at least, of the period of his life whose ending the writing marks). Then is it motivated by an event as momentous as the "breaking of his natural relation to movies," a loss so traumatic it "seemed to demand repairing, or commemorating, by taking thought"? (Cavell 1979b, xix).

Can we say, for example, that the writing of "Excerpts" is motivated by the breaking of its writer's "natural relation" to his own memories, his own past, his own life? What could that mean? Before he awakened to the realization that his natural relation to movies was already broken, Cavell never intended to write a study of movies. The writing of *The World Viewed* was never postponed. But in "Excerpts" he notes that in recent years he had often had the intention writing his autobiography. The writing of *The World Viewed* was never in the same way postponed. Why telling the story of his life will no longer be postponed *is*, in a sense, the story his autobiography is telling.

In writing about movies, Cavell recognized the need for prose capable of evoking film's "ever-shifting moods of faces and motions and settings," as he put it in a Sorbonne colloquium on *The World Viewed*, and capable, at the same time, of capturing what remains fixed in the physiognomy of the world on film—what in *The World Viewed* he calls the "reality of the unsayable," the "unmoving ground" that makes film capable of exhibiting the world. The double existence—the transience and permanence—vouchsafed by film's ontological conditions became an aspiration of all his philosophical writing, not only his writing about movies.

But how could he begin to achieve this by telling the story of his life? It was not a traumatic loss that caused him to stop postponing the telling of the story, Cavell suggests in "Excerpts from Memory." It was a "pre-compositional agreement" he made with himself—one that solved the problem, which had been stopping him, of how he could begin. What freed him "to press onward with my necessity to find an account of myself without denying that I may be at a loss as to who it is or for whom at any time, varying no doubt with varying times, I am writing," was his decision—or was it his coming accidentally upon the simple thought?—to begin entries of memories by dating himself on each day of writing (Cavell 2010, 9).

By following this "double time scheme," he could "accept an invitation in any present from or to any past, as memory serves and demands to be served" (Cavell 2010, 9). Thus, his writing could bring attention back regularly to the fact that the most he could expect to provide would be excerpts from a life—so that he could finesse the question of beginnings by repeatedly bringing a day's or an hour's writing to a close without anticipating when a further time for beginning, of inspiration or of opportunity, will present itself. It is this "double time scheme," in other words, that enables the writing of his autobiography to be at once improvised and composed—to acknowledge, and to achieve, the double existence, the transience and permanence, of the "accidental, anonymous, in a sense posthumous, days" it evokes.

In a climactic passage of our reading of the ending of *The World Viewed*, Marian Keane and I wrote the following:

> St. Augustine stole a pear; lots of children have. Rousseau, like lots of little boys, got a spanking with his pants down. For years, going to the movies was a normal part of Cavell's week, as it was for millions of Americans. And for the writer of *The World Viewed*, as for most regular moviegoers, the natural relation to movies has been broken. Why seems this so particular to him? Because among all of us who have involved movies massively in our lives, among all of us who have lost our "natural relation" to movies, he is the one prompted by that loss to think philosophically about what movies are and what makes them important. He is the one prompted to step forward to write this book, to take upon himself the burden of its writing, to accept the necessity of the loss it mourns, to confess his own implication, to make himself intelligible, to open himself, like Joan of Arc, to interrogation and rejection. (Rothman and Keane 2000, 258)

Again, who is this "he"? Whose lives have been incorporated in his life? What identities are "compacted" in his identity as a writer? These are questions that *The World Viewed* postpones. "Excerpts from Memory" addresses them directly, opening his life, his writing, to an interrogation that will no longer be postponed.

In *The World Viewed* Cavell writes, "I think everyone knows odd moments at which it seems uncanny that one should find oneself just here now, that one's life should have come to this verge of time and place, that one's history should have unwound to this room, this road, this promontory" (Cavell 1979b, 156). (This conference. This paper. This book.) "Movies bring home the knowledge, or self-knowledge, that we exist in the condition of myth, that we do not require the gods to show that our lives illustrate a story which escapes us; and it requires no major recognition or reversal to bring its meaning home" (Rothman and Keane 2000, 243).

In telling the story of his life in a way that makes philosophy, Cavell hopes to show that, and how, the "excerpts"—the days, the moments—his prose evokes mark out for him recognizable efforts to achieve his own death. He hopes to show that, and how, these "excerpts," told the way he wants to tell them, enable him to recognize—however partially, however belatedly—the myth his life illustrates, a story that has, until now, escaped him—the story of how his life should have come to this, to just these words, to telling just this story. And he hopes to show that this is a story that is not his alone.

20

Stanley Cavell, Victor Perkins, and the Personal

Stanley Cavell hadn't read a word of Victor Perkins's writings when he published *The World Viewed*, nor had Perkins read any of Cavell's writings when he published *Film as Film*. Nonetheless, the two books have innumerable parallels. Nearly every feature of the medium that Cavell cites, Perkins cites, too. Both offer virtually identical explanations of the way film, a photographic medium, can render fantasy as readily as reality. Perkins's discussion of Hitchcock's two Albert Hall sequences highlights a fact Cavell, too, ponders, that film is capable of dissolving the difference between seeing and reading, between what our eyes literally see and what we know. And I could go on and on. Are such parallels surprising? These were supremely smart men committed to finding the truth of the matter. All it took was to trust good films to teach how to think about them—and to not let some theory blind them to their own experience.

The theory whose grip both felt the need to loosen was what *Film as Film* calls the "orthodox theory," which defines film as a purely visual art. Both had more sympathy for André Bazin's opposing theory, but distanced themselves from it, too. Both took popular movies at their best to be exemplary of the art of film and stuck to their guns when academic film studies embraced a new orthodoxy and it became dogma that the kind of movies they affirmed were pernicious ideological constructs, not works of art to be valued. And both kept faith with their conviction that, as

---

Paper presented at the conference "*Film as Film* Today: On the Criticism and Theory of V. F. Perkins" at the University of Warwick, 2018. My gratitude to the organizers of this memorable conference, James MacDwell and Andrew Klevan. Later published as "*Film as Film* and the Personal" in *The Thought of Stanley Cavell and Cinema*, ed. David LaRocca (New York: Bloomsbury Academic, 2020), 121–26. Reprinted with permission.

Cavell put it, the study of film cannot be a worthwhile human enterprise if it isolates itself from the kind of criticism that seeks to articulate a work's *idea*—not a thought lying *behind* the work, but a thought the work expresses, in its own way, in its own medium—the kind of criticism Perkins, like Cavell, was inspired to write.

I say this even though *Film as Film* characterizes its goal as providing a rational basis for aesthetic judgments of films. For Perkins didn't actually write criticism as if its primary task were *judging* films or directors, in effect weighing how many Michelin stars, if any, to award them. Rather, his criticism, like Cavell's, bespeaks a conviction that its value resides in discerning what a given film is about and what it has to say about what it is about—what Cavell calls the film's *idea*.

I cannot honestly say, though, as many of you can, that Perkins's work taught me how to think about films. In the 1960s, I wasn't a regular reader of *Movie*. I wish I had been, for it would have been sweet, over these all too many years, to have been able to count all the *Movie* regulars, not just Perkins, as dear friends. But it was Andrew Sarris's articles in the *Village Voice*, later expanded into his 1968 book *The American Cinema*, that awakened me to the fact that within the popular American cinema there were directors who left personal stamps on their films.

As a critic, Sarris wasn't in the same league as Perkins. Sarris *did* take his main task to be ranking films and directors. And he lacked the critical tools to justify his rankings in terms that satisfied a young me, or even to explain what made some directors "auteurs" and others not. His claim was that the films of auteur directors expressed their *personalities*. I knew that couldn't be right, since directors, on screen, are generally outside the projected world, invisible and voiceless. Then what part of a director's "self" might a film express?

That some directors' films are profoundly personal is an idea important to *Film as Film*, as it was—and is—to me. But what it *means* for a film to be profoundly personal is a question Perkins's book doesn't address. It is a *philosophical* question that can only be addressed by writing, like *The World Viewed*, that *is* philosophy. Philosophy, for Cavell, is "any place at which the human spirit allows itself to be under its own question, indeed, that allows that questioning to happen" (Fleming and Payne 1989, 66). *The World Viewed* is a "place at which the human spirit allows itself to be under its own question." *Film as Film* is not.

In 1964, Cavell, newly arrived at Harvard, offered a graduate seminar on the aesthetics of film he allowed me, a lowly junior, to take. In *The World Viewed* he calls this seminar a failure. As I never tire of saying, it didn't fail me. But I no more learned how to think about film from Cavell than from Perkins. What Cavell taught me was that when I think about film my way, I was doing philosophy. In many respects, my writing about film is more like Perkins's than like Cavell's. It's the aspiration to philosophy that has pulled me into Cavell's orbit.

"Film is an interest of mine, or say a love," Cavell writes, "not separate from my interest in, or love of, philosophy. So, when drawn to think through a film, I do not regard the reading that results as over, even provisionally, until I have said how it bears on the nature of film generally and on philosophy" (Cavell and Rothman 2005, 153). In *The World Viewed*, reflections on the historical significance of the *event* of film, its significance for Western art and philosophy, are strand over strand with reflections on film's significance for its author personally. *Film as Film* is not concerned with such matters. Marian Keane and I argued, in our book about *The World Viewed*, that what motivates its writing is a question the entirety of the book is concerned with answering. In this "metaphysical memoir" about the period of his life when going to the movies was a regular part of his week. Cavell shares intimate confidences with the reader. In his early *Movie* articles and in *Film as Film*, Perkins does not. When he writes, in his great 1963 essay on Nicholas Ray, "Almost every man acts from a position of profound uncertainty and insecurity," Perkins leaves open the possibility that he—perhaps Ray, too—is an exception (Perkins and Pye 2020, 172). But in his late book on *The Rules of the Game*—surely, there is no finer book of film criticism—he uses the phrase "like all of us" to acknowledge that he, too, acts—writes—from such a position. But he voices his confession in a tone that's anything but confessional. Cavell once observed, in a passage I have found myself repeatedly invoking, that the need he felt in writing about film to "become evocative in capturing the moods of faces and motions and settings" left "permanent marks" on his philosophical prose (Cavell and Rothman 2005, xiii). Perkins's prose *avoids* becoming evocative. His assertions seem made with certainty—disinterestedly, dispassionately, from the security of an aesthetic distance. *Rationally*. And yet, surely, expressing himself in this impersonally rational voice was this man's *way* of being personal—a mask that revealed, revealed *by* masking, who he was. Who was he?

When Archie Leach willed himself to become Cary Grant, it was an instance of what Jean Rouch characterized as a fictional part of oneself being the most real part of one's self. I still say "cawffee," if little else, in my native Brooklynese, but once a Brooklyn boy, always a Brooklyn boy. Perkins had his reasons, obvious and not, for willing himself to become the person for whom that familiar voice of impersonal rationality was the "most real" expression of who he was. Still, once a working-class Devonshire lad, always a working-class Devonshire lad. The Victor Perkins he had once been no longer existed, but the Victor Perkins he had become, he also was not. He had made his own the voice, still endemic among analytical philosophers, of those articles in academic philosophy journals that were a cross I had to bear on the road to my PhD—a voice ideal for dismissing other philosophers as if they were social inferiors one was entitled to put down with impunity. But when Perkins, in that voice, expressed disdain for directors who stoop to "weepfests" or when he unsparingly criticized students, it was different. He was asserting, not his *personal* superiority, but the superiority of being rational—a path open to all.

There's a country music song that begins, "Beneath still waters, there's a strong undertow. The surface won't tell you what the deep waters know." In his Nicholas Ray essay, Perkins attributes to the director's latest films a quality he calls "passionate placidity"—a perfect description of his own writing. Beneath the placid surface of his impersonally rational prose is a strong undertow of passion—his love of film, inseparable from his empathy for characters whose uncertainty and insecurity he recognized as also his own—that threatens or, better, *promises* to sweep us from the safe harbor of reason into turbulent, uncharted waters.

Like Cavell, Perkins hewed to the discipline of meaning everything he said, but not to Cavell's further discipline of saying everything he meant—even, or especially, when it seemed unsayable. There are depths of emotion in the films Perkins loved that he couldn't speak about in that voice of impersonal rationality—depths he acknowledged only by what he consigned to silence. That silence doesn't *express*, but neither does it *disavow*, his emotion. If it did, Perkins wouldn't have been the great film critic he was.

In *Film as Film*, Perkins analyzes the scene in *55 Days in Peking* in which the Charlton Heston character has the unpleasant duty of informing a young half-Chinese girl that her American father had been killed in action (Perkins and Pye 2020, 78–83). Rejecting the temptation to milk easy tears, Ray focuses not on the girl, but on the Heston character's unwillingness to deal with her emotion—or his own. Perkins leaves it unsaid, however, that a parallel can be drawn between the Heston character and Ray, whose decision to avoid dwelling on the girl might be seen as manifesting his own reluctance to deal with emotion. And the same parallel can be drawn with Perkins, who praises Ray for not letting the girl distract from his study of the Heston character—as if the director, like a scientist, were viewing the character from a secure, dispassionate position. Perkins leaves it unsaid that Ray's study—it's also a devastating *critique*—could be of a character he sees as akin to himself. If the sequence didn't have a confessional dimension, what would make it profoundly personal to Ray? And what, if anything, would make Perkins's "study" of Ray's "study" profoundly personal, as I do not doubt it is?

Cavell writes, in another passage I have found myself repeatedly invoking, "What I found in turning to think about film was a medium which seemed simultaneously to be free of the imperative to philosophy and at the same time inevitably to reflect upon itself—as though the condition of philosophy were its natural condition" (Cavell and Rothman 2005, xxii). Painting only brought itself "under its own question" when painters like Manet could no longer make paintings they believed in without breaking with the tradition they wished to keep alive. But being "under its own question" *is* film's tradition, *The World Viewed* argues. That a film could express an idea about itself, itself *as* a film, is a possibility *Film as Film* consigns to silence.

Nowhere does that silence speak more loudly than in Perkins's analysis of *Psycho*'s shower murder sequence. He argues, brilliantly, that Marion "is destroyed by an explosion of forces existing within her own personality: the savage equation of sex and punishment, the self-comforting contempt for others' desires. Implicated as we have been in Marion's thought, we cannot entirely refuse the guilt of Mother's action" (Perkins 1972, 113). But from what position did Hitchcock express this thought? It's an idea central to *The Murderous Gaze*—an idea profoundly personal to me—that Hitchcock films are "under their own question." In a Hitchcock film, as I wrote in *The Murderous Gaze*, my first book, "the nature of love, murder, sexuality, marriage, and theater are at issue, but so is the nature of the camera, the act of viewing, and directing as a calling" (Rothman 2012, ix). What it revealed about

Hitchcock, personally, and what it made of him, that he made the role of director his own in the particular way he did, and what that way wa*s*, can't be separated from *Psycho*'s "idea." Hitchcock's films aren't dispassionate "studies." The fate of his soul was at stake, as Perkins later acknowledged in his 2000 *I Confess* essay, which ends with this strongly Cavell- (and perhaps Rothman-) inflected passage: "If, as I believe, Hitchcock's ambition was to shape this film as his own confession he was making an avowal of his riven nature, his inability to find a point of rest between the desire for recognition and the terror of being known. So he was one of us, after all" (Perkins 2000, 39).

Whenever I find myself choking up reading my own paper at a conference—an experience I doubt Perkins ever had—I take it as a sign that I've gotten it right. I'm as American as Perkins was English. I respect his writing, and he respected mine, but I no more want to write like him than he wanted to write like me. To write in my voice, he would have had to risk the sentimentality he detested. To write in his, I'd have to consign to silence what I have at heart to say about films I love, films that to me are philosophy, films that move me to write about them in a way that makes philosophy. Don't get me wrong. That *Film as Film* is not a book of philosophy doesn't make it inferior to *The World Viewed*, much less to *The Murderous Gaze*. Philosophy isn't everyone's cup of tea. But it was Cavell's. And it is mine. I fervently believe it was Hitchcock's cup of tea, too, even if his films served it with a pinch of arsenic.

Perkins writes, "Ray's films show man as an intruder in a turbulent and indifferent, or hostile, universe. His hero often journeys into a primitive landscape like that of the Everglades in search of a lost certainty, a lost harmony between man and his environment. But he brings with him his own inner conflicts, which make that harmony unattainable" (Perkins and Pye 2020, 175). Ray himself, journeying into the primitive landscape of Hollywood, was such a hero. So was that Devonshire lad who journeyed into the turbulent and hostile or indifferent universe of the English academic world. When Perkins writes, "Ray looks toward an ideal relationship of man to nature, like that of man to man, in which the struggle for domination is resolved by the recognition of interdependence," he leaves it unsaid that Ray's dream was his own as well (Perkins and Pye 2020, 175). It was also Cavell's, and Emerson's before him. In *The World Viewed*, it was already a theme, which Cavell was only later to connect with Emerson's way of thinking, that human beings are *in* nature, that nature is in *us*, and that our alienation was our turning away from nature, from our own nature. If we view Ray, as Perkins's essay portrays him, from the perspective of Cavell's later writings, we can see that the achievement of Ray's last Hollywood films was to undo the repression of the Emersonian philosophy that was ascendant in the American cinema, as it was in America, in the New Deal era. Then again, films that achieve what Cavell calls "the poetry of film" are inherently egalitarian, inherently Emersonian. Perkins ends his Ray essay on a hopeful note: "All Ray's films balance an immediate conflict against an ultimate unity, but his more recent work suggests a place for man within that unity" (Perkins and Pye 2020, 176). But

Perkins couldn't know then what we know now—that Ray's inner conflicts, along with Hollywood's hostility or indifference, would make the harmony he sought unattainable. Cavell attained it. So did Perkins.

    I first met Perkins in the early 1970s, when I was teaching in the NYU Cinema Studies Department. He had come down to New York from Boston, where he had made a pilgrimage to meet Cavell, and was on his way to see Nicholas Ray. He stayed a night with Kitty and me at our home in Brooklyn Heights. We talked and talked and talked, as we were to do over the next forty-five years whenever our paths crossed. Victor and Stanley had profound respect for each other, but after that first meeting, *their* paths rarely crossed. Now that they have both taken that long journey to the place where the river of no return flows into the sea, I like to imagine them spending eternity watching movies together and talking, talking, talking.

Afterword

In a passage of *Pursuits of Happiness* I have invoked more than once in my writings, Stanley Cavell observes that in *The Philadelphia Story* the Cary Grant character's demand "to determine for himself what is truly important is a claim to the status of a philosopher." Then he asks, "Is what Dexter claims to be enormously important, a matter of his most personal existence, of *national* importance?" (Cavell 1981b, 150).

Here, Cavell cites Matthew Arnold, for whom the rule of the best was the antidote to society's loss of authority. Arnold wished, in Cavell's words, "to work out the rule of the best to mean the rule of the best *self*, something he understood as existing in each of us—a potential in the human self not normally open to view, or not open to the normal view. Call this one's invisible self" (Cavell 1981b, 158). And he adds—this is a key to why *movies* have been of national importance—that the movie camera can make the invisible self visible—as it does in the book's frontispiece—that glorious shot of Cary Grant in *The Awful Truth*, captioned with an Emerson quote, that reveals that this star *does* "carry the holiday in his eye" and *is* "fit to stand the gaze of millions."

Adapted from remarks presented at the memorial tribute to Stanley Cavell at Harvard University, 2018.

Arnold distinguished the two forms of authority, which he named "Hebraism" and "Hellenism," that, as Cavell puts it, "still impel us on the quest for perfection or salvation." The governing idea of Hellenism "is spontaneity of consciousness; that of Hebraism, strictness of conscience" (Cavell 1981b, 158). *The Philadelphia Story* is of national importance, Cavell proposes, because the remarriage of Dexter and Tracy comes to, or fantasizes, "a marriage or balance between Western culture's two forces of authority, so that American mankind can refind its dedication to a more perfect union, toward the perfected human community, its right to the pursuit of happiness" (Cavell 1981b, 159).

Dexter *becomes* a philosopher—it happens offscreen—when he finds in himself the saving balance between Hellenizing and Hebraizing that gives him the authority to help Tracy balance her Hebraism with Hellenism and recognize her own "best self"—and his. "He not busy being born is busy dying," Bob Dylan sang, channeling Emerson, who knew that what he called the "wonderful way of *life*" must be *strictly* followed if one's "best self" is to rule.

Cavell's wish was to achieve, within philosophy and in his life, a marriage or balance between Hellenizing and Hebraizing, between philosophy *and* life, between saying what he meant and meaning what he said, between rationality and morality and, when he was tickling the ivories—or the keys of his beloved manual typewriter—between improvisation and structure.

We can call Cavell a philosopher of intuition as long as we keep in mind his conviction in the necessity of paying the tuition for our intuitions by *expressing* ourselves, apart from which we cannot know our own minds, cannot make ourselves known to others, cannot achieve the acknowledgment of others—our acknowledgment of them, theirs of us—requisite to walking in the direction of an unattained but attainable self, as Ralph Waldo Emerson put it. Cavell liked to invoke Henry James's advice to the aspiring writer to "write from experience, and experience only"—but also to strive to be a person on whom no experience is lost.

When Stanley Cavell came to Harvard in 1963, he had published little, but had already achieved that saving balance. As I put it in the preface, "The charismatic young professor allowed me, a skinny undergraduate philosophy major with a penchant for mathematical logic, a love of movies, and a full head of hair, to enroll in a graduate aesthetics seminar devoted to film. In *The World Viewed*, Cavell calls that seminar a failure. As I never tire of saying, it didn't fail me." It taught me to see film as not only a subject *for* philosophy, but as a medium *of* philosophy. And to think of philosophy, as he was later to put it, as "any place at which the human spirit allows itself to be under its own question, indeed, that allows that questioning to happen"— as it *does* happen, my writings have aspired to demonstrate, in films by the likes of Alfred Hitchcock, Jean Renoir, Yasujiro Ozu, Eric Rohmer, Agnes Varda, Jean Rouch, Donn Pennebaker, Chantal Akerman, Abbas Kiarostami, Terrence Malick, Robert Gardner, Ross McElwee, and Jean-Pierre and Luc Dardenne. Cavell didn't teach me my way of thinking about film. He taught me that when I think about film my way, determining for myself what makes them truly important, I am claiming—with his blessing—the status of a philosopher.

Cavell was the first person I'd ever known, certainly the first who knew me, that I saw as possessing the kind of authority I found in the films I passionately desired to write about. I didn't see him as balding; I saw him as having, to borrow an admiring contemporary's description of Kant, "a broad forehead built for thinking." With a heart to match. And what did he see in me? He saw in me then what he never stopped seeing, what he inspired me to see: my "best self."

What I learned from Stanley Cavell—from his teaching, his writing, his conversation, his friendship, his humor, his unfailing graciousness, his democratic spirit, his generosity in encouraging everyone he conversed with to be a person on whom no experience is lost, and above all his love—is something enormously important to me, a matter of my most personal existence. So many can say the same! If it weren't also of *national* importance, now more than ever with our democracy in peril, I wouldn't have written this book.

Thank you, Stanley.

Works Cited

Allen, Richard. 2006. "Hitchcock and Cavell." In "Thinking through Cinema: Film as Philosophy." Special issue, *Journal of Aesthetics and Art Criticism* 64, no. 1 (Winter): 43–53.

Allen, Richard, and Malcolm Turvey, eds. 2011. *Wittgenstein, Theory and the Arts*. London: Routledge.

Barbash, Ilisa, and Lucien Taylor, eds. 2007. *The Cinema of Robert Gardner*. Oxford: Berg.

Bazin, André. 1967. *What Is Cinema?* Edited and translated by Hugh Gray. Berkeley: University of California Press.

Biskind, Peter. 1983. *Seeing Is Believing*. New York: Pantheon.

Bogle, Donald. 1973. *Toms, Coons, Mulattoes, Mammies, and Bucks: An Interpretive History of Blacks in American Films*. New York: Bloomsbury Academic.

Carroll, Noel. 2020. "Revisiting *The World Viewed*." In *The Thought of Stanley Cavell and Cinema*, edited by David LaRocca, 41–62. New York: Bloomsbury Academic.

———. 1988. *Philosophical Problems of Classical Film Theory*. Princeton: Princeton University Press.

Cavell, Stanley. 2010. *Little Did I Know: Excerpts from Memory*. Palo Alto: Stanford University Press.

———. 2005a. *Cities of Words: Pedagogical Letters on a Register of the Moral Life*. Cambridge, MA: Harvard University Press.

———. 2005b. *Philosophy the Day After Tomorrow*. Cambridge, MA: Harvard University Press.

———. 2002. *Must We Mean What We Say?* New York: Cambridge University Press. First published 1969.

———. 1996. *Contesting Tears: The Hollywood Melodrama of the Unknown Woman*. Chicago: University of Chicago Press, 1996.

———. 1995. *Philosophical Passages: Wittgenstein, Emerson, Austin, Derrida*. Cambridge, MA: Blackwell.

———. 1994. *A Pitch of Philosophy: Autobiographical Exercises*. Cambridge, MA: Harvard University Press.

———. 1990. *Conditions Handsome and Unhandsome: The Constitution of Emersonian Perfectionism*. Chicago: University of Chicago Press.

———. 1988. *In Quest of the Ordinary: Lines of Skepticism and Romanticism*. Chicago: University of Chicago Press.

———. 1987. *Disowning Knowledge: In Six Plays of Shakespeare*. Cambridge: Cambridge University Press.

———. 1984. *Themes Out of School: Effects and Causes*. San Francisco: North Point Press.

———. 1981a. "North by Northwest." *Critical Inquiry* 7, no. 4 (Summer): 761–77.

———. 1981b. *Pursuits of Happiness: The Hollywood Comedy of Remarriage*. Cambridge, MA: Harvard University Press.

———. 1979a. *The Claim of Reason: Wittgenstein, Skepticism, Morality, and Tragedy*. New York: Oxford University Press. New edition 1999.

———. 1979b. *The World Viewed: Reflections on the Ontology of Film*. Enlarged edition. Cambridge, MA: Harvard University Press.

Cavell, Stanley, and David Justin Hodge. 2003. *Emerson's Transcendental Etudes*. Stanford: Stanford University Press.

Cavell, Stanley, and William Rothman. 2005. *Cavell on Film*. Albany: State University of New York Press.

Cohen, Ted, Paul Guyer, and Hilary Putnam, eds. 1993. *Pursuits of Reason: Essays in Honor of Stanley Cavell*. Lubbock: Texas Tech University Press.

Conant, James, and Stanley Cavell. 1989. "An Interview with Stanley Cavell." In *The Senses of Stanley Cavell*, edited by Richard Fleming and Michael Payne, 21–73. Lewisburg, PA: Bucknell University Press.

Emerson, Ralph Waldo. 2000. *The Essential Writings of Ralph Waldo Emerson*. New York: Modern Library.

———. 1911. *The Conduct of Life, Nature, and Other Essays*. Chicago: University of Chicago Press.

———. 1903. *Emerson's Complete Works: Essays*. 1st series. Boston: Houghton Mifflin.

Emerson, Ralph Waldo, and Joel Porte. 1983. *Ralph Waldo Emerson: Essays and Lectures*. New York: Library of America.

Fay, Jennifer, and Daniel Morgan. 2021. Introduction to "Cinema, Modernism, and the Perplexing Methods of Stanley Cavell." Special issue, *Discourse: Journal for Theoretical Studies in Media and Culture* 42, nos. 1–2.

Fleming, Richard, and Michael Payne, eds. 1989. *The Senses of Stanley Cavell*. Lewisburg, PA: Bucknell University Press.

Fried, Michael. 1968. "Art and Objecthood." In *Minimal Art*, edited by Gregory Battock, 16–47. New York: E. P. Dutton.

Glitre, Kathrina. 2006. *Hollywood Romantic Comedy: States of the Union, 1934–1965*. Manchester: Manchester University Press.

Goodman, Russell, ed. 2005. *Contending with Stanley Cavell*. Oxford: Oxford University Press.

Guzzetti, Alfred. 1981. *Two or Three Things I Know about Her: Analysis of a Film by Godard*. Cambridge, MA: Harvard University Press.

Keane, Marian. 1991. "Acting About Acting: John Barrymore's Performances on Stage and Screen." Doctoral dissertation, New York University Department of Cinema Studies.

———. "The Authority of Connection in Stanley Cavell's *Pursuits of Happiness*." *Journal of Popular Film and Television* 13, no. 3 (Fall): 139–50.

Lackey, Douglas. 1973. "Reflections on Cavell's Ontology of Film." *Journal of Aesthetics and Art Criticism* 32, 271–73.

LaRocca, David, ed. 2020. *The Thought of Stanley Cavell and Cinema*. New York: Bloomsbury Academic.

Leab, Daniel. 1976. *From Sambo to Superspade: The Black Experience in Motion Pictures*. Boston: Houghton Mifflin.

Meyers, Rebecca, William Rothman, and Charles Warren, eds. 2016. *Looking with Robert Gardner*. Albany: State University of New York Press.
Michelson, Annette. 1968. "*What Is Cinema?*" *Artforum* (Summer). Reprinted in *Performing Arts Journal* 17, no. 2/3 (May–September 1995): 20–29.
Morgan, Daniel. 2013. *Late Godard and the Possibilities of Cinema*. Berkeley: University of California Press.
———. 2006. "Rethinking Bazin: Ontology and Realist Aesthetics." *Critical Inquiry* 32, no. 3 (Spring). https://doi.org/10.1086/505375.
Noble, Peter. 1948. *The Negro in Films*. London: Skelton Robinson.
Perkins, Victor. 2012. *La Règle du Jeu*. London: Palgrave Macmillan.
———. 2000. "*I Confess*: Photographs of People Speaking." *CineAction* 52 (September): 28–39.
———. 1972. *Film as Film: Understanding and Judging Movies*. New York: Penguin.
Perkins, Victor, and Douglas Pye. 2000. *V. F. Perkins on Movies: Collected Shorter Film Criticism*. Detroit: Wayne State University Press.
Putnam, Hilary. 2008. *Jewish Philosophy as a Guide to Life: Rosenzweig, Buber, Levinas, Wittgenstein*. Bloomington: Indiana University Press.
Rothman, William. 2019. *Tuitions and Intuitions: Essays at the Intersection of Film Criticism and Philosophy*. Albany: State University of New York Press.
———. 2014. *Must We Kill the Thing We Love? Emersonian Perfectionism and the Films of Alfred Hitchcock*. New York: Columbia University Press.
———. 2012. *Hitchcock—The Murderous Gaze*, 2nd edition. Albany: State University of New York Press.
———. 2004. *The "I" of the Camera: Essays in Film History, Criticism and Aesthetics*, 2nd edition. New York: Cambridge University Press.
———. 1997. *Documentary Film Classics*. New York: Cambridge University Press.
Rothman, William, and Marian Keane. 2000. *Reading Cavell's "The World Viewed": A Philosophical Perspective on Film*. Detroit: Wayne State University Press.
Shumway, David R. 1991. "Screwball Comedies: Constructing Romance, Mystifying Marriage." *Cinema Journal* 30, no. 4 (Summer): 7–23.
Sobchack, Vivian. 1991. *The Address of the Eye: A Phenomenology of Film Experience*. Princeton: Princeton University Press.
Turvey, Malcolm. 2001. "Is Skepticism a 'Natural Possibility' of Language?" In *Wittgenstein, Theory and the Arts*, edited by Richard Allen and Malcolm Turvey, 117–36. London: Routledge.

Index

39 Steps, The (Alfred Hitchcock, 1935), 177, 206
55 Days in Peking (Nicholas Ray, 1963), 254

Ace in the Hole (Billy Wilder, 1951), 129
Address of the Eye, The (Sobchack) xxi, 67–70
Affeldt, Steven, xxvii
Affair to Remember, An (Leo McCarey, 1959), 76
African Queen, The (John Huston, 1951), 49
Akerman, Chantal, xiii
Allen, Richard, xvii, xxi, xxvii, 187–202
Althusser, Louis, 15, 59n
Antonioni, Michelangelo, 11
Aravindan, G., xv
Arnold, Matthew, 73–76, 139, 257–58
Astaire, Fred, 217–40 *passim*
Austin, J.L., xix, 78, 114, 173, 246
Awful Truth, The (Leo McCarey, 1937), 84, 85, 86, 87, 197

Backman, Joyce, xxiii
Bad and the Beautiful, The (Vincente Minnelli, 1952), 232
Bambi (James Algar *et al*, 1942), 122
Band Wagon, The (Vincente Minnelli, 1953), 128, 217–40
Barrymore, Joh, 107, 107n
Barthes, Roland, 15, 59n
Batkin, Norton, xiii
Baudelaire, Charles, 78

Baz, Avner, xxvii
Bazin, André, 10–11, 17, 23, 24, 26, 28–31, 46
Benjamin, Walter, xiv, 4, 165
Bergman, Ingmar, 11
Bergson, Henri, 8, 79
Best Years of Our Lives, The (William Wyler, 1946), 10
Bicycle Thieves (Vittorio DeSica, 1948), 10
Blonde Venus (Josef von Sternberg, 1932), 94–95, 101
Bogle, Donald, 94–95, 96, 97–99
Bohème, La (Giacomo Puccini), 151
Bordwell, David, 9
Brakhage, Stan, xxiv
Brecht, Berthold, 43
Bresson, Robert, 11
Bringing Up Baby (Howard Hawks, 1938), 206
Browne, Nick, xii
Bruno, Giuliana, xiii
Butler, Rex, xxvii

Cabin in the Sky (Vincente Minnelli, 1943), 223
Cahiers du Cinéma, 11, 12, 15–16, 24
Cantor, Jay, xxvii
Carroll, Noel, xxiii–xxvi, 9, 28–30
Carmen (Cecil B. DeMille, 1915), 151
Cavell, Cathleen, xxxii
Cavell, Stanley
  "Avoidance of Love, The," 3, 20, 44, 51
  "Being Odd, Getting Even," 141

Cavell, Stanley *(continued)*
  "Capra Moment, A," 72, 168
  Cities of words, xiv, xxx, 6, 79, 167–74, 176–77, 186, 189, 205–206
  Claim of Reason, The, xxx, 2, 5, 6, 8, 21, 71, 190, 193
  Conditions Handsome and Unhandsome, 6, 19, 72
  Contesting Tears, xvi, 2, 21, 50, 85, 138–46, 153, 195
  Disowning Knowledge, 18
  "Emerson Mood, An," 5, 72, 78
  Emerson's Transcendental Etudes, 6, 72
  "Excerpts from Memory," 241–48
  "Fact of Television, The," 135, 136–38
  "Fred Astaire Asserts the Right to Praise," 217–18, 232, 239–40
  "Good of Film, The," 160–61
  In Quest of the Ordinary, 6, 72, 190, 191
  "Knowing and Acknowledging," 223
  Little Did I Know, xiv, xvi, xxx, 2, 5, 7, 8, 79, 170–72, 174, 193
  "Matter of Meaning It, A," 6, 7
  "Moral Reasoning" course, xiv, 168
  "More of *The World Viewed*," 2, 23, 48, 49, 56
  Must We Mean What We Say?, xix, xxvi, xxx, 1–8, 10, 15, 21, 38, 71–72, 155–57, 172, 192–93
  "*North by Northwest*," xxvi, 6, 112, 158–59, 161
  "Opera and the Lease of Voice," 148–50
  "Opera in and As Film," 150–52
  "Performative and Passionate Utterances," xxviii
  Philosophy the Day After Tomorrow, xxviii, 79, 85, 163, 193
  Pitch of Philosophy, A, xvi, 50, 79, 142
  Pursuits of Happiness, 2, 6, 7, 15, 21, 71–79, 81–87, 106, 107, 108, 112, 117, 123, 139, 151, 167–76, 192, 201
  Senses of Walden, The, 5
  "Something Out of the Ordinary," 217–34 *passim*, 239–40
  "Stella's Taste," 10, 108–11, 113, 142, 201
  Themes Out of School, 153–55
  "Thinking of Emerson," 5, 21, 72, 78, 168
  This New Yet Unapproachable America, 6, 72
  "Thought of Movies, The," 72, 168
  "Two Cheers for Romance," 219
  "What Becomes of Things on Film?," 24, 157
  "What is the Scandal of Skepticism?," 74, 194
  "World as Things: Collecting Thoughts on Collecting, The," 153
  World Viewed, The, xi, xvii–xix, xxii, xxv, xxviii, 5, 7, 9–35, 78, 82, 84, 115, 123, 136, 138, 147, 155–57, 246–57, 251–53
Cavell, Stanley and William Rothman, *Cavell on Film*, 153–65
Chabrol, Claude, 11
Chaplin, Charles, 45
Cholodenko, Alan, xiii
City Lights (Charles Chaplin, 1931), 79
Clément, Catherine, 146
Conant, James, 16
Cukor, George, 107, 108, 112, 113

Davis, Bette, 141
Day, Bill, xxvii
Deleuze, Gilles, xx, 8, 79
Derrida, Jacques, 31, 31n, 59n, 64
Descartes, René, 74
Dietrich, Marlene, 94–95
Doll's House, A (Ibsen), 85, 139, 143, 189
Domenach, Elise, xvii, xxvii
Donatelli, Piergiorgio, xxvii
Don't Look Back (D. A. Pennebaker, 1967), 212–13
Double Indemnity (Billy Wilder, 1944), 124, 127–28
Dreyer, Carl, 11, 49

Egelman, Robert, xxvii
Eisenstein, Sergei, 11
Emerson, Ralph Waldo, xxiii, 5, 19, 76–79, 107, 114
  "Behavior," 183
  "Circles," 208
  "Experience," 2, 179, 180, 186, 208, 209–10
  "Intellect," 184–85, 210
  "Manners," v, 186, 212
  "Self-Reliance," 171

Emersonian perfectionism, xxix, 8, 19, 77, 79, 125, 126, 138, 154, 160, 169, 170, 172–79, 182, 186, 199–200, 205–209

Fay, Jennifer, xxi
Fellini, Federico, 11, 49
Female (Michael Curtiz, 1933, 85
Figueroa, Gabriel, xiv
Film as Film (Perkins), 251–56
Floyd, Juliet, xxvii
Ford, John, 11, 15
Foucault, Michel, 59n
Franks, Paul, xxvii
Freud, Sigmund, xiv, 14, 113–15, 141, 149, 201, 244
Fried, Michael, 24, 24n, 39, 78
Friedlander, Eli, xxvii
Frozen (Chris Buck and Jennifer Lee, 2013), 122–23

Gardner, Robert, xi, xiii
Garland, Judy, 122, 125
Gaslight (George Cukor, 1944), 8 9, 141, 197, 198
Glitre, Kathrina, 83–87, 126
Goodman, Russell, xxvii
Goodrich, Frances, 125
Godard, Jean-Luc, 11, 160
Gould, Tim, xxvii
Grant, Cary, 76, 106, 107, 112, 113, 212
Greenberg, Clement, 17
Groundhog Day (Harold Ramis, 1993), 160
Gudel, Paul, 24n
Guzzetti, Alfred, xi, xii, xiii

Hackett, Albert, 125
Happy Mother's Day, A (Richard Leacock and Joyce Chopra, 1963), 103–105
Hawks, Howard, 11, 15, 107
Heidegger, Martin, 8, 17, 51, 79, 114, 172, 187
Hepburn, Katharine, 106, 107, 126–27
Herwitz, Daniel, 107n
High Society (Charles Walters, 1956), 126
Hiroshima, mon amour (Alain Resnais, 1959), 51, 54
Hitchcock, Alfred, 11, 12, 196–202
"Hitchcock and Cavell" (Allen), 187–202

Hollywood Romantic Comedy: States of the Union, 1934–196 (Glitre), 83–87, 126
How Green was My Valley (John Ford, 1941), 119, 120–21, 124

Imitation of Life (John Stahl, 1934), 98–102
In the Good Old Summertime (Peter Fitzgerald, 1949), 125, 126
I Remember Mama (George Stevens, 1948), 120
It Happened One Night (Frank Capra, 1934), 84, 85, 87, 99, 191–92, 206
It's a Wonderful Life (Frank Capra, 1946), 10

James, Henry, 258
Jazz Singer, The (Alan Crosland, 1927), 96

Kant, Immanuel, 149, 220, 222, 234
Karmel, Pepe, xiii
Keane, Marian, xii, xvii–xviii, 107, 107n
Keaton, Buster, 40, 45
Kierkegaard, Søren, 40
Klevan, Andrew, xxvii, xxxii
Krebs, Victor xxvii
Kripke, Saul, 163
Kristeva, Julia, 59n
Kurosawa, Akira, 10

Lacan, Jacques, xx, 15, 59n
Lackey, Douglas, 32
Lady Eve, The (Preston Sturges, 1941), 21, 84, 85, 131, 151, 197
Lady Gaga, 122
Lady Vanishes, The (Alfred Hitchcock, 1938), 206
Langlois, Henri, 11
LaRocca, David, xxiii, xxvii
Late Spring (Yasujiro Ozu, 1949), 76, 78, 86, 128
Laugier, Sandra, xvii, xxvii, xxxii, 4
Leacock, Richard, 103–105
Letter from an Unknown Woman (Max Ophuls, 1948), 86, 89, 141
Lévinas, Emmanuel, 74, 174
Lévi-Strauss, Claude, 15
Life with Father (Michael Curtiz, 1947), 120

Lodger, The (Alfred Hitchcock, 1926), 207
Looking with Robert Gardner, xi, xv
Lorenzini, Daniele, xxvii

Makavejev, Dušan, xii
Mallick, Terrence, 123
Man Who Knew Too Much, The (Alfred Hitchcock, 1934 and 1956), 125
Man with a Movie Camera (Dziga Vertov, 1929), xxiv
Marnie (Alfred Hitchcock, 1964), 181, 209
Marrati, Paula, xxvii
Maysles, Al and Dave, 105
McElwee, Ross, xiii
Meeting Venus (Istvan Scabo, 1991), 151
Meet John Doe (Frank Capra, 1941), 84, 86
Meet Me in St. Louis (Vincent Minnelli, 1944), 127–28
Mekas, Jonas, 12
Metz, Christian, 15
Michelson, Annette, xxiv
Mineelli, Vincente, 11, 128
Misoguchi, Kenji, 10
modernism, xx, xvi, 6, 7, 8, 12, 18, 24, 32–34. 47, 57, 78–79, 154, 156, 159, 172, 200
Modleski, Tania, xvi, 109
Moi, Toril, xxvii
Monteverdi, Claudio, 147
Moonstruck (Norman Jewison, 1989), 151
Moran, Richard, xxvii
Morgan, Daniel, xxi, xxii
Morgan, Kitty, xiv, xv, xxxii
Morocco (Josef von Sternberg, 1930), 78, 95
Moss, Robb, xiii
Mr. Deeds Goes to Town (Frank Capra, 1936), 150–51
Mulhall, Stephen, xxvii
Mulvey, Laura, 60

Nair, Mira, xii
Negro in Films, The (Noble), 98
New American Cinema, 12
Nietzsche, Friedrich, 8, 40, 79, 172
Noble, Peter, 98
North by Northwest (Alfred Hitchcock, 1959), 76, 158–59, 185–87, 193–94, 210

Notorious (Alfred Hitchcock, 1946), 180, 197
Now, Voyager (Irving Rapper, 1942), 89, 90–91, 141, 142
Nozick, Robert, xii

One Sunday Afternoon (Stephen Roberts, 1933), 126
One Sunday Afternoon (Raoul Walsh, 1948), 126
Only Angels Have Wings (Howard Hawks, 1939), 78
Our Vines Have Tender Grapes (Roy Rowland, 1945), 119
Orfeo (Monteverdi), 147
Ozu, Yasuriro, 10

Panofsky, Erwin, 12, 23, 24
Passion of Joan of Arc, The (Carl Dreyer, 1928), 49–57 *passim*
Pelléas and Mélisande (Debussy-Maeterlinck), 243
Pena, Richard, xii
Pennebaker, Donn, 106
Perez, Gilberto, xii, xxxii
Perkins, Victor, xxxii, 251–56
Petric, Vlada, xi, xii, xiii
Philadelphia Story, The (George Cukor, 1940), 73, 75–77, 85, 86, 106, 108, 112, 156, 167–74, 181, 204–205
Philosophical Investigations (Wittgenstein) xix, 3, 6, 47, 163, 246
Pomerance, Murray, xxxi
Psycho (Alfred Hitchcock, 1960), 180–81, 264–65
Putnam, Hilary, xii

Queen Kelly (Erich von Stroheim, 1929), 130
Quiet Man, The (John Ford, 1952), 125

Raphaelson, Samson, 126
Ray, Nicholas, 11, 254–56
Reading Cavell's "The World Viewed," xiii, xvi, xvii–xix, xxv
Rear Window (Alfred Hitchcock, 1954), 197
Rennebohm, Kate, xxvii
Renoir, Jean, 11

Rivette, Jacques, 11
Robeson, Paul, 96–98
Rodowick, David, xiv
Rohmer, Eric, 11
Rome, Open City (Roberto Rossellini, 1945), 10
Rothman, William
  "Cavell, Emerson, Hitchcock," xiv, xxviii
  Cavell on Film, xxix, 155–68
  "Cavell Reading Cavell," xxxi, 1–8, 172
  "Cavell on Film, Television and Opera," 135–52
  "Cavell's Creation," xvi
  "Cavell's Philosophy and What Film Studies Calls 'Theory,'" xvi, xvii
  Documentary Film Classics, xv
  "Excerpts from Memory," xiii
  Hitchcock: The Murderous Gaze, xiii, xv, 70, 175–77, 198–99, 203–204, 206–207, 213–15, 242, 254–55
  "I" of the Camera, The, xiii, xv, 106, 125
  Jean Rouch: A Celebration of Life and Film, xv
  Three Documentary Filmmakers, xv
  Must We Kill the Thing We Love? xv, 178, 186, 199, 203–15
  "On Stanley Cavell's *Band Wagon*," xxviii
  "Stanley Cavell, Victor Perkins, and the Personal," xxvi
  "Same Again, Only a Little Different, The," 200
  Tuitions and intuitions, xv, xx–xxi, xxx, xxxi
Rothman, William and Marian Keane, *Reading Cavell's "The World Viewed,"* xiii, xvi, xvii–xix, xxv, 155, 9–58, 161, 248
Ruiz, Raul, xiii

Sabotage (Alfred Hitchcock, 1936), 206
Saito, Naoko, xxvii
Sarris, Andrew, 12, 252
Scheman, Naomi, xxvii
"Screwball Comedies: Constructing Romance, Mystifying Marriage" (Shumway), 81–83
Secret Agent (Alfred Hitchcock, 1936), 206
Shadow of a Doubt (Alfred Hitchcock, 1943), 102, 198

Shakespeare, William, xiv, xix, 18, 19, 32, 74, 85–87, 107, 114, 139, 147, 150, 154, 158, 160, 164, 176, 189, 197, 223
Sherlock, Jr (Buster Keaton, 1924), 40
Shop Around the Corner, The (Ernst Lubitsch, 1940), 125, 126
Show Boat (James Whale, 1937), 96–98
Shumway, David, 81–83
Singin' in the Rain (Stanley Donen and Gene Kelly, 1951), 128, 133
Sinnebrink, Robert, xxvii
Sirk, Douglas, 125
skepticism, xvi, 6, 18, 23–24, 34–35, 62–63, 116–17, 121, 141, 147, 154, 157, 162, 188–202, 223–24, 233
Snow, Michael, xxiv
Sobchack, Vivian, xxi, 67–70
Stage Fright (Alfred Hitchcock, 2950), 77, 78, 86
Stahl, John, 125
Standish, Paul, xxvii
Stanislavski, Konstantin, 40
Stanwyck, Barbara, 112
Star is Born, A (George Cukor, 1954), 122
Star is Born, A (Bradley Cooper, 2018), 122
Stella Dallas (King Vidor, 1937), 89, 90–94, 108–14, 116, 141, 142–48, 201
Strangers on a Train (Alfred Hitchcock, 1951), 180
Strawberry Blonde, The (Raoul Walsh, 1941), 126
Sublett, John "Bubbles," 228
Sunrise (F. W. Murnau, 1927), 78
Sunset Blvd. (Billy Wilder, 1950), 128–33
Swanson, Gloria, 130
Sweet Movie (Dušan Makavejev, 1974), 159

Tale of Winter, A (Eric Rohmer, 1992), 160
Talk of the Town, The (George Stevens, 1942), 187
Tannhäuser (Richard Wagner), 151
Terra Trema, La (Luchino Visconti, 1948), 10
Teuber, Andreas, xxvii
Text of Light, The (Stan Brakhage, 1974), xxiv
Thin Man, The (W. S. Van Dyke, 1934), 125, 204

Thoreau, Henry David, 8, 40, 57, 76, 79, 113, 172
Toles, George, xxxii
Toms, Coons, Mulattos, Mammies, and Bucks (Bogle), 94, 95–96, 97–99
Treasure of the Sierra Madre, The (John Huston, 1948), 49
Tree of Life, The (Terrence Malick, 2011), 123
Trouble in Paradise (Ernst Lubitsch, 1932), 78
Trouble with Harry, The (Alfred Hitchcock, 1955), 178
True Heart Susie (D. W. Griffith, 1919), 78
Truffaut, François, 11
Turvey, Malcolm, 194–96
Twentieth Century (Howard Hawks, 1934), 78

Unni (G. Aravindan, 1989), xv

Vertigo (Alfred Hitchcock, 1958), 194, 207, 208

Von Stroheim, Erich, 130

Wallach, Eli, xiv
Warren, Charles, xi, xiii, xxxii
Welles, Orson, 11
Whatever Happened to Baby Jane? (Robert Aldrich, 1962), 130
Wheatley, Catherine, xx, xxii–xxiii
Wilder, Billy, 128–33
Wittgenstein, Ludwig, xix, 3, 6, 7, 8, 14, 17, 47, 48, 50, 78, 113, 114, 163, 172, 173, 188, 195–96, 247
Wollen, Peter, 15, 60
Woman of the Year (George Stevens, 1942), 126–27
Wordsworth, William, 245

Young and Innocent (Alfred Hitchcock, 1937), 206
Young Mr. Lincoln, The (John Ford, 1939), 15–16

THE SUNY SERIES

HORIZONS OF CINEMA

MURRAY POMERANCE | EDITOR

Also in the series

William Rothman, editor, *Cavell on Film*

J. David Slocum, editor, *Rebel Without a Cause*

Joe McElhaney, *The Death of Classical Cinema*

Kirsten Moana Thompson, *Apocalyptic Dread*

Frances Gateward, editor, *Seoul Searching*

Michael Atkinson, editor, *Exile Cinema*

Paul S. Moore, *Now Playing*

Robin L. Murray and Joseph K. Heumann, *Ecology and Popular Film*

William Rothman, editor, *Three Documentary Filmmakers*

Sean Griffin, editor, *Hetero*

Jean-Michel Frodon, editor, *Cinema and the Shoah*

Carolyn Jess-Cooke and Constantine Verevis, editors, *Second Takes*

Matthew Solomon, editor, *Fantastic Voyages of the Cinematic Imagination*

R. Barton Palmer and David Boyd, editors, *Hitchcock at the Source*

William Rothman, *Hitchcock: The Murderous Gaze, Second Edition*

Joanna Hearne, *Native Recognition*

Marc Raymond, *Hollywood's New Yorker*

Steven Rybin and Will Scheibel, editors, *Lonely Places, Dangerous Ground*

Claire Perkins and Constantine Verevis, editors, *B Is for Bad Cinema*

Dominic Lennard, *Bad Seeds and Holy Terrors*

Rosie Thomas, *Bombay before Bollywood*

Scott M. MacDonald, *Binghamton Babylon*

Sudhir Mahadevan, *A Very Old Machine*

David Greven, *Ghost Faces*

James S. Williams, *Encounters with Godard*

William H. Epstein and R. Barton Palmer, editors, *Invented Lives, Imagined Communities*

Lee Carruthers, *Doing Time*

Rebecca Meyers, William Rothman, and Charles Warren, editors, *Looking with Robert Gardner*

Belinda Smaill, *Regarding Life*

Douglas McFarland and Wesley King, editors, *John Huston as Adaptor*
R. Barton Palmer, Homer B. Pettey, and Steven M. Sanders, editors, *Hitchcock's Moral Gaze*
Nenad Jovanovic, *Brechtian Cinemas*
Will Scheibel, *American Stranger*
Amy Rust, *Passionate Detachments*
Steven Rybin, *Gestures of Love*
Seth Friedman, *Are You Watching Closely?*
Roger Rawlings, *Ripping England!*
Michael DeAngelis, *Rx Hollywood*
Ricardo E. Zulueta, *Queer Art Camp Superstar*
John Caruana and Mark Cauchi, editors, *Immanent Frames*
Nathan Holmes, *Welcome to Fear City*
Homer B. Pettey and R. Barton Palmer, editors, *Rule, Britannia!*
Milo Sweedler, *Rumble and Crash*
Ken Windrum, *From El Dorado to Lost Horizons*
Matthew Lau, *Sounds Like Helicopters*
Dominic Lennard, *Brute Force*
William Rothman, *Tuitions and Intuitions*
Michael Hammond, *The Great War in Hollywood Memory, 1918–1939*
Burke Hilsabeck, *The Slapstick Camera*
Niels Niessen, *Miraculous Realism*
Alex Clayton, *Funny How?*
Bill Krohn, *Letters from Hollywood*
Alexia Kannas, *Giallo!*
Homer B. Pettey, editor, *Mind Reeling*
Matthew Leggatt, editor, *Was It Yesterday?*
Merrill Schleier, editor, *Race and the Suburbs in American Film*
Neil Badmington, *Perpetual Movement*
George Toles, *Curtains of Light*
Erica Stein, *Seeing Symphonically*
Alexander Sergeant, *Encountering the Impossible*
Brendan Hennessey, *Luchino Visconti and the Alchemy of Adaptation*